The Best
AMERICAN
SPORTS
WRITING
2003

GUEST EDITORS OF
THE BEST AMERICAN SPORTS WRITING

The Best AMERICAN SPORTS WRITING™ 2003

Edited and with an Introduction
by Buzz Bissinger

Glenn Stout, Series Editor

HOUGHTON MIFFLIN COMPANY
BOSTON • NEW YORK 2003

Visit our Web site: www.houghtonmifflinbooks.com.

ISSN 1056-8034
ISBN 0-618-25130-8
ISBN 0-618-25132-4 (pbk.)

Printed in the United States of America

DOC 10 9 8 7 6 5 4 3 2 1

"Lucky Jim" by Elizabeth Gilbert. First published in *GQ*, May 2002. Copyright © 2002 by Elizabeth Gilbert. Reprinted by permission of the author.

"Fowled Away" by Bill Plaschke. First published in *The Los Angeles Times*, August 24, 2002. Copyright © 2002 by *The Los Angeles Times*. All rights reserved. Reprinted by permission.

"The Ball (An American Story)" by Gary Smith. First published in *Sports Illustrated*, July 29, 2002. Copyright © 2002 by Time Inc. Reprinted courtesy of *Sports Illustrated*.

"Baseball Without Metaphor" by David Grann. First published in *The New York Times Magazine*, September 1, 2002. Copyright © 2002 by David Grann. Reprinted by permission of the author.

"The Lone Wolf" by S. L. Price. First published in *Sports Illustrated*, June 24, 2002. Copyright © 2002 by Time Inc. Reprinted courtesy of *Sports Illustrated*.

"Bobby Fischer's Pathetic Endgame" by Rene Chun. First published in *The Atlantic Monthly*, December 2002. Copyright © 2002 by Rene Chun. Reprinted by permission of the author.

"When the Terror Began" by Alexander Wolff, with additional reporting by Don Yaeger. First published in *Sports Illustrated*, August 26, 2002. Copyright © 2002 by Time Inc. Reprinted courtesy of *Sports Illustrated*.

"Power Pact: Champion Lifter and Former Steroid Abuser Training Teenage Son" by Juliet Macur. First published in *The Dallas Morning News*, December 22, 2002. Copyright © 2002 by *The Dallas Morning News*. Reprinted by permission of *The Dallas Morning News*.

*Dedicated to the memory of Mark Kram Sr.,
a fine writer and friend of this series*

Contents

Foreword

Since our last installment, *The Best American Sports Writing* franchise has moved from the cozy confines of Uxbridge, Massachusetts, both north and slightly west for the usual reasons — a better stadium deal — so that after first working out of a hallway and then a basement I may finally get to move to the first floor in a room with both a window and heat. O glorious day. Writers, editors, and anyone else who cares to submit material for the next edition of this book, *The Best American Sports Writing 2004*, would do well to pay attention and note the address change at the end of the foreword. Otherwise, your submissions may well become lost in the Möbius strip of forwarded mail.

After nine seasons here in Uxbridge and thirteen overall, I have to admit that this "series editor" racket doesn't come so easy anymore. I'm ready for a change and a fresh start. Oh, I know, you think I've got it easy, that all I do is sit around in my jammies, smoking a pipe, fending off journo-groupies, and trying to affect a cultured accent when I answer the phone, but all that's only a fiction of the media. Although for most people reading is an enjoyable pastime, something they do to fall asleep at home or to stay awake and impress people while taking public transportation, here in the pros it's a whole different game. There's no such thing as an off-season. I have to get my work in, stay within myself, and bring it every week so I can step up just before deadline and peak at the right time. When I'm on, it looks easy, but the fans never see the real costs. All they care about is the table of contents and the guest editor's name on the coffee table.

When I came up more than a decade or so ago, I was just a fresh-faced, long-haired, wide-eyed kid with 20–10 vision who sped-read through a couple of dozen sports stories before breakfast, gulped some coffee, read all day, and then, when it was over, regaled my friends at the bar with stories of split infinitives and bad leads lifted from T. S. Eliot and Charles Dickens. Then I got up and did it again and never worried for a second about squinting or getting a headache. When I saw someone walking around with a pair of bifocals hanging from his neck, I'd laugh. Of course, this was a long, long time ago, in the dark ages before spell-check, voice mail, Infotrac, and Internet-influenced magazine design took the soul out of the page. Once upon a time — and I remember when — words were always black on white in an easily recognized font. Of course, that was a time when all the authors touch-typed, used Wite-Out, and carried around a hardcover dictionary, then termed a "hefty tome."

Oh, how things have changed. Now I put sunblock on my head and receive e-mails that start "Yo, Mr. Stout."

As much as I enjoy editing this series, it hasn't been easy, let me tell you. There's always someone out there sniping, accusing me of playing favorites, being PC, hating football, not being PC, or even worse, *skimming.* Then there are those who never read the foreword and call me up in June asking if it's too late to submit material, even though the deadline has *always* been February 1 and *always* will be. And there are still the ignorant few who think this book is a collection of *sportswriting,* not *sports writing,* which is much like confusing checkers with chess. But there is a difference, so please don't ask me why there isn't a special category for badminton columns written in the dark on deadline during a natural disaster.

Fortunately, the stalkers have been few and far between, and where I've lived has either been a high-crime neighborhood or inaccessible to public transportation. As I enter my fourteenth season in the league I know that if it weren't for the fans I'd be pouring concrete somewhere and watching pro wrestling instead of, well, pouring something else and watching for the mail. I have been blessed.

And right now, believe me, I know that out there somewhere is some fresh-faced kid who started reading this series after running out of Matt Christopher books, sneaking it off Mom and Dad's night table to read in the dark, and then getting hooked on this stuff. And now she's just graduated from college with references and a much sought-after internship in her pocket. She's polishing up the résumé, reading this, and thinking, "He can't have much left. That Stout guy has been around *forever* and that 'series editor' moniker sure would look good on my CV while I pursue my Pulitzer and land one of those cushy writing camp jobs back at the university."

Well, good luck, kid. Give it your best shot. But I'm warning you. This isn't like making it big in figure skating or skateboarding. In that line you peak at fourteen, go through rehab a year later, then write the comeback biography and get the TV movie your junior year of high school. But not here. Although I know better than anyone that I'm not a rookie anymore, I'm not close to being finished. According to Bill James's latest calculations, I'm just entering my prime. Although my rapid eye movement has slowed a little, I can still read about baseball, boxing, the aforementioned badminton, and even skateboarding back-to-back-to-back while scanning the agate page with one eye closed and calling up my favorite website on the laptop. And there has yet to be a day when I've gone to the post office and couldn't carry my own mail back to the car.

But you're probably right about one thing, kid. There will be a woman in this slot someday. If not you, then maybe your daughter. Or mine. Just take a look at the table of contents in this year's book — one-quarter female. Ten or twelve years ago a story written by a woman was a rarity. Not now. Sports writing isn't a closed shop anymore, and that raises everybody's game. And this despite the fact that outlets that target "women sports fans" and tend to use more female writers, like the late *Sports Illustrated Women* and *Condé Nast's Women's Sports and Fitness,* keep going belly up. I always thought those magazines got it wrong anyway. They seem to think that women won't read about sports unless it's wrapped between low-carb recipes and ads featuring models wearing spandex. I beg to differ. I believe that would actually be more effective as a way of attracting male readers — I'm a low-carb man myself. The attentive reader will note that *The Best American Sports Writing* features neither recipes nor models, yet based on the feedback I get, I'd be willing to bet that half our readers are women in spite of this, or maybe because of it. They are special.

In fact, all readers of this book are special, primarily because, well, they actually do read the book. Now, you might not think that this is a big deal, but I have plenty of books myself and have noticed that I don't read half of them, maybe even a bit less than half if I'm not allowed to count the ones I've written myself and therefore had to. But this book, unlike many, actually gets *read.* I find this event as remarkable as any in the natural world, such as spring training. The writers represented in these pages know this, too, because every single year, without fail, they write words that people want to read and then read again. They are always in their prime, and my task is always a joy.

Each year I read as many stories as possible in hundreds of sports and general interest publications in a quest for stories that our guest editor might feel worthy of inclusion in this book. In addition, I contact the editors and sports editors of hundreds of magazines, asking for either submissions or complimentary subscriptions. I also contact sports editors of a like number of newspapers and ask them to submit material.

Writers are *always* encouraged to submit their own work, as are readers who come across eligible work they would like to see included in this book. In early February I select about seventy-five stories that I want to read again with our guest editor, who makes the final selection. Buzz Bissinger stepped up to the task this season with unusual veracity.

As you read this, I am already reading stories for consideration for *The Best American Sports Writing 2004.* Each *nonfiction story* must have been published in 2003 in either a newspaper, magazine, or online publication in either the United States or Canada, and it must be *column-length or longer.* Reprints are not eligible. I must receive all submissions by February 1, 2004.

Every submission should include the title, the name of the author, the date of publication, and the publication's name and address. Photocopies, tearsheets, or clean copies are fine — reductions to 8½ × 11" are best. Newspaper stories should be mounted on paper, if possible, as loose clippings are often damaged and difficult to read. URLs of online versions can be helpful. Because of the volume of material I receive, *submissions will be neither returned nor acknowledged.* Neither is it appropriate for me to make any comments about any individual submission.

Please note the change in address listed below. Publications that want to make absolutely certain that I see their material are advised to send a complimentary subscription to this address. This is not a requirement, but receiving a publication regularly allows me to survey material over the course of the year rather than in a deluge each January.

Submissions and subscriptions should be sent to this precise address:

Glenn Stout
Series Editor
The Best American Sports Writing
PO Box 549
Alburg, VT 05440

I may be contacted by e-mail at baswed@sover.net. If this should ever change, a current e-mail address will always be available on my Web site, glennstout.net. But please note that no submissions will be accepted electronically, either pasted in or as an attachment. Earlier editions of this book can be ordered through most book dealers or online sources. An index of stories through year 2000 is available on glennstout.net.

Thanks again to Eamon Dolan and Emily Little of Houghton Mifflin for their trust and help each year, to my able assistant Amanda Hicks, and to Buzz Bissinger for his understanding during a trying time. As I did much of the work for this book this year, my young daughter Saorla was hospitalized for several weeks and hooked up to all manner of medical equipment. I've had the misfortune of spending a great deal of time in the hospital myself, but I never had to go through anything remotely similar to what she did. Words like *bravery* and *courage* get thrown around pretty easily in the world of sports, but Saorla and her mother, who never left her side, showed me more grit than anybody I've ever seen with either a ball in their hand or a magazine in their lap.

Thanks, guys.

GLENN STOUT

Introduction

IF YOU CARE, as I do, with a love and passion that is almost mysterious because of the very depths of it, this was the year that pushed me overboard.

To hell with sports. To hell with all of it. To hell with the greed and the pettiness. To hell with that insouciant arrogant athlete swagger of I-could-care-less, man-boys making their millions and not putting out a dime's worth of effort for it.

The hype got to me, the towering Babel of Kornheiser and Wilbon and Rome and Tom Arnold, *Tom Arnold for godsakes*. The saturation got to me, college football games around the clock, NCAA basketball for every mood swing, the NFL draft receiving almost as much bad seat-of-the-pants analysis as the War in Iraq. The scandals got to me, the pathetic shame of the Harricks at Georgia and the decision by St. Bonaventure, when confronted with cheating, to simply cancel the rest of the basketball season as if it never happened. I got tired of sports pages reading like rap sheets. I got tired of wondering whether Shaq liked Kobe or Kobe liked Shaq. I got tired of checking the box score every night to see how many times Rasheed Wallace had pouted. The more I read about high school basketball wunderkind LeBron James, the more it seemed like a nasty little morality play, big-time magazines and big-time networks making this kid larger than life only to chisel away at him when he began to act like the entitled smack-ass monster that they of course had created.

I went to a couple of Major League Baseball games, but they were at Veterans Stadium in Philly where I live. The stadium is amorphous and atmosphere-less, everything about it drab except for the hideous glaring green of the artificial-surface field and the increasingly desperate prancings of the Phanatic. By the time it got into the fifth inning, the players seemed like they were in slow motion in the thick soupy summer Philly heat, and I knew it wasn't just the beer that was inducing such bleary-eyed lethargy.

I went to an NBA game in Seattle. Thanks to a friend, I had a great seat on the floor right opposite the Seattle SuperSonics' bench. The SuperSonics were playing Indiana, and the game was pretty good, actually damn good since it went into overtime. You couldn't help but admire the intensity of Gary Payton even if his scowl did cast the entire arena in shadow. But it was the conduct of the players on the Seattle bench that drew my attention, the way they rose for a team huddle during a time-out with all the enthusiasm of arthritic octogenarians, the cool little nods they gave during the game to friends in the stands, as if what happened after the game was a whole lot more important than what was happening during it.

I went to a pro football game in Tennessee. It was a big game, a Monday Night game on ABC, the Titans versus the Patriots. As a result, there was a lot of hype, and it seemed to me that for some of the players, in particular Jevon Kearse, the pregame intro was far more important than the game itself, the way he ran onto the field like a gyrating drum major, swiveling his head back and forth with slightly less effect than when Linda Blair did her 360 in *The Exorcist*. It was a grand entrance, a great entrance. The fans loved it. The cameras loved it. Kearse loved it most of all, making his invisible play during the game almost incidental. *Face time, baby. Face time.* And he had gotten lots of face time in that preening cockadoodle strut, better than any sack.

The disillusionment I felt wasn't something conjured up. Sports truly has defined my life, a presence as powerful in my forties as it was in my prepubescence. Drawing ever closer to the no-man's-land of fifty, I am shocked by the slippage of so many facts that were once at my fingertips. And yet, there is all this sports knowledge that still crams my head, as if there is a specific part of the brain actually dedicated to the gathering and permanent collection of it, a frontal sports lobe.

I can't tell you where I was last week, but I can tell you exactly

where I was when Joe Pepitone hit a grand slam for the Yankees
in game 6 of the 1964 World Series — on the Eighty-sixth Street
cross-town bus just as it was leaving Fifth Avenue, the sublime
knowledge of it coming from men in coats and ties with transistor
radios glued to their ears. I can't come close to telling you who the
presidents of our nation were in the twentieth century, but I can list
off the top of my head all the World Series champions from 1957
to 1980. Before September 11 I had no idea where Afghanistan
was, much less its political climate, but I do know that the great
Dartmouth football team of 1970, where my father went to college,
shut out six of nine opponents in its undefeated season and gave
up only forty-two points.

I remember sitting in the Yale Bowl in tears as a child when the
Elis handed the Big Green a particularly humiliating 56–15 defeat,
and I still can feel the arm of my father cupping my skinny shoulder blades, trying to console me in the cold shiver of that barren
hateful place. Close to forty years later, in 2001, as my father lay in
a hospital bed in New York trying to stave off the cancer that would
kill him and I groped for words of reassurance that would not come
because there was no reassurance that I could give, the bond that
held us together was the sweet music of the Yankees. We watched
the American League Championship Series games together
against the Mariners, and it gave my father and me something to
care about, unite over, share together, without having to confront
what neither of us could confront. He loved the Yankees, and he
had passed that love on to me. We didn't say much as we watched.
We let the games do the talking for us. But as they unfolded, he
suddenly blurted out that he had actually seen both Ruth and
DiMaggio at Yankee Stadium, and that for his money DiMaggio was
the best he ever saw, the grace of him like magic.

We reminisced over game 4 of the 1964 World Series, Yankees
versus the Cardinals at Yankee Stadium, when he had somehow
copped a pair of tickets and had decided to take me. I was nine at
the time, and in that hospital room I could still recall the score, a
devastating 4–3 Yankee loss after the Bombers had gone up 3–0 in
the first. I remembered the circumstances that had caused it as if it
had happened yesterday, an error by my favorite player, second
baseman Bobby Richardson, on an easy double-play ball that
loaded the bases, followed by a grand slam by Ken Boyer off of Al
Downing into left field that I mercifully didn't have to witness be-

cause there was a big fat concrete girder in front of us like there was in front of most seats in the old Yankee Stadium.

In fact, I didn't move out of my seat at all on the crack of Boyer's bat. The instant I heard it I knew it was bad, but my father rose, as did all the thousands around us, moving in unison with outstretched necks a little bit like a Bill Gallo cartoon in the *New York Daily News*, then cranking their necks back in when the havoc Boyer had just wrought became sadly apparent. When my father looked back at me, there was such a sweet sense of concern in his eyes, as if he knew I would impale myself on the nearest mustard dispenser if left to my own devices. I was crushed, totally crushed, the slap-in-the-face of Ken Boyer's home run only made worse by the fact that he had a brother Clete who played for the Yankees (how could you do something like that to your own brother?), not to mention the shame of Bobby Richardson, who never made an error. Never. *Never.* Until now when I was there to witness it.

I did not do any harm to myself, as it turned out. But I did not speak for the rest of the day. I simply could not, and maybe that sounds extreme, although it really wasn't if you were a kid discovering the thrill of first love in your hometown sports team.

As I related the details to my father, he looked at me and asked how it was possible that I still remembered "all this shit," particularly when he acknowledged that he couldn't remember what he had had for dinner two hours earlier, which was maybe not such a bad thing given that it was hospital food. We laughed, something we so rarely did anymore. In the orb of that hospital room where he lay dying, watching the Yankees was somehow enough to make us forget, at least for a little bit. Like the father and son we once had been, or maybe just like little kids at a sleepover, we turned off the lights, the glow of that television set enough to make us feel safe. We could not talk about what was really happening. But we could talk about the magnificence of the Rocket's longevity. We could marvel at the fluid serenity of Bernie's swing. We could both agree that no place in the world was more lonely than the batter's box from the left side when Mariano threw one of those wicked cutters.

Maybe it all sounds overdone and silly. Maybe this idea of sports having such a hold, even in the face of the death of someone you love, is the reflection of an empty life, or at least a life with odd priorities. But the place of sports had been that powerful, which made the potential loss of it over the past year not a matter of defiant anger, one man's fuck-you to the spoiled brats who increasingly dominated it, but the genuine loss of something essential.

Even the football-mad chaos of Odessa, Texas, where I had spent a year while researching the book *Friday Night Lights,* had not filled me with the profound sense of deflation that I now felt. The excesses that I witnessed as I chronicled the Panthers of Permian High School were no doubt shocking and disturbing — racism, a warped sense of values in which the culture of football was considered of far greater worth than the culture of academics, more money spent on athletic tape and travel by chartered jet than on books for the English department. But even in the obsession of Odessa there was a saving grace — the nobility of the kids who played, their dedication to a goal so far beyond the immediacy of themselves. The games across the windswept West Texas plains on a Friday night were unlike anything I had ever witnessed — exciting, valiant, even poetic, in the sense of these boys sacrificing themselves for the sake of a town that so depended on them.

I was disturbed by what I saw, terribly disturbed, but I wasn't turned off. Not like the past twelve months. With more and more regularity, the television went on and then went off after a quarter, or an inning, or a period. I watched the 2002 World Series between the Anaheim Angels and the San Francisco Giants, but it felt like obligatory duty. Being a Yankees fan had no doubt spoiled me, but the games started too late and then seemed to go on for days. You could get up in the middle to take a nap, have a shower, go to the 7-Eleven for a box of Sugar Pops, make a bank deposit, have a garage sale, and still find yourself in the top of the eighth with Tim McCarver making the same point he had made in the second. The Super Bowl? I know the Tampa Bay Buccaneers were in it, but it just took me a good minute to remember whom they played. The NBA finals between the San Antonio Spurs and the New Jersey Nets? Don't be ridiculous . . .

And then something strange happened.

A query asking if I might be interested in serving as the guest editor for the 2003 edition of *The Best American Sports Writing.* An answer of yes, largely because of the flattery of being asked and following in the footsteps of such figures as David Halberstam and Richard Ford. Followed by a feeling of dread that it would be a chore and a pain in the ass, having to read some eighty-odd entries with some fair degree of seriousness and then cull them down to the twenty-five best, assuming there were twenty-five best. Like most things in my life, what started as something joyful psychologically mutated into an albatross around my neck. Why did I say yes?

But once the entries started arriving, something truly unexpected happened. From the very first story I read, and continuing until they had all been exhausted, I found myself enthralled and delighted. It made the job easy, dread replaced by craving as I waited for the next packet of stories to arrive. I also found myself feeling a sense of gratitude, the best funkiest qualities of sports not lost at all, but there all along in the hands of exquisite writers with the eye and appetite to scoop it out.

It's there in Susy Buchanan's piece on demolition derby in Arizona, where among the cast of deliciously deranged wackos is a pair of brothers known as the Shoeless boys:

> Shoeless Jim is twenty-six years old with thick glasses and a permanently dazed look on his face. He's been racing since he was thirteen. The shoeless nickname stems from the fact that he and his kin don't wear shoes — ever — because "that's the way our daddy raised us. That's how everyone is back home."

It's there in Bill Plaschke's ability to literally get inside the head of the San Diego Chicken and report that it's "sour, steamy, a moldy shower stall in a darkened locker room." It's there in Ted Levin's piece on bird watching in Camden Yards, which gives a whole new method for coping with a rain delay:

> At 6:34 P.M., Casey spots ten great egrets flying in loose formation above left field, white birds against a dark sky, like a bevy of outfielders dressed in immaculate home jerseys. A ring-billed gull lands in shallow center field, walks around in tight circles, wet to the bone. Mercifully, the game is canceled.

It is there in David Grann's profile of Barry Bonds, which gives us an insight into Bonds that makes him seem almost sympathetic given his puzzling and pathetic layers of persecution:

> He had spies up in the press booth, Bonds explained to me, that reported back to him the things reporters and broadcasters said to one

another. "They don't know I have ears up there, but I do. I know everything they say. Everything."

And it's there in Rebecca Mead's ability to capture Shaq's very strange world by describing the utilitarian act of using a cell phone:

> He holds it in front of his mouth and talks into it as if it were a walkie-talkie, and then swivels it up to his ear to listen, as if the phone were a tiny planet making a quarter-orbit around the sun of his enormous head.

It's there in these stories and twenty more just as good. They span a spectrum of subjects from Bonds to Shaq to Michael Jordan to Bobby Fischer to Pancho Gonzalez to Jud Heathcote to the San Diego Chicken. They tap into a host of subjects, some on the beaten path and some off — the well-meaning but inept ludicrousness of the NFL trying to teach pro football rookies how not to behave badly by handing out condoms; the bitter fight over the ownership of a baseball that ends up in the hands of a federal judge; crouching in a tiny three-by-four-foot cubbyhole of an America's Cup sailboat as it cuts the water at forty-five degrees in seventeen-knot winds.

Some of the stories, like Elizabeth Gilbert's about a former Ironman competitor named Jim MacLaren, reveal a resolve in the face of tragedy as uplifting as it is incomprehensible. Some of them, like Rene Chun's piece about Bobby Fischer, reveal shocking disgrace. Some of them, like Josh Sens's piece about playing a round of golf with a Tibetan lama, are sweet and hilarious. Some of them, like S. L. Price's profile of Pancho Gonzalez, or Bill Donahue's chronicle of the rise and fall of former Olympic gold medalist skier Bill Johnson, are so sad and haunting they will linger long after you have read them.

Each story is different, of course. Each stands alone. But there is a cumulative force to them, an evocation of sports sometimes glorious and sometimes inglorious but with a momentum and weight powerful enough to convince even the most disillusioned member of the flock that there is reason after all to stick with the church.

To hell with sports?

Not when it's your religion.

BUZZ BISSINGER

The Best
AMERICAN
SPORTS
WRITING
2003

ELIZABETH GILBERT

Lucky Jim

FROM GQ

JIM MACLAREN DOESN'T HAVE any memory of the first accident. He can't tell you what it feels like to be hit by a New York City bus and thrown eighty-nine feet in the air, to have your bones shattered and your legs crushed, to have your organs pulverized and to be pronounced dead on arrival at the hospital, because he can't recall any part of it.

The last thing he remembers about that accident is happily cruising down Fifth Avenue on his motorcycle, on "one of those balmy October nights when anything seems possible." As well it should have. Jim MacLaren was, as of that moment, a handsome, intelligent, ambitious, and well-liked twenty-two-year-old who had the world on a string. He'd recently graduated from Yale, where he'd excelled as a scholar, a football player, and a theater star — not a bad trifecta for a fatherless kid from a moneyless family. He'd spent the previous evening dancing with debutantes at a society party and was returning home from a job interview that had gone extremely well. He was wearing a crisp white oxford shirt, his favorite jeans, and a brand-new pair of Italian shoes. He looked wonderful, and he felt wonderful.

He never saw the 40,000-pound bus that ran the red light on Thirty-fourth Street and demolished him. Nor does he have any memory of the paramedics who scraped him off the sidewalk (certain he was already a corpse) and delivered him to Bellevue Hospital. The next thing Jim remembers — after disappearing into a coma for eight days — is waking up in intensive care and learning that his left leg had been amputated below the knee.

So that was the first accident.

Over the next eight years, Jim MacLaren made a concerted effort to become the best one-legged man he possibly could. He endured a brutally painful rehabilitation but was ever uncomplaining about his loss. He graduated from the prestigious Yale School of Drama, acted on stage and television, found plenty of girlfriends. What's most astonishing, though, is that Jim now became a more accomplished athlete as an amputee than he'd ever been as an able-bodied man.

He initially took up swimming to get back in shape after the accident. Then he began riding his bicycle with a special prosthetic. Within a year of losing his leg, Jim was running. First limping, then walking, then hopping, then running. He started signing up for 10-K road races. During his first race, Jim's prosthetic rubbed the stump of his amputated leg so raw and bloody that he had to walk and stumble the last four miles, stopping frequently to change his bandages and dress his open wound, but he did finish and was exhilarated by the accomplishment. Which is why, the following November, he ran the New York City Marathon. Then it was on to the Boston Marathon, where he broke the world speed record for amputee contenders. Jim MacLaren was now the fastest one-legged endurance runner on earth.

Still as engaging a personality as ever, Jim started making a living as a motivational speaker, encouraging people with and without physical disabilities to never accept the notion of personal limitations. He also pursued a serious study of Eastern philosophy, which helped put his amputation into a larger metaphysical context. He was moved and edified by the Buddhist idea that all pain comes from attachment and that therefore we must not become attached to anything in this universe that is impermanent — including, for example, our own bodies. Our bodies are temporary vessels, after all. Attaching our identities to some ego-based perception of physical self is a sure path to misery. Instead, we must define ourselves only by what is eternal within us — namely, our highest level of pure consciousness, our divinity, our one true self. The more attachments we can shed, the closer we can come to enlightenment.

Even as he studied this idea, though, Jim kept pushing that temporary body of his to higher limits. He found extreme physical challenge to be a means of knowing himself better. Pain and endurance were becoming doorways through which he could pass toward greater self-awareness.

How strong is my will? How far can I go without fear? Who am I, really?
Soon he could run a marathon in just over three hours, routinely finishing in the top third of able-bodied contenders. And then he took up triathlons. Yes, triathlons. Once he'd survived a few of those, he set out to conquer the Ironman, one of the most brutal organized sporting events ever imagined. Two and a half miles of swimming, 112 miles of biking, and a full 26.2-mile marathon, all in one race, all in one day. And all on one leg.

Which explains what Jim MacLaren was doing in southern California on that cool June afternoon in 1993. He was participating in an Ironman. Jim was excelling. He was speeding through the town of Mission Viejo on his bicycle, tearing ass at thirty-five miles per hour. The sidewalks were crowded with spectators, and he was dimly aware of their cheers. He had just pulled ahead of a thick snarl of cyclists. He was leading the pack. Suddenly, Jim heard the crowd gasp. He turned his head to see what was going on, and there was the steel grille of a black van heading straight toward him. He realized he was about to be hit by a goddamn car.

It was supposed to have been a closed racecourse. But for some unknown reason, a cop guarding an intersection decided to let one car through, and he misjudged how fast the bicyclists were coming. As Jim MacLaren was approaching, the cop was gesturing to the driver of the van to hit the gas. The driver, a fifty-year-old man on his way to church, was merely obeying orders. He floored it. He didn't see Jim until Jim was on his windshield.

This time Jim vividly remembers being hit. He remembers the screams from the crowd. He remembers his body flying across the street and smashing into a lamppost headfirst, snapping his neck. He remembers riding in the ambulance and being aware that he could not feel his limbs. He was put under anesthesia for emergency surgery on his spine, and when he woke up he was in the trauma ward. He could not move. His head was shaved. There was a bolt screwed into the back of his skull, preventing him from shifting his head even a millimeter. Jim remembers this well. But what he remembers most clearly is this image: all the nurses were in tears.

"We're so sorry," they kept saying.

Jim MacLaren was now a quadriplegic. He was thirty years old. And this is where his story begins.

*

I first heard about Jim from a friend who had been a roommate of his at Yale and who described him as "a marvel and a mystery."

"What happens to a person after two accidents like that?" I asked. "How does he survive? How does he reconcile? How does he not kill himself?"

"That's the mystery part."

I first spoke with Jim MacLaren on the telephone one morning in the spring. I told him I wanted to write about him.

"For *GQ?*" he asked, and laughed. "Okay, but I don't really look the part these days. Armani doesn't exactly make Velcro flies on their pants, you know?"

And I first met Jim MacLaren on the side of a road. It was a sunny afternoon in coastal California. Jim had suggested I come over and meet him at the campus of the Pacifica Institute, where he is currently working on his doctorate. The Pacifica Institute is a small private university buried in the hills of Santa Barbara and dedicated to the graduate study of mythology and psychology. The school is also home to papers of the great mythologist Joseph Campbell. Jim is writing his dissertation on wounds and the wounded male throughout mythological history.

"Meet me down on the road by the front entrance," he said. "We can go up to the campus and have lunch."

The day was cool and dry. The landscape was all parched browns and olive greens. I drove until I reached the gates of Pacifica, and there, waiting on the shoulder of the lonely and dusty road, was Jim MacLaren — Yale graduate, football star, actor, amputee, triathlete, quadriplegic, scholar. He was in a wheelchair, but he did not look anything close to helpless. He was a big and handsome man, broad through the chest. He was wearing shorts, and there was a peglike prosthesis attached to the stump of his left leg. His other leg was muscular and tan. A catheter bag half filled with urine hung from the side of his wheelchair, and a thin hose snaked up from it and disappeared under his shorts. He was lighting a cigarette with fingers that were frozen into painful-looking talons, bent and twisted like little Joshua trees. I rolled down my window.

"Jim MacLaren, I presume?"

He smiled. "How'd you recognize me?"

"You *smoke?*" I said.

"Don't start," he warned.

*

The reason Jim MacLaren can light his own cigarettes has to do with the nature of his spinal injury. He is what is known as an incomplete quadriplegic. This means that although all four limbs were damaged when he broke his neck, he still has limited nerve activity, allowing him some movement and sensation. He can raise his arms a bit, he can bend forward in his wheelchair, he can use his hands somewhat (twisted though they are), and sometimes he can even lift his legs by a few degrees. This tiny range of movement means everything — the difference between an independent life and one with round-the-clock caretakers. The incompleteness of Jim's injury is why he can live alone. With excruciatingly protracted effort, Jim can bathe himself, dress himself, feed himself, and even drive a van (specially outfitted with only hand controls). This all came as a big surprise to Jim's doctors; they'd initially diagnosed him as a complete quadriplegic, meaning he would never have any feeling or motion below the point of injury.

"So I've been very lucky," Jim told me.

We were now sitting in the garden of the Pacifica Institute, eating lunch in the sun. Jim is a true sun lizard. His body is deadly intolerant to cold; chills burrow down into his bones and nerves and torment him without mercy, but sunlight can bake out the pain even better than codeine sometimes. And Jim is almost always in pain. This is the kicker about an incomplete spinal injury — there is still just enough damaged-nerve activity left in his spine to keep him in agony. It's a terrible biological irony. If Jim's injury were more serious, it would actually cause him less suffering. He would feel nothing from the neck down. His limbs would atrophy, and he could forget about his body. As it stands, though, his nerves are spastic and unpredictable. He wakes up some mornings, he says, "feeling like I'm encased in wet cement with electrical currents running through it." His legs convulse uncontrollably, his bowels revolt, he goes blind with pain. Other days he's fine. Day by day, he never knows what he's going to get from his body, or when.

So when Jim says he's been "very lucky," well . . . go ahead and take that with the biggest grain of salt you need to get it down.

What they do in hospitals to someone who has suffered a major spinal injury is unthinkable and torturous, something from a nightmare or the basement of a serial killer. After another surgery to clean the bone chips from Jim's spinal fluid, the doctors put him in a halo — a steel ring that encircled his head and bolted directly into his skull. They had to do this procedure without anesthesia, and Jim screamed for mercy while they drilled the screws into his forehead. Then the halo was attached with four long bars to steel plates clamped tightly on either side of Jim's body. This was to keep him immobilized during recovery, so his spine would risk no further injury. Jim was locked in this halo for three months. There has never been a more dreadfully misnamed apparatus than the medical device known as "the halo."

During his time in the halo, Jim got such bad respiratory infections that an orderly had to come by every few hours with a long tube, forcing it up his nose and down into his lungs to clean out the infected fluid. Other people came to dig inside his rectum with their hands, pulling out the feces because he could not empty his own bowels. Others came to take his blood, to catheterize his bladder, to force-feed him, or to tighten the screws on his halo.

Jim had known physical agony before. After his first accident, he'd been sent to a rehab center legendary for its toughness, a kind of boot camp for new amputees. There Jim worked with a physical-therapy aide named Oscar, a big, bald, muscular black guy who was tougher, Jim says, "than Apollo Creed." Oscar used to hoist Jim onto a machine to exercise what was left of his leg, make him do squats and lifts. Jim would do a few repetitions, and then Oscar would gently lift him off, lay him down on the ground, cover him with a towel, and let him sob uncontrollably for a while. Then they'd do it all over again. So Jim had endured pain before.

But not like this.

The nights were interminable. Paralyzed and in the halo, he couldn't reach the call button for the nurse. He lay awake, anguished at being left alone but equally frightened of whoever might come into his room next and what they might do to him. His body was a hot chaos of pain. Every time someone touched him, he screamed. "I was all body," he remembers. "I was all animal impulses, operating from the most primitive core of my being. I was too afraid to cry — I'd lost control of my diaphragm muscle and was physically unable to cough. I was afraid that if I started crying, all my tears would fill up in my lungs and throat and literally choke me to death."

As he describes it now, he had no soul anymore. He had no self.

He had no identity, no "Jim MacLaren," no history, no future, no hope. Because all this stuff is a luxury in the face of real trauma. The metaphysical question of *Who am I?* — that universal question of humanity that had echoed through Jim's consciousness for years — was now brutally silenced. He wasn't even a "who" anymore; he was a "what."

After three months in this dark underworld of pain, Jim was released from the steel halo. Moved to a rehabilitation center in Colorado, he was assigned to a floor with thirty-seven other patients who had recently become quadriplegics or paraplegics. Like Jim, most of these patients were young men. They were athletic, healthy men who'd been out there in the world only a few weeks earlier, living at their prime and doing the things that snap guys' necks — climbing rocks, racing motorcycles, driving with the top down, and riding in rodeos.

"There was a lot of anger on that ward," Jim says. "But it was good anger. Funny anger. Sarcastic, brave, young man's anger. It wasn't as grim as you might think."

Tentatively, in this battered company, Jim's sense of self began to reemerge. His human consciousness crept out from hiding, and he began to recognize that there was something familiar about his situation. Loss, pain, incapacitation, rehabilitation, endurance? Jim had been through this already. The amputee-triathlete-survivor within him took over. This was the inner voice that said, "You know how to do this, Jim. Work your ass off in rehab, eat the pain, focus on regaining your independence, keep your spirits up, and get the hell out of this place."

Over the next months, Jim became — to nobody's surprise — the model recovering quadriplegic. He was upbeat and stoic and unflinchingly focused. He kept his distance from the other patients so that he could concentrate instead on his own recuperation. He lobbied to get the best therapist in the place and then arranged to have an old issue of a triathlon magazine sent to the guy, featuring an article about this wondrous amputee athlete.

"Look," Jim said. "I want you to read this. This is who I am. This is how hard I'm willing to work."

There is a particular energy to the momentum of recovery, and Jim now swung his whole existence into that energy. He advanced, he pushed, he strove. He defied prognosis after prognosis and recovered faster than anyone had expected. But here's the thing — everyone *had* expected that. Because he's *Jim MacLaren,* damn it, and that's what Jim MacLaren does when he's beaten down. He rises up. He never quits. He's a marvel and a mystery, right?

Which is why, just six months after breaking his neck, Jim was back in the world. He was living on his own, with only visits from caretakers. About a year after his accident, he made a difficult voyage to Hawaii to speak before a convention of Ironman athletes. He was wheeled out onstage to a standing ovation. When the applause finally died down, Jim began with, of all things, a dark joke: "For years I sat out there in that audience and listened to the best Ironman champions in the world speak from this very podium. I always wondered what it would take for a guy like me to be invited up here. I never realized it would be so simple — all I had to do was break my neck."

There was a bone-chilling silence.

Jim thought, *Whoops . . .*

Apparently, these people weren't ready for a joke like that. Nobody in the real world was ready for this. Quickly, Jim changed his tone, went back to his old rousing motivational-speaker oration about endurance and the strength of the human spirit. He gave the people what they wanted, and they (with considerable relief) rewarded him with riotous applause and tears of emotion. After the speech, they all gathered around him, telling him what a hero he was, how healthy he seemed, how they all expected to see him running in the Ironman next year.

"Doesn't Jimmy look *great?*" everyone said. "Isn't Jimmy doing incredibly well?"

In fact, though, he wasn't. He wasn't doing well at all.

Yes, there is a galvanizing momentum to recovery, but then there comes a moment when the recovery has gone as far as it can possibly go and momentum can't carry you anymore. There eventually comes a wall where healing stops and the truth of what you're left with settles in. And Jim had just hit that wall. His body had healed as much as it was ever going to. And all the determination in the world could not change these facts: he would never be out of pain again; he would never lift his arms above his head again; he would never be able to control his bladder again. And he would absolutely never walk again. Not even if he spent ten hours a day in physical therapy, as his old triathlete buddies kept suggesting he do. ("Why aren't you in the gym right now?" they'd ask. "Why aren't you trying harder to beat this, Jimmy?")

Because it couldn't be beat, that's why. That was it — the truth, plain and simple. And the day he realized that truth was the day the invincible Jim MacLaren finally began to lose it.

The next year was an ugly tailspin of rage, sorrow, calamity, and dysfunction. Jim won a big settlement for his accident — $3.7 million. After considerable medical and attorney's fees, that still left him with a fair amount of money. He decided to move to Kona, Hawaii, putting an ocean between himself and everyone who loved him.

"I announced to all my friends that I was moving to the beach to spend my time contemplating my destiny and writing my memoirs," Jim recalls. "Everyone thought this was a great idea and believed it. Everyone supported it. But it was bullshit. I was just running away."

Jim was running away because he didn't want anyone to know the truth, which was that he had become addicted to cocaine. He'd started using the drug about two years after he broke his neck. He'd met this woman, and she'd offered some coke to him. ("Go ahead," she'd said, full of sympathy. "You've suffered so much, you deserve it.") And Jim thought, *Yeah, I do deserve it.* He took the stuff, and it made him disappear for a little while. It took the nightmare of his reality away. Soon he was buying it, doing it alone, needing it — and surrounding himself with the kinds of friends who encouraged the behavior. Junkies, prostitutes, dealers, and lost souls.

"You wouldn't believe how many people were willing to give me cocaine and let me kill myself because they felt sorry for me," he says. "These weren't cruel people, but they were just like, 'Dude, have another line — what else are you gonna do with your damn life?'"

And he drank. There's nothing worse he could have done to his battered body, but he drank and did cocaine every night until his body went away from him, until he didn't have to belong to it anymore.

His old friends called from California, from Colorado, from Yale. Left messages. *How you doin', Jim?* He wouldn't call them back for weeks; then he'd apologize — *Sorry, I've been really busy, been working on my book. . . . Yeah, it's going great. . . .*

Then one night, he found himself drunk out of his mind and drugged to the gills at three in the morning, wheeling his chair up the middle lane of some desolate highway. He realized he was on Alii Drive — the most famous stretch of road on the Hawaiian Ironman racecourse. He'd been here before — had run marathons up this road. Now he shut his eyes and could almost hear the lost echo of the crowd's roar. Alii Drive had been the site of Jim MacLaren's greatest triumph, but now look at him. Wheeling around at night, seeing double, trying to figure out where he could score more cocaine at this hour. Unwashed, alone, crippled. He looked up, or as far up as he could, given that his head couldn't tilt back and he was too blind drunk to see the sky.

"Why are you doing this to me?" he yelled. "Why are you fucking doing this?"

As a human being, you have two choices as to how you view the events of your life. Either you can believe every act is random, or you can believe every act occurs for a preordained reason. But what if you believe every act occurs for a reason and then hideous, unspeakable things happen to you? Well, you are faced with two choices once more. Either you can believe you are cursed, or you can believe you are somehow blessed. Jim MacLaren — who lost a leg at twenty-two and became a quadriplegic at thirty — has decided to believe he is blessed.

This has indeed been a decision. Jim made it shortly after that dark night on Alii Drive. He woke up and knew there was a choice he had to make, and soon. Was he going to die, or was he going to live? He'd surrounded himself with people who were essentially saying to him with each gram of cocaine and each grimace of pity, "Go ahead and kill yourself, Jim. You've suffered enough. I give you permission to leave this life."

"But I didn't *want* to leave this life," he says. "I was thirty-three years old. That's too young to say you're finished. I wanted to live. I didn't want to live as a fucking quadriplegic, but I couldn't change that. And since I couldn't change it, I knew I'd have to make some kind of peace with it."

Not some facile, life-is-beautiful, made-for-television, triumph-of-the-human-spirit peace but a true and sustaining and deeply personal peace. And the only chance he had for gaining any peace, he realized, was to start seeing things very differently. He needed a total change in perception, a paradigm shift. He wasn't sure exactly how to do this yet, but he knew one thing: if he couldn't start finding some serious blessings in all this disaster, he did not stand a chance in hell.

So he went inside. What else could he do? He took his intellect, his energy, and his spiritual hunger and he turned it all inward, setting forth on a journey to find out all over again, but with a newfound humility, "okay, seriously now — who am I? Who am I *really?*"

"The first thing I had to do was identify my absolute deepest fear about all this," Jim says. "What was it? What was the worst thing about having to spend life as a quadriplegic? Was I afraid of death? Not really. I'd had two near-death experiences already, with the white light and the tunnel and the whole deal. They were both amazing encounters, not scary either time. I knew that death no longer frightened me. Was I afraid of losing my sexuality? No. I knew as long as I had taste and smell and sensation, I could lead a sensual life. Was I afraid of helplessness? Not really. Managing on my own is a drag, but it's just logistics. Was I afraid of pain? No. I know how to deal with pain. Pain is a bitch, but I know how to beat it, how to wrestle physical pain to the ground. So what was I afraid of? The answer was pretty clear: I was afraid of being alone with myself, with my mind, with the dark things that lived in me, like fear and doubt and loneliness and confusion. I was afraid of *metaphysical pain.*"

Jim MacLaren knew he was going to have to spend much of his life in solitude and stillness. He was often confined to his bed for days at a time. As though wrestled to the ground by God Himself, he had been forced into his own company. This was petrifying, but now Jim faced this terror and wondered if he could learn to see it differently.

"Maybe, I thought to myself, this wasn't really a curse at all. Maybe it was actually the most exquisite blessing of my life. Maybe it was the opportunity for true catharsis, if I chose to make it one — an opportunity to see my true self beyond all the noise."

Jim MacLaren? Meet Jim MacLaren.

Continuing to seek answers, Jim began to speculate that maybe he needed to have the second accident because he'd never fully learned the correct metaphysical lessons from the first one.

"Yeah, sure, after I lost my leg, I talked the talk about how *I am not this body,* but did I really understand that yet? I had the words down, and I appreciated the concept, but I didn't really have the experience yet to carry that wisdom beyond words. As an amputee, I was still vain about my looks, still seeking attention and affirmation from women, still getting approval from the world through applause, still trapped in my ego."

So maybe destiny had looked down at Jim MacLaren and said, "Hate to do this, pal, but you still don't quite get it," and then pushed him in front of a van — not as a punishment but as a favor — saying, "*Now* will you let go of all your attachment to this mortal body? Now will you examine who you really are?"

Or, as Goethe said, "Die, so you can live."

Inspired, Jim turned to his books. He went back to the ancients. He examined all the classical images of wounded men — the crippled god Hephaestus, the blinded Oedipus, the long-suffering Job. What was God trying to do to Job, anyhow, by stripping him so ruthlessly of his family, his health, his fortune? Testing his faith, right? But something more than that, Jim suspected. And then Jim finally saw it on the tenth reading of that biblical book. God was trying to bring Job closer to Him. After all, Job starts off the story as a faithful but somehow detached worshiper of the Lord. By the end, however, his suffering has erased all formality and he speaks to God directly, challengingly, intimately — just the way God speaks to him.

Maybe this is what had happened to Jim that dark night in Kona in his wheelchair when he'd yelled up at the sky. No priests or rituals or prayers were needed — he had been able to yell directly in God's face, *I am here right now and I am talking to you. Answer me!* Jim had believed that was his low point, but now he saw another possible truth: perhaps he had been closer than ever to the divine. Perhaps that had been his *highest* moment.

Jim came to believe there were other blessings. For the first time, he could see something most people go through their entire lives blind to — namely, that we are not in charge of what happens to us in this lifetime. We are in charge only of how we *perceive* what happens to us in this lifetime.

"I started looking around and seeing people everywhere — especially successful middle-class American men — walking around in complete denial, smugly thinking to themselves, *I sure am doing a good job running my life here.* But I could see now that their sense of control was nothing but a mirage. Safety, entitlement, power — these are all fantasies. We don't drive our destinies. Not in that way."

Jim realized, to his relief, that once you stop trying to control events you can't control anyway, you can drop all that wasted energy and focus on the one thing you *are* in charge of. As the teachings of Buddha and Socrates show, you have only one task as a human being: to know yourself.

"Look," Jim says. "I have honestly come to believe that I needed these accidents in my life. I completely believe that. Not in terms of paying dues or getting punished by God, but in terms of getting my attention and bringing me deeper inside myself to a place where I could find honesty and peace. Was it destined? Did I literally choose to have these awful things happen to me? No, not in so many words, I don't believe so. But I do believe this — I believe I was born *begging* for experiences that would show me who I really am. And that's what I've been given."

Sitting across from Jim at lunch, listening to him recount his story, I suddenly decided to interrupt and tell him a story of my own. I told him about a bicycle accident I'd had a few weeks before I met him. I was riding my bike at night in New York City, going too fast, getting thrills from dodging taxis and passing buses. I was crossing Thirty-seventh Street, thinking, *I am so cool!* when I hit a pothole and went flying. I landed on my head, broke my helmet, took all the skin off my shoulder. But after a few minutes of shaking with adrenaline and pain, I was able to get back on my bike and — very gingerly — ease my way home.

I told this story to Jim only because I'd just realized that my little accident took place a mere three blocks from the street where he'd lost his leg. Raising the inevitable question: *Why?* Two separate accidents in two isolated moments. Why did they have such astonishingly different consequences?

"Is it even worth asking why I got *this,*" I say, lifting my sleeve and showing the tiny scar on my shoulder, "and you got . . . *that?*"

"Sure, it's worth asking. Any question is worth asking. Why do different people have different destinies? It's an interesting intellectual subject. We could sit here and speculate about it forever, if that's what you want to do. But we'll never know why. And if we did somehow miraculously find out why, would that change anything?"

"So should we just move on to some other question?" I asked.

Jim smiled. "Well, that's what I've done."

These days, Jim lives in a huge loft in downtown Pasadena. On good mornings, he can get out of bed, eat, clean out his bowels, attach his catheter, shower, dress, and be ready to leave the apartment in just under three hours. Almost the same amount of time it used to take him to run a marathon, and nearly as physically grueling. It's painful, but he gives his body the time it needs, and then the rest of the day belongs to him. If the weather is nice and he feels strong enough and doesn't have a paper to write, he'll get in his wheelchair and head into the city's Old Town. He'll park at an outdoor café, order up a triple espresso, and read in the sun, blissfully alone and blissfully comfortable with his own company.

Or sometimes he spends the day with his girlfriend. Her name is Alessandra. Jim calls her Ally, or Ally-mander, or Ally-cat. She's beautiful, blond, smart. They met in an Internet chat room and have been together for two years.

"People look at me and call me a saint for being with a guy in a wheelchair," says Ally, "and it's so insulting. First of all — the idea of *me* as a saint . . ."

This makes both Jim and Ally laugh so hard that the conversation has to stop for several minutes.

"Anyway," Ally continues, wiping her eyes. "I'm with him because he's the most intelligent and sexy man I've ever known. Period."

As for the sex, yes, they have it. Maybe not the way you have it, but they do have it. Jim does have limited sensation in his penis, but he has to be careful because an orgasm could be a serious health risk. (It could put him into a state of hyperreflexia — pulse goes down, blood pressure goes up; he could have a stroke or a spasm or even die.) So he expresses his sexuality differently now — with hands, mouth, voice, imagination, and lots of time.

Of course, Jim and Ally have to deal with the limitations of his body every day. For one thing, they don't get a lot of privacy in public. People stare at Jim. People stare shamelessly. After all these years, Jim is used to this sort of thing. He recognizes that his is a public body now. But it still drives his girlfriend nuts when people stare. The three of us all headed into the Old Town one afternoon, with Jim rolling along as Ally and I walked beside him. Every person we passed either gaped openly at Jim, did a double take, or stared with purpose at the ground before his own feet, fiercely determined not to gawk at the quadriplegic. Jim took no notice of this, but Ally grew increasingly tense. By the time a young couple nudged each other with absolute indiscretion and actually pointed at Jim, Ally lost it.

"What the fuck is the *matter* with people?" she exploded.

"They're just curious, Ally-mander," Jim said, reaching for her hand. "It's nothing."

Indeed, Jim attracts an enormous amount of attention. And it's not only gruesome fascination, either. He has earned a strange kind of status through his injury. People constantly come to Jim with their own tragedies in hand, seeking solace or wisdom from him. Even perfect strangers see him as some holy sage of pain, someone who can help them heal their own wounds.

"I'm a walking projection," Jim says, and then clarifies, "No — I'm a *rolling* projection."

Acquaintances who barely know Jim make him the first person they consult when calamity strikes. People call him at all hours from hospitals, jails, funeral homes, and rehab centers, everybody begging for the same thing — *Please, help lead me out of this fear.* Jim tries to help when he can, but he says sometimes it's hard to come across as completely sympathetic. For instance, when he gets a desperate midnight phone call from someone whose brother or son or wife has been in a dreadful car accident and he hears that the loved one has lost a limb, it's all Jim can do to affect a somber tone and not say what he's thinking. Which is, Thank God! Hallelujah! Just an amputation? That's *nothing*. We can *totally* handle that.

And it isn't always easy, because Jim still struggles. Jim MacLaren, let's be very clear about this, did not enjoy losing his leg, and he does not enjoy being in a wheelchair. He looks for the blessings where he can find them, and he tries to keep a sense of humor, but there are days when it's not funny and it's not enlightening. Days when he wakes up in so much pain he can't get out of bed at all. Days when he can no longer stand the endless battle over trying to control his bowels. ("I'm more obsessed with my feces than the

Marquis de Sade," he jokes darkly.) Days when yet another infec-
tion lodges in his catheter incision and his testicles swell to the size
of softballs. Days when he wonders how he's going to possibly survive this abuse for another forty years.

"There are moments when I realize all over again what happened to me," Jim says, "and it's still unbelievable. I mean, come
on! Jesus Christ, for fuck's sake, how much can one person endure?
But I can't stay in that place for long or I'll lose my mind. Instead, I
have to ask, What is wholeness, really? What is a full life? What are
my actual obstacles? And whenever I find myself frustrated with my
handicap or looking with envy at an able-bodied man, I ask myself
this: If I could get up out of this wheelchair right now and walk
across the room, would that really get me there? I mean, would that
really get me to the place I most want to go with my life? Because
let's be honest here — the other side of this room is not my ultimate destination. My ultimate destination is self-knowledge and
enlightenment. Do I have to get there on foot? Or can I find some
other path?"

The day before Jim MacLaren broke his neck, he woke up in his
house in Boulder, Colorado, stirred out of bed earlier than usual
by some strange and unfamiliar energy. He left his then girlfriend,
Pam, sleeping and went outside to sit in his back yard to eat his
breakfast alone. The sun was coming up, reflecting off the mountains, and the morning light was filmy and gold. Jim could hear
his neighbor's young children playing next door. He could hear
birdsong and the tremor of leaves. He'd brought a book outside
with him to read, but it lay in his lap unopened; he couldn't focus
on it. He couldn't pay attention to his breakfast, either. He wasn't
even thinking about the Ironman he'd be competing in the next
day. None of this mattered, suddenly. All Jim wanted was to sit in
stillness and experience the inexplicable bliss that was surrounding
him in this moment.

And then the bliss started to grow, to rise within him. Jim moved
from a state of contentment into a state of joy, and soon even the
joy could not be contained, and it became a euphoria that spilled
out over his whole body, lifting the hair on the back of his neck and
running goose bumps across his skin. He was overcome by a thrilling sense of what he could later only describe as *anticipation*. He'd

never felt anything like this, and he never wanted it to end. He was laughing and crying at the same time, elated beyond his senses.

Jim's girlfriend heard the noise and rushed out of the house to see what was wrong.

"What is it, Jim?" she asked. "What's going on?"

He looked up at her through his tears and smiled. He was thirty years old. He was twenty-four hours away from becoming a quadriplegic, and he could not contain his excitement.

"Pam," he said, and he was never more certain of anything in his life, "Pam — listen! Something *amazing* is about to happen to me!"

Fowled Away

FROM THE LOS ANGELES TIMES

SALEM, ORE. — The Chicken is barking.

His breath comes in short, loud bursts, straining to escape the narrow opening in his foam beak.

He sprints through the warm night, off the faded field, into a windowless concrete storage room, plopping down on a folding chair.

Outside, in the aluminum bleachers that ring this tiny baseball stadium in the Northwest woods, the laughter dies.

Inside, the Chicken gasps.

"Was it funny?" he asks.

He tears off his costume head, swallows air in giant breaths, chugs a twenty-ounce bottle of water, gulps more air.

His blue vest is stained dark with sweat. His yellow leotard is dotted with infield dirt.

His black hair is plastered to a face that is pale from nearly three decades of hiding. It is the smooth face of a boy on the thickening body of a man who next year will turn fifty.

"Well," he asks again. "Was it funny?"

Yes, he is told. It was great.

He looked devious throwing the water balloons at the first base coach. He looked helpless when players retaliated by showering him with their own water balloons.

He is told that many fans smiled, chuckled, held up little children, and pointed them toward this strange and wonderful creature who has made this Saturday night so memorable.

He frowns. That's not what he asked. He wants to know about the roar. Where was the roar?

Nearly every summer night for most of his adult life, he has surrendered his identity and hidden his face and changed his voice in search of the roar.

Did he somehow miss the roar?

Outside, the inning is nearly over, an expectant hush descending upon several thousand fans who have put down their Killer Kielbasas and Dippin' Dots ice cream to watch what may be the final webbed footsteps of a legend.

Inside, the Chicken growls.

"But was it funny????"

Put on the head.

Go ahead, pick up the one-pound clump of feathers and baseball-sized eyes and giant beak and put it on.

Feel what Ted Giannoulas has felt for twenty-nine years.

Good luck enduring it for more than twenty-nine seconds.

The inside of the head of the San Diego Chicken is sour, steamy, a moldy shower stall in a darkened locker room.

"First time I put it on, I couldn't believe it," said his sister Chris. "I thought, 'How does he do this?'"

And how does he see? The holes in the beak through which he views the world are only inches wide, like a couple of cracks in a Venetian blind. He cannot look below him, or above him, or beside him.

Put on the chicken head and realize, Ted Giannoulas has gone through life with the unique blessing of being exposed only to what is directly in front of his face.

He sees the children's smiles. He doesn't see the uncomfortable stares from those who watch him increasingly strain to create that joy.

He sees baseball in all its flannel-and-leather-covered romance. He didn't see the game's creeping selfishness and greed until it was too late.

Today, the most recognizable mascot uniform is no longer a uniform, but a time warp, one in which Giannoulas finds himself seemingly trapped.

He is the best-known, highest-paid baseball mascot in history, a star who still fills minor league stadiums and attracts autograph lines that stretch for blocks.

But for the first time, he did not work a major league park this season, because the big leaguers no longer have the time or the interest.

In the Chicken's final days in major league clubhouses, players cursed him, ran from him, even purposely missed throws that might have hit him.

"It's so sad, there's such acrimony in there now," Giannoulas said. "The players are way too cool. Guys who I had fun with in the minor leagues wouldn't even say hello to me anymore."

He is the father of modern sports entertainment, an accomplished vaudevillian who invented the art of toying with an umpire and dancing with a player.

But there are nearly a dozen imitators out there now, slick and hip traveling mascots with names like BirdZerk! and ZOOperstars!, acts that allegedly steal the Chicken's material and send him screeching.

"Few things stick in my craw, but this is one of them," Giannoulas said. "Those laughs are my babies. My babies!"

While never missing an event in twenty-nine years — more than six thousand consecutive games — Giannoulas has thrilled three generations of children.

But he wakes up today at forty-nine with no children of his own because he never had the time.

"You know how everyone always says that if they lived their life over again, they wouldn't change a thing?" Giannoulas said. "Well, that's bull. I would change things. I would have given more time to myself."

Observers agree his unique style of physical humor and mime would make Giannoulas a great entertainer on any stage.

But because he refuses to allow himself to be photographed outside of his suit, nobody would recognize him.

Twenty-nine years of standing ovations for the Chicken, and not once has anybody cheered Ted Giannoulas.

Twenty-nine years of fame, yet nobody has seen his face.

"Sometimes it's like I don't have a real life," he said.

Unlike the owners of other mascot costumes, Giannoulas also will not allow anyone else to wear the suit and learn the trade.

"I'm not a department store Santa Claus," he said. "There is only one Chicken."

So when Giannoulas retires, the Chicken will disappear forever. Then what will happen to the man?

It is a question he faces daily, yet never really faces, still working more than one hundred dates a year, hugging a happy child in Wyoming one moment, dealing with a jerky first baseman in Fresno the next.

Have you seen him? Do you remember your favorite gag?

Was it when he marched onto the field followed by a line of children dressed like baby chickens, a skit that ended with the kids lifting their legs on the umpire? Or was it when he lost a dance contest to a Barney look-alike, then punched him out?

He's still doing the same things, only this summer, for the first time, one of his gigs was a softball tournament. And while the San Diego Padres hired a mascot to work one game at his home Qualcomm Stadium, it wasn't him.

In serving baseball, the San Diego Chicken has become like baseball itself: a brilliant idea, born of innocence, bred with joy, but now struggling to age gracefully through a building cloud of impertinence and indifference.

"Ted invented mascots, he was the first and funniest, I have nothing but respect for him," said Dave Raymond, who spent years wearing the costume of the popular Philly Phanatic. "But if you're not careful, you can lose yourself in that suit."

The Chicken is dripping.

Running off the field in ninety-degree Fresno heat, he grabs for a towel as he drops to a chair in a humid tunnel behind the dugout.

As always, the head is the first thing to come off. But this time, because of a skit involving a special costume, he must also peel off the rest of his leotard and feathers.

"Can you help me take off my suit, sir?" he asks a team employee, gasping as he buries his exposed face in the towel.

The usher doesn't understand.

The Chicken pauses, stares up, asks again, a little louder.

"Sir, please, can you help me get out of this suit?"

The employee shrugs and steps forward, grunting and grabbing and pulling and yanking and slowly stripping away the wet layers until the Chicken becomes a man again.

At which point Giannoulas, his face still in the towel, drops breathless back into his chair.

"I've seen him for the last five years," whispers a nearby guard. "But I've never seen him like this."

The search for the Chicken began earlier this summer during a meeting with a five-foot-five, middle-aged man standing outside a budget hotel in Lake Elsinore.

He was wearing blue jean shorts, an untucked blue Hawaiian shirt, and reading glasses propped on a full head of black hair. He looked like a tourist. He looked like a science teacher. He looked like anything but . . .

"Ted Giannoulas," he said, extending his hand.

He saw the surprised look on his visitor's face. He shrugged. He is used to the disbelief. It really doesn't matter. It's never about him, anyway.

"I have plenty of Chicken stories," he said. "I'm afraid I don't have any Ted stories."

Oh, but he does.

As the essence of baseball remains curiously timeless, so, too, does the man underneath its mascot.

The Chicken is a multimillionaire who commands in the neighborhood of $7,500 an appearance.

Yet Ted Giannoulas has lived in the same modest suburban San Diego house for twenty-two years.

This is partly because it is within a mile of the home of his mother, who still makes his costumes. This is also because the house is near a good library. After spending his summer chasing a roar, he spends his winters soaking in silence.

The Chicken is also an effective salesman who makes big money in affordable merchandising that includes everything from dolls to videos.

Yet Ted Giannoulas doesn't have an ATM card. No pager. No personal e-mail address. Can't use the computer printer.

When he arrives every night at the ballpark on his leased luxury bus — he hasn't flown regularly for ten years because of the hassle — he is not carrying a wallet, keys, or a cell phone.

The Chicken is a perfectionist who carefully choreographs every move and understands every nuance. He knows the size of every minor league foul territory, the nature of every sound system, the location of every bathroom.

Yet when he talks to small children afterward in the autograph line, he uses the words and high-pitched tones of a character from Looney Tunes.

"Hey, Pork Chop!" "Hello, Wiener!" "Howyadoin', Sugar Cube?"

Folks say this is part of what makes the Chicken different — and more enduring — than other mascots.

The other ones don't talk. They can't talk. To open their mouth is to risk ruining the illusion by sounding different from the person who wore the costume the previous year.

Because the Chicken is the Chicken forever, he can talk, and so he does, cackling on the dugout, whispering to the children, and engaging in a running patter with fans in postgame autograph lines that often last past midnight.

Incidentally, he signs for free. He signs everything. He poses for anything.

On that summer night in Salem, seated at the head of a long line winding through the rightfield playground, how he chirps.

"Have some Kentucky Fried Chicken!" announces one brave little boy, plopping down a trademark bucket on the autograph table.

"I hope that's nobody I know," says the Chicken, staring at the chicken.

"Thanks for helping us win tonight," mumbles a shy little girl.

"I'm your good-cluck charm," says the Chicken.

"Why did the chicken cross the road?" ask a couple of teenage boys.

"To get away from stupid questions," says the Chicken with a laugh.

The question he is most often asked, of course, is a more basic one.

Is that really still him?

It is asked by adult fans who bring him twenty-year-old autographs in search of comparative proof. It is asked by senior citizens who test him with questions about an act in El Paso in 1978.

In Tucson, the question stunned Giannoulas when it was asked by a man in his midtwenties who brought him a photo of the Chicken performing his trademark biting of a baby's head.

"That baby was me," said the man.

It is also a question increasingly asked by friends and family members.

Said Chris: "I'd like to see him finally relax and enjoy the fruits of his labor. After a while, you've got to say, maybe I should go home now."

Said former mascot Raymond: "Can you imagine if he had decided to share his knowledge, to teach others his craft? He would be running the entire mascot industry today. He would be his own little Disney."

Instead, the Chicken remains a huge man in a small world, unfolding eye charts for young umpires, literally stealing bases for old laughs, signing autographs that begin "Best Wishbones . . ."

"He's thought about retiring," said his wife, Jane. "But how do you retire from yourself?"

The Chicken is crying.

All night in this tiny ballpark in Butte, Montana, people have told him that he must meet a boy named Matthew.

"Matthew is looking for you."

"Matthew wants to see you."

Late in the game, the Chicken is finally directed to the child, a four-year-old with huge eyes.

"How are you doing, you little wiener?" the Chicken asks.

"I'm really enjoying you," Matthew says.

"Having fun?" the Chicken asks.

"You are very funny," Matthew says.

As Matthew tentatively reaches out to stroke the Chicken's suit, his father leans over and whispers into Giannoulas's ear.

"My son has been blind since birth."

Giannoulas spends the rest of the game in tears.

"Imagine allowing a child to see with his ears," he says later.

That night is what convinced him that, even after all these years, this is what he must do.

"That night," he says later, "laughter was the most powerful force in the universe."

His father never liked it. Up until two months before his death of lung cancer in 1979, John Giannoulas was not proud that his son was the Chicken.

Growing up the only son of Greek immigrants in London, Ontario, young Ted liked to rearrange the furniture, wear a cape, and jump around like Mighty Mouse.

His father wanted him to stop clowning around.

"My husband wanted Ted to be a doctor, something big, something serious," Helen Giannoulas said. "He was a very traditional Greek man."

After third grade, Ted obeyed his father, turned his emotions inward, tried to become that model man.

"I always wanted to be the class clown, but I never had the nerve," Giannoulas recalled. "So I would always sit next to the class clown."

Until that spring afternoon in 1974 at San Diego State.

Giannoulas, a student, was sitting with other fellow workers at the campus radio station when an executive from a local rock station walked in and asked if anybody wanted to wear a chicken suit and pass out promotional eggs during spring break.

Nobody said anything. The executive looked at Ted.

"You're the shortest," he said. "You can start tomorrow."

Eager for the money and pining for adventure, Giannoulas said yes.

"Sixty seconds that changed my life," he said.

That first job was boring, it was embarrassing, the chicken suit looked awful.

But something happened when Giannoulas put it on.

Where he was once worried about behaving like a man, suddenly he could act like a fool.

What Ted Giannoulas could never do, the Chicken could do with abandon.

"I discovered an untapped personality in that suit," he said. "It was like, now I have freedom. Now I'm no longer Ted."

When the gig ended, he convinced the radio station owners to allow him to remain in the suit long enough to attend 1974 opening day for the Padres.

"I just wanted a free ticket, and I figured that was a way to get it," Giannoulas said.

People tend to stare at a chicken in a seat. Giannoulas liked those stares. He started performing gags in the stands.

He became so popular that, several months later, Padre officials invited him to the field during the game to shoot a commercial.

He lifted his leg on an umpire, and a star was born.

When he won a lawsuit that freed him from the radio station and allowed him to wear the chicken suit anywhere, that star became national.

He has since performed at the White House, worked with Elvis Presley, written top-selling memoirs, appeared on every sort of national stage and screen.

But the one performance he will never forget is the only one witnessed by his father.

John Giannoulas never really accepted his son's job. He scoffed at the suit.

"Don't worry about my boy," he would tell friends. "Even the president of the United States used to wash dishes."

But in 1979, while fighting lung cancer that would take his life less than two months later, he finally agreed to watch Ted's act.

"I remember him wearing a beret, and pulling an oxygen tank," Ted said.

He paused, and it was clear that wasn't all he remembered.

"My father laughed," said Ted softly, his eyes wide, as if he had just heard that roar.

The Chicken is fuming.

He shows up in a Chicago White Sox clubhouse to say hello to old friend Frank Thomas, and the player starts shouting.

"Don't come near me," Thomas says. "Don't look at me, don't talk to me, I want nothing to do with you."

The Chicken shows up in a Boston Red Sox clubhouse, and several players are suddenly too injured to help.

The Chicken shows up in Philadelphia, and catcher Bo Diaz agrees to be part of a gag, but only for money.

The Chicken arrives in Baltimore, and Eddie Murray refuses to give him a warmup ball for a trick.

"If only these players knew how much the fans needed to see them having fun," Giannoulas says later. "If only they had a clue."

Amy Schneider, a young marketing assistant with the Cincinnati Reds, was asked about the Chicken.

"I've never heard of the Chicken," she said. "There's a level of seriousness at a major league park now that doesn't lend itself to outside entertainment. The players and umpires don't want to be distracted."

Charlie Seraphin, marketing vice president of the Kansas City Royals, was asked about the Chicken.

"It's all economics," he said. "The gap between the size of a Chicken crowd and a regular crowd has declined."

Dave Oldham, president of the Class-A San Bernardino Stampede, was asked about the Chicken.

He answered in a different language.

"I want to raise my son to be a Chicken," Oldham said. "He's a living legend, the best, he can still fill a minor league park, still make a five-figure difference that night."

On this night in Salem, the game had long since ended, but the entertainment continues.

The line for autographs is filled with fidgety kids and laughing adults. After two hours, a guy named Ray Woods shows up in front of the Chicken with nothing in his hands.

"I don't need an autograph, I don't need anything," he says. "It was my kid's first game and I just wanted to say thank you."

The Chicken shakes his head. Sometimes there is nothing even he can say.

The clock ticks past midnight when two teenage girls appear out of the darkness for one final photo.

The seventh inning was hours ago. The players have long since departed. The balls and bats and gloves are locked up.

Yet as the girls approach the Chicken they are singing, softly, soulfully, their words softening the night like an old friend.

"Take me out to the ballgame, take me out to the crowd . . ."

It is not a roar. It will have to do.

GARY SMITH

The Ball

An American Story

FROM SPORTS ILLUSTRATED

INSIDE A LOCKED METAL BOX. Inside a thick gray vault. Inside a yellow stucco building. In a town named Milpitas, California. There lies a baseball.

No one may play with this ball. No one may touch it or see it. Mr. Hayashi and Mr. Popov are just too angry — each insists the ball is his — and there's simply too much riding on it. Mr. Hayashi's reputation is at stake, and his obligation to the spirit that steered the baseball into his hands. So are much of Mr. Popov's savings, a year of his life, and his self-esteem as an outfielder. So are $1.5 million. That's how much the baseball is said to be worth.

It looks like such a simple thing, the ball in the metal box. But if you were to begin to pull it apart to know it at its core, you'd have to unstitch 88 inches of waxed thread sewn in a factory on the slopes of a Costa Rican volcano, peel back two swaths of cowhide taken from a tannery in Tennessee, unravel 369 yards of Vermont wool, and pare away a layer of rubber applied in Batesville, Mississippi — and you still wouldn't have gotten to its heart. It's sort of like this story.

It's the tale of a record-setting baseball struck by a wooden stick swung by the descendant of slaves from Africa, smacked into the glove of the son of a Russian immigrant who'd been captured and forced into labor by the Nazis, popped into the fingers of the child of Japanese Americans once locked away in internment camps, and finally landed in a safe-deposit box whose key is held by a San Francisco judge, the grandson of Mexican immigrants who fled Pancho

Villa. That's Bonds to Popov to Hayashi to Garcia, if you're scoring at home. And now the lawyers — third-generation Japanese, Chinese, and Italian Americans — are in feverish preparation for an October trial to settle the lawsuit over who will possess this ball. That's right. It's a genuine American story.

Ah, but this is the America that makes your stomach turn. The one in which pettiness and greed and lawyers chasing contingency fees can sully anything, even a thing so pure as a baseball sailing through the sky on a Sunday afternoon. You're forgetting already: nothing's simple. Wait till the stitches come off and the yarn starts unfolding. Wait till you see how far back, back, back Barry Bonds's maple bat made that baseball go.

Their eyes met, a few minutes before their fates did. Two strangers, on last season's final day, standing upon the loveliest piece of baseball real estate on earth, the rightfield arcade at Pac Bell Park — a brick reef poised between the glorious green of a ball field and blue of a bay. Two strangers gazing together upon the festival in McCovey Cove, Frisbees and foam balls flying over a flotilla of canoes, kayaks, surfboards, rowboats, and motorboats, over women in wet suits and guys in bull's-eye T-shirts and Batman and Robin suits and barking retrievers and fishing nets lashed to broomsticks, all waiting for treasure to drop from the sky.

Something else, that very moment, was dropping from the sky. The U.S. assault on Afghanistan had commenced just a few hours earlier. Knots of people were staring at TV monitors near the concession stands as F-16s and cruise missiles screamed through the clouds and Special Forces parachuted behind enemy lines. We were all in this together. We'd all just learned, the hard way, what really mattered. Just twenty-five days had passed since September 11.

Looking down from the arcade at all their bobbing brothers, Alexander Nikolaivich Popov and Patrick Mitsuo Hayashi exchanged a smile.

They shared things, the two strangers, that they never could have guessed. Both had graduated from Cal Poly–San Luis Obispo. Both had become fascinated by computers and had majored in electrical engineering. Both had gone on to market high-tech equipment in Silicon Valley. Both were passionate golfers and still bachelors in their midthirties. Both had come to Pac Bell Park wearing baseball

gloves and accompanied by brothers with whom they'd shared bedrooms and front-yard ball games growing up.

It was time to be boys again. Alex Popov, waiting with a baseball
outside the subway station near the stadium, had tossed it to his
brother, Michael, the moment he emerged, and the two of them
had weaved through pedestrians, flinging fly balls to each other
for a half-dozen blocks in preparation for the big one. As soon as
they reached the ballpark, Alex traded his $40 lower box seat to a
scalper in exchange for a ten-buck standing-room-only ticket, like
the one his brother already held, so they'd both be able to stand on
the rightfield arcade walkway.

Patrick Hayashi, picking up his brother Lane at the San Jose airport, had spoken excitedly about their chances as they drove to the
ballpark. Patrick likened the SRO tickets they'd purchased on eBay
to lottery tickets. Lane said no, their odds were much better than
the lottery's — why, if Bonds pulled one to right, as was his habit,
and *didn't* get quite enough of it to blast it into San Francisco Bay,
Lane and Patrick would be two of perhaps 1,500 people in the
sweepstakes.

A few minutes before Bonds's first-inning at-bat, both pairs of
brothers split up. So they could cover more ground — that's what
they told themselves. So brother wouldn't be clawing brother over
a ball whose value, memorabilia marketing agent Michael Barnes
estimated, was between $1 million and $2 million — that's what
they didn't say.

By pure chance Michael Popov and Lane Hayashi ended up a
few feet from each other, in dead right, while Patrick Hayashi and
Alex Popov ended up likewise, just behind the 365-foot sign nearer
to right center, where Alex's online research had told him the biggest number of Bonds's bombs had gone.

Bonds approached the plate. Two outs, nobody on. The brothers
sized up their neighbors. Their *enemies*. Alex Popov, six feet and
two hundred pounds, decided he was taller than anyone within
arm's reach, but just in case, he planted one foot on a box containing television cable so he could make himself even taller. He took
no notice of the KNTV reporter beside him with a microphone
stuffed inside his jacket, angling for the big story, nor of the reporter's cameraman a dozen feet away. Kathryn Sorenson, a Xerox
repairwoman in a wool cap, surveyed the eager mass of males in

their thirties and forties and noticed the five-foot-five-inch Patrick Hayashi. *How's that little short guy gonna get the ball?* she thought. *He doesn't have a chance in hell. He's gonna get stomped.*

Three balls, two strikes to Bonds. Had the slugger mulled the ethical question staring him in the eye? He'd already smashed the all-time home run record held by Mark McGwire, hitting numbers 71 and 72 two days earlier. The 72 ball ricocheted back onto the field and was presented to Bonds, which meant that all he had to do now, in a game that was meaningless in the standings, was to hit anything except a home run, and the 72 ball he possessed would be the million-dollar ball. What should he do?

Dodgers pitcher Dennis Springer coiled. The Hayashis and Popovs tensed. Springer slung a 3-and-2 knuckler. Bonds dropped his hands and lifted, a launching-pad lick, perhaps the most unselfish act of his life. The ball shot up, up, and farther up — could a ball hit that high travel far enough? Up over a city where the gold rushers had thronged a century and a half earlier in quest of instant wealth. Up over a town where the rush had just happened all over again, a dotcom boom in which websites and high-tech firms had sprouted and monetized, in the locals' lingo, overnight. Where everyone had babbled of click-through rates and vested stock options and rents tripling and condos that couldn't be built quickly enough to accommodate the wave of worldwidewebbers washing in. Up over the stadium at the epicenter of it all, the cyberbarons' playground where Yahoo.com, Schwab.com, Webvan, CNET, TicketWeb, TiVo, Blue Mountain, and *Wired* magazine had hung their 10,000-watt shingles from the façades, and where every spiderwebbed warehouse within a ten-block radius had been converted into a dotcommer's office or his two-bedroom pad.

Up, up over a mob that had just seen the four-year bubble burst, the dot detonate, instant riches vaporizing and the lights blinking out on those ballpark billboards one by one as the city of San Francisco discovered, to its shock, that the world didn't need a dozen online pet-supply companies.

High above Hayashi, one of 40,000 people laid off by Nortel Networks just a few months before, and Popov, whose online venture, Man.com, had gone up in smoke. High against a gray sky, one last dot worth a million bucks.

*

Oh . . . my . . . God. Slowly it dawned on Popov. That ball wasn't just
high. That ball was deep. That ball was . . . monetized. And coming
straight toward him.

As well it should. Who else in the entire ballpark had awakened
that Sunday morning, pulled out a packet of flash cards, and begun
reciting a dozen statements crafted as neurolinguistic tools to play
on his subconscious and improve his life?

> Each and every morning I plan my day in an efficient and productive
> manner to maximize the hours . . .
> My lean waistline is an indication of my attitude toward life . . .

Who else had awakened that morning and reminded himself of
the ten things he had pledged to do daily: plan his day, clean his
one-bedroom San Francisco apartment, stretch, read, exercise, account for his expenditures, utter the twelve affirmations from the
flash cards in the morning and then again at night, guess at something that might happen that day (to build anticipation), and practice his golf swing? Who else had awakened and, because it was the
first weekend of a new month, checked a monthly review sheet to
make sure he'd lived up to his vows during the previous month,
that he'd bathed at least twice (baths are more contemplative than
showers), read both a business and nonbusiness book, gotten his
monthly massage, visited his parents at least twice, reviewed his file
of photographs that elicited positive emotions, and graded himself
from 1 to 100 on his relationships, health, nutrition, finances, career, education, spiritual life, and golf game?

The beauty of it was, it worked! That baseball was flying, as
if magnetized, straight toward the most enthusiastic, most determined, most optimistic American in the whole damn ballpark. Toward the one voted by high school classmates the likeliest to succeed, the one who hadn't let the twenty intervening years wilt any
of his wonder at the world or his belief in himself. The guy who'd
spend fourteen hours writing up a business plan for a start-up venture, hop in the car at 10:00 P.M., drive an hour and a half out of
San Fran to lay a sleeping bag on the hood and watch a meteor
shower on a mountaintop till 3:00 A.M., and then decide, What
better capper on a meteor shower than to watch the sunrise? The
one who had called a pal on his cell phone just a few minutes earlier in the game and informed him that number 73 was coming,
baby, and he was going to snag it.

The headphones piping play-by-play into Alex's ears disconnected him from the world, cocooned him from everything except the ball soaring toward him. All sound ceased. The dot in the sky grew larger. Time became taffy tugged at both ends: 5.7 seconds became forever. He didn't have to move.

Clearly, he'd think later — for he believed in such things — the ball was meant for him. He lifted his glove, unaware of what was happening around him. Unaware of how many other human beings believed that Barry's ball was meant for them.

This was what Todd McFarlane had feared. This lust, this frenzy, this stampede was what he'd felt in his bones, the premonition he'd had the moment he purchased McGwire's 70th home run ball for $3 million two years before. That was twenty-five times the amount paid for the next-most-expensive baseball in history: Babe Ruth's first Yankee homer, auctioned off in 1998 for 120 grand. *I've just given people a false sense of how much a baseball is worth,* he remembered thinking. *I've just turned people into lunatics.*

The ball struck the top of the webbing of a glove whose pliability Alex Popov so prized that he'd appropriated it from his girlfriend a year and a half earlier. There was an explosion of noise from 41,000 throats, then darkness as he fell to the cement floor beneath a wall of flesh and bone. All sounds — the crowd's roar, the blasting home run music, the shrieks of treasure-seekers entangled in the pile *(Help! Get off me!)* — grew muffled and distant, as if heard through water. Alex's headphones were ripped off, a lens of his glasses knocked out. Michael Popov, a surfer, felt as if he were being lifted and carried by a wave, only the liquid below and above him was human, the man on his back was Lane Hayashi, and suddenly he couldn't breathe.

What was occurring in that heap? Each survivor tells a different tale.

KNTV reporter Ted Rowlands says his first flush of ecstasy at finding himself at the bottom, literally, of a big story was replaced by panic as he was crushed against Alex Popov, the air driven from his lungs.

Kathryn Sorenson, who played tackle football with boys while growing up, says it felt like the middle of a blitz with Alex Popov as the quarterback. Says she saw people raking at him and kneeing him to obtain the ball she's sure he caught and took to the ground.

Says she saw Patrick Hayashi bite a teenage boy and thrust his hand underneath Popov's crotch to try to get the ball.

Jim Callahan, a piano-shop proprietor whom Sorenson identifies as one of the ball-rakers, says no, the experience was neither scary nor violent — that he, in fact, said, "Sorry, excuse me," as he foraged for the nugget beneath a man's buttocks. Besides, he adds, he was looking right into Alex's glove one second after Alex hit the ground, and the ball he saw inside it wasn't the Bonds ball, but somehow another one, with black felt-tip lettering on it.

Doug Yarris, a dentist, says that's not possible, that he landed with his head two or three feet from Popov's glove as it lay tucked near Alex's torso, and that the ball inside the glove was the one Bonds hit.

Kevin Griffin, a plumbing contractor who agrees that the ball should be Popov's, reeled away with a new insight into his species: "I felt bad for Alex. I felt bad for humanity. It opened my eyes to how ruthless human beings can be."

Jeff Hacker and Paul Castro, who design display panels for military aircraft, insist that no theft or atrocity occurred and that Popov himself told them a half-hour later — which Alex denies — that he must have lost the ball after transferring it into his clothing in an attempt to protect the million-dollar one by pulling a switcheroo with a second ball.

Alex? He says he had the ball for at least forty-five seconds but that no man could be expected to withstand such an assault, and that he can't recall transferring it from his glove to his clothing, but God knows, in that madness he might've considered it.

On and on went the scrum, new bodies joining in whooping celebration as if it were a mosh pit, some in hope that a TV eye was watching and making them immortal, others determined to keep scavenging because no one had yet stood and displayed ownership of the ball. Somehow, the million-dollar nugget seemed to have vanished.

And where was security? Nearly half the security guards that the Giants had contracted to supervise the stands that day were no-shows. A half-minute elapsed before a Major League Baseball security officer could reach the maelstrom, another half-minute before two reinforcements arrived, all in plain clothes. "Where is it? Cough it up!" they demanded, yanking bodies out by the scalp and scruff of the neck, but because they wore no uniforms the chaos multiplied, the treasure-seekers believing that three more bullies were bent on becoming rich by hook or by crook.

At last Alex was excavated, gouged and dazed. All eyes fixed on him. The ball in his hand was a squishy impostor, one he'd just picked up as he felt around for the Bonds ball now missing from his glove. "This isn't it!" he cried. Ted Rowlands, still convinced Alex was the new millionaire, whipped his microphone out of his jacket to interview him. Kathryn Sorenson flinched — she thought the flash of metal was a gun. Alex's hands groped his jacket and pants pocket in bewilderment. "I caught it!" he cried. "It f——' hit my glove!"

Slowly, a few people began to notice a small Asian man behind Alex wearing a wide grin . . . and holding up a baseball. Who was he, the littlest guy in the bunch — and how could he possibly have come up with the treasure? "Who's got it?" Patrick Hayashi quietly asked. "I got it."

The security men's eyes flashed: yes, it bore the markings of a big league ball. People blinked. People cheered. People began coming to their senses. An African American man, blood running down his nose, hurried to his crying daughter. A wheelchair was summoned for an injured woman. An Asian woman sobbed.

Popov spluttered as the security men formed a wedge around Hayashi and the sacred ball, and swept them away.

The world needed to know who possessed the pearl. A Giants official placed a pen and notepad in Hayashi's hand. Patrick tried to write his name and gave up. His hand shook so much, he couldn't grip the pen.

In the quiet of the Giants' ballpark operations office, he stared at the ball. What had he just done? He'd gone to the concrete amid the tangled heap. He'd seen the ball — just lying there on the cement, he says. Opportunity: the thing that his grandparents and mother had left war-decimated Japan in search of. He'd extended his hand. . . .

Him. The boy who'd always been careful not to do anything that would make anyone look at him. Not to sing. Not to dance. Not to argue. Not to sign up for any extracurricular activity at school nor to raise his hand from his seat in the back of every classroom, even when he knew he knew the answer. The chunky second baseman who might've played more than just two years of Little League ball if not for that part when you had to step to the plate with everyone watching you.

Lane kept bopping him on the shoulder, crowing, "You got the ball! It's the biggest record in all of sports! You've got *history!*" Even Patrick, nowhere near the sports fan Lane was, felt its power. It was as if the ball had sailed through the century, from Babe Ruth to Roger Maris to Mark McGwire to Barry Bonds . . . to him. What should he do with it? Just walk out of here with it in his hand? The Giants suggested placing it in the vault of a local hotel, and he nodded. His lips and tongue couldn't form words.

Just once before in his life had he taken a risk, lit a match to a piece of paper when he was seven, and whoosh, the pine tree that stood a foot from the house next door had shot up in flames, and in another few seconds, if his father hadn't raced over with a hose. . . .

His father. What else could explain how the ball had ended up, out of all those hungry hands, in Patrick's? Nothing else made sense. In almost all his memories of his dad — repairing dents and repainting cars in the driveway for friends, puttering around the house, taking walks with Patrick to feed the ducks at the pond — there was a Giants hat on his father's head and a Giants game on his transistor. There was that yelp and hand clap that jolted his wife every time Bonds jolted one. There was that easy thing to talk about whenever Patrick wished to feel close to him. Right up to the end, when the clot formed in his father's brain two years earlier and all but snuffed out that happy-go-lucky man, leaving him on life support while the family frantically tried to find Patrick, who was driving home from San Diego. Two days later Patrick walked through the front door, expecting the welcoming goody bag his father always prepared for his visits, and got the wallop of his life.

He spent his dad's last night watching and talking and crying over the near-lifeless body, and he spent the days leading up to this historic Giants game thinking, God, how much I wish Dad could be right there with us watching his guy, Barry, launch one into eternity.

Maybe . . . yes, he *must've.* Suddenly Patrick was filled with a certainty that it was his father who had guided the ball into his sight amid that snarl of fingers and elbows and knees. That Barry Bonds and a baseball had brought Patrick and Larry Hayashi together again. He pictured, at that very moment, his dad smiling down at him.

Now Patrick might meet his father's hero. A mob of media would be waiting to speak to Bonds and Patrick both at a press conference as soon as the game was over.

Patrick sagged into his chair as his brother left with a police escort to store the baseball. Two Giants employees were talking in the next room. Patrick couldn't help eavesdropping. "That guy's life's about to change forever," one said. "His neighbors will know who he is, people will recognize him wherever he goes."

Dread began to grow in some part of Patrick that wasn't numb. He was so simple and unadorned a man that he never hung anything on his apartment walls, so private a man that his personal life was a blank to his family. He hadn't thought of fame — of having all America's eyes on him — when he'd reached for the ball. Now he became aware of a stir outside the door. Someone else besides the media, he was told, was waiting out there. Some fan claiming that the sacred ball had been stolen from him.

No, Patrick told Giants officials. He didn't want to meet the media horde. He just wanted to go home and begin sorting through another tangled heap, the pile of emotions inside him. It had all seemed so simple, just reaching out and taking hold of the ball. Or had the ball taken hold of him?

So many people all across the Mediterranean basin once craved possession of John the Baptist's skull that soon there were John the Baptist skulls all across the Mediterranean basin. The Shroud of Turin, purported to be the burial cloth of Jesus Christ, was reportedly stolen from Constantinople and taken to France during the Fourth Crusade. Jesus's crown of thorns is said to reside in the church of Sainte Chappelle in Paris — never mind that twenty-five cathedrals across Europe claim to own thorns from that crown. In the sixth century the bodies of saints were dug up and cut into pieces to be distributed or sold.

Ownership of objects once touched by or belonging to someone who has attained immortality makes a man matter — and maybe immortal, too. Such objects have always been worth lying, stealing, and pillaging for.

Something deep and powerful began to stir inside Alex as it sunk in that his relic was gone. By the second inning ushers and police were arriving to sort out the mushrooming controversy, and a few dozen people who had seen the ball enter his glove began chanting, "Do the right thing! Do the right thing!" By the fourth inning he'd collected a pocketful of telephone numbers from witnesses. Doug Yarris had offered his because, as a twelve-year-old at a Stanford game, he had caught a football that had been kicked into the stands on an extra point, and it had been ripped from his arms by two kids. Sorenson offered hers because, she says, "I'm tired of seeing injustice. I'm tired of seeing O. J. Simpson get away with murder."

By the fifth inning Alex had received a shrug from Giants officials — they said he'd have to pursue his claim on his own — and the attention of four reporters intrigued by his story. By the eighth he'd received a business card from a lawyer who offered to represent him. And a question from the KNTV reporter: "Are you gonna sue?"

By 6:00 P.M. he was standing in his underwear as his girlfriend snapped photos of the abrasions on his elbows and knees and the welts on his head.

By 1:30 A.M. he was waiting outside the *San Francisco Chronicle*'s offices to get the story hot off the presses, the first-edition headline hitting him like a shovel in the gut: "Man Loses Fortune at Bottom of Pile."

By 6:00 A.M. — after a sleepless night spent combing the Internet for information about Bonds's 73rd, Hayashi, and record home runs — Alex was calling local sports talk radio host Gary Radnich to tell his tale.

By 9:00 A.M. his phone was jangling, one local and national reporter after another calling.

By 1:00 P.M. he was sitting in an office at KNTV, his mouth agape. There it all was on the video that cameraman Josh Keppel had shot, the ball flying into Alex's glove, the glove quickly disappearing from view, the rabble toppling him, the long struggle before the ball was produced and — wait, what was that, when the video was played in slow motion? Why, you couldn't see teeth, but it appeared that Hayashi, on his hands and knees in the pile, was doing what witness Sorenson had claimed he'd done: biting the leg of a teenager in a Dallas Cowboys hat!

By 4:00 P.M. Alex was visiting the first of two newsrooms, presenting the video and a list of witnesses to the *Chronicle* and then to KRON-TV.

The days blurred for Alex. There he was at San Francisco police headquarters, a thirty-seven-year-old man reporting that his baseball had been stolen. There he was dialing Hayashi, leaving a voice mail asking if they could meet over a beer and sort this out. There he was hiring lawyer Marty Triano. There he was on BBC Radio and Radio New Zealand. There he was — having received no return call from Hayashi and having read that Patrick had talked with Michael Barnes, the sports marketing agent who'd brokered the sale of Big Mac's 70th home run ball — filing a lawsuit against Hayashi for damages and to take possession of the ball.

September 11's ashes had barely cooled, but materialism was back in full blaze — that's what commentators and columnists howled. A San Francisco sports anchor called it perhaps the most ridiculous story the station had ever covered. An e-mailer to CNN sneered, "If you can't play nicely, you'll have to go to your rooms," and a CNN commentator called Alex's claim and his hiring of a lawyer "pathetic." How could an artifact from a ball game mean that much, people wondered. What's happening to us?

In the Middle Ages so many splinters of Christ's cross were sold to or bestowed upon the reverent that if the splinters had been laid end to end, it is said, they'd have circled the globe.

Splinters of major league ballplayers' bats, along with threads from their jerseys, are being encased in plastic and sold today in a hobby shop near you.

Nineteen hours after he'd given the world the slip, Patrick climbed into his car to go to work and glanced into his rearview mirror. A news van had penned him in. He refused to do an interview on air and, after the van backed away, hurried to work.

He returned home at dusk. Two more reporters awaited him outside his door.

He turned on the TV. There was Popov's head, telling the world that a great injustice had been done and that Patrick had his ball.

He went out to eat. A stranger approached his table and asked him if he'd go say hello to a friend, as if Patrick were a celebrity.

He went to work at Cisco Systems, where he'd been on the job

for only two weeks. He wasn't just imagining it, was he? Everyone
was staring at him. He could barely concentrate. His stomach was
in knots.

At home he picked up the phone to check messages: more reporters. And Popov's lawyer, threatening legal action. He picked
up the newspaper. The media were licking their chops over allegations that Patrick had taken a chomp out of the leg of a teenage boy
and participated in a mugging — both preposterous, he insisted. A
Los Angeles Times columnist wrote that Patrick had "slithered into
the pack like a snake after a rat."

Who was this Popov, what else might he spread, and why, Patrick
kept wondering, couldn't the man admit that he'd dropped the
ball? Everywhere Patrick turned — on radio, television, and in
newspapers — there was Popov again, accusing him.

Patrick confided in no one, not even his relatives, for fear they
would be subpoenaed and dragged into court. He couldn't sleep.
He got headaches and chills. Somehow, without ever having chosen to take a journey, he'd stepped onto a train he couldn't get off,
a train whose destination was unknowable.

Why not end this agony? Why not settle out of court with Popov,
sell the ball in the metal box, split the bounty, and melt back into
his levelheaded life, marketing telecommunications devices? Settle
rather than confront, acquiesce rather than assert: that's what he'd
been raised to do. But then . . . wasn't that what his parents and
grandparents and 120,000 others of Japanese descent had done in
America in 1942? Bowed their heads and complied when they were
given forty-eight hours to gather whatever they could jam into two
suitcases, climb onto a bus full of dazed and weeping people wearing name tags, and report to a camp surrounded by barbed wire,
gun towers, and armed soldiers who they had thought were their
countrymen?

Not a whisper of it had been breathed in his house as he grew
up, but in his thirties Patrick had become fascinated by TV documentaries on the subject and had begun piecing together the
story through relatives. His mother had been six years old, his
dad twenty-two, when they and their families were swept away to
ease America's terror in the wake of the sneak attack at Pearl Harbor. Both families, who didn't know each other at the time, were
transported by train at gunpoint from a camp in Fresno to a camp

in the wastelands outside Jerome, Arkansas, where for two years they would sleep in cramped barracks on folding cots and hang blankets across rooms for a semblance of privacy.

Patrick's maternal grandfather, Jinkichi Fukui — sickened at the treatment of a people who had never committed an act of sabotage in America during the war — refused to vow allegiance to the U.S. government on a questionnaire. He was branded an enemy alien and banished to a camp in South Dakota for a half-year, then was returned to his family and sent with it to yet another internment camp, for those considered suspect or disloyal, at Tule Lake in northern California, surrounded by tanks and troops. For the third time in three years Patrick's mother carried her clothes and her doll to start over again amid strangers.

The Fukuis flushed the American dream and returned at war's end to Japan, where they lived, often racked by hunger, in a relative's barn, cold-shouldered as outcasts for all the years they'd spent in America. Twelve harsh years later Patrick's grandfather admitted that no soil grew opportunity like America's, even with its weeds, and so he brought the family back to California. After years of barbed wire, all that Patrick's mother wanted when she returned at age twenty-two was a white picket fence. She soon married a man who'd left his internment camp to work in a factory making ammunition for U.S. troops and had then been drafted into the U.S. Army and assigned to the Military Intelligence Service.

In a Sacramento house so small that a few family members had to sleep in a backyard camper, the Hayashis raised six children, sealing off their past so completely that their children knew nothing of their parents' internment, and so completely from each other that neither of them realized that they'd been locked up at the same time in the same camps, in Fresno and Jerome. They introduced none of the old rituals or language to Patrick and his siblings, so the children would have no accent and would blend in as swiftly and quietly as possible. So they would become like the people around them, quick to recognize opportunity and grab it: Americans.

Patrick scraped and sacrificed, working his way through college, and when he moved into his own apartment, he began watching documentaries on TV that showed all those impounded people staring from train windows, standing in food lines, wasting away lives they no longer recognized, never screaming no. He came to realize that he was staring at his parents, and maybe even himself. What would he do when his turn came, when someone tried to take what he felt was his and cast suspicion on him when he felt he'd done nothing wrong? What would he do?

"In Japanese culture you just go along with things, you don't create controversy," Patrick says. "But to give up now and give away what's mine would feel like what my grandparents and parents went through. I know that my parents had to buckle. I decided, no more."

Patrick hired Don Tamaki, a Japanese American lawyer who in 1983 helped overturn the forty-year-old conviction of Fred Korematsu, one of three Japanese Americans jailed for refusing internment. Patrick decided not to settle with Popov. He'd swallow his dread, step outside the shadows, outside his culture, outside himself, and fight this to the end. He'd scream no. For a baseball.

Here's a valuable object hit right to you, Alex, and then taken from your grasp. How are you going to react? Who are you as a person? What are you made of?

These are Alex's words. This is Alex's view of his war with Hayashi: a test, contrived by the cosmos, of Alex's character and will. What are you going to do? Here's what:

Wake up most days in darkness, on four to six hours' sleep, lift weights, do aerobics, shower, recite his twelve affirmations, and report for duty on the twenty-fifth floor of the Shell Building early enough to greet his attorneys and their office assistants by first name as they file in. Plug in his laptop in the office assigned to him for the year, sip from a deep cup of green tea, slip on his headphones, and cue up one of the 96 Kruder & Dorfmeister tunes he's downloaded — why not *Deep S——, Parts 1 & 2*? Dig into one of the 300 computer files he's compiled on the case or the 250 hardcopy files he's jammed into four cardboard boxes.

Speed-dial the fast-food health-food restaurant he opened in Berkeley six years ago after quitting his job as a marketing engineer. Make sure the veggie burgers and air-baked fries are still sizzling across the counter and that his girlfriend, Stephanie Dodson, is still vertical after months of managing the operation so he can keep chasing that baseball and keep paying the $120,000 in lawyers' fees, phone bills, airfare, and miscellaneous costs — likely to reach nearly a quarter-million dollars by the end of the trial — of preparing for his cosmic exam.

Risk. Big. Bet that he'll win, retaining his attorneys' services at $200 per hour rather than the contingency fee of less than 33 percent that Hayashi will likely pay his.

It feels sometimes like my head is about to explode. The ball has become my life.

Cram for the eight-hour deposition that his opponent's lawyers would put him through — a duel of words in which one misspoken phrase could impeach him and cost him the million-dollar ball — and walk away deciding that he could play this game. That he would compose the line of questioning for every witness his lawyers would depose: forty pages' worth of queries, forty hours of work, for Hayashi's deposition alone. How else could he afford his gamble, keep the $200-an-hour meter from running wild?

I'm not afraid to want something. Show me your fear, and I'll show you who you are.

Learn a whole new language and spend hours on the Internet studying case law so he can fling *ex partes* and *pursuants* and *motions to compel* right back in his foes' faces. Analyze each word of each deposition for new leads, discrepancies, impeachable testimony, cross-referencing it with dozens of other witnesses' statements, with law journal notes, and with media interviews he records and transcribes and can flash on his laptop screen with a blur of his fingers. Work all day at the law offices, then go home and work some more.

Don't be afraid that you don't know. Just learn as you go and trust that you'll overcome the problems as they come up. You don't know where you're going to go and what obstacles you'll face — but that's the excitement of it!

Pay a videographer $1,500 to enlarge and enhance critical images during the four-and-a-half-minute Keppel tape. Break the video down into individual images, each lasting one thirtieth of a second, then burn those images onto a CD and into his brain. Watch it in slow motion so many hundreds of times — with sound run through his stereo system and headphones so he can hear every utterance, or with no sound so he can focus on the most minute movements, with an erasable marker poised to scrawl lines and circles on the screen and compose a color-coded aerial map of witnesses — that he can tell you the names of a couple dozen people in the tangled heap and exactly what each will do next: *Watch! My brother's about to get his hair pulled! Listen! Did you hear that? That was me calling for help. That sliver of black jacket you see here? That's Paul Castro. There's Russ Reynolds, see the back of his hair? There's the Asian girl. Look at her face — it's like the fall of Saigon!*

Dart to Wal-Mart to purchase sixty blank tapes. Record the Keppel tape on each one while you're showering or sleeping, and mail them to media outlets across America.

Start a website, of course: www.bonds73rd.com, with pie charts and quotes from witnesses and a pop-up box with a photo of the unidentified, allegedly bitten teenager over a caption reading, "Do you know this person?"

Create a Christmas card, a three-photo strip showing him and his brother at the ballpark, Bonds's 73rd home run swing, and Alex making the snag, along with the greeting, "Happy Holidays! May your New Year be filled with unexpected opportunity!" Invite strangers he has met to the "touching party" he will throw if he wins the case and the ball. Why not have some fun?

Even if the judge looks me in the eye and tells me I'm wrong, there's a chance to grow from this. Because at the end of the day, life is about experiences — not possessions.

Fire off a 1:00 A.M. e-mail on the day's developments to his brother. Repeat his affirmations. Scan the net for new developments. Keep chipping away at his 50-page reply to the 42 Requests for Admissions and 105 Specially Prepared Interrogatories that Hayashi's lawyers have unloaded on him.

They want to see how much I can endure. Their strategy is to break me. They won't. Show me the size of the problem that bugs the man, and I'll show you the size of the man.

Look over, as his eyelids sag, at that photograph on his book shelf: the blond boy in the Little League uniform and blue cap. The kid whom people expected to bash balls off fences because he was taller and thicker than his peers, the one with asthma whose dad had that funny accent and no idea how to teach his son the game. The twelve-year-old who found himself on second base with two outs in the last inning of a playoff game, his team trailing by one.

"Two outs, Alex!" cried the third base coach. "Run on anything!

You're moving with the crack of the bat!" Crack! Alex obediently dashed toward third. The ball rolled to the one place those instructions didn't apply — third base! — and the third baseman gratefully slapped the season-ending tag on Alex. *Incompetent!* That's what everyone was thinking — he could see it in their eyes.

People can pile on and take the ball, but they can't take away that I caught it. I executed. They can't take that away from me.

He walked off the field in shame, his family about to depart for a summer on his grandfather's farm in Bethel, New York. He would never play organized sports again.

That boy in the picture, that's who was robbed.

Is there precedent in this case? Yes. The baseball is like the whale that Swift and Gifford were chasing in 1872 and the fox that Pierson and Post were pursuing seven decades earlier: an unowned moving object whose possession comes into dispute between two parties. That much, the lawyers of Mr. Popov and Mr. Hayashi agree on.

The whale was awarded to Gifford because his harpoon entered it first, and the fox to Pierson because his bullet mortally wounded it — each man thus exerting dominion over the contested object.

Surprise! Popov's and Hayashi's lawyers disagree dramatically over what constitutes dominion when the wild animal is Barry Bonds's 73rd.

Hayashi's lawyer, Tamaki — along with Cal law professor John Dwyer, his legal consultant — contend that that dominion is exerted over a baseball in the stands, by common practice established over decades, when a customer holds up the ball to display ownership, as Patrick was first to do. "It's not enough to throw a harpoon that grazes the whale or to shoot a bullet that hits the fox's ear," declares Dwyer. "The harpoon's got to stick in the whale. The bullet's got to *kill* the fox. You have to successfully assert ownership in the rule of capture." The moral of their story: a fan should be able to pursue a ball in the stands without fear of being sued.

Popov's attorney, Triano — along with Tulsa law professor Paul Finkelman, his expert witness — believe that Alex achieved dominion by spearing the ball from the sky with his glove. Any other interpretation, they say, rewards the violent behavior of those who separated him from the ball. "The rule of capture is designed to prevent the melee over the whale or the fox," says Finkelman. "[Tamaki's] interpretation of it encourages the melee. If the San Francisco police were doing their job, they'd go through the video and arrest everyone who can be identified and charge him with assault." The moral of their story: a fan should be able to pursue a ball in the stands without fear of being mugged.

"If Hayashi wins, would you bring your children into the bleachers when A-Rod's going for number 756?" asks Todd McFarlane, the comic-book and toy tycoon who watched the value of his McGwire number 70 ball plummet an estimated 75 percent thanks to Barry Bonds. "How do you know some 250-pound guy won't do a belly flop for the ball and permanently compress your child into the bleachers? Whoever catches it first should be the guy who gets it. But we'll probably wait till an eight-year-old gets his rib cage crushed."

"Mr. Popov's crying over spilt milk," counters Michael Barnes, the agent who helped broker the sale of the ball to McFarlane. "He had a *glove* on and couldn't hang on to it. Popov has nothing to blame except his own lack of baseball skill."

If Solomon were deciding the case, he'd no doubt award the ball to both men and have them split the proceeds from its sale — or award it to neither, and use the million bucks to buy baseballs for kids who can't afford one. But Solomon wouldn't have a prayer in an American civil courtroom, where it's all or nothing, and one party or the other must win the lawsuit and get the ball.

A twelve-person jury will decide the case, which is scheduled to begin on October 7 — by sheer chance, one year to the day after the event — and Popov will have to convince at least nine of the jurors in order to win. Jury selection will be critical because informal polls have shown that blue-collar males tend to favor Hayashi and the last-man-standing rule in bleacher baseball ethics, while females tend to side with Popov.

Clearly, the thick vault that contains the baseball under Judge David Garcia's temporary dominion hasn't diminished the ball's power over human beings. It lured Mike Wranovics, a young filmmaker from Stanford, to begin filming a documentary entitled *Up for Grabs*. It led a fan, who mistakenly believed that he'd photographed the Bonds ball in Popov's hand, to try to sell the picture to him for $100,000. It made witness Yarris take out an extra million dollars' worth of life insurance, in case his testimony somehow leads to his elimination, and it haunted his sleep: he kept dreaming that in the chaos he couldn't find his way back to the son he left behind to pursue the relic that day.

It filled one gay witness with the fear of being outed by the trial and attendant publicity. It set off a security alert for Bonds's 600th home run, coming soon. It reduced Giants employees and Bonds himself to silence — none would comment on the case. It made the father of cameraman Josh Keppel wish his son's lens had never caught the ball's flight, for without the video there would probably never have been a lawsuit. It drove Patrick to move to a new apartment and change his phone number. It flushed him out of the woodwork and onto the network morning shows so the world would hear more than Popov's claims.

Still, eight months after the event, each visit to the mailbox churns Patrick's dread, for he knows another letter full of bewildering legalese and mysterious ramifications likely awaits him. Still, he broods over questions Popov's lawyer asked him during the deposition that his own attorneys angrily terminated. Why did the lawyer ask for Patrick's driver's license number? Why did he want to know how much memory and RAM Patrick's home computer has? Patrick doesn't know when or if he'll ever go to a ball game at Pac Bell Park again.

"It's a curse, getting that ball," says Ray Scarbosio, a friend of Popov's. "Look what Alex is going through. Look at Hayashi — how'd you like to be him? And what do you do with the ball, anyway? You can't wear it around your neck. You can't leave it in your apartment. Someone could steal it, or the dog could eat it. It's no fun leaving it in a safe. So you sell it, and people call you a greedy son of a bitch. Or you don't sell it — and you're a fool. I'm telling you, it's a curse."

One Saturday in April, Popov took his glove and his seventy-two-year-old father, Nikolai, to the spot where he'd caught and lost that lovely curse. Picture the old Russian, who had never been to a big league ball game before, listening with furrowed brow as his son excitedly demonstrated everything that had happened there.

Picture Alex breathlessly explaining the loss of a cowhide-covered sphere to a man whose family had its 125-acre farm in

Ukraine confiscated by the Soviet government and collectivized in 1929. Picture Alex describing his trauma to a man who, when he was twelve years old, was on his way to visit his uncle, grandfather, step-grandmother and step-uncle when they were executed by the German army that had swept in and taken over their valleys and towns. Who hid with his father for a week beneath an overturned, manure-covered hay wagon so the counterattacking Soviet army wouldn't find them and force them into service. And who finally fled the horror with his parents, a 700-mile migration that ended when German soldiers rounded them up on the Hungarian border and shipped them off to forced labor in Poland.

Picture Alex, with his wide-eyed fervor, decrying the injustice he'd suffered to a man whose own dad was not only put in forced labor but also later locked away in a German concentration camp. To a man who, when the war ended, spent three years in a refugee camp in Germany with his family, hungering to emigrate to America, to freedom and opportunity, but was unable to get the necessary documents. Who moved with his parents to Venezuela for nine years instead and finally, at twenty-six, got the visa that put him on a freighter to Philadelphia in 1957 with a dozen words of English. Who helped his father establish his 170-acre farm in Bethel, then went cross-country with his Scottish bride to start on his own as a machinist for Hewlett-Packard in Silicon Valley.

Barry Bonds? Nikolai didn't even know who the fellow was that day last autumn when his son called, babbling something about having just caught Bonds's 73rd. So imagine what the old man said a few weeks later when his son explained to him that he needed to file a restraining order to prevent a Japanese American man from selling a baseball before Alex had a chance to prove that the baseball belonged to him, and that because the worth of the ball could plummet while it was locked away in a Bank of America vault awaiting the trial — see, this Barry Bonds or someone else might hit 75 and knock a couple of zeroes right off the price tag — Alex needed, uh . . . well . . . he needed his father to pledge $100,000 worth of his property as collateral against the potential devaluation of this, uh . . . baseball.

Yes. That's what Nikolai said. Yes, because who knew better how it felt to have everything taken away, uncles and grandfathers, land and bread, in a place where there was nowhere to appeal? Yes, because if his son didn't fight to the end for justice when he felt he'd been wronged, then why had Nikolai trudged through Moldavia and Romania, through blizzards and mountains?

Yes, because of that Saturday when he'd sat in the car with Alex for hours in stoic vigilance outside the home of the boy who'd stolen Alex's skateboard, until at last he caught the boy on it and got it back.

Yes, because when one more horde overtook Nikolai's father's land in Bethel, in 1969 — hippies trashing his farm as they overflowed the Woodstock Festival on Max Yasgur's place next door — Grandpa Popov, who could barely speak English, had a voice, had a lawyer, had a five-figure compensation that helped pay off the mortgage on the farm. And so he called Nikolai to come from California and walk the land with him. At last, said the old man in trembling Russian, he was back on his feet. At last he had what was taken from him nearly a half-century before. He said he felt like an American.

At the core of the ball in the metal box is a pellet of cork that once was bark on a tree that grew on the Iberian Peninsula. It was shipped to Maryland, ground into granules, and transported to a plant in Batesville, Mississippi, where it was mixed with tiny flecks of rubber and cooked in molds to form the tiny ball inside the ball, giving it the pop, when struck properly with a bat, to rise toward a fence, toward a horizon, toward all those hands reaching for the sky.

DAVID GRANN

Baseball Without Metaphor

FROM THE NEW YORK TIMES MAGAZINE

ONE NIGHT LAST FALL Barry Bonds, the demon of America's pastime, caught a glimpse of his own redemption. The player who had been called a "prima donna," a "phony," "overrated," "a cancer," and a "spiritual drain on baseball" was about to do what no one had ever done. He was having the greatest season in the history of the game, and now the thirty-seven-year-old San Francisco Giant was on the verge of breaking the single-season home run record set by Mark McGwire only three years earlier — and finally, as he had always vowed, "melt" his critics' pens.

For the moment, though, he tried to concentrate only on the pitcher, Chan Ho Park, a mercurial right-hander. Recently, almost no one had pitched to Bonds; as he neared the record, opposing teams increasingly walked him, prompting many to wonder if they were intentionally denying him a shot at history. His daughters had begun to hold signs that read: "Please pitch to our daddy" and "Give our daddy a chance."

Outside the stadium, people seemed even more determined to thwart him. A few weeks earlier, Dusty Baker, the Giants manager, knocked on Bonds's hotel room door with an FBI agent at his side: Bonds had received a death threat. A man had called a Houston television station and vowed to shoot him before he could break the record. Bonds thought it was because of his race, that he was being threatened the way they had once threatened Hank Aaron, but the caller insisted it was something else: like so many fans, he just hated him.

But now as Bonds watched the pitcher go through his motion he didn't think about any of that. He waited until the pitch was almost past him, then uncoiled his bat, swinging so hard that he pulled the ball into the deepest part of the park. As it vanished over the wall, the crowd rose to its feet. Many in the press box, reporters and broadcasters who had often badmouthed Bonds publicly and privately, stopped typing and stood. His teammates — who in April, when Bonds hit his 500th home run, left him standing alone at the plate — descended upon him as he crossed home and picked up Nikolai, his eleven-year-old son and the team's bat boy, and pointed to the sky. Two innings later, Bonds did it again.

Although the game didn't end until after midnight, a podium was set up near home plate and a ceremony was held in Bonds's honor. Once, while watching a similar tribute to Cal Ripken after he broke the record for most consecutive games, Bonds confided to a reporter that he would be too scared to get so close to the fans — "If you could hear the things they say to me" — but now as the crowd beckoned him, Bonds appeared from the dugout, still in his uniform and cap. It was at this point, as he looked out at the thousands that had lingered into the early-morning hours just to see him, that he seemed to contemplate his redemption. "We've come a long way," he said to the fans. "We've had our ups and downs." And then, as his teammates stood behind him and the crowd chanted his name, Bonds lowered his head and began to cry.

Within days, though, the fans' appreciation had reverted to antipathy. On talk radio and in the sports pages around the country, he was being blamed for everything from overpriced athletes to players' surly attitudes. "It is a shame that a jerk like Barry Bonds . . . now is the home run record holder," read one letter from the *Los Angeles Times*. "Hopefully, someone with style and integrity will knock him out of the top spot. I, for one, will never buy another ticket to a Major League game." When Bonds's contract expired at the end of his record-breaking season, not a single team reportedly expressed public interest in luring away the greatest player in the game.

Then this season, as Bonds approached 600 career home runs, a feat achieved only by Hank Aaron, Babe Ruth, and Willie Mays, and as his batting average skyrocketed above .350, the rumors came on full force that Bonds was juiced on steroids. There was no evidence

— and Bonds vehemently denied it — but as allegations engulfed the game people began to look at him differently, studying his muscle mass for the telltale signs of chemical enhancement.

By summer, as word of another possible strike spread, things had only gotten worse. After Bonds casually commented that baseball could survive its ninth work stoppage in the last thirty years ("It's entertainment," he told the *Washington Post*. "It will come back. A lot of companies go on strike . . . And people still ride the bus"), he was again roundly denounced as the embodiment of everything that was wrong with the sport. "I yearn for the day that Bonds leaves Major League Baseball," said Chet Coppock, a host on *Sporting News Radio*. "He won't be missed for ten seconds."

Baseball, of course, has long been played under the burden of metaphor. More so than basketball or football, it is supposed to represent something larger than itself. As the former baseball commissioner A. Bartlett Giamatti once claimed, "It is a dream of ourselves as better than we are."

Although baseball actually began as a game played largely by urban toughs, its image was soon reconstructed to mirror the country's pastoral myth. And in the constant search for meaning in the flick of a glove or a routine hit, most of the game's greatest players, no matter how ordinary or reprehensible off the field, were also transformed into something more than they actually were. (There were exceptions, of course, like Ty Cobb, whose official biographer referred to him as "psychotic.") In his recent book on Joe DiMaggio, Richard Ben Cramer described how the owners, along with a complicit media, created an unofficial "hero machine" that invented entire personalities around the best sluggers. Many of the writers, whose travel and food and lodging were paid for by the owners, turned Ruth's appetite for female fans into an appetite for hot dogs.

The country became so steeped in the metaphoric nature of the game that when the Supreme Court in 1972 upheld its antitrust exemption, it cited the words from a New York district judge and said that baseball is on a "higher ground" and that "it behooves everyone to keep it there."

Even after the writers were no longer plied with free travel and bottles of scotch, the machine remained sufficiently intact to reinvent recent sluggers, most notably McGwire, who despite a reputation for arrogance and rudeness became known as the antidote to Bonds. "From his 20-inch biceps to his 500-foot blasts, everything about Mark McGwire is Bunyanesque — including his heart," wrote *Sports Illustrated* in 1998.

But as the latest strike looms, it has become harder and harder to deny the true nature of baseball — that it is, at its core, a business like any other, filled with labor disputes, petty disagreements, greed, and drugs. Still, rather than view the threat of a strike as the ordinary jostling of competing self-interests, it has been spoken of as a moral catastrophe and a violation of some sacred trust. And alongside the old hero machine there has, over the last decade of strife, emerged a kind of antihero machine, in which the most ordinary weakness — from conceit to carousing to even a divorce — can be seized upon as proof of some larger rot.

Perhaps no one has been more ravaged by this new machine than Barry Bonds, the most dominant player of the modern era. At the very moment when Bonds is edging closer to the all-time home run record, when in another age he would be lionized for his grace and strength, he has become a new kind of archetype — "The poster boy for the modern spoiled athlete" and "a symbol of baseball's creeping greed and selfishness, complete with diamond earring."

When I arrived in San Francisco this July, Bonds was once again refusing to engage in the rituals required of a celebrity athlete. He wasn't giving press conferences or posing for pictures, and after another series of negative articles focusing on steroids and his disagreements with teammates, he had imposed a "boycott" on the local sportswriters. He devised elaborate strategies to keep them at bay, using an army of sentries: his imposing personal trainer; the Giants' bevy of public relations officials; and his childhood friend, Steve Hoskins, who sometimes served as his informal "publicist," a job that mostly meant refusing requests, including one from George Will, whom Hoskins said he had never heard of. Usually, though, Bonds simply greeted anyone who invaded his space with a cold stare.

One afternoon before a game against the World Series champion Arizona Diamondbacks, while the union was still contemplating a strike date, the press, increasingly desperate for even a routine quote, was deciding whether to dare invade his space. The more Bonds denied reporters access the more they seemed to despise him. As Bonds suddenly walked through the pack, his eyes smoldering at them, one of the writers said under his breath, "There goes Mr. Personality."

Later he appeared in the batter's box. Curt Schilling, the Diamondbacks' All-Star pitcher, came out and leaned against the cage. In 2000, Schilling had told reporters, "Barry Bonds is a first-ballot Hall of Famer . . . but when he retires, he's still going to be the biggest ass who ever lived. Ask his teammates. Ask anyone on their team or in their clubhouse." Now, as Schilling and the press looked on, Bonds compressed his hands around the handle of the bat, rubbing the wood between his fingers. He smacked a line shot into deep left field. Then he smacked another, this one even farther, ricocheting off the wall. When Bonds finished his turn, he twirled his bat like a baton and walked off the field.

Despite his boycott of the local press, Bonds had agreed to talk with me, and as he approached the dugout, I tried to introduce myself. I extended my hand, but he kept walking, his eyes on a knot of reporters and cameramen moving toward him. He put his palm in front of one of the TV cameras, bumped my shoulder, and vanished inside.

For days I tried unsuccessfully to approach him. Then one afternoon, Bonds suddenly sat down beside me in the dugout shortly before a day game in Los Angeles. Most of the players were still in the clubhouse or stretching on the field, and we had the area to ourselves.

Bonds had hurt his hamstring the night before, collapsing in midstride as he ran toward the wall, and now he had a bandage on his thigh. His head was shaved, setting off his handsome, if blunt, features. It was his eyes, though, that caught my attention. They can be frank and expressive one minute, then cold and impassive the next. At the moment, they seemed to be deciding between the two. "Dude, I've seen you watching me," Bonds finally said.

As I began to pepper him with questions, he was polite but guarded. When I asked how he thought the fans and media perceived him, he insisted he didn't know. When I asked how all the public criticism had affected him after his monumental season, he said: "I don't think about it. I don't read the paper that much. I read the business section."

The dugout began filling with players. Someone brought out a bucket with sunflower seeds, and several players stuffed them in their pockets while others hastily rubbed pine tar on their bats. Bonds said he had been scratched from the lineup due to his injury and that he needed to see the trainer.

I assumed that was the end of the interview, but instead he led me down a long corridor that echoed with the clicking of his spikes. The locker room was empty, except for an elderly man folding towels. In a tiny back room scattered with weights and bandages, Bonds pulled up a chair and, leaning back against the wall, began to talk openly. "People who say they're not afraid of anything are liars," he said. "I'm afraid every time I go up there, not of being hit, but of failure." He said he tried to succeed by concentrating on only what he did on the field. But then he admitted, "I know how I'm perceived. I know I'm supposed to be some kind of monster."

Once on KBNR, a San Francisco sports radio station, after a fan denounced him and said he should be traded, the show's host took the next call. "We have a call from a Barry in San Francisco. Barry, what would you like to talk about?"

"I hear this all the time," the caller said plaintively. "'He's arrogant, he's this . . .' I'm not arrogant. I'm good. There's a difference."

The host seemed stunned when he realized it was Barry Bonds on the line. "I'm sorry that I had to get on the phone like this," Bonds said.

When I asked him now about the incident, Bonds shrugged and said, "My wife was listening to it." He seemed aware of almost every slight, even those that never appeared in print. He had spies up in the press booth, Bonds explained to me, that reported back to him the things reporters and broadcasters said to one another. "They don't know I have ears up there, but I do. I know everything they say. Everything." He sounded more tired than angry, as if he had given up trying to change people's views. "If you sit up in the booth and call me all these names, then why do you come down and look me in the face and say hi?"

His trainer peered in the room, but Bonds seemed to want to keep talking. "They expect you to be who they want you to be, not who you are," he said. "If they could only judge a player by their own eyes, if they could just watch me play, what I do on the field."

In the background, we could hear the sound of the national anthem being sung and the players being introduced. Bonds leaned forward in his chair, preparing to go, then settled back for a moment. "There are times I've thought about quitting," he said. "A lot of times."

Barry Bonds has a hero's pedigree. His father, Bobby, was an All-Star outfielder, his godfather is Willie Mays, his distant cousin is Reggie Jackson. "The thing you need to understand," Bonds tells me, "is that I was born into this game."

After the San Francisco Giants called up his dad in 1968, Barry, then no more than four or five years old, hung out in the locker room eyeing the aging Mays. "He was always watching me," Mays tells me, always trying "to take my glove." Although Barry relished being in the clubhouse, he was aware even then of how he was being perceived. "You don't know who your friends are at times," he says. "You don't know if they want to be your friend because you're the son of Bobby Bonds."

An instinctive player like his father, in high school Barry was already being called "a superstar." He was so fast, his teammates say, that he would steal bases and never slide. Yet in his senior year in high school, in a kind of harbinger of his entire career, another player was named the MVP, even though Bonds put up the best numbers. "That had to do with the fact that Barry was perceived even then to be cocky and arrogant," Dave Canziani, Bonds's high school teammate, told me. "He clearly deserved the award."

His high school coach has said, "He wanted to be liked, tried so damn hard to have people like him . . . But then he'd say things he didn't mean, wild statements. Still, he'd be hurt. People don't realize he can be hurt, and is, fairly often."

In 1985, the Pittsburgh Pirates drafted the twenty-year-old outfielder in the first round. Lanky, with long, graceful strides and a lightning-quick, powerful swing, Bonds wore a thin mustache and, before long, his trademark diamond earring.

As he tore through the minors, his story — from his birthright to his natural swing — eventually became part of the baseball lore that burnished all of the game's greatest hitters. There was the tale, for instance, of how in 1986 Syd Thrift, the Pirates general manager, watched Bonds pull five balls over the fence in right field during batting practice. As Thrift often recalled, he told Bonds that was great, now how about a few over the left-field fence? Bonds hit the next few over the left-field fence and said, "How's that?" That night, the story goes, was the last game Barry Bonds played in the minor leagues.

But there was trouble with the myth of Barry Bonds from the start. First of all, to be Barry Bonds, the heir to baseball's mythic past, he needed to both be like his father but also surpass him, to achieve what Bobby hadn't been able to and become the "next Willie Mays." "I don't call them expectations," Bonds says today. "I call them manipulations. You're a young kid and you have other people brainwashing you, making you believe that you're something you may not be able to be."

Often when he was in the clubhouse reporters would stop at his locker and start asking him about his father, how he compared to him and to his godfather, Mays. They would frequently call him Bobby by mistake, and he would stop the interview and say: "I'm Barry. Bobby's my father."

It wasn't just that he was in his father's shadow. "My father and I were never really close when I was growing up," he once told ESPN, "because he was never around. I wanted my dad at my Little League games, because everybody else's parents were there. My parents weren't there, just my mom." Bobby has said that he often came to the games but stayed in the car, not wanting to make a scene. "He said he was there," Barry said, "but I never saw him."

In Pittsburgh, when for the first time he seemed to collapse under the expectations, when the can't-miss prospect started missing all the time, getting only 17 hits in his first 100 at-bats, he grew increasingly defiant. Some players grumbled that Bonds refused to heed any instructions and that he was more concerned with himself than with the team. To compound that image, Bonds rarely spoke. Even after knocking in 114 runs, stealing 52 bases, and crushing 33 home runs in 1990, he would often refuse to give interviews or mingle with fans, telling writers and autograph-seekers to stay out of his face.

And when he did talk, he never sounded like a conventional superstar. Rather than speak of the game in mystical terms he referred to it openly as a business. As he still says today: "I was asked, when was baseball a game to you? The last game I played in college.

Ever since then it's been a business. This is a business. We provide for our families. There are people we have to deal with that
manipulate and con and try, you know, to cheat. It's not a game
anymore."

Whereas other players let their agents negotiate behind the scenes
while they smiled at the cameras, Bonds came right out and said he
should be paid millions by the Pirates or be traded. "The Pirates
can't keep crying broke," he said of the owners. "You can't own half
of Pittsburgh and say you're on welfare."

Then came the day at spring training in 1991 when Bonds says
one of his coaches accused him of sulking over his salary. Bonds
started shouting at him while the TV and print guys zoomed in on
the fray. Jim Leyland, the Pirates head coach, tried to intercede,
and now they were going at it, too, the manager and the star. "I've
been kissing your butt for three years," Leyland yelled. "If guys
don't want to be here, aren't happy with the money they're making, don't take it out on everybody else."

After that — and an ugly divorce played out in the tabloids — it
didn't seem to matter what Bonds did on the field. It didn't matter
that Leyland pleaded with the fans to let up on the booing ("That
is getting old — it's gone too far") or that Bobby Bonds begged reporters, "Give my boy a chance." It didn't matter that Bonds won
three MVPs in four years or that he would become the first player
ever to hit 400 home runs and steal 400 bases or that he was majes-
tic in left field, climbing the wall and catching the ball in the web of
his mitt, winning eight Gold Gloves. It didn't matter that, unlike
many players, Bonds never actually held out for more money or
that, as his former teammate Bobby Bonilla put it to me, "once he
knows you, he'll give you the shirt off his back."

He was now Barry Bonds, "the Pirates' MDP — Most Despised
Player," as the Pittsburgh media began to call him, and by 1993, after the Giants acquired him and made him the highest-paid player
in baseball, he was now the spoiled face of America's pastime.

One July afternoon, Bonds was sitting by himself at his locker. The
area is only a few square feet, but slightly grander in scale than
those around it. Rather than one or two wood-panel cubbies, he
has three in a row. There is also, instead of the typical metal folding
chair, a large leather recliner, which reportedly cost $3,000.

Although Bonds paid for the chair himself, and it is designed to help his ailing back ("They pay me millions of dollars to play baseball," Bonds says. "What would they say if I hurt my back and couldn't play?"); and though one of the lockers is for his son, the bat boy, the entire area — the "kingdom," as it's sometimes called — has been a constant fixture in the countless Bonds takedowns written in recent years. "In the San Francisco Giants' clubhouse," Rick Reilly wrote in *Sports Illustrated* last year, "everybody knows the score: 24–1. There are 24 teammates, and there's Barry Bonds."

The romantic notion of the clubhouse as a traveling fraternity of working-class heroes — the boys of summer — is perhaps the most potent in all of baseball. But while the notion is still propagated, the reality is less and less like that, if it ever was. Most clubhouses have become rather businesslike affairs, where the players cautiously refrain from saying anything candid to the press trolling the clubhouse, instead offering the same platitudes about wanting to win and personal numbers not mattering, as if they were revealing a profound baseball truth.

In recent years, few players have been held up as representatives of the old ideal more than Jeff Kent, the Giants' slender, tightly coiled second baseman, who in 2000 beat out Bonds for the MVP and is said to despise Bonds more than anyone in baseball. "They've hated each other since the day Kent came to town in 1997," Ray Ratto of the *San Francisco Chronicle* observed. "They hate each other today, and . . . the one who lives longer will attend the other's funeral, just to make sure he's dead."

Last year, while Bonds was on the verge of breaking the home run record, Kent told Rick Reilly of *Sports Illustrated:* "I was raised to be a team guy, and I am, but Barry's Barry. It took me two years to learn to live with it, but I learned." Although Kent was publicly taking a teammate to task during a pennant race, which isn't quite the act of a "team guy," there was little criticism of this in the sports media.

One day when I was in the locker room, not long after Kent and Bonds came to blows in the dugout in which Bonds appeared to put his forearm in Kent's throat, Kent, about to take off his towel, asked a pack of reporters if there were any "queers" or "women" among them — a remark that, especially in San Francisco, would have created a certain stir. Although he was surrounded by at least a dozen reporters half of whom have seized upon any number of Bonds's remarks, none, as far as I know, reported this. "Is there a double standard because Kent talks to us?" one sports radio announcer told me. "Definitely."

In contrast to Kent, there were unofficial rules, I was told by reporters, to get to Bonds. Don't talk to him when he is getting dressed. Don't talk to him just before or after batting practice. Don't talk to him when he is sitting in his chair. Don't talk to him when he is talking to the trainer or to his son.

One day I decided to break the rules. I approached Bonds as he was reclining in the chair next to his conditioning coach. His shirt was off, and I could see the muscles along his stomach. Circling one of his giant biceps was a chain-link tattoo. He normally fell silent when a reporter intruded, but now he became vocal, nodding and complaining about all his vacation houses, how he has so many he doesn't know what to do, how he has a place in the mountains and a place in the Caribbean, how he has his own private ski slope, and how in addition to keeping up his properties he also has to support everyone in his family.

For several minutes I stood there, listening. At one point, without a hint of remorse or self-consciousness, he said in a loud voice: "My grandmother wants me to get her some wheelchair that drives like a car. Why do I need to get her some wheelchair when she's gonna die anyway?"

The next morning, when I warily approached him again, Bonds looked at me for a long time. Then he began to smile and said: "Dude, I was just dawging you yesterday. I was just testing you, man. I wanted to see if you'd write that stuff in the paper." My first thought, beyond realizing that Bonds mistakenly thought I was a reporter for a daily newspaper, was that he had suspected that he'd been too loud and too obnoxious, and now he was manipulating me. But as I considered this, Bonds went on to describe what appeared to be an elaborate and mysterious defense mechanism. The theory, as far as I could tell, was that it was always better to strike first, to manipulate his own image, even if that meant creating a caricature of himself, than to be misunderstood and misrepresented by somebody else. "No writer can ever know me," he said, as if to finally explain.

When I asked him why he had devised such an elaborate ruse, especially since it only made him look worse, he seemed surprised. "When you come to the ballpark," he said, "you're walking into a place that is all deception and lies."

"The truth is," Bobby Bonds tells me one day, "whatever you put down, whatever you say, that's what the world is going to believe about Barry. Not his friends, not me, not his family — we know who Barry is — but the world. You can make my son into a hero or you can make him into the devil."

Barry Bonds was still young when his father's fall began. Although Bobby still continued to put up good numbers year after year, he never lived up to expectations. "Anything I did that wasn't what Willie Mays did meant I never lived up to my potential," Bobby once said. Yet there were whispers that Bobby's failure was not just the result of the pressure of having to play in the shadow of Mays. In 1974 and 1975, when Bobby was playing for the Giants and the Yankees, stories began to appear in the papers with headlines like: "Bonds Charged With Drunk Driving" and "Bonds Confronts Rumors About Drugs, Drinking."

Of course, Bobby Bonds wasn't the first player ever to get torn up in the press. But in the past most of the beat writers went out of their way to protect players' off-the-field foibles. If a player was so drunk that during the national anthem he was puking in the showers, Cramer noted in his biography, the writers simply banged out a line about his "stomach flu."

But by the 1970s, when Mays was getting ready to retire and Bobby Bonds was embarking on his own career, the old codes were being broken. Part of it was due to the growth of televised games, which made it harder for reporters simply to cover what happened on the field. But part of it, too, was a revolution in the business of baseball. In 1972, the players, whose average salary was only $34,000, went on strike for the first time. Delaying the opening of the season by thirteen days, the strike eventually paved the way for free agency, which liberated the players but created a system in which the best players increasingly moved from team to team, shattering a sense of loyalty with the fans. After Bobby Bonds and several other popular Yankees left in 1975, an article appeared in the *New York Times* under the headline: "A 5-Year-Old Boy Loses His Heroes." It asked: "Do you tell this boy that baseball is not really

just a game? . . . Is it correct to say that Bobby Bonds, whom he idolized, did not have fun playing here in New York, that he will be
playing in some back yard in California next year? Can this young-
ster, precocious though he is, comprehend the complex web of the
baseball superstructure? . . . Will he love baseball as his dad did, or
will he be turned off?"

Bobby Bonds, as much as any player of the time, came to be seen
as a part of "the complex web of the baseball superstructure," offering his electric but erratic talents to the highest bidder. After he
was traded seven times in seven years, the rumors about his personal problems only increased. "What I was doing," he said, "was
probably no different than Mickey Mantle or a bunch of 'em,"
Bobby once said of his drinking. Finally, in 1981, one year after another strike-shortened season, he unceremoniously packed up his
locker and left the sport.

Perhaps no one was more affected by the constant trades and
gossip than his eldest son. "Bobby went through a lot," Dusty Baker
once said, "and Barry has shared a lot of his dad's pain."

Barry himself has stated, "They never gave him the respect he
deserves. Why should I believe things will be any different for me?"

According to Barry, one day, after Bobby had left the game and
stopped drinking, he pulled his son aside. "He told me to play the
game for as long as I could because it all goes so fast," Barry said.
"And he told me to keep my mouth shut. I guess that second one
got by me."

"You can watch," Bonds said, as he walked into World Gym at 8:00
A.M. "You're not here to ask questions. I don't want it to be like the
FBI." Whereas his father was once rumored to have fallen short of
his potential because of drugs, his son was now rumored to have
exceeded his because of drugs.

He wore black sweat pants and black gloves. Lying down on one
of the benches, he began to press several dumbbells while his
strength coach, Greg Anderson, stood above him. "I hate doing
this," Bonds said, as he got up and looked in the mirror. "In three
years this is all coming off. My wife likes me this big, but I can't
stand it."

When Bonds first entered the National League in 1986 he had a
sprinter's build. But after a few years, he became one of the first of

the new generation of players who lifted weights, gradually trans-
forming himself from a 185-pound leadoff hitter into a 230-pound
slugger. "I think Barry saw all this potential that my dad had, and it
was just wasted," Barry's brother, Bobby Jr., told ESPN.

Bonds often gets up at five in the morning and runs sprints, even
after night games. He lifts every day, isolating one segment of his
body — his shoulders or calves or abdomen. "I had the lowest body
fat of anyone on the team in spring training," Bonds said, suddenly
talking with me after his initial refusal.

"It was too low," said Anderson.

"6.2," said Bonds.

To stay in such condition he eats six specially prepared meals a
day, consisting of fish, chicken, turkey, vegetables, or, in rare in-
stances, beef; each meal has 350 to 450 calories. "Every month we
take his blood and test his mineral levels to make sure they're in
line so that if he's ten milligrams off in zinc or six off in magnesium
or five milligrams off in copper, that's what we replace," Anderson
explained. "That's how he stays in such good condition."

Last year, as Bonds approached the record, he seemed in awe of
his own power. During a humid series against the Atlanta Braves,
with his uniform soaked through with sweat and his body crouched
over the plate, he hit three home runs in a single game. When
asked about his sudden surge, Bonds, who had never treated hitting as a rarefied science, told reporters: "Call God. Ask him. It's
like, wow. I can't understand it, either. I try to figure it out, and I
can't figure it out. So I stopped trying."

But this year, after two former All-Stars admitted that they had
used illegal steroids during their careers, many began to openly
question whether Bonds's production was fueled by steroids. "The
running bet in the office is that Barry's head has grown," which is a
sign of steroids, a local reporter told me one day in the press box.

As fans began to yell "Barry's on 'roids" whenever he came up to
bat, Bonds vehemently denied using them. At a game at Yankee
Stadium, he seemed irate that the rumors were still circulating.
"I'm tired of it," he said. "One minute I do this, and I'm good. The
next minute I'm accused of other stuff. That's how you make a living," he said to the reporters gathered around him. "The more
blood you can drain, the more successful you can be."

Now, as he sat up on the bench dropping two weights on the

ground, Bonds said, "It affects you when this stuff comes into your home. When my son comes up to me and says kids at school are asking him if his father is on drugs, that's when it bothers me."

He paused, picking up another weight and studying it for a minute. "My cap has been 7½ forever," he said when I asked him about the speculation over whether his head has grown. He said he took the protein supplement creatine, which is legal and sold over the counter, but nothing more. "I don't need to take anything illegal. Why do I need to cheat? I'm already good."

He did several reps, sweat starting to soak through his shirt. "No one wants to believe that someone is just good," he said. "They always want to find something. There has to be some reason. They have to believe there's a catch to why he's different from anyone else. They have to think you're cheating." He continued, "The problem with me is that they don't have anything on me. You really think about my career, honestly think about my career, what do they really got on me? Nothing. I don't do drugs. I don't go with prostitutes. I got divorced. That's it. Nothing."

After an hour of working out he went into the lobby, where Anderson ordered him one of his meals, scrambled egg whites and turkey sausage. He seemed like a different person here than the one in the clubhouse, almost unguarded. Every few minutes someone came by to hug or chat with him and he smiled and laughed, tilting his head back and embracing him or her in his giant arms.

"You got to try one of these, man," he said to me, holding out a piece of sausage on the end of his fork. "You're gonna pass out. You've never had anything like that in your life. And they have this barbecue chicken . . ."

I started to ask him a question, but before I could finish he asked it himself: "Why do I change at the ballpark? There's nothing truthful at the ballpark. Except the game." He picked up the paper, where there was a story on the potential strike. A poll said that more fans blamed the rich players than the rich owners for the endless disputes over salary caps. He studied the article for a long time, then put down the paper: "They say: 'You should just be happy. You're making a whole lot of money.' Baby, I earned this money. I don't give a damn. You can say whatever you want. I earned this money. I worked for this money. I didn't work to be called names all day."

Oddly, by being one of the few players who spoke candidly about the business of baseball, he was often shunned by the business world itself. Although he has dominated his sport for several years (*Total Baseball,* the bible of statistics, concluded that he was the best player in the National League in 1990, 1991, 1992, 1993, 1995, 1996, 1998, 2000, and 2001), he has never received the kind of corporate endorsements that other sports stars have. "They don't like me," he once acknowledged.

After he broke the home run record, Bonds cut commercials for Charles Schwab and KFC, including one in which he appeared with Hank Aaron. But he said of all the commercials and banquets and engagements off the field: "This isn't me. The game is my stage. That's where I'm happiest."

"I'm a ballplayer," Bonds told me of his negative image. "I'm not a PR man. I'm a ballplayer. You know how many words I got to say out on the baseball field? 'I got it!'" At one point, when I asked him if he ever wanted to be revered like his godfather, he thought about it for a long time. "I want to be a ballplayer," he said. "A damn good one." Then he stood up to go. "I got to take my kids to school," he said.

"How long is it gonna take? I'm watching the golf game."

It was Willie Mays. His voice was hard to hear over the phone, almost a whisper. He is seventy-one, and when he shows up at Pacific Bell Park — where there is a statue and a plaza named after him — to watch his godson, fans, many of them too young to have seen him play, still surround him.

At first when I asked him about Barry he seemed hesitant to talk. "This isn't my thing," Mays told me, and the more we spoke, the more striking it was how much he sounded like his godson. When I asked him why Barry was criticized so vehemently, he paused for a while, as if searching for the precise reason. "Whatever you ask him," he finally said, "he'll tell you the truth."

Mays said he still offered Bonds advice when he was struggling at the plate, but lately he had nothing to offer: "He hasn't been in a rut."

Indeed, Barry Bonds is fast approaching the heights of his godfather, the only player of his generation to ever do so. Already the only player ever to hit 400 home runs and steal 400 bases, as of late August, Bonds was only 11 bases short of creating a new club: 500/500. It is not inconceivable that he will end his career with more runs batted in than any other player, passing Hank Aaron's 2,297. And while his fielding and lifetime batting average may never reach Mays's, he is likely in the next few seasons, barring injury, to surpass Mays in total home runs (660) and is potentially within reach of Hank Aaron's all-time record of 755. "He has often said to me, 'Willie, I don't want to pass you,' and I always say, 'Wait a minute,'" Mays recently said. "I tell him: 'Home runs are there to be hit. If you pass me, pass Ruth, pass Hank, then just go ahead and do it. You can't lay back and not pass who you want. This is just baseball.'"

On a recent summer night, shortly before the players' union set the strike date, Bonds, only 2 home runs shy of becoming the fourth player in history ever to hit 600, broke his boycott of the local media and held a press conference. He sat at the dais in his uniform, facing the three dozen or so reporters and cameramen who had filled the tiny room in the bowels of the stadium. There were no questions about steroids or the strike. For the moment, with the season in jeopardy and the opportunities for greatness running out, the reporters appeared happy just to be talking with Bonds again, and Bonds seemed happy to be talking to them without having to defend himself. "I don't understand how I got here yet," Bonds said in a soft-spoken voice. "I just got done doing one thing that was shocking, and now there's another chapter, another shock."

After a few minutes he walked into the clubhouse and sat in his corner by himself, getting ready for the game against the Chicago Cubs. Normally, his son got dressed beside him, then went milling around the clubhouse the way Barry once had. He was already known in Little League as a rising superstar, the son of Barry Bonds. "At least one of us," Barry often jokes, "has won a championship." When the press circles around his father he often looks at them with the same wary, blank eyes. Once when a crush appeared around his dad he seemed almost scared. "I'm out of here," he said, pushing his way out.

"He's not gonna be the next Barry Bonds," Bonds told me. "He's gonna be his own man."

But now, to my surprise, instead of his son, who was on vacation, his father suddenly appeared at Barry's side. Bobby had recently undergone surgery to remove a tumor and still looked frail. He wore blue jeans and a black T-shirt. "We had a little talk," Bobby told me after he left the clubhouse. "I was getting his mind to where it's supposed to be. Making sure that he stays relaxed and realizes how much fun this is. Don't take it out of context of what it really is."

Upstairs, we sat with Barry's mother and second wife and one of his daughters. It was a cool night, and every seat was filled. Out in San Francisco Bay, out past right field where Barry often hit his longest balls, boats gathered hoping to fish out of the water his 599th and, ultimately, the one that counted — the 600th home run. When Bonds first stepped into the batter's box with two men on, the stadium lit up with flash bulbs. The Cubs had a rookie left-hander on the mound, and no one knew if he'd pitch to him. After two balls, the crowd started to boo; but then, with one strike, the lefty came right at him, and Bonds lined a shot into right center. The crowd rose in expectation, but it skidded into the alley. Only a double. "He's more relaxed than I've ever seen him," Bobby said.

As we waited for another turn, Bobby shook his head. "You know what's a shame?" he said. "A lot of people will have missed all that he's done — missed the entire parade." He looked around at the people gathered into the stadium. "Sometimes in this park he can hit a home run and everyone will cheer and think he's the greatest in the world, but they will still dislike him when the day's over with." He shook his head, his voice trailing off. Barry's wife, a pretty, slender woman, handed him a plate with hot dogs and started to clap as Bonds came up again. Before he stepped into the batter's box he waved to his family. "Look for him to do something," Bobby said.

Once again, the rookie came right at him. "Here it comes," said Bobby. This time, on a one-two pitch, Bonds uncorked his bat, crushing the ball into the farthest reaches of the park, more than 420 feet away. Bonds dropped his bat and watched. The crowd roared as the scoreboard flashed his latest total: 599. "Do I know my son?" Bobby said, standing up, trying to peer over the tops of hundreds of heads as his son crossed home plate. No one in the stadium sat down, and after a minute Barry came out of the dugout and tipped his hat.

As he stood there, smiling as the crowd chanted his name, I thought for the first time I could see him for what he really is, the true face of baseball — a game that at its best and stripped of the dead weight of metaphor, satisfies everyone's self-interest: the fans, the owners, and Bonds himself, who gets to play the game he loves and is better at, arguably, than anyone who has ever played.

After a few minutes he ducked into the dugout, then took the field, resting his hands on both knees. He would still have three more at-bats to try for his 600th. But for the moment, as the crowd settled back into its seats, there were no heroes or demons. Just baseball. Isn't that enough?

S. L. PRICE

The Lone Wolf

FROM SPORTS ILLUSTRATED

BETWEEN HANDSHAKES AND HELLOS, with the cool clang of money and the pop and hum of the MGM's endless night echoing in his ears, Mike Agassi stood in his good suit with a smile on his face and wondered how he was going to kill Pancho Gonzalez. Should he do it himself? Scrape up $20,000 and hire a hit man? It was 1981, in a Las Vegas still proud of its gangster soul, and Agassi had been on its front lines for years as a casino greeter. He knew people who knew people. It was only a matter of calculating the real cost, because Agassi had no illusions about getting away with murder. He'd spend the rest of his life in jail, he was sure. Then again, he'd have the satisfaction of seeing the man dead.

Agassi had come to America twenty-five years earlier, a tennis fanatic who'd boxed on the 1952 Iranian Olympic team, and in recent years his obsessive stewardship of the tennis career of his oldest daughter, Rita, had hit the shoals of teenage burnout and rebellion. There was great promise in Mike's eleven-year-old son, Andre — who years earlier, using a sawed-off racket, had wowed crowds at the Alan King Desert Classic by rallying with Gonzalez before the final — but there was reason to think that Andre, too, would wither under Mike's punishing critiques and 5,000-balls-a-day regimen. Gonzalez said Andre was too soft, too scared, and who knew better than Pancho? In Vegas he was the tennis king.

There was no more perfect match than Pancho and Vegas: both dark and disreputable, both hard and mean and impossible to ignore. At fifty-three he was still a big man in every way, six-foot-three, with a thunderclap voice and a career that had anticipated nearly every major stage in the evolution of modern tennis. Locked out of prestigious amateur tournaments such as Wimbledon and the U.S. Championships during his prime, Gonzalez nonetheless dominated the game as a pro in the 1950s and early 1960s and left its landscape scorched by the fire of his all-consuming bitterness. Before the groundbreaking wins by Althea Gibson and Arthur Ashe in the 1950s and 1960s, before the brattiness of Jimmy Connors and John McEnroe in the 1970s and 1980s, before the complaints about Pete Sampras's untouchable serve in the 1990s, Gonzalez smashed through the game's class and ethnic barriers, abused officials verbally, and paralyzed opponents with a serve so powerful that it inspired cries to remake the sport. Ion Tiriac, the Romanian player of the early Open era and eventual manager of Guillermo Vilas, Boris Becker, and other pros, has called Gonzalez "the beginning of professional tennis as we know it . . . the father of everything we have today."

Now, in the raging autumn of his life, the man who'd beaten Don Budge and Connors and everyone in between had insinuated himself into the Agassi clan. And Mike Agassi had no one to blame but himself. It was Mike, after all, who in 1973 had taken thirteen-year-old Rita to be coached at Caesars Palace, where Gonzalez worked as tennis director. This wasn't easy for Mike. Like everyone else in the Vegas tennis community, he'd endured Gonzalez's moods, but few people knew how far back their enmity went: seventeen years earlier in Chicago, Mike had worked as a line judge during a match between Gonzalez and Ken Rosewall. Gonzalez harangued Agassi so viciously that night that Agassi rose from his chair, refused to work another point, and stalked off into the bleachers.

Still, Mike was desperate; Rita wouldn't listen anymore, and her game was slipping away. He turned her over to Gonzalez. When Rita was fifteen, Mike, suspecting she had a crush on Gonzalez, demanded that she stop training with him. She refused. At seventeen, she was teaching at Caesars and in love with her coach, a man thirty-two years her senior. At eighteen, she left her parents' house and moved into her own apartment. At nineteen, she and Gonzalez became an official item. At twenty, she moved in with him.

Mike was livid. He railed in public, telling relatives that he wanted to hire a hit man. He thought about what might happen to his wife and the three other kids if he went to jail. "There were two things to do," he says. "Kill him, or stay away and forget him."

Mike cut off relations with Rita. "I had no daughter," he says. He and Gonzalez would pass each other at tennis events without speaking, but Agassi was sure he could read what Gonzalez was thinking. "'I'm f—— your daughter,'" Agassi says. "The guy enjoyed that I didn't like him. I knew what kind of person he was."

Pancho, fifty-five, and Rita, twenty-three, were married in March 1984 — he for the sixth time, she for the first — in their back yard, in a windstorm. Mike didn't attend the ceremony. Nearly two decades later and seven years after Gonzalez's death, Mike still spews obscenities about Pancho and the storm he stirred. Though tennis helped Agassi realize the immigrant's ultimate dream, though the sport gave his son immortality and untold riches, Agassi wishes he'd never heard of the game. Tennis made him deliver his child into the hands of a man he despised.

He could be a real son of a bitch. Everyone knew that about Richard "Pancho" Gonzalez — friend, foe, wife, and family. But when his contemporaries use the phrase "real son of a bitch" to describe him, their anger is often lightened by a weird lilt of admiration. No: joy. You have to hear his old friend Pancho Segura describe how Gonzalez hated to lose. You have to hear another opponent speak of how Gonzalez once stormed into the locker room and shattered his second-place trophy against the wall, or how he growled to a man who'd defeated him, "Give your money back, you a——. You're never going to beat me again." In 1952 Segura, seven years older than Gonzalez and not nearly as talented, had the day of his life and crushed Gonzalez at a pro event 6–2, 6–2, 6–2. "He wouldn't talk to me for days," Segura says, laughing, and then he shouts gleefully, "He was a p——!"

Days? "I was one of his friends, and when I beat him, he wouldn't talk to me for three months," says 1959 Wimbledon champion Alex Olmedo. It didn't matter if the match was played before thousands or no one. In 1964 Gonzalez and his protégé Charlie Pasarell, a top U.S. amateur, were playing practice sets at the Los Angeles Tennis Club: loser paid for the balls. Gonzalez won the first set easily and went up 5–2 in the second when he noticed a hitch in Pasarell's backhand volley. Gonzalez stopped to give a fifteen-minute tutorial. When play resumed, Pasarell won the set.

"He went ballistic," Pasarell says. "Threw the racket against the fence: *athwoonnng!* Grabbed the racket again and hit all the balls over the fence, beyond Wilcox Avenue. Picked up his equipment, slammed open the gate, slammed it shut, and drove off, tearing down the street. I figured, Jeez, I guess I've got to pay for the balls."

Pasarell got off easy. Segura once joked that the nicest thing Gonzalez said to any of his wives was "Shut up." For all but the last of his eight children he was a glowering critic who came and went bearing suitcases and rackets. Pancho and Richard Jr. won a couple of father-son tournaments together, but what Richard Jr. remembers about those matches is being loudly upbraided by his father. Sometimes Pancho would call his son a "dumb f——."

When, in late 1956, Gonzalez briefly went home to Los Angeles during a pro tour against Rosewall, he learned that the mother of his wife, Henrietta, had been murdered. A bereft Henrietta talked with Pancho about whether he should go back on tour immediately. To others he expressed no doubt. He told one intimate, "If it had been Richard Jr., I'd still go."

"He was such a complex person," says Madelyn Gonzalez, who married Pancho in 1960, two years after he divorced Henrietta. "He really wanted to be a good guy, but he just couldn't. It wasn't in him." In 1965 Pancho was playing Chile's Luis Ayala in Newport, Rhode Island, when he noticed Madelyn walking to her seat. He stopped play and snarled, "You'd be late to your own father's funeral."

Yet two years after their divorce in '68, Madelyn remarried Pancho. They divorced again in '75 and almost remarried in '78. She keeps a picture of him on her dresser. "I've had many chances to marry very wealthy men," she says, "but he's a tough act to follow. It's that fire, that larger-than-life thing."

She isn't the only one who feels that way. Forty years after his prime as a player, Gonzalez still invades the dreams of the men he beat, still evokes tears in those who idolized him. Men's tennis is obsessed with numbers: as Sampras neared his record-breaking thirteenth major singles title, the debate over who was the greatest player in history boiled down to him and Rod Laver, the only man to win the Grand Slam twice. Gonzalez won only two majors, the U.S. Championships in 1948 and '49, but the figure he cut, the game he played, the rage and need that rose off him like vapor were unlike anything tennis had ever seen. "He was just so beautiful to watch," says Jennie Hoad, the widow of Lew Hoad, one of Gonzalez's fiercest — and most elegant — rivals. "Being tall, he was a little more graceful, more natural. I don't think he ever moved in an unattractive way."

To see Gonzalez play, said Gussy Moran, the flamboyant women's tennis star of the 1940s, was to watch "a god patrolling his personal heaven." Writers compared Gonzalez's movement to that of a jungle cat, his strokes to music or poetry. His serve — falling as straight and deadly as an executioner's blade — was so clean that other players beheld it with wonder, and generations of coaches held it up as the paragon. In 1969 Danish pro Torben Ulrich lost to Gonzalez in the third round of the U.S. Open but seemed grateful to have been on the receiving end of genius. "Pancho gives great happiness," he said. "It is good to watch the master."

Ulrich, a jazz aficionado whose son had saxophone legend Dexter Gordon for a godfather, calls Gonzalez an artist. "You ask if I understood Pancho. I did not," Ulrich says. "But if there's real greatness, you're not supposed to understand it." Still, his genius never tripped into McEnrovian self-destructiveness. It was the rest of the world Gonzalez wanted to hurt, and he flew at his target like a guided missile.

Ulrich tells of a night he had with Gonzalez in 1974, on the Grand Masters Tour. The two stayed up for five hours in a hotel, drinking beer and eating, and Gonzalez regaled Ulrich with stories about Las Vegas and his early days as a drag racer. "Come the next day, the draw had been made, but I didn't know," Ulrich says. "The matches had started, and Pancho's watching. I sit next to him and say, softly, 'Good morning, Pancho. Did you get some rest?' He doesn't answer. So I raise my voice a little and say, 'Good morning.' He didn't make the smallest acknowledgment that I was there — because we were playing each other that day."

As a professional, Gonzalez did as he pleased. His selfishness was unalloyed. On the pro tour of the 1950s and 1960s the players were expected to travel together and pitch in with promotions. Gonzalez would have none of it. He did few interviews. The sport then was a social whirl, with sponsors' cocktail parties and the like, but Gonzalez did not schmooze. He drove from town to town in his Thunderbird, showed up late, slept through appointments.

"He was like a lonely wolf," Olmedo says. "But he had his reasons."

He didn't start out mean. After Gonzalez won the 1948 U.S. Championships at Forest Hills at age twenty, *Life* magazine called him "happy-go-lucky" and "good-natured." He was constantly portrayed as a carefree champion, casual in his approach to training, open to everyone. "He was really happy," Segura says, "but he wasn't ready."

Gonzalez was no innocent, but nothing had prepared him for the WASP-dominated, moneyed world in which he was suddenly moving. When his father, Manuel, was a child, he walked nine hundred miles from Chihuahua, Mexico, to Arizona with his own father. Manuel eventually settled in South Central L.A., where he met his wife, Carmen, with whom he would have seven children.

Manuel worked as a house painter, and despite his heavy hand Pancho grew up loose and wild. He hustled pool, but he spent just as much energy teaching himself to play tennis on L.A.'s public courts with a fifty-one-cent racket he had gotten for Christmas. Rising fast in southern California boys' tennis, Pancho quit high school after two years to play full-time, but he was banned from junior tournaments because he was a dropout. He got busted for burglarizing houses at fifteen. "You don't know the thrill of going out the back window when someone's coming in the front door," Pancho told his brother Ralph.

Put him away, Manuel told the judge. Pancho spent a year in detention, then joined the Navy and swabbed decks in the Pacific. One AWOL and a couple of late returns from leave earned him a bad-conduct discharge in 1947, and he came home. He married Henrietta Pedrin and quickly dominated the powerful men's tennis scene in southern California. Along the way he took note of every slight, such as Anglos' habit of calling every Mexican Pancho. He entered the '48 U.S. Championships ranked seventeenth in the country and, to everyone's shock, won. The next year, cocky and still knowing nothing about conditioning, he defended his title in a five-set classic against Ted Schroeder. By then he and Henrietta had one son, Richard Jr., and another on the way. They needed money. Bobby Riggs dangled a $75,000 pro contract, and Pancho bit.

In that pre-Open era, the pro tour was a Darwinian death march.

While winners of Wimbledon and the U.S. Championships were feted in the mainstream press, no one had any illusion that those amateurs were the best players in the game. Top pros like Riggs and Jack Kramer waited for amateurs to make names for themselves and then hired them for barnstorming tours in which a seasoned pro played a series of matches against a newly signed "challenger." The tours were sold on the prestige of the challengers, who were paid more as a result and whom the pros proceeded to beat without mercy. Riggs pitted Gonzalez against Kramer, who at twenty-eight was considered the world's best player. For Gonzalez, that would spell disaster.

For 123 nights the two men played on canvas stretched over wood in high school gyms, armories, even an opera house. Kramer won by a punishing margin of 96–27. Gonzalez nevertheless enjoyed himself, gulping Cokes during matches and smoking afterward, oblivious to the fact that his reputation was slipping away. The twenty-one-year-old didn't understand that once an amateur was established as a loser, his value as a gate attraction plummeted. Kramer, tough and principled, wasn't willing to carry him. Almost as quickly as it had begun, Gonzalez's pro career was done.

For the next four years Gonzalez diddled away his early prime as a player, spending most of his time racing hot rods, bowling, breeding dogs, stringing rackets at his soon-to-fail tennis shop in L.A.'s Exposition Park. In 1952 he and Henrietta separated. Finally, in late 1954, Kramer, who was playing less and promoting more, invited Gonzalez to join a round-robin tour he had organized for top pros Budge, Frank Sedgman, and Segura. Gonzalez beat the other men consistently, positioning himself to take apart the next amateur challenger.

Tony Trabert won Wimbledon and the French and U.S. Championships in 1955, then went for the money. But Kramer kept Gonzalez waiting as he mulled whether to play Trabert himself. "Jack completely demoralized him," says Henrietta, who had reunited with Pancho after a year and a half apart. Kramer finally took himself out of the running and signed Gonzalez to a seven-year contract. Pancho was back — and different from the man who'd left the tour a few years earlier. "A loner," says Schroeder, "and always the unhappiest man in town."

"His nature had changed completely," Kramer says. "He became difficult and arrogant. Losing had changed him. When he got his next chance, he understood that you either win or you're out of a job."

Gonzalez resented Trabert, who, Henrietta says, corrected Pancho's English and dismissed his interest in cars. The challenger was making a minimum of $80,000, while Gonzalez, the best pro in the world, was guaranteed only $15,000. Gonzalez wanted to make him pay. Over six months of singles matches he crushed Trabert 74–27.

Trabert, for his part, grew to loathe Gonzalez. To him the selfish, irascible, bullying Gonzalez broke all the rules of tennis. He made it personal. He turned a genteel sport into a street fight. In 1956, after a doubles match in which a dispute over a point led to an exchange of smashes aimed at the body, Gonzalez marched off the court without shaking hands with Trabert or his partner. Then, as Gonzalez stood by, Trabert told a reporter, "You just saw one of the most chickens —— things in sports." Another time Trabert told Gonzalez, "Somebody's going to flush you down the toilet before your life's over — and I just might be the one to pull the handle."

When the Gonzalez-Trabert tour ended in '56, Gonzalez dismantled Frank Parker and Dinny Pails in a round-robin 45–7. Then came Rosewall. Then Hoad. Gonzalez beat them all. He also beheaded the microphone of a chair ump who refused to overrule a call during one match, and shattered a wall clock when he smacked a ball away in frustration during another match. He blew off promoters. He shredded opponents' concentration by stopping play to pose for pictures. Hoad's Aussie contemporaries say he braced Gonzalez against a locker one night and threatened to beat him senseless. But Gonzalez drew crowds like no one else in the game.

That's why he resented Kramer more than any opponent. Kramer stuck to his policy of offering far more money to the amateur challenger, insisting that the tour's appeal lay in seeing if the amateur could dethrone the king. Gonzalez, the established number one, wanted to be paid like it. He sued Kramer to get out of the contract and lost. Pancho told Ralph, who often accompanied him on tour, "I'm just a piece of meat. They cut off a piece, and they sell it. I'm hanging on the goddam hook."

"He took it too personally," Ralph says. Told that Trabert once said Pancho had "a persecution complex," Ralph nods in agreement. "Born a——," he says of Trabert, "but he's right."

If Gonzalez had no time for his fellow players, he had little for Henrietta or their three young sons: Richard Jr., Michael, and Daniel. Pancho and Henrietta separated again and headed for divorce. One evening in 1958 Lew and Jennie Hoad and their little daughter went to visit Henrietta at her house and found her passed out from an accidental overdose of sleeping pills. They called Pancho, who came over and brought Henrietta out of her stupor by tossing her into the shower. He was furious. He roared and threw furniture around. Jennie locked herself and her daughter in the study. "She no doubt was looking for sympathy from Pancho," Jennie says of Henrietta. "She didn't get it. He left the house in a mess and charged out."

The end of that marriage also marked a beginning for Pancho. In Madelyn Darrow, a recently minted Miss Rheingold, he collided head-on with the one person who could make him as miserable as he made everyone else. For an outsider like Pancho she was inside incarnate: haughty and accustomed to getting her way. They fell instantly for each other, but Madelyn didn't want anything to do with hot rods. She wanted cocktail parties, famous faces, and a house in the hills. She and Pancho married and moved to Malibu, then Brentwood, and finally Holmby Hills.

"She destroyed him," says Segura. "I told him, 'You made a mistake divorcing Henrietta. You could eat standing up and nobody cared. You didn't have to worry about using a knife or fork.' Madelyn tried to improve him. This is a man who hated ties. She told him he had to put on a jacket and tie. It always happens to athletes. Your tennis brings you up around these people — a lot of horses——! It kills your soul."

Pancho adored drag racing, but most of all he loved tinkering with engines, stripping them down and making them sing. "I hated those cars," Madelyn says. "He poured the little bit of money we had into those stupid cars, or the crap tables." He moved his tools and auto parts to Ralph's house and spent hours there. Often he met his sons at the races. On the way home he would stop to scrub his fingernails clean. "It was sad," says Richard Jr.

Pancho and Madelyn had three daughters together: twins Mariessa and Christina, born in 1961, and Andrea, born in '63. Ralph never felt comfortable in Madelyn and Pancho's home. Pancho's sons later worked with their dad at the tennis ranch he opened in Malibu in '66, but only Richard Jr. went to his house much. "Once I was in the kitchen, and I heard [Madelyn] say my father's friends were a bunch of rubes," says Richard Jr. "I didn't know what a rube was. I thought it might be good."

Madelyn had little in common with her in-laws, but she says it was Pancho who kept them at a distance. He told Henrietta that the only family he had then was Madelyn and their daughters.

In truth, winning was his pride and joy. After beating Hoad 51–36 in 1958, Gonzalez spent the next few years dispatching all comers: Ashley Cooper, Mal Anderson, Rosewall, Olmedo, Andrés Gimeno, Barry MacKay. He retired in 1961, at the end of his contract with Kramer, then returned for a humiliating first-round loss to Olmedo at the U.S. Professional Grass Court Championships at Forest Hills. There, after cautioning reporters not to write him off, Pancho took Madelyn's hand and sat while his eyes filled with tears.

In '63 Gonzalez coached the U.S. team to the Davis Cup final, against Australia, in Adelaide. The team arrived Down Under in mid-December, and, says Dennis Ralston, one of the U.S. players, "Madelyn would refuse Pancho's collect phone calls." According to Ralston, she was angry at Pancho because he wouldn't be home for the holidays. (Madelyn says she doesn't recall this.) "She wouldn't let him talk to his kids at Christmas," Ralston says. "He'd slam the phone down and take four or five drinks."

Gonzalez headed home before the matches began. "Trying to keep peace in the family," he said in a TV interview.

When he felt like it, Gonzalez could turn on a radiant charm. He made room in his life to tutor young U.S. players such as Ashe, Cliff Richey, Pasarell, and Ralston, who all held him in awe, but his generosity often lost out to his rage. On that same Davis Cup trip to Australia, Gonzalez and Ralston were playing a practice match in front of some 1,500 people, five dollars a set. Ralston lost the first 6–4 and said playfully, "Double or nothing, but you got to give me a game and the serve."

Gonzalez glared at him. "Get out the way you got in, punk," he said. Ralston went up 4–0, and Gonzalez gathered his rackets. "Listen, you son of a bitch, you crybaby, all you do is cry," he snapped at Ralston. Then he walked off the court. The crowd heard it all.

"I was heartbroken," Ralston says. "This was my idol. There was a party that night at the U.S. ambassador's, and I didn't want to go. Pancho came over and apologized: 'I'm sorry, kid; I just lost it.'"

In 1965, seventeen-year-old Richard Jr. gave his father some bad news: Richard's girlfriend was pregnant. Richard expected anger, disdain — anything but what happened next. Pancho began to cry. He wrapped Richard in his arms and held him close, tears streaming down his cheeks. Richard had never seen his father weep, and he thought Pancho was looking back at his own life, at his marriage to Henrietta and the son he'd had at twenty, the son whose life had now changed for good. Richard had never known a moment like this.

It would be another thirty years before he got that close to his father again.

The boy was hungry. He knew few people in London on that June day in 1969, and he was alone and far from home. His mother would've told him to eat, to spend his fifty pence of dinner money, but Vijay Amritraj had no intention of eating. Pancho Gonzalez was playing at Wimbledon that evening, and the fifteen-year-old Amritraj knew he had to be there. As a rising junior player in India, poring over newspaper stories and photos, Amritraj had worshiped Gonzalez without ever having seen him play. Stomach growling, he spent the fifty pence on a standing-room ticket for Centre Court.

Just before 6:00 P.M. Gonzalez stepped out of a black-and-white past into Technicolor, swaggering onto the grass for his first-round match with Pasarell. "He lived up to my dreams," Amritraj says of Gonzalez that evening "I still don't see anybody who devoured the sport as he did."

In truth, Gonzalez didn't look so good. He was forty-one and had not played consistently in recent years. Sensing the onset of the Open era and convinced that to compete with the young guns he had to weigh less than he did at twenty, he had indulged in wild diets to keep at 180 pounds. He drank little water. "He said you had to be like the [American] Indians, who he said never drank water," says Richey. In 1968, in a tournament at Bournemouth, England, Gonzalez inaugurated the Open era of tennis by losing to British amateur Mark Cox in five sets. "After waiting for it all these years," Gonzalez had said, "I had to be here when it finally happened." He played Wimbledon for the first time since 1949 but lost early: tennis history, it seemed, was going to leave him behind.

Gonzalez decided not to let it. He spent the last few months before Wimbledon '69 punishing his body for the last push of his playing career. "He would eat nothing but soup," Ulrich says. "He was fearsome on himself."

A dashing gray streak cut through his still-thick hair, but deep wrinkles creased his elbows, and his sun-baked skin seemed stretched over his thin frame, his gaunt face. Age had made him even more of a craftsman. His aluminum rackets were strung at widely different tensions — tighter for receiving, looser for serving. For Wimbledon he had prepared an arsenal, drilling holes from the handles to the heads of the rackets (twelve to fifteen holes per racket) to lighten them for touch and as a hedge against fatigue. In long matches he'd work all the way through his quiver, from the weapon with the fewest holes to the one with the most.

He would need every one against the twenty-five-year-old Pasarell. The son of Puerto Rican tennis champions, Pasarell was a younger, prettier, nicer version of Gonzalez, with perfect strokes and a classic serve-and-volley game. The match began as a service war, with neither man close to breaking the other as the daylight dimmed. Pasarell looked to wear the old man down, moving him around relentlessly and lobbing over his head, and in the first set the strategy worked — eventually. This was before the introduction of the tie-breaker; in numbing and increasingly riveting fashion, the games of the first set mounted to the equivalent of nearly *five* sets played on today's tour. Finally, in the forty-sixth game, on Pasarell's twelfth set point, the younger man broke serve by throwing up one more lob that Gonzalez couldn't run down. It was 8:00 P.M., and as the unreal score of 24–22 lit up the scoreboard, Gonzalez hunched over gasping. "He looked half dead," Amritraj says.

It got only worse. After Pasarell won the first point of the second set, Gonzalez asked the chair umpire, "How much longer do we have to play in this absolute darkness?" He asked again after the first game and threatened to default if the remainder of the match wasn't postponed. Referee Mike Gibson said no. Furious, Gonzalez spent most of the set screaming about the poor visibility. The crowd jeered at him to play on. "I've never seen this happen at Wimbledon before," intoned BBC broadcaster Dan Maskell. But Maskell's partner in the booth was hardly surprised. Jack Kramer had been watching Gonzalez behave this way for two decades.

Pasarell understood what was happening: *Pancho knows he's in trouble.* He abandoned his chip-and-lob tactics and began driving his returns, sure that Gonzalez couldn't pick them up in the dark. As Gonzalez served at 1–4, 15–30, the umpire mistakenly awarded him a point to make it 30–30. "Umpire, it's 15–40," Gonzalez shouted in disgust across the court. His subsequent cursing was drowned out by cheers for his sportsmanship. But Pasarell won the last two games to take the second set 6–1.

Gibson then suspended play. Gonzalez hurled his racket at the umpire's chair, gathered his other rackets, and stomped off. He didn't wait for Pasarell. He didn't stop to bow to the royal box. For perhaps the first time in the history of Wimbledon a player was booed off the court. Everyone began writing Gonzalez's professional obituary.

The next day, on the drive to Wimbledon for the resumption of the match, Pancho said to Madelyn, "I'm going to win." Amritraj, who would one day be coached into the top ten by Gonzalez, arrived early and stood in line for hours, lunch money in hand.

The third set began like the first, with both men easily holding serve, but as the games piled up, it became clear that Pasarell's level of play had dropped. People kept filing into Centre Court, packing it to capacity. Finally, with Pasarell serving at 15–40 in the thirtieth game, Gonzalez drove a hard, flat forehand up the line. His racket made a sound it hadn't made all match, like an ax biting into dead oak. Pasarell hit a backhand volley wide. Gonzalez had the break and the third set, 16–14, and as the cheers rose, he flicked his head back as if to say, *Here I am, you bastards.*

"What a monumental fighter this fellow is, Dan," Kramer said over the BBC. In the fourth set Gonzalez took complete charge. He pounced on balls, the years falling off him with every step, and won the set 6–3 to even the match.

The fifth set was another marathon, but Gonzalez only seemed stronger, even moving backward with astonishing speed. Serving at 4–5, however, he buckled and went down 0–40: three match points for Pasarell. Gonzalez calmly won the next two points and then watched as a lob by Pasarell fell an inch wide to bring the game back to deuce. Two points later Gonzalez dived for a ball, fell, and lay flat on his stomach. For a moment he didn't move. Pasarell approached and asked if he was okay. Gonzalez struggled to his feet, propping himself up with the racket like a man with a cane. Pasarell thought, *Why doesn't he just give up?*

Gonzalez held serve. Two games later Pasarell again had him

pinned, triple match point, only to watch Gonzalez wriggle free: an overhead smash, a drop volley, a service winner. Five of six times he had faced match point, Gonzalez had pounded his first serve in. "I've seen Sampras lose many matches because his serve wasn't working," says Pasarell, who now runs the ATP tournament at Indian Wells. "I never saw Gonzalez lose because his serve let him down."

Gonzalez held again, but as the roars shook Centre Court, he looked indifferent. He may have raged between points the evening before, but this afternoon he was strangely calm. He gave nothing away.

Pasarell had one more shot, his seventh and last. At 7–8, ad out, match point for the younger player, Gonzalez plunked his first serve into the net. He didn't hesitate: he drove his second serve so deep in the box that it took Pasarell by surprise. He managed a return, but Gonzalez struck a biting volley, and Pasarell lofted one last backhand lob — and a prayer. This time he died with it; the lob went way long. Gonzalez served out easily, flipping his head back like a prancing thoroughbred. Pasarell rebounded to go up 9–8, and by then no one doubted the match was destined for legend. "I don't think I've ever seen one like this," Kramer said.

Gonzalez held again, and at 9–9 Pasarell finally cracked. He went down 0–30 on his serve, and Gonzalez gave him some of his own medicine, lofting a backhand lob that kissed the inside of the baseline. Facing three break points, Pasarell showed none of Gonzalez's grit; he struck a forehand volley long. Break in hand, Gonzalez stepped on Pasarell's air hose, serving a love game to win the match by the lunatic score of 22–24, 1–6, 16–14, 6–3, 11–9.

"Seven match points," Pasarell says all these years later. "The son of a bitch." The crowd that had booed Gonzalez less than twenty-four hours earlier stood and flooded him with adulation. Later he found the humiliated Pasarell in the corner of the locker room, sobbing. Gonzalez, who never apologized for winning, sat down next to the young man, put his arm on his shoulders, and said, "Kid, I'm sorry. I was really lucky to win."

Luck had nothing to do with it. Kramer rates Gonzalez a better player than Sampras or Laver. Ashe called Gonzalez the only idol he ever had. Segura, Olmedo, and Ralston say Gonzalez was the best player in history. Connors said once that if he needed someone to play for his life, he'd pick Gonzalez. Pasarell agrees: "He was the toughest competitor who ever played. He just fought and fought and fought until he died."

The five-hour, twelve-minute epic between Gonzalez and Pasarell made Wimbledon history: longest match, most games played. For tennis aficionados it's surpassed in drama only by the 1980 final between McEnroe and Bjorn Borg, but in one sense it had more impact. In 1970, using Gonzalez-Pasarell as Exhibit A, the U.S. Open instituted the tiebreaker — the biggest structural change in tennis in a century.

Still, by the end of that first week of Wimbledon '69, Gonzalez was gone, having lost to Ashe in the round of sixteen. At the U.S. Open, Gonzalez battled severe cramps to beat Ulrich in five sets. In the locker room afterward his bony frame seized up grotesquely. "I can't do this anymore," he croaked to Ralph. He wondered if he was losing his mind. "I feel like Van Gogh out there."

Ralph tried to lighten the mood. "Don't cut off your ear!" he said.

"Goddammit, you don't understand!" Pancho yelled. "Nobody understands what I'm trying to do on the court, nobody — and I can't do it anymore."

But he could. Four weeks later he rolled through the cream of the tennis crop at the Howard Hughes Open in Vegas, swatting aside John Newcombe, Rosewall, Stan Smith, and Ashe. Then, in January 1970, at Madison Square Garden, Gonzalez beat Laver — the number-one player in the world, four months removed from winning his second Grand Slam — in five sets. A few months later, in 102-degree heat in Vegas, he beat Laver again.

The following year the forty-three-year-old Gonzalez beat a nineteen-year-old Connors *from the baseline* in the Pacific Southwest Open. "Nobody remembers," Olmedo says of that match. Once, in the early 1990s, Sampras was at dinner with commentator Mary Carillo when the subject of Gonzalez came up. "Pete had never heard of him," Carillo says, "because he'd never won Wimbledon." Andre Agassi isn't surprised to hear this. "The history of tennis is pretty complex," says Agassi, who was never close to his onetime brother-in-law, "and unless you're aware, you might not have a sense of how important a figure Pancho Gonzalez was."

Pancho was always aware. One night after a match at the L.A.

Coliseum he drank a few beers with the twenty-six-year-old Newcombe and then staggered out to the parking lot. As Gonzalez
started his hotted-up Mustang, Newcombe jumped on the hood
and playfully gave him the finger. Gonzalez floored it, lurched
ahead, and stomped on the brakes. Newcombe catapulted off, and
as he lay in a heap on the asphalt, pants torn, Gonzalez rolled
down the window and rasped, "Don't f—— with me, kid," before
driving off.

Beg? Take a handout? No. Ralph Gonzalez once accused Pancho
of drawing a three-foot circle around himself and leaving room
for no one else inside. "That's right," Pancho replied. He hadn't
let the world in when he was on top, and he wouldn't now that he
was broke. It was the early 1990s. Segura wanted to put on a benefit
for him. No, Gonzalez said. "So he chose to be down-and-out,"
Madelyn says, "and live in this nasty little house."

It wasn't nasty. It was his own idea of peace. Five minutes from
the Vegas airport, it was a runty yellow-stucco affair — but he had it
all to himself. At last Gonzalez was alone. He had carved his life
down to the barest bones. He and Madelyn had split up for good in
1980. Since then he had had three other wives and two children,
ending with Rita Agassi and their son, Skylar, but women and kids
just complicated things. Pancho and Rita divorced in 1989 after
nearly ten years together. For a while Pancho lived in a motor
home in an RV park. The little yellow house was better.

There he had things the way he'd always wanted: a hook on a
wall to hang his rackets, a workbench in the kitchen, a row of
shelves for the groceries. He slept on a mattress on the bedroom
floor. He used the same plastic cup and plate for every meal.

"I want a simple life," he said when Ralph tried to give him some
drinking glasses. "If it breaks, I've got to clean it up." For a time he
rode around in an old U-Haul van. "He was happy," Ralph says.
Pancho told his kids not to expect any money when he died.

All his bridges had been burned. He had made $75,000 a year
from an endorsement deal with Spalding, but he treated company
employees as if he were a lord, and in 1981, after a nearly thirty-
year association, Spalding didn't renew his annual contract. For
sixteen years he'd had the best professional relationship of his life
working for Cliff Perlman as the tournament director at Caesars
Palace, but Perlman left and the new man had no history with Gon-

zalez. It didn't help that Gonzalez only grudgingly agreed to his boss's request that he hit with Colin Powell and refused to give private lessons to the boss's wife. In 1985 Caesars cut Gonzalez loose. "He didn't know how to treat people," Olmedo says. "He was very proud, and that's what made him a great champion. He was like a goddam lion. But off the court he didn't know how to behave."

"He became impossible to be around," Rita says. His one redeeming relationship was with Skylar. When the boy was ten months old, Rita had found him sinking in their swimming pool and had him rushed to the hospital. (Pancho was asleep inside the house.) Pancho's daughter Mariessa had died at age eleven after being thrown by a horse. Pancho hadn't been close to her. He made sure, once Skylar was out of danger, not to be a stranger to the youngest of his children.

He opened himself to the boy as he had to no one else in his life. Most nights Skylar would stay with Rita or her parents, but he spent his days, while Rita was working, with Pancho. With Skylar, Pancho was warm and patient. They would ride dirt bikes and go-carts and hit golf balls into the desert. All the love Pancho had held back from his brothers and his women and his other children he poured into Skylar. The boy would curl up in a ball and nap by his side. Pancho's friends were stunned. "I just want to be around long enough to get him through high school," Pancho would say.

During the 1994 U.S. Open, as Andre Agassi was beating Michael Chang in the fourth round, Gonzalez lay in his hotel room in New York City, racked with back and abdominal spasms. When he returned home, X-rays revealed cancer in his stomach, esophagus, chin, and brain. For the next few months, as he underwent chemotherapy and radiation treatments, he kept saying he was going to beat the cancer, but he knew better. In March he told Laver not to feel sorry for him. He'd lived a good life. He was happy. He made peace with Kramer. "For the first time in my life, I'm open," he told a reporter. "I'm no longer selfish."

But flashes of the old Pancho remained. Ralph, too, had learned he had cancer — of the prostate — but he and his wife, Ona, moved into Pancho's house to help him. They soon chafed at his arrogance and neediness. One night the two stooped men in their sixties lunged at each other with their fists. "Die like a man, you son of a bitch!" Ralph yelled. Later that night the two brothers sat in the bedroom together and cried.

In late June, Pancho, his skin gone yellow, entered the hospital. After a few days he phoned Mike Agassi — whose house he refused to set foot in. The hostility between the two men had ratcheted down a level since Skylar's pool accident. "I cannot take care of my son," Gonzalez told Agassi. Sure that Skylar would carry some of his traits, Pancho added, "It's going to be hard for Rita because he's mine. Please raise him."

Mike came to the hospital carrying a jug of mushroom tea. He told Pancho, "Don't worry. We'll take care of him."

"It was sad," Mike says. "A great man, flat broke; a great man, his life is finished; a great man, has no friends."

On July 2, the day before he died, Gonzalez tried to watch Wimbledon on TV. Skylar came to say good-bye. Pancho faded in and out of consciousness, pillowed by morphine. He and Richard Jr. hadn't spoken for a few months because of a petty argument, but now Richard Jr. came and sat with him. Pancho went to the bathroom but was too weak to clean himself, so Richard Jr. did the job as that loud voice barked out intricate instructions. "I never could say no to him," Richard Jr. says, "and there I was again at the end." Later he took his father's hand. For the second time in his life he felt like a son should. "I sat with him the whole night," he says. "He held my hand, and he just kept squeezing it."

Skylar Gonzalez is sixteen. He has spent most of the last seven years with Rita. Every year, from May until July 3, he falls into a funk. Occasionally he goes to his father's grave and stares at the stone as the sound of traffic rumbles over the grass.

Pictures of Pancho paper Skylar's bedrooms at Mike's house and Rita's house. "He says, 'Daddy, I love you,' to the picture," Mike says. "Anytime there's something about Pancho on TV, he stands and watches with tears in his eyes. Skylar says, 'Everybody has a father. I wonder sometimes why I can't have a father.'" He dreams of his father still, and in his dreams the old wolf is always wise and kind.

Andre Agassi paid for Pancho's funeral. The crowd was small, everyone's memories a mix of good and bad. Mike Agassi opened up his home to the mourners and fed them. He didn't kill Pancho Gonzalez, but he saw him humbled, and he saw him dead.

RENE CHUN

Bobby Fischer's
Pathetic Endgame

FROM THE ATLANTIC MONTHLY

BOBBY FISCHER was singing the blues. As he wailed along with a 1965 recording by Jackie ("Mr. Excitement") Wilson, his voice — a gravelly baritone ravaged by age but steeled by anger — rumbled through the microphone like a broken-down freight train on rusty wheels. With each note he became increasingly strident. Even if you knew nothing about Bobby Fischer, listening to him sing this song would tell you all you needed to know. *"There just ain't no pity. No, no, no, in the naked city, yeah — New York City."*

This unlikely duet, featuring Jackie Wilson and the world's first and only chess grand master fugitive from justice, was broadcast live, on July 6, 2001, by DZSR Sports Radio, a Manila-based AM station that has embraced Fischer as a ratings booster. In exchange for these rare interviews (Fischer hasn't given a magazine or TV interview in thirty years), Sports Radio management has happily provided Fischer with hours of free airtime to spin his classic R&B records and to lash out at his enemies, both real and imagined. Fischer categorizes these enemies — including the former New York mayor Ed Koch, both Presidents Bush, and the Times Mirror Corporation — as "Jews, secret Jews, or CIA rats who work for the Jews."

This radio broadcast was Fischer's seventeenth in the Philippines. The bizarre karaoke interlude was a departure of sorts, but otherwise the broadcast was no different from the previous sixteen. Fischer's talking points never vary.

- Bobby Fischer is being persecuted by world Jewry.
- The United States government is a "brutal, evil dictatorship" that has falsely accused Bobby Fischer of a crime and forced him to live in exile.
- Bobby Fischer has been swindled out of a "vast fortune" in royalties by book publishers, movie studios, and clock manufacturers (yes, clock manufacturers), who have brazenly pilfered his brand name, patents, and copyrights.
- The Jews are a "filthy, lying bastard people" bent on world domination through such insidious schemes as the Holocaust ("a money-making invention"), the mass murder of Christian children ("their blood is used for black-magic ceremonies"), and junk food (William Rosenberg, the founder of Dunkin' Donuts, is singled out as a culprit).

For chess buffs who tune in for some shoptalk from the game's most revered icon, there is this:

- Chess is nothing more than "mental masturbation." Not only is the game dead, it's fixed. Garry Kasparov, the world's top-rated player, is a "crook" and a former KGB spy who hasn't played a match in his life in which the outcome wasn't prearranged.

The number-one transgression, however, the thing that has devastated Fischer, embittered him, and made him screech at night, alone in his apartment, is the "Bekins heist."

- Millions of dollars' worth of personal memorabilia, painstakingly collected and stockpiled by Bobby Fischer in a ten-by-ten-foot Bekins storage room in Pasadena, California, has been stolen from him in a secret plot involving the Rothschilds (Jews), Bill Clinton (a secret Jew), and unnamed Bekins executives (CIA rats who work for the Jews).

The international chess community, which tracks Fischer's downward spiral the way astronomers track the orbit of a dying comet, has been monitoring his radio interviews since the first one aired, back in January of 1999. For the most part chess people have for years downplayed the importance of his outlandish outbursts, explaining that Fischer's raging anti-Semitism, acute paranoia, and tenuous grasp on reality are hyped by the media and misunderstood by the public. In the early 1990s Fischer's girlfriend at the time said, "He's like a child. Very, very simple." A friend who spent a lot of time with him in the 1990s says, "Aside from his controversial views, as a person Bobby is very kind, very nice, and very human." Another friend, asked how he could stand by someone so blatantly anti-Semitic, replies, "A lot of people wouldn't care if Michael Jordan was an anti-Semite if they could play a game of Horse with him."

Many Fischer apologists argue that Bobby Fischer is in fact deranged, and that as such he deserves not public castigation but psychiatric help. They are quick to point out that he was raised in a Jewish neighborhood in Brooklyn, has had close friends who were Jewish, and in fact had a Jewish mother (information he has gone to great lengths to deny). It seems hard to imagine that his hate-filled rhetoric isn't an unfortunate manifestation of some underlying illness.

But even the Fischer apologists had to throw up their hands when he took to the Philippine airwaves on September 11, 2001. In an interview broadcast this time by Bombo Radyo, a small public-radio station in Baguio City, Fischer revealed views so loathsome that it was impossible to indulge him any longer. Just hours after the most devastating attack on the United States in history, in which thousands had died, Fischer could barely contain his delight. "This is all wonderful news" he announced. "I applaud the act. The U.S. and Israel have been slaughtering the Palestinians, just slaughtering them for years. Robbing them and slaughtering them. Nobody gave a shit. Now it's coming back to the U.S. Fuck the U.S. I want to see the U.S. wiped out."

Fischer added that the events of September 11 provided the ideal opportunity to stage a long-overdue coup d'état. He envisioned, he said, a "*Seven Days in May* scenario," with the country taken over by the military; he also hoped to see all its synagogues closed, and hundreds of thousands of Jews executed. "Ultimately the white man should leave the United States and the black people should go back to Africa," he said. "The white people should go back to Europe, and the country should be returned to the American Indians. This is the future I would like to see for the so-called United States." Before signing off Fischer cried out, "Death to the U.S.!"

The United States Chess Federation had always been willing to ignore Fischer's public antics, no matter how embarrassing. He was, after all, Bobby Fischer — the greatest player in the history of the game. But this was too much. On October 28 of last year the USCF unanimously passed a motion denouncing Fischer's incendiary broadcast. "Bobby has driven some more nails in his coffin," Frank Camaratta Jr., a USCF board member, says. The backlash has reached all the way to grassroots chess clubs. "It's because of Fischer that I'm involved in chess," says Larry Tamarkin, a manager at the Marshall Chess Club, a legendary New York parlor frequented by Fischer in his teens. "But I can't help feeling a sense of betrayal, anger, and sadness. You devote your entire life to one player and find out he's completely off his rocker. It ruins everything. He's an embarrassment." Asked about the possibility of a Fischer comeback, Tamarkin can't conceal his disgust. "We prefer that he doesn't come back. Because if he does, it will destroy the last vestige of magic."

In reality the magic has been gone for some thirty years. That's how long it has been since Fischer played his first and only world-championship match. Why he stopped playing tournaments, and how his life unraveled so pathetically, is a story one can learn only by seeking out those who actually know Fischer. There are surprisingly few such people — and fewer yet are willing to talk. Fischer doesn't tolerate friends who give interviews. His address book is a graveyard of crossed-out names of people who have been quoted in articles about him.

But some formerly loyal Fischer associates, appalled at his recent behavior, are finally talking about him. They reveal that Fischer's story doesn't follow the usual celebrity-gone-to-seed arc. He has not been brought low by drugs or alcohol, by sex scandals or profligate spending. Instead he is a victim of his own mind — and of the inordinate attention that the world has given it. Fischer's paranoia, rage, and hubris have been enough to transform him into an enemy of the state; they have been enough to sabotage a brilliant career and turn a confident, charismatic figure into a dithering recluse; and, sadly, they have been enough to make us forget that when Bobby Fischer played chess, it was absolutely riveting theater, even for those who didn't play the game.

In many ways Fischer's story resembles that of the mentally unstable Nobel Prize winner John Forbes Nash Jr., the mathematician who inspired the book and Oscar-winning movie *A Beautiful Mind,* but without the happy ending. Both Fischer and Nash were the best at their chosen professions. Both were widely considered to be geniuses. Both were also supremely arrogant, rebellious, eccentric, and — although respected — not necessarily well liked by colleagues. Fischer left the United States to live in exile. So did Nash. Even eerier, while in the grip of schizophrenia Nash was an anti-Semite and was convinced that Communists (the men at MIT wearing red ties) were observing him.

Contrary to popular belief, Fischer didn't emerge from the womb a full-blown grand master. While he was learning the game, as a child in Brooklyn, he was essentially a hotshot club player — a prodigy, to be sure, but not obviously world-championship material. But at age thirteen, in 1956, Fischer made a colossal leap. That year he became the youngest player ever to win the U.S. Junior Championship. He also dominated the U.S. tournament circuit. What was astounding wasn't simply that a gawky thirteen-year-old kid in blue jeans was suddenly winning chess tournaments. It was the way he was winning. He didn't just beat people — he humiliated them. The thing he relished most was watching his opponents squirm. "I like the moment when I break a man's ego," he once said, during a Dick Cavett interview.

Later in the year he played a game so remarkable that it was immediately dubbed "the Game of the Century." Fischer faced Donald Byrne, then one of the top ten U.S. players, at the Rosenwald Memorial Tournament, in New York. The now legendary battle was packed with more chess pyrotechnics than are typically seen during the course of an entire match. There were complex combinations, ingenious sacrifices, danger and apparent danger — enough to make Fischer, who won, a chess god overnight. Asked to explain his sudden emergence on the world stage of chess, Fischer shrugged and said, "I just got good."

The Fischer-Byrne duel was dissected in newspapers and magazines around the world and won Fischer the Brilliancy Prize, an annual chess award that recognizes particularly imaginative play. Chess analysts, a decidedly reserved lot not given to spasms of hyperbole, peppered their dry annotations with exclamation marks ("Be6!"). "While we have learned to distrust superlatives, this is one game that deserves all the praise lavished on it," wrote Fred Reinfeld, a leading chess journalist of the day. Even the Russians, loath to acknowledge so much as the existence of American players, grudgingly tipped their hats. After the Fischer-Byrne game, Mikhail Botvinnik, the reigning world champion, reportedly said, "We will have to start keeping an eye on this boy."

That is exactly what the chess world did from that moment forward. Fischer's achievements were staggering: In his time he was the youngest U.S. master (at fourteen years and five months), the youngest international grand master, and the youngest candidate for the world championship (at fifteen years and six months). He also won eight U.S. chess championship titles — a record not likely to be broken. In 1966 he co-authored *Bobby Fischer Teaches Chess,* the best-selling chess book ever, and in 1969 he published *My 60 Memorable Games,* arguably the best chess book ever.

Fischer also just won a lot of games — an impressive fact given that draws among grand masters are commonplace. At the highest level of competitive chess, players are so familiar with one another's games that they can practically read their opponents' minds. The memorization of opening theory and the intensive study of an opponent's oeuvre so dominate the modern game that when two grand masters square off, the first twenty moves unfold like a stale sitcom plot. Players often lament that "draw death" is killing the game.

But Fischer didn't play for draws. He was always on the attack — even rhetorically. Of the Soviet champions who had dominated the game so completely, he said, "They have nothing on me, those guys. They can't even touch me."

The Soviets were not amused. They dismissed the young American upstart as *nyekulturni* — literally, "uncultured." This wasn't far from the truth, and Fischer knew it. He lacked education, and had always been insecure about this. His deficiency was particularly glaring now that most of his interaction was with adults, many of whom were sophisticated and well-read.

The answer, Fischer thought, was to upgrade his wardrobe. So at sixteen, using his chess winnings, he traded in his uniform of sneakers, flannel shirt, and jeans for luxurious bespoke suits. He reveled in his new Beau Brummell image. When he traveled abroad for tournaments, he frequently visited local tailors and had suits cut for his gangly, broad-shouldered physique. He liked to brag that he owned seventeen such suits, which he rotated to ensure even wear. "I hate ready-made suits, button-down collars, and sports shirts," he once said. "I don't want to look like a bum. I get up in the morning, I put on a suit."

The change did wonders for Fischer's self-esteem. He boasted that once he had defeated the Russians and become the world champion, he'd take on all challengers. Like the boxing champ Joe Louis, he'd have his own bum-of-the-month club. He boldly promised that he was "gonna put chess on the map." He envisioned a rock-star existence for himself: a $50,000 custom-made Rolls-Royce, a yacht, a private jet, and a mansion — in either Beverly Hills or Hong Kong — "built exactly like a rook." Asked what his long-term goals were, he replied, "All I want to do, ever, is play chess."

But the sartorial façade of sophistication was a flimsy one. Those close to Fischer knew that when it came to art, politics, or anything else the cosmopolitan set talked about, he was at a total loss. "If you were out to dinner with Bobby in the sixties, he wouldn't be able to follow the conversation," says Don Schultz, a former friend. "He would have his little pocket set out and he'd play chess at the table. He had a one-dimensional outlook on life."

This limited worldview prompted Fischer to drop out of Brooklyn's Erasmus Hall High School midway through his junior year. It was hardly a case of a promising academic life being cut short. Pulling courtesy Ds, ostracized by the other students, Fischer was going nowhere. Many chess insiders have insisted that the poor grades were a direct result of an abnormally high IQ — that is, Bobby wasn't stupid, he was just bored. (Although Fischer was a poor student, he was regularly reading Russian chess journals.) It's a point that has long been debated. Everybody agrees that Fischer is no dummy, including Fischer himself (during one interview he said, "I object to being called a chess genius, because I consider myself to be an all-around genius who just happens to play chess"), but chess champions aren't necessarily geniuses. What they need for success is powerful memories, the ability to concentrate deeply, refined recognition and problem-solving skills, decisiveness, stamina, and a killer instinct.

When he dropped out of high school, Fischer was living in Brooklyn with his older sister, Joan, and his mother, Regina. Regina was a registered nurse, a secular Jew, and a single mother with a bohemian lifestyle that included leftist politics and social activism but not chess. (When Fischer was born, his mother was married to Hans-Gerhardt Fischer, a German biophysicist, who is generally assumed to be Bobby's father, although Bobby's paternity is the subject of some speculation.) Fischer's relationship with his mother was strained, in part because of her politics, her religious heritage, and her general eccentricity. "Bobby's mother was a cuckoo," the *New York Times* chess columnist Robert Byrne says. "She was an intelligent neurotic full of far-fetched ideas." As Fischer developed as a chess player, he distanced himself from his mother. In 1962, three years after dropping out of high school, he began living alone in the family apartment (his mother and Joan had moved out).

Fischer began to devote fourteen hours a day to studying chess. According to a 1962 interview in *Harper's*, he had some two hundred chess books and countless foreign chess journals stacked on his floor. He had an exquisite inlaid chess table, made to order in Switzerland, and three additional boards, one beside each bed in his apartment. As part of a Spartan training regime he would play matches against himself that lasted for days, sleeping in the three beds in rotation. Asked how he spent his free time, Fischer once replied, "I'll see a movie or something. There's really nothing for me to do. Maybe I'll study some chess books."

As Fischer became more successful, he began to generate more and more criticism. In a very short time he managed to offend and estrange almost everyone who was in a position to advance his career, including USCF officials, patrons, journalists, and sponsors. He frequently backed out of tournaments. He'd threaten a no-show unless the promoters ponied up more prize money. He also regularly groused about noise and light levels.

The press loved it. Fischer was labeled an insufferable diva and a psych-out artist who made life hell for tournament officials and tried to rattle opponents by complaining about, among other things, high-frequency sounds that only he and several species of nonhuman mammals could detect. The press also loved to talk about his greed. But Fischer never cared about money per se. "Bobby wanted to get all kinds of money for everything," says Arnold Denker, a former U.S. chess champion, "and yet when he got it, he pissed it away. In Reykjavík [the site of the 1972 world-championship match between Fischer and Boris Spassky] the maids who cleaned up his room made thousands of dollars because he left money under the pillows and all over. He wanted money because to him it meant that people thought he was important."

Fischer demanded richer purses not only to validate his self-worth but because he was convinced that tournament promoters were out to fleece him. He would sign a tournament contract only to obsess later about how quickly his demands had been met. Although the prize money involved was always more than fair, Fischer's paranoia invariably got the best of him. "Away from the board, Bobby suffered from a terrible inferiority complex," says Allan Kaufman, the former director of the American Chess Foundation. "In his mind he concocted lots of excuses: people were taking advantage of him; they were smarter than he was; if he had only had their education, he would know what to ask for in negotiations." Often before the ink on a contract was dry, Fischer would refuse to play unless the purse was raised. Promoters would cave, only to receive word later that Fischer was demanding even more money. Frequently the negotiations became so impossible that frustrated promoters simply walked. These confrontations prolonged his quest for the world title. "A couple of times Bobby dropped out of tournaments that would have led to him playing for the world championship earlier," says Shelby Lyman, a chess pundit who analyzed Fischer's famous 1972 match with Boris Spassky on PBS

The Russians certainly weren't willing to lend support to Fischer's title bid — especially after *Sports Illustrated* in 1962 published an interview with Fischer in which he accused the Soviet chess establishment of cheating in an effort to deny him what he viewed as his birthright: the world chess championship. In the interview, titled "The Russians Have Fixed World Chess," Fischer alleged that Soviet grand masters were forced to lose or draw games in order to advance the careers of favored players who were being groomed as potential world champs. Fischer argued that he was at a great disadvantage, because during a tournament he had to endure a grueling schedule of games while several anointed Soviet grand masters cruised from one victory to the next, conserving their strength for the real competition — which more often than not was Fischer himself in the finals.

Published after Fischer had finished a disappointing fourth in the 1962 Curaçao Candidates tournament, the interview was denounced by the Soviets as a classic case of sour grapes. Those familiar with the palace intrigue of the Soviet Chess Federation, however, knew better. Nikolai Krogius, a Soviet grand master now living in Staten Island, acknowledges that Fischer's allegations of foul play were valid. "There were some agreed draws at Curaçao," he admits. According to Arnold Denker, beating the Soviet chess machine during that era was all but impossible. "In 1946," he says, "I had an adjourned game with Mikhail Botvinnik in which I was ahead. During the break I saw Botvinnik eating dinner and relaxing. I didn't have dinner. I went to my room and studied. When the game resumed, Botvinnik remarkably found the only move to draw the game. I said, 'How is that possible?' Someone told me, 'Listen, young man, all of these people were analyzing for him while he was having his dinner.' I was naive in those days."

"I'll never play in one of those rigged tournaments again," Fischer fumed after losing to the Soviet Armenian champion Tigran Petrosian at Curaçao. "[The Soviets] clobber us easy in team play. But man to man, I'd take Petrosian on any time." The five-time U.S. chess champion Larry Evans agrees that the Soviets were less than good sportsmen when it came to defending their world title. But he also believes that Fischer was looking for a convenient excuse for losing. "The fact of the matter is," Evans says, "that in '62 at Curaçao, Bobby just wasn't good enough yet."

After Curaçao, Fischer dropped out of international competition for several years. His cash flow, which was about $5,000 a year, slowed to a trickle. Money was so scarce that he began living at a YMCA. When he couldn't afford that, he moved in with friends, hopping from apartment to apartment and running up phone bills he couldn't pay. Broke and feeling increasingly detached from New York's insular chess community, he moved to California in the spring of 1968. He was twenty-five years old.

Fischer's move to the West Coast has sometimes been considered the beginning of his so-called "wilderness years." Although he wasn't playing in many tournaments, his work ethic never wavered: he continued studying chess during most of his waking hours. But late at night, Arnold Denker recalls, Fischer began prowling parking lots, slipping white-supremacist pamphlets under windshield wipers. He began studying anti-Semitic classics such as *Mein Kampf* and *The Protocols of the Elders of Zion*. He became obsessed with German history and the Third Reich, and collected Nazi memorabilia. It was rumored that he slept with a picture of Adolf Hitler hanging over his bed. Larry Evans says that Fischer's admiration for the Führer had less to do with anti-Semitism than with insatiable ego. "We once went to see a documentary on Hitler," Evans recalls. "When we came out of the theater, Bobby said that he admired Hitler. I asked him why, and he said, 'Because he imposed his will on the world.'" (Fischer has never made an effort to conceal his distaste for Jews. As early as 1962, in the *Harper's* interview, he expressed his prejudice, mentioning what he perceived to be a growing problem affecting the upper ranks of his profession. "Yeah, there are too many Jews in chess," he said. "They seem to have taken away the class of the game. They don't seem to dress so nicely. That's what I don't like.")

In the fall of 1968 Fischer walked out of the Chess Olympiad in Switzerland. He refused to play for another eighteen months, and some feared that his competitive drive had stalled, but that wasn't the case. He was still training fourteen hours a day and playing chess privately. And in 1970 and 1971 he returned to public competition and had the longest winning streak in tournament chess, when he won twenty consecutive outright victories against the world's top grand masters, a record unrivaled in the modern era.

By 1972 Fischer had reached his peak. That year the reigning world champion, Boris Spassky, agreed to meet him in Reykjavík to play what would be the most carefully scrutinized match ever, a contest the press heralded as "the chess match of the century."

Inescapably, the match became a Cold War battleground. The world's two superpowers were about to lock horns across a chess board. The political stakes were high enough that President Richard Nixon ordered Secretary of State Henry Kissinger to intercede personally when Fischer began hinting that he might not play. "In short," Kissinger reportedly said at the time, "I told Fischer to get his butt over to Iceland." According to the *Boston Globe* chess columnist Harold Dondis, however, "Kissinger tried to call Bobby, but Bobby wouldn't take the call."

Although Fischer had worked his entire life for an opportunity to play for the world chess crown, now that he finally had the chance, he began to be taken over by anxiety, self-doubt, and paranoia (he feared the Soviets would shoot down his plane). All the youthful bravado and swagger — the bum-of-the-month club, the taunting of the Russians — was a memory. "They had to drag Bobby kicking and screaming to play in Iceland," Shelby Lyman says.

The prize money troubled Fischer, too. Up to this point the world-championship chess purse had not been particularly noteworthy. When Spassky won the world title, in 1969, his take was a paltry $1,400. The promoters in Iceland were willing to pump the prize money up some, but not to a level Fischer deemed sufficient. When a handsome five-figure purse was suggested, Fischer balked and threatened a no-show. When Spassky and his entourage were in Reykjavík for the opening festivities, Fischer was still in New York, grumbling about indentured servitude.

After a series of escalating demands, Fischer managed to drive up the match's prize money to $250,000 and was guaranteed a considerable slice of film or TV revenues. But even then the match hit a snag. Fischer refused to play because his favorite television program, *The Jack LaLanne Show,* wasn't available on Icelandic TV. It was Lina Grumette, a Los Angeles chess promoter and Fischer's "chess mother" at the time, who finally managed to talk Fischer into playing.

Fischer's performance in Iceland was no disappointment. He put on a show that was equal parts Ionesco play, soap opera, and political potboiler. Between acts he managed to play some brilliant chess. The games were an instant hit. *World Chess Championship,* the Shelby Lyman program created by PBS to cover the tournament, was at the time the highest-rated PBS show ever — an amazing fact, considering that it consisted of little more than a giant wall-mounted chess board on which each move was recorded and then discussed by several analysts.

Fischer played poorly in the beginning, and Spassky easily won the first game, on July 12. Fischer refused to play the second game unless all cameras were removed from the hall. The match organizers tried to minimize the intrusiveness of the cameras, but still he refused to play. Finally Fischer was warned that if his demands didn't stop, game two would be awarded to Spassky. Fischer thought, wrongly, that they were bluffing, and ended up forfeiting the game. Suddenly he was in a hole, with Spassky ahead 2 to 0. At this juncture Spassky could easily have retreated to Moscow still in possession of his crown, and nobody would have blamed him because of Fischer's behavior.

To placate Fischer the third game was played in another room and broadcast to the dismayed audience on closed-circuit television. He won handily. The players returned to the exhibition hall for the rest of the match, and Fischer soon grabbed the lead and held it, albeit still complaining about the presence of cameras (in the end very little of the match was filmed), the surface of the chess board (too shiny), the proximity of the audience (he insisted that the first seven rows of seats be removed), and the ambient noise. Distressed at their countryman's poor showing, members of the Soviet delegation began to make their own unreasonable demands, hoping to unnerve Fischer. They accused him of using a concealed device to interfere with Spassky's brain waves. The match was halted while police officers searched the playing hall. Fischer's chair was taken apart, light fixtures were dismantled, the entire auditorium was swept for suspicious electronic signals. Nothing was found. (In a subsequent investigation a Soviet chemist waved a plastic bag around the stage and then sealed it for lab analysis. The label affixed to the bag read "Air from stage.")

Fischer wasn't flustered. If anything, his play became stronger. As the week wore on, Spassky began slowly to crack, and on September 1 he resigned.

Fischer's accomplishment cannot be overstated. A brash twenty-nine-year-old high school dropout, armed with little more than a pocket chess set and a dog-eared book documenting Spassky's important games, had single-handedly defeated the Soviet chess juggernaut. Spassky had a wealth of resources at his disposal to help him plot moves, including thirty-five grand masters back in the Soviet Union. Fischer, on the other hand, had two administrative seconds who served essentially as companions, and Bill Lombardy, a grand master, whose role was to help analyze games. However, Fischer did almost all the analysis himself — when he bothered to do anything. "After the games were adjourned, all the Soviets would go back to Spassky's hotel room to plan for the next position," recalls Don Schultz, one of the seconds. "Lombardy said to Fischer, 'That's a difficult position. Let's go back to the hotel and analyze it.' Fischer said, 'What do you mean, analyze? That guy's a fish. Let's go bowling.'"

Fischer returned home to a hero's welcome. In a televised ceremony at New York's City Hall, Mayor John Lindsay presented him with the key to the city. Shelby Lyman recalls, "Here's Bobby in his great moment of triumph. He's resplendent in this beautiful suit. The world is his: he's young, handsome, women adore him, there's all this money if he wants it. And he later said to a reporter, 'The creeps are beginning to gather.' He was referring to press, lawyers, agents — everyone he thought was out to take advantage of him. After that his whole life was about avoiding the creeps."

Fischer didn't in fact get the full hero treatment. "I was never invited to the White House," he said in one of his radio interviews. "They invited that Olympic Russian gymnast — that little Communist, Olga Korbut." In his notorious September 11 interview he elaborated. "Look what I have done for the U.S.," he said. "Nobody has single-handedly done more for the U.S. than me. When I won the world championship, in 1972, the United States had an image of, you know, a football country, a baseball country, but nobody thought of it as an intellectual country. I turned all that around single-handedly, right? But I was useful then because there was the Cold War, right? But now I'm not useful anymore. You see, the Cold War is over and now they want to wipe me out, steal everything I have, and put me in prison."

Following the City Hall ceremony Fischer returned to Pasadena, leaving $5 million worth of unsigned endorsement contracts on his lawyer's desk. It wasn't that he didn't want the extra income; he just couldn't deal with the creeps.

He also stopped playing tournament chess. And in 1975 the World Chess Federation (known by its French acronym, FIDE) stripped him of his world-championship title for failure to defend his crown against the Russian grand master Anatoly Karpov. Such stonewalling was difficult for chess people to fathom, given that Fischer was so much stronger than the competition. The truth was that Bobby Fischer was running scared. "Bobby was always afraid of losing," Arnold Denker says. "I don't know why, but he was. The fear was in him. He said that if he played Karpov, he was going to insist on a long match. After not playing for three years, he was very

concerned about how good he would be." Shelby Lyman echoes
that assessment. "Hating to lose, and having the myth destroyed,"
he says, "was a big part of him not playing."

Instead of playing tournaments, Fischer retreated to the protective cocoon of the Worldwide Church of God, an apocalyptic
cult that predicted the end of the world every four to seven years
and whose members tithed up to 30 percent of their income. Such
protection came at a steep price. It was reported that out of his
$200,000 income that year he donated $61,200 to the WCG.
"They cleaned out my pockets," he later said. "Now my only income is a few royalty checks from my books. I was really very foolish." To show its appreciation for such a generous contribution,
the WCG treated Fischer almost as if he were the very deity the
Church's members had been waiting for. He lived in WCG-owned
apartments, was entertained at fancy restaurants, and flew to exotic
spots in the Church's private jet. And Fischer was set up on the first
dates of his life, with attractive WCG members. A fellow WCG member, Harry Sneider, says that this hedonistic lifestyle had a detrimental effect on Fischer: "He got pampered and got a lot of attention. It made him soft."

Fischer's relationship with the WCG, like all the others in his
life, didn't last. In 1977, after a bitter falling-out that led Fischer
to claim that the WCG was taking its orders from a "satanical secret world government," he cut all ties with the Church. Then he
crawled even further into his own netherworld. He began dressing
like a hobo. He took up residence in seedy hotels. He began worry-
ing about the purity of his bodily fluids. He bought great quantities
of exotic herbal potions, which he carried in a suitcase, to stave
off the toxins he feared might be secretly put in his food and water
by Soviet agents. According to a 1985 article in *Sports Illustrated,*
Fischer medicated himself with such esoteric remedies as Mexican
rattlesnake pills ("good for general health") and Chinese healthy-
brain pills ("good for headaches"). His suitcase also contained a
large orange-juice squeezer and lots and lots of vitamins. He always
kept the suitcase locked, even when he was staying with friends.
"If the Commies come to poison me, I don't want to make it easy
for them," he explained to a friend. Perhaps the most telling sign
of his rapid mental deterioration was that he insisted on having
all his dental fillings removed. "If somebody took a filling out and

put in an electronic device, he could influence your thinking," Fischer confided to a friend. "I don't want anything artificial in my head."

The low point of Fischer's California sojourn came on May 26, 1981, when two Pasadena police officers stopped him for an ID check. By then he had unkempt hair, a scraggly beard, and tattered clothes, and looked like an aging hippie down on his luck. He also generally fit the description of a man who had recently committed two bank robberies in the neighborhood. He refused to answer questions and was taken to jail, where he spent forty-eight hours. "All he had to do was tell the police he was Bobby Fischer, the chess player, and the whole thing would have been over," a friend says. "But he just couldn't bring himself to do it. Submitting to authority is a foreign concept to Bobby." A year later Fischer privately published a fourteen-page pamphlet titled "I Was Tortured in the Pasadena Jailhouse!" The pamphlet, which became a surprise best-seller in chess shops across the country, is a melodramatic account of Fischer's confinement. The subheadings say it all: "Brutally Handcuffed." "Choked." "Isolation & Torture." "Sick Cop."

Meanwhile, he was turning down big money to come out of retirement. Caesars Palace in Las Vegas offered him $250,000 for a single exhibition game. After Fischer had agreed to the terms and a date had been set, he reneged. "I'm risking my title," he griped. "I should get a million dollars." According to a 1992 article in *Esquire,* despots and rogue millionaires were also willing to pay outrageous purses to Fischer: Ferdinand Marcos offered him $3 million to play a tournament in the Philippines; the Shah of Iran offered $2 million; Qatar, South Africa, Chile, and Argentina are believed to have put similar deals on the table. When a Francoist millionaire from Spain offered $4 million, Fischer replied, "Nah. The figure's too low."

What Fischer craved far more than wealth was anonymity. To achieve it he assumed a new identity and began carrying a Nevada driver's license and a Social Security card bearing the pseudonym Robert D. James. This is the name that appears on the 1981 Pasadena police report. (His full name is Robert James Fischer.)

To generate income, however, he resorted to selling himself to chess fans and curiosity seekers. The going rate for an hour's phone conversation was $2,500. Bob Dylan is said to have received a call from Fischer as a gift from his manager. For $5,000 a personal meeting could be arranged. A student of the three-time U.S. chess champion Lev Alburt once paid $10,000 for several "chess consultations." Alburt says his student considered the money well spent.

In the years to come insiders knew that Fischer was still the man to beat. In 1981 the grand master Peter Biyiasas played seventeen straight games of speed chess against Fischer and lost every one. "He was too good," Biyiasas said at the time. "There was no use in playing him. It wasn't like I made this mistake or that mistake. It was like I was being gradually outplayed from the start. He wasn't taking any time to think. The most depressing thing about it is that I wasn't even getting out of the middle game to an endgame. I don't ever remember an endgame."

In 1992 Fischer came out of retirement to play Boris Spassky in a $5 million rematch that commemorated the twenty-year anniversary of their meeting in Reykjavík. Aficionados dismissed the match as meaningless, since Fischer was no longer the world champion, and Spassky was then ranked ninety-ninth in the world. But the press had reason to celebrate: Fischer was a big draw; there was the nostalgic superpower angle; and the setting was Yugoslavia. United Nations sanctions had been imposed in an effort to halt the fighting in the country, and Americans were forbidden to do any business there, even in the form of a chess match. Fischer spoke arrogantly to the press about the irrelevance of the sanctions, and practically dared the United States to keep him from playing. Annoyed, Washington decided to make an example of him; the Department of the Treasury issued a cease-and-desist letter to Fischer, stating that if he played chess in Yugoslavia, he would be in violation of Executive Order 12810. The penalty for defying the order was a $250,000 fine, ten years in prison, or both. Fischer appeared untroubled.

He had signed on for the match because he desperately needed money. This was to be his big payday. After all the missed endorsements and spurned multimillion-dollar matches, he was prepared to play one last time, to ensure his financial security: the winner's share would be $3.65 million.

In the end, though, Fischer didn't play for money. He played for love. Not for love of the game but for the love of Zita Rajcsanyi, an eighteen-year-old Hungarian chess prodigy who had leveraged a pen-pal relationship with Fischer into a full-fledged romance. With glasses, a long ponytail, and Converse high-tops, Rajcsanyi was hardly a goddess. But she was exactly what was needed to coax Fischer out of his shell. "Zita wrote Bobby beautiful letters telling him how wonderful it was for her to be inspired by his great genius," Harry Sneider, the WCG member, says. "She had a lot to do with him coming back. Actually, it was she who inspired him."

That Rajcsanyi was able to talk Fischer out of his apartment, much less onto a plane bound for Yugoslavia, is miraculous. By this time his paranoia had intensified. Several months before the match Darnay Hoffman, who produced a 1972 TV exposé about Fischer and was working on another TV project about him, had tracked Fischer to Orange Street — in the heart, curiously, of the Fairfax district, then L.A.'s largest Jewish neighborhood. When a film-crew member knocked on the door to request an interview, he heard Fischer inside frantically dialing a rotary phone and screaming into the receiver, "They've found me!"

Once Fischer arrived in Yugoslavia, however, he showed not the slightest indication of mental trouble. He wore a suit and appeared healthy, robust, almost happy. "Bobby is so kind, so friendly," Spassky marveled at the time. "He is normal!" Lev Alburt ventures an explanation. "Chess is a game that forces you to be objective and to take into account an opponent's views," he says. "It forces you to make reasonable judgments and to be sane. When Bobby quit playing, it was really the end of his rational existence. And he began filling that void with crazy ideas."

This was made painfully evident when Fischer kicked off the pre-match festivities in Yugoslavia with a press conference on September 1. After the usual battery of chess-related questions a journalist finally asked the question that was on everybody's mind: "Are you worried by U.S. government threats over your defiance of sanctions?" Fischer calmly reached into a briefcase, pulled out the Treasury Department letter, held it up, and said, "Here is my reply to their order not to defend my title here." He then spat on the paper.

Fischer proceeded to rattle off a series of astonishing proclamations: he hadn't paid his taxes since 1976 (and wasn't about to start now); he was going to write a book that would prove that Russian grand masters ("some of the lowest dogs around") had "destroyed chess" through "immoral, unethical, prearranged games"; he really wasn't an anti-Semite, because he was pro-Arab, and Arabs are Semites, too. His assertion that Soviet communism was "basically a mask for Bolshevism, which is a mask for Judaism," elicited the most quizzical expressions.

The old Bobby Fischer was back, and more bizarre than ever. This was made eminently clear when Fischer informed tournament officials that he wanted the toilet in his bathroom to rise higher in the air than anyone else's.

Fischer played beautifully in the first game. Spassky resigned on his forty-ninth move. Considering that Fischer had been away from formal competitive chess for two decades, this was no small accomplishment. But the rest of the match featured less-inspiring play. Although Spassky was clearly outclassed, the contest dragged on for almost six weeks before Fischer was finally declared the victor, with ten wins, five losses, and fifteen draws. Today Fischer attacks critics who dismiss the significance of the rematch. "I hadn't played in twenty years!" he bellowed during one of his Philippine radio broadcasts. "I did what was utterly impossible. It's still my greatest match."

The Bush administration wasn't impressed. Fischer was immediately indicted, and an arrest warrant was issued. He hasn't returned to the United States since.

Fischer stayed in Yugoslavia after the rematch, and began promoting what he called Fischer Random Chess — a tweaked version of shuffle chess, in which both players' back-row pieces are arranged according to the same random shuffle before play begins. Although not revolutionary, the premise of FRC is compelling: with 960 different starting positions, opening theory becomes obsolete, and the strongest player — not necessarily the player who has memorized more strategies or has the most expensive chess-analysis software — is assured victory.

Fischer envisioned FRC as a means of democratizing chess and as a lucrative business venture — and as an easy way to reinsert himself into the world of competitive chess without having to immerse himself in opening theory. He had designed and patented two electronic devices that he hoped to sell to FRC enthusiasts: a clock for timing games, and a pyramid-shaped "shuffler" to determine the starting positions. A 1996 press release described the two instruments as "essential to playing according to the new rules for the game of chess." Fischer desperately wanted the Tokyo-based watch company Seiko to manufacture his FRC products but couldn't generate interest.

Worse than Seiko's snub was the loss of Zita. After less than a year she left Fischer and, against his protestations, eventually wrote a book that chronicled their relationship. After the book's release he accused Zita of being a spy hired by the Jews to lure him out of retirement.

Following the breakup Fischer roamed around Central Europe for several years. He ended up being befriended by Susan and Judit Polgar, two young Hungarian Jews who were at the time the Venus and Serena Williams of the chess world. "I first met Bobby with my family," Susan recalls. "I told him rather than spending the rest of his life hiding . . . he should move to Budapest, where there are a lot of chess players."

Fischer did, and was welcomed as a guest in the Polgar household. He appears to have behaved himself. "I remember happy times in the kitchen cutting mushrooms," Susan says. "He's very normal in that sense, very pleasant." Although Fischer refused to play classic chess, he graciously helped the Polgar sisters with their games. When he wasn't sharing his expert analysis with them, he was playing FRC games against them. He was astounded at how accomplished the sisters were. Seeing that he was impressed by the Polgars' play, a friend of Fischer's suggested a publicized match to promote FRC. Fischer agreed.

Fischer was well aware that a high-stakes match pitting the game's strongest male player (in his own mind, anyway) against Judit Polgar, the game's strongest female player (now ranked in the top ten in the world), would interest the media. But the battle-of-the-sexes extravaganza was not to be. "The Jewish-nonsense stuff caused a problem between Bobby and the girls' father," says a Fischer confidant. "One day Bobby just changed his mind. He said, 'No, they're Jewish!' He just couldn't handle it and walked away."

Would Fischer be able to beat a top grand master in an FRC match today? Doubtful. He played numerous FRC games with Susan, who concedes that the results were "mixed." She isn't optimistic about the prospect of a Fischer comeback, either. "He's not that young anymore," she says.

This may explain why Fischer now lives in Tokyo, where chess buffs are virtually nonexistent and he can live in complete anonymity. He walks into bars unrecognized and converses with women who have no idea who he is. "Bobby has always liked Japan," says Larry Evans, the five-time U.S. chess champion. "He likes their subservient women." The culture, too, is a draw, according to Harry Sneider. "Bobby loves Japanese food," Sneider says, "the great mineral baths, and the electronics." Others, however, insist that Fischer chose Japan for a different reason. "Bobby needs to be in a place away from the Jews," one woman says.

But Tokyo is only a home base. Fischer spends much of his time traveling around the world, spreading his gospel of hate. Live radio is his medium of choice. His modus operandi is to lull his audience into a false sense of security by reminiscing about past chess glories. Then, like clockwork, five minutes into the interview the conversation takes a detour — as it did on January 13, 1999, during Fischer's very first live blitzkrieg, on Budapest's Radio Calypso. After politely answering the stock questions, Fischer became noticeably agitated and launched into his now familiar diatribe.

"We might as well get to the heart of the matter and then we can come back to chitchat," he curtly said to his host. "What is going on is that I am being persecuted night and day by the Jews!" Fischer proceeded to recite his bizarre list of grievances: the emergence and sale of FRC-clock knockoffs; a fortune owed him in unpaid book royalties; the unauthorized use of his name to promote the movie *Searching for Bobby Fischer*. His rage reached a peak when he began detailing the precious memorabilia allegedly stolen from his Bekins storage room in Pasadena. Lost treasures supposedly include a book from President Nixon and a letter from Ferdinand Marcos.

Fischer's claims range from suspect to spurious. All U.S. book royalties due him have been paid (since 2000 they have been held in escrow by the State of California, because Fischer has not provided a taxpayer-identification number). A movie can be titled *Searching for Bobby Fischer* without his consent. Unauthorized "Fischer Method" clocks, which he claims infringe on his patent (expired in November of 2001, because of overdue maintenance fees), may or may not be legal. But the issue is irrelevant, because Fischer refuses to file suit ("The Jews control the courts").

As for the Bekins theft, it, too, is a fiction. He did maintain a Bekins storage room in Pasadena for twelve years, and the memorabilia inside it were confiscated, but not in some nefarious plot. The contents of the storage room were sold at a public auction, because Fischer's account — maintained by a Pasadena businessman named Bob Ellsworth, whom Fischer had met through the Worldwide Church of God — was in arrears. The Pasadena storage facility had been sold in the late 1990s, and the new owners noticed that the account was overdue. "It was my responsibility to pay the bill, and I didn't pay it because I didn't know there were new owners," Ellsworth says. "So they put Bobby's stuff up for auction. I felt really bad and spent about eight thousand dollars of my own money buying back all the significant memorabilia."

The storage room was not a treasure trove worth "hundreds of millions of dollars," as Fischer has claimed. "A lot of it," Ellsworth says, "was old magazines and things that were of personal interest to Bobby: books on conspiracy theories, racy Mexican comics, lots of John Gunther books. Things you could go down to Olvera Street and replace for a dime a copy. That stuff I passed on. But anything of intrinsic value I snagged." At the auction Ellsworth acquired "about 80 percent" of the various lots.

Harry Sneider corroborates Ellsworth's story, and says that his son personally delivered the reclaimed memorabilia to Fischer in Budapest. When a list of the numbered lots was read off to him, Sneider confirmed that each one is again in Fischer's possession. Lot 151: Box Lot of Telegrams to Bobby Fischer During Word Chess Championship. "Delivered." Lot 152: Box Lot of Books Inscribed to Bobby Fischer (not by authors). "Delivered." Lot 153: From the People of New York given to Bobby Fischer — Leather Scrapbook with Letter and Telegram from Mayor John V. Lindsay of New York City. "Delivered."

Fischer denies all of this, and would like nothing better than to see Ellsworth drop dead — literally. During a Philippine radio interview broadcast on January 27, 1999, he instructed the host to read Ellsworth's home address on the air. "Some Filipino who loves me should say hello to that motherfucker," Fischer said. "Bob Ellsworth is worthy of death for this shit he pulled on me, in cahoots with Bekins. This was all orchestrated by the Jewish world governments."

Despite such conduct, friends in recent years have thought they detected a glimmer of light amid the darkness of Fischer's tortured psyche. For one thing, he has a girlfriend — Justine, a twenty-two-year-old Chinese-Filipina living in Manila, who couldn't care less about chess and has no intention of writing a tell-all memoir. And Fischer is now a parent: Justine gave birth to a baby girl in 2000. Fischer's fatherhood has until now been a well-kept secret, shared by his Philippine friends, who hope that this child will fill the void in Fischer's life that chess once occupied.

But their hope appears to be in vain. Fischer is a far cry from being a doting papa. According to one source, he "regularly sends money to his girlfriend and child" but visits them only "once every two months." Nobody has rescued him from his paranoid fantasies, either. During his most recent radio interview, broadcast live from Reykjavík on January 27, 2002, Fischer rattled off the same Bekins "mega-robbery" drivel. He described the fictitious crime as "probably, in monetary terms, one of the biggest, if not the biggest robbery, in the history of the United States." He also encouraged the Icelandic government to close the local U.S. naval base. "If they refuse to go," Fischer said, "send them some letters with anthrax. They'll get the message."

For all the anti-American bluster, those closest to Fischer say he'd secretly like to return to his homeland. Sam Sloan, a chess writer and longtime friend of Fischer's, says, "If he knew he wouldn't be prosecuted for this executive order, I think he'd come back." It seems that Fischer has a sentimental side. Difficult as it is for some former friends to believe, he still thinks about them. "Bobby called someone in New York recently," says Stuart Margulies, a co-author (with Fischer and Donn Mosenfelder) of *Bobby Fischer Teaches Chess* (1966). "He wanted to know how all his old friends were doing."

This covert homesickness may explain why for a time Fischer continued to pay property taxes on a piece of Florida real estate he was unable to set foot on. But returning to America is no more real a possibility than the rook-shaped house he once dreamed of building. The federal arrest warrant issued in 1992 will not expire, and it is unlikely that Fischer will be shown much leniency — especially since he referred to George W. Bush during one of his radio interviews as "borderline retarded."

It's almost certain that he won't play chess competitively again. But the chess world continues to sing his praises. Last December, for example, the World Chess Hall of Fame opened for business — a rook-shaped building situated on an unlikely strip of land just off the Florida Turnpike, in South Miami-Dade County — and inducted the initial five members. One of them was Bobby Fischer.

Nevertheless, Fischer is now more alone than ever before. His mother and sister both died in the late 1990s. According to friends, he was extremely close to Joan and had reconciled with Regina; not being able to attend their funerals is said to have been a great blow to him. The New York chess players he periodically inquires about have broken all contact with him. As for Justine and his daughter, they appear to be an inconvenience, a distraction best kept at arm's length. Once one of the most famous men in the world, Fischer is now nothing more than a ghost — a shrill, disembodied voice heard only in faraway countries.

ALEXANDER WOLFF
Additional reporting by Don Yaeger

When the Terror Began

FROM SPORTS ILLUSTRATED

FOR A CITIZEN of a country manacled to its past, Dr. Georg Sieber had a remarkable knack for seeing the future. In the months leading up to the 1972 Olympic Games in Munich, West German organizers asked Sieber, then a thirty-nine-year-old police psychologist, to "tabletop" the event, as security experts call the exercise of sketching out worst-case scenarios. Sieber looks a bit like the writer Tom Clancy, and the crises he limned drew from every element of the airport novelist's genre: kidnappers and hostages, superpower patrons and smuggled arms, hijacked jets and remote-controlled bombs. Studying the most ruthless groups of that era, from the Irish Republican Army and the Palestine Liberation Organization to the Basque separatist group ETA and West Germany's own Baader-Meinhof Gang, he came up with twenty-six cases, each imagined in apocalyptic detail. Most of Sieber's scenarios focused on the Olympic Village, the Games' symbolic global community; one that did not — a jet hired by a Swedish right-wing group crashes into an Olympic Stadium filled with people — foreshadowed a September day in another city many years later.

But on September 5, 1972, at the Munich Olympics, history would not wait. It hastened to crib from one of Sieber's scenarios virtually horror for horror. The psychologist had submitted to organizers Situation 21, which comprised the following particulars: At 5:00 one morning, a dozen armed Palestinians would scale the perimeter fence of the Village. They would invade the building that housed the Israeli delegation, kill a hostage or two ("To enforce discipline," Sieber says today), then demand the release of prisoners held in Israeli jails and a plane to fly to some Arab capital. Even if the Palestinians failed to liberate their comrades, Sieber predicted, they would "turn the Games into a political demonstration" and would be "prepared to die . . . On no account can they be expected to surrender."

To Sieber, every terrorist organization has an MO that makes it a kind of text to be read. With the Black September faction of the PLO he hardly had to read between the lines. "I was simply trying to answer the question, If they were to do it, how would they do it?" Sieber says, in his house in the Nymphenburg district of Munich, the Bavarian capital.

There was only one problem with Sieber's "situations." To guard against them, organizers would have to scrap plans to stage the Games they had been planning for years — a sporting jubilee to repudiate the last Olympics on German soil, the 1936 Nazi Games in Berlin. The Munich Olympics were to be "the Carefree Games." There would be no place for barbed wire, troops, or police bristling with sidearms. Why, at an Olympic test event at Munich's Dante Stadium in 1971, when police deployed nothing more menacing than German shepherds, foreign journalists had teed off on the organizers, accusing them of forgetting that Dachau lay only twelve miles away. *Nein,* the organizers came to agree, where Berlin had been festooned with swastikas and totalitarian red, Munich would feature a one-worldish logo and pastel bunting. Where Hitler's Olympics had opened and closed with cannon salutes and der Führer himself presiding, these would showcase a new, forward-looking Germany, fired with the idealism pervading the world at the time. Security personnel, called Olys, were to be sparse and inconspicuous, prepared for little more than ticket fraud and drunkenness. They would wear turquoise blazers and, during the day, carry nothing but walkie-talkies.

The organizers asked Sieber if he might get back to them with less-frightful scenarios — threats better scaled to the Games they intended to stage.

Thirty years later Sieber recalls all this with neither bitterness nor any apparent sense of vindication. He betrays only the clinical detachment characteristic of his profession. "The American psychologist Lionel Festinger developed the theory of cognitive dissonance," he says. "If you have two propositions in conflict, it's human nature to disregard one of them."

*

With security tossed aside, the Olympics became one big party. Mimes, jugglers, bands, and Waldi, the dachshund mascot, gamboled through the Village, while uncredentialed interlopers slipped easily past its gates. After late-night runs to the Hofbräuhaus, why would virile young athletes bother to detour to an official entrance when they could scale a chain-link fence only six and a half feet high? The Olys learned to look the other way. A police inspector supervising security in the Village eventually cut back nighttime patrols because, as he put it, "at night nothing happens." Early in the Games, when several hundred young Maoist demonstrators congregated on a hill in the Olympic Park, guards dispersed them by distributing candy. Indeed, in a storeroom in the Olympic Stadium, police kept bouquets of flowers in case of another such incident. Hans-Jochen Vogel, who as mayor had led Munich's campaign to land the Games, today recalls the prevailing atmosphere: "People stood on the small hills that had been carved out of the rubble from the war. They could see into some of the venues without a ticket. And then this fifth of September happened. Nobody foresaw such an attack."

Nobody except Sieber. To be sure, he turned out to have been slightly off. Black September commandos climbed the fence about fifty minutes earlier than envisioned in Situation 21. To gain entry to the Israelis' ground-floor apartment at 31 Connollystrasse, they did not, as Sieber had imagined, have to ignite a blasting compound because they were able to jimmy the door open. But the rest of his details — from the commandos' demands for a prisoner exchange and an airliner; to the eventual change of venue from the Village; even to the two Israelis killed in the first moments of the takeover — played out with a spooky accuracy. By the early hours of the next day nine more Israelis were dead, along with five of the terrorists and a Munich policeman, after an oafish rescue attempt at a military airfield in the suburb of Fürstenfeldbruck.

Following indignant words from the paladins of the Olympic movement, after a little mournful Beethoven, the Games of Munich went on. It's an article of faith that The Games Must Go On. For the thirty years since, the Olympics — indeed, all sports events of any great scale — have carried on, even if permanently altered by the awareness that terrorists could again strike.

To revisit the Munich attack is to go slack-jawed at the official lassitude and incompetence, and to realize how much has changed.

The Munich organizers spent less than $2 million to make their Games secure; in Athens two years from now the Olympic security bill will total at least $600 million, none of which will go toward candy or flowers. "I don't see how the Germans could have made any mistakes that they didn't make," says Michael Hershman, a senior executive at Decision Strategies, a Fairfax, Virginia–based security consulting firm that has been involved in five Olympics. "Over the years Munich has served as a model of what not to do in every conceivable way."

But today the Munich attack is irrelevant in a sense, for terrorists are unlikely to try to duplicate it. In the cat-and-mouse world of terrorism and counterterrorism, the bad guys strive for audacity, as only the unthinkable will both confound security planners and achieve what terrorists truly hope for, which is to galvanize the attention of the world. So organizers think and think, to close that window of vulnerability. For the most recent Summer Games, in Sydney, they tabletopped 800 scenarios, even as they girded for that unthinkable 801st. "You can't prepare for everything," says Alex Gilady, an Israeli member of the International Olympic Committee. "In Atlanta one of the scenarios was that a bomb would go off in Centennial Park. When you're at the barn, you don't believe the horse will run away until it runs away."

Late on the morning of September 5, 1972, several hours after the horse had left the barn, the director of security for the Games, Munich police chief Manfred Schreiber, told Georg Sieber that his help was no longer needed. "[Israeli prime minister] Golda Meir is involved," he said. "This is no longer a psychological matter, but a political one."

At this, Sieber resigned from the department. He returned to his home in Nymphenburg, flicked on the TV, and poured a cup of coffee.

The Plot: "Consider Yourself Dead"

Details about the massacre in Munich have dribbled out since 1972, slowly at first, and then, over the past decade, in a rush. First came interviews during the 1970s with the surviving terrorists in France's *Jeune Afrique* and Germany's *Stern*. Then came the 1978 memoir of late Black September leader Abu Iyad, in which he explained how he handpicked the two commandos who led the attack within the Village: Issa, who served as lead negotiator and became known to millions of TV viewers as "the man in the white hat"; and Tony, a short but fiery fedayee, or "fighter for the faith," who was in charge of operations. Excerpts from a long-suppressed Bavarian State Prosecutor's Office report on the debacle surfaced in 1992, after an anonymous whistle-blower leaked documents to the families of the Israeli victims when he learned how his government had for fifteen years stonewalled their efforts to learn the truth about what happened that night. In 1999 the lone terrorist to have survived Israel's furious revenge operation, Jamal Al-Gashey, spoke to the producers of *One Day in September,* the Academy Award–winning documentary about the attack. And another Black Septembrist, Abu Daoud, perhaps gulled by the false peace of the 1993 Oslo Accords, published a memoir in which he described how he and Abu Iyad masterminded the operation. In late July, Abu Daoud also answered *SI*'s questions about the attack. These accounts, most self-serving and some maddeningly incomplete and contradictory, nonetheless reveal how a kind of perfect storm gathered over the Munich Olympics, a confluence of determination and naïveté.

It turns out that Georg Sieber envisioned the events of September 5 even before Black September had planned them. The plot wasn't hatched until July 15, when Abu Daoud and Abu Iyad joined another Black September leader, Abu Mohammed, at a café in Rome's Piazza della Rotonda. Leafing through an Arabic newspaper, they spotted a report that the IOC had failed even to respond to two requests from the Palestinian Youth Federation that Palestine be permitted to take to Munich an Olympic team of its own. "If they refuse to let us participate, why shouldn't we penetrate the Games in our own way?" Abu Mohammed asked. They conceived their plan, giving it the code name Biraam and Ikrit, after two Palestinian villages from which Zionists had evicted Arab residents in 1948.

Two days later Abu Daoud was in Munich to reconnoiter the Olympic Village, then still under construction. On August 7 he returned, this time with Tony. Together they determined that the commandos could hurdle the fence now ringing the Village by jumping off one another's backs. "Each of you will boost the other," Abu Daoud said, likening the maneuver to what tumblers do when they dismount from human pyramids.

"But then one of us will be left behind," Tony replied.

"I'll be there to help the last man over," Abu Daoud told him.

On August 24, two days before the opening ceremonies, Abu Iyad flew from Algiers to Frankfurt via Paris with a male and a female associate and five identical Samsonite suitcases as checked luggage. As Abu Daoud watched through plate glass outside the baggage claim, customs officials picked out one of the five bags and popped it open. They saw nothing but lingerie. The female associate looked on indignantly, which may explain why the other four bags went uninspected. Taking a separate taxi, Abu Daoud met Abu Iyad and his colleagues at a hotel in downtown Frankfurt, where they consolidated the contents of the five suitcases — six Kalashnikovs and two submachine guns, plus rounds of ammunition — into two bags. Later that day Abu Daoud transported the weaponry by train to Munich, where he stored it in lockers at the railway station.

Over the following days Abu Daoud took delivery of another two Kalashnikovs and a cache of grenades, and regularly moved the weapons from locker to locker. And he returned once more to the Village, this time with a Syrian woman, a friend who was visiting a sister married to a professor in Munich. As a group of Brazilian athletes, back from training, made their way through one of the gates, she told the guard, in German, "My friend here is Brazilian and just recognized an old schoolmate. Can we say hello? Only for ten minutes." The guard waved them through. It made sense to pass as Brazilian, Abu Daoud says, given his complexion and the unlikelihood that anyone would chat him up in Portuguese. On this visit he was able to inspect the quarters of the Saudis and the Sudanese, thereby getting a sense of the layout of Village housing.

Two days later, back this time with Tony and Issa, Abu Daoud approached the same guard.

"Ah! You come every day!"

"Naturally — we've come all the way from Brazil to cheer our guys on."

The guard gestured at Abu Daoud's two companions. "Brazilians, too?" he said.

"My friends are upset with me. I told them yesterday that I'd been able to enter the Village and meet our athletes."

"They're jealous?"

"That's why I'm asking this favor."

"Fine, go with your friends."

In his memoir Abu Daoud writes, "It couldn't have begun better — but the best was yet to come. Five minutes later we arrived in front of 31 Connollystrasse, and suddenly I saw a young, tanned woman coming out the door."

She was attached to the Israeli delegation. They chatted her up, telling her they were Brazilians who had always wanted to visit Israel. She escorted them through the foyer by the stairwell and through the doorway into the ground-floor apartment, a duplex with an interior stairway. "For six or seven people, this is sensible, don't you think?" she said. "The rest of the delegation is in other apartments just like this." Inside, the Palestinians took note of the details of each room, including the locations of telephones and TV sets and the sightlines from each window.

"She gave us a fistful of flags, and we had no recourse but to thank her," Abu Daoud writes. "She had no way of knowing that she had considerably facilitated our task. We now knew our first mission would be to take control of this ground-floor apartment. It had the most exits and controlled access to the upper floors and basement. Once the building was taken, the commandos would regroup here with the captured Israelis."

In the meantime six junior Palestinians — mostly *shabab,* "young guys" culled from refugee camps in Lebanon — were training in Libya, with an emphasis on hand-to-hand combat and jumping from high walls. Black September commanders told them that they had been selected for an unspecified mission in a foreign country. Using fake passports, they converged on Munich in pairs soon after the Games began. Although it is unclear where in the city they stayed, some attended Olympic events. Only on the eve of the attack did they assemble and learn the details of their mission.

That evening, in his room at the Hotel Eden Wolff, near the train station, Abu Daoud stuffed ammunition, grenades, food, and a first-aid kit into eight sport duffel bags, each graced with the Olympic rings. He also included nylon stockings for making masks, rope precut to use for binding hostages, and a supply of the amphetamine Predulin for keeping his men alert. Before Abu Daoud added the Kalashnikovs, Issa and Tony kissed each of the weapons and said, "Oh, my love!"

At 9:00 P.M. the Palestinians gathered at a restaurant in the train station for final instructions. Once the Israelis had been seized, no one was to be admitted to the building except a senior German official who might want to check on the condition of the hostages. Abu Daoud says he told the eight fedayeen to exercise restraint: "The operation for which you've been chosen is essentially a political one . . . to capture these Israelis alive . . . No one can deny you the right to use your weapons to defend yourselves. Nonetheless, only fire if you truly can't do otherwise . . . It's not a matter of liquidating your enemies, but seizing them as prisoners for future exchanges. The grenades are for later, to impress your German negotiating partners and defend yourselves to the death."

To which Issa added, "From now on, consider yourself dead. As killed in action for the Palestinian cause."

Each was issued a packed duffel and a track suit with the name of an Arab nation. Abu Daoud collected everyone's passports. Sometime after 3:30 A.M. they took off in taxis for the Village.

As they approached the fence, they noticed another group in warmup gear: American athletes back from a night on the town, laughing and tipsy. Abu Daoud urged his comrades to join them, to use the Americans' innocent comportment as cover while they all scaled the fence. "Not only did our men mix in with the Americans, we helped them over," he says. "And they helped us. 'Hey, man, give me your bag.' This was surreal — to see the Americans, obviously far from imagining they were helping Black September get into the Village."

Much of the Israeli delegation had been out on the town that night, too — at a performance of *Fiddler on the Roof.*

The Takeover: "Danger, Guys! Terrorists!"

Perhaps Yossef Gutfreund was at the Games to provide security for his fellow Israelis. Perhaps not. An Israeli government report, commissioned by the Knesset in the aftermath of the massacre, surely settled that question, but the earliest the report would be made public was 2003. In its next-day account of the incident, the

New York Times suggested that both Gutfreund, a wrestling referee, and Jacov Springer, a weightlifting judge, doubled as security personnel. "Rubbish," says Gilady, the Israeli IOC member. "Simply not true."

In any case Gutfreund apparently heard the rattling of the door at the threshold of that ground-floor duplex, the apartment the other Israelis called the Big Wheels' Inn because it housed senior members of the delegation. When the door cracked open in the darkness, he could make out the barrels of several weapons. He threw his 290 pounds against the door and shouted a warning: "Danger, guys! Terrorists!" For critical seconds Gutfreund succeeded in staying their entrance, allowing his roommate, weightlifting coach Tuvia Sokolovsky, to shatter a rear window and flee to safety through a backyard garden. But the terrorists, using their rifle barrels to crowbar their way inside, soon had Gutfreund subdued on the floor. Quickly they prized track coach Amitzur Shapira and shooting coach Kehat Shorr from one downstairs bedroom. When Issa opened the door to the other downstairs bedroom, wrestling coach Moshe Weinberg lunged at him with a kitchen knife that had been lying on a bedside table. Issa stumbled to the side, unhurt, while another fedayee fired a round from his Kalashnikov that tore through the side of Weinberg's mouth.

The terrorists pushed their unharmed captives up the stairs of the duplex and overpowered the two occupants of the bedroom there, Springer and fencing coach André Spitzer. Leaving their first group of captives behind, under guard, Tony and five other fedayeen nudged Weinberg — he was able to walk, holding a scarf to his bleeding mouth — out onto Connollystrasse and two doors down, where another apartment filled with Israelis issued directly onto the street. There they seized David Berger, a weightlifter from Shaker Heights, Ohio, who had recently immigrated to Israel; another weightlifter, Yossef Romano, who was on crutches from an injury suffered in competition; and wrestlers Eliezer Halfin, Mark Slavin, and Gad Tsabari. Most had heard the shot that wounded Weinberg, and, curious, left their rooms, only to walk into captivity. The fedayeen led their five new hostages the few steps back to join the others.

The stairwell by that first apartment led up to other lodgings, but also down to a parking garage. As soon as the group had reentered the foyer, Tsabari made a dash down the stairs and into the garage, where he zigged and zagged, taking cover behind concrete support posts as a Palestinian shot after him. Weinberg tried to take advantage of the chaos. He tackled one of the fedayeen, knocking his gun free — whereupon another terrorist gave up on Tsabari, who escaped, and finished Weinberg off.

The commandos herded their captives to the second floor of that first duplex apartment. Romano, a Libyan-born weightlifter and veteran of the Six Day War, gimped along, but here he threw down his crutches and grabbed a Kalashnikov from one of the terrorists. Another fedayee shot him dead. For the next seventeen hours the pulpy corpse of their countryman would keep the Israelis company.

A cleaning woman on her way to work had called the Olympic security office at 4:47 A.M. to report the sound of gunfire. An unarmed Oly dispatched to 31 Connollystrasse found a hooded commando with a Kalashnikov in the doorway. "What is the meaning of this?" he demanded. The gunman ignored him, but the intentions of Black September — a group that took its name from the loss in September 1970 of 4,000 fedayeen in fighting in Jordan with King Hussein's Jordanian army — would become clear soon enough. The fedayeen rolled Weinberg's body into the street as a sign of their seriousness.

At 5:08 A.M., a half-hour before dawn would break over the Village, two sheets of paper fluttered down from the balcony, into the hands of a policeman. The communiqué listed the names of 234 prisoners held in Israeli jails, and, in a gesture to win the sympathy of radical Europeans, those of Andreas Baader and Ulrike Meinhof, Germany's most notorious urban guerrillas. If the lot weren't released by 9:00 A.M., a hostage would be executed. "One each hour," Issa told the policeman. "And we'll throw their bodies into the street."

At 8:15 A.M. an equestrian event, the grand prix in dressage, went off as scheduled.

The Standoff: "Trying to Bring the Dead Back to Life"

That morning the Germans assembled a crisis team whose composition further underscored the shadow cast by Germany's past. The council included both city police chief Schreiber and West German interior minister Hans-Dietrich Genscher. To further distance itself from the Nazi era, the West German government strictly limited federal power, leaving responsibility for domestic security to the country's eleven states. So the triumvirate also included Genscher's Bavarian counterpart, Bruno Merk — perhaps one too many cooks for a simmering broth.

Soon came word, through West German chancellor Willy Brandt, of Meir's summary response to the Black September demands: "Under no conditions will Israel make the slightest concession to terrorist blackmail." That position remained firm throughout the day. The Germans, however, desperate to buy time, would keep feeding the Palestinians excuses: that some members of the Israeli cabinet couldn't be reached; that not all the prisoners could be located; that phone lines to Jerusalem had broken down.

The fedayeen knew all along that the Israelis weren't likely to accede to their demands. Still, they extended their deadline to noon. Issa would emerge from the building from time to time to confer with German officials, usually with a grenade conspicuous in his shirt pocket, its pin sometimes pulled.

The crisis team groped for a plan. First Schreiber offered the terrorists an unlimited amount of money. Genscher, who would later become West Germany's foreign minister, pleaded with Issa not to subject Jews once more to death on German soil, then offered himself as a substitute hostage. Vogel, Schreiber, Merk, and Walther Tröger, the ceremonial mayor of the Olympic Village, joined Genscher in that offer, but Issa refused. Avery Brundage, the president of the IOC, said he recalled that in the 1920s, the Chicago police had piped knockout gas into buildings to overpower gangsters. But after placing fruitless calls to U.S. police departments asking for more information, the authorities abandoned Brundage's idea. They tried to have policemen disguised as cooks deliver food to the compound and overpower the terrorists, perhaps after igniting a "blitz bomb" to blind them. But the fedayeen weren't going to fall for that; they ordered that provisions be left at the building's threshold.

The terrorists pushed back their deadline twice more, to 3:00 P.M., then to 5:00, knowing that each postponement only redoubled the TV audience. "The demand to free our imprisoned brothers had only symbolic value," Al-Gashey would say later. "The only aim of the action was to scare the world public during their 'happy Olympic Games' and make them aware of the fate of the Palestinians."

In the late afternoon one more plan — to have thirteen policemen infiltrate the building through the heating ducts — advanced far enough that the men, dressed ludicrously in track suits, began to loosen ventilation grates on the roof. But this operation, too, was called off, mercifully: television cameras had long since been trained on the building and were broadcasting the police team's movements live to a worldwide audience, including the fedayeen.

Shortly before 5:00 P.M. the terrorists made a new demand. They wanted a jet to fly them and their captives to Cairo. "I did not believe [the Israelis] would negotiate with us in Germany, and that is why we made a plan to take a plane and the hostages to another Arab country," Abu Daoud told *SI*. "From there I believed they would negotiate the release of our prisoners." The freed Palestinians were to be waiting on the tarmac in Cairo by 8:00 the following morning, Issa told the Germans. If not, Black September would execute the hostages before leaving the plane.

"These are innocent people," Genscher told Issa.

"I am a soldier," Issa said. "We are at war."

Yet here, finally, the Germans saw a potential opening. If the crisis relocated, there would be buses and helicopters and planes, embarkations and disembarkations, the agora of an airport tarmac — perhaps an opportunity to draw a bead on the fedayeen. But before going forward, the Germans wanted to make sure of two things: that the hostages were still alive and that they were willing to fly to Cairo.

Genscher and Tröger were escorted into the second-floor room of Apartment 1. The hostages told them that yes, if they had to be routed through an Arab capital to freedom, they would be willing to go. But the hostages' spokesman, Shorr, the senior member of the delegation and a resistance fighter during World War II, added that in such a case, they assumed that "our government would meet the demands of the terrorists. For otherwise we would all be shot."

"In other words," said Genscher, "if your government did not agree to the prisoner exchange, you would not be willing to leave German territory."

"There'd be no point to it," Shorr said.

Genscher tried a stab at bravado with his reply: "You will not be abandoned." But to be an Israeli is to know well your government's policy toward terrorists. Surely each hostage must have suspected that his fate rested in the hands of the German government — that the episode would end in Munich, not Cairo, for better or worse.

Nonetheless, Brandt would try for hours to reach Egyptian president Anwar Sadat, to secure permission for an aircraft to land and a guarantee of safety for the hostages. Sadat didn't come to the phone. Finally, at 8:20 P.M., Brandt spoke to Prime Minister Aziz Sidky, who would not or could not pledge his government's help.

The Egyptian response plunged the Germans back into despair. Issa had set a final deadline, 9:00 P.M., and renewed his promise to kill one hostage an hour until the Germans provided the jet. The Israeli government would never countenance the kidnapping of its citizens to a hostile destination. Certainly Germany, given its history, couldn't acquiesce in such an endgame. Perhaps a jet could appear to be at the disposal of the terrorists, but under no circumstances could it be permitted to take off.

The Germans entertained one last plan to liberate the hostages before they were to be helicoptered out of the Village to this supposed jet to Cairo. Schreiber proposed to place police gunmen behind the concrete pillars of the underground garage, the same obstructions that had saved Gad Tsabari's life. The police would pick off the fedayeen while they walked the hostages from the apartment complex to the helicopters. But a suspicious Issa demanded that the transfer be by bus; the bus pulled up to the doorway, and the fedayeen with their captives piled directly into the vehicle, affording the police no clear shot. Moments later, in the plaza of the Village, seventeen captors and captives boarded two Iroquois helicopters.

By now, the crisis team had essentially accepted the hostages' deaths as inevitable. "We were 99 percent sure that we wouldn't be able to achieve our objective," Schreiber would later say. "We felt like doctors trying to bring the dead back to life."

No Israelis survive to dispute him, but if you believe Al-Gashey, the mood on board the helicopter was lighter, if only from the change of scenery. "Everyone seemed to be relaxed, even the Israelis," he has said of the flight to Fürstenfeldbruck. "For our part, in the air we had the feeling that somehow we had achieved what we'd wanted. For the first time I really thought about the hostages sitting so close — in physical contact. My cousin [Adnan Al-Gashey, another commando] was talking above the noise of the blades with an Israeli about personal things. I think they talked about his wife and kids. Even the Israelis realized our lives were inextricably linked.

"I remembered our orders to kill the hostages if it were to become a hopeless military situation. But I also thought how nobody had trained us how to kill bound, unarmed people."

The Shootout: "Condemned to Fail from the Beginning"

Schreiber had entrusted the operation at Fürstenfeldbruck to his deputy, Georg Wolf, and Wolf had a plan. The two helicopters would land one hundred or so yards from a Lufthansa 727 ostensibly ready to fly to Cairo. After the terrorists brought their captives over to the plane, seventeen police officers, some disguised as crew, would ambush them — if, that is, police sharpshooters couldn't get a clear shot at the fedayeen as they made their way across the tarmac.

But on the plane, not fifteen minutes before the helicopters touched down, the policemen were in an uproar over what they regarded as a suicide mission. Most of the officers were to be holed up in the rear of the aircraft, where they believed a single terrorist grenade could incinerate them. As for the officers posing as pilots, they would be in the line of fire from the police at the rear of the plane — and were unpersuasively disguised besides, having been issued incomplete Lufthansa uniforms. After hearing them out, the officer in charge, Reinhold Reich, polled his men, who voted unanimously to abandon the mission. It was a mutiny inconceivable to an Israeli, and Ankie Spitzer, André Spitzer's widow, still fumes at the Germans' lack of courage. But West Germany, not to be trusted with soldiers and guns, had no special-forces unit, nothing like Israel's Sayeret Matkal or the U.S. Army's Delta Force.

With the helicopters moments from touchdown, Wolf's plan, such as it was, now rested on the police sharpshooters — five of them.

The helicopter pilots had flitted about the sky to give the Germans time to prepare the assault and permit a third helicopter, carrying Schreiber, Genscher, and Merk, to beat the others to the airfield.

"Lousy thing to happen at the last minute," Schreiber told Wolf when he found him.

"What lousy thing?" asked Wolf.

"That there are eight of them."

"What? You don't mean there are eight Arabs?"

"You mean you're just finding that out from me?"

Wolf was. For unknown reasons, he thought that there were only five terrorists. No one had told him that three postal workers headed for work that morning had seen the Palestinians scaling the fence and had already provided police with their best guess as to the number: seven or eight, according to two of the postmen; ten or twelve, according to the third. In the underground garage, a policeman had counted the eight terrorists boarding the bus.

Yet now, critically, the snipers didn't know they were outnumbered, even though German TV had reported the postal workers' accounts. Schreiber's testimony to investigators from the Bavarian Prosecutor's Office as to why he hadn't focused early in the day on the number of terrorists would reflect the crossed signals characterizing the operation: "I was sure somebody" — somebody else — "would count them as soon as an opportunity presented itself."

Now the plan rested on the accuracy of five sharpshooters, none of whom deserved the title. Two had been picked from the Bavarian riot police. The other three were Munich police officers. None had any special training. All had been chosen simply because they shot competitively on weekends.

Nevertheless, three took positions on the terrace of the control tower. A fourth lay on the tarmac, behind a low concrete parapet. The fifth took cover behind a fire truck.

The helicopters touched down at 10:35 P.M. The four pilots and six of the fedayeen emerged. As other Black Septembrists held the pilots at gunpoint, Issa and Tony walked over to inspect the jet. Their suspicions already aroused by the lengthy helicopter transfer, they must have gone on full alert when they found the plane empty. As they jogged hastily back toward the helicopters, Wolf gave the order to open fire.

The events that followed are still a *Rashomon*-like fog of chaos, gore, and contradiction. This much seems likely, however: gunfire filled the air for the first four minutes. With six terrorists visible, snipers killed two and mortally wounded a third. But the other three, including Issa and Tony, scrambled to safety. As the pilots dashed for cover, the Palestinian survivors of that first fusillade ducked beneath and behind the helicopters, from where they shot out as many of the airport lights as they could. Anton Fliegerbauer, a police brigadier posted near a window at the base of the control tower, took a fatal bullet.

That flurry of gunfire gave way to an eerie stalemate of more than an hour, during which neither side got off more than a few shots. At this point some sort of SWAT team might have stormed the Palestinian positions. But a police "special assault unit," helicoptered in about an hour after the shooting began, for some reason landed at the far end of the airfield, more than a mile from the action, and was never deployed. "The biggest failure was not having enough sharpshooters," says Ulrich Wegener, a lieutenant colonel in the Bundeswehr who served as Genscher's aide-de-camp that day and went on to lead the GSG-9, the special-forces unit that the West German government established within two weeks of the fiasco. "The second biggest failure was not having special forces that could storm the helicopters."

Alternatively, German forces might have attacked with armored personnel carriers. But six such carriers ordered to the scene had gotten stuck in traffic, much of it caused by curiosity seekers flocking to Fürstenfeldbruck, as if it were the venue for another Olympic event. One carrier had mistakenly lit out for Riem, Munich's civilian airport, on the other side of town, as had scores of police. In a Keystone Kops moment, the driver of one police car happened to hear the correct destination on the radio, slammed on the brakes, and caused a pileup.

Just before midnight the carriers finally arrived to bear down on the helicopters. Only here did the hostages lose their lives, to judge by what can be pieced together from portions of that long-suppressed Bavarian Prosecutor's Office report. A terrorist strafed the four hostages inside one helicopter, killing Springer, Halfin, and Ze'ev Friedman and wounding Berger. Then he sprang to the ground, wheeled, and flung a grenade back into the cockpit before being shot dead as he fled.

Before fire from that explosion reached the fuel tank and turned the helicopter into an inferno, Issa emerged defiantly from beneath the other chopper with Kalashnikov blazing, strafing the Germans. Police killed him and a second fedayeen with return fire. At this point another commando, believed to be Jamal Al-Gashey's cousin Adnan, raked the remaining five hostages — Gutfreund, Schorr, Slavin, Spitzer, and Shapira — with fatal gunfire.

Berger would be the last hostage to die. He had taken two non-lethal bullets in his lower extremities, only to perish of smoke inhalation. (Firefighters at one point braved gunfire to douse the helicopter with foam but were forced to retreat to cover.) Three fedayeen, alive and largely unhurt, lay on their stomachs nearby, two of them playing dead. They were captured, and forty minutes later, with the help of dogs and tear gas, police tracked Tony to the refuge he had taken beneath a railroad car on the fringe of the airfield, killing him during a brief gun battle.

The last shot, fired at about 12:30 A.M., ended nearly three hours of an operation that, as an official involved later put it, "was condemned to fail from the beginning." To this day the Germans have never satisfactorily explained why they didn't deploy two or three snipers for each terrorist. The gunmen had neither precision rifles nor bulletproof vests. The military airfield was only moderately lit, so the police had erected three mobile lighting towers, but on this moonless night the towers cast stark shadows, as did the helicopters' long rotor blades, and none of the snipers had been issued night-vision goggles. Several nights later, during a reconstruction exercise, members of a team from the Bavarian Prosecutor's Office positioned themselves exactly where the five police gunmen had been. With night-vision goggles, each was able to distinguish figures within the helicopters.

Indeed, the police shot as much in the figurative as the literal dark. They hadn't merely been kept ignorant of how many terrorists to expect; no one had told them precisely where the helicopters would be landing and hence what might be the optimal positions to take up. "The helicopters landed directly in front of me and thus exactly in the line of fire of the shooters on the tower," the policeman behind the concrete parapet told the inquiry of the prosecutor's office. "Had I known they were landing where they actually did, I would have chosen another position."

Finally, the policemen had no two-way radios with which to coordinate an operation that had to take out the commandos virtually at a stroke. When Wolf, from his post in the tower, gave the order to fire, only three gunmen were in a position to hear him; the other two, who were to begin shooting when they noticed the first three doing so, found themselves in the line of fire of their comrades and had to take cover. So in effect three riflemen were left to take out the eight terrorists. That trio's shooting was only enough to disable three of the fedayeen immediately and to alert the other five that the day's negotiations had been a ruse.

In their negligence suit the families of the victims charged that saving the hostages became subordinate to Brundage's desire to remove the crisis from the Olympic Village. Wegener suggests as much. "The Village," he says, "was like a church, a cathedral." It was almost as if the Germans had said, There's no way we can save the hostages. Let's at least save the Games.

Even as the shootout continued at the airport, a rumor had cruelly mutated into fact. At 11:00 P.M. Conrad Ahlers, a spokesman for the West German federal government, told reporters that all the hostages had been liberated. The wire services sent this misinformation around the world, and Israeli newspapers hit the streets on September 6 repeating it in banner headlines. Even Golda Meir went to bed believing the Germans had freed the nine captives.

On the morning of the sixth the grim truth became known. "Until today, we always thought of Dachau as being near Munich," said Israeli interior minister Josef Burg. "From now on, unfortunately, we'll say that Munich is near Dachau."

Willi Daume, the president of the Munich organizing committee, at first wanted the remainder of the Games called off, but Brundage and others talked him out of it. "I, too, questioned the decision to continue," says Vogel, the former mayor of Munich, "but over time I came to believe that we couldn't let the Olympics come to a halt from the hand of terrorism."

So, after a memorial service on September 6, the Carefree Games resumed. Many of the eighty thousand people who filled the Olympic Stadium for West Germany's soccer match with Hungary carried noisemakers and waved flags, while authorities did nothing to intervene in the name of decorum. Yet when several spectators unfurled a banner reading 17 DEAD, ALREADY FORGOTTEN? security sprang into action. Officials seized the sign and expelled the offenders from the grounds.

It's part of the protocol of every Olympics that organizers shall publish an official report of great scope and heft. Munich's is Teutonically comprehensive. It praises Mark Spitz for his feats in the pool and Olga Korbut for hers on the mats, and the informal Olympic Village for its contribution to the relaxed spirit of the Games. And it recounts the atrocities perpetrated on members of the Israeli delegation in dispassionate, mostly exculpatory prose. Then it adds this grotesque rationalization: "After the terrible events of September 5, 1972, it was once again the atmosphere of the Olympic Village which contributed a great deal to calming down and preserving peace among the athletes."

Thirty Years Later: "This Will Be a Very Secure Place"

Today most of the apartment block at 31 Connollystrasse is filled with middle-class Germans going about the banal business of living. Well-tended flowers spill from windowsills. A young girl prances off with her bicycle. A memorial plaque by the main doorway is in temporary storage, but it will return in the spring, after renovations are complete on the pedestrian-only street.

If you know what went on there, however, the scene hints at the sinister. The plastic tape of the construction cordon suggests the crime scene the spot once was. Chain-link fencing is a reminder of what the Black Septembrists scaled to steal into the Village. On the side of the building, faded graffiti evokes the ferment of another time, of shouted slogans and violent means.

The door that leads from the street to the foyer and stairwell is locked. During the 1972 Olympics that door was never locked.

The entryway and apartment where Moshe Weinberg and Yossef Romano were murdered now belong to the Max Planck Institute, a scientific think tank. A sign reads PLEASE RESPECT THE PRIVACY OF OUR GUESTS. "Of course we all know what happened," one of the three residents, all Russian scientists on contract with the institute, recently told a stranger who knocked on his door anyway, "but none of us knows exactly where the guys were murdered. We don't want to know. If we knew, it would make it very hard to live here."

In their negligence suit the families of the victims argued that the Germans should have anticipated some attack. If it wasn't enough that Georg Sieber laid out the entire plan, Black September had staged five operations in Europe over the previous ten months, including three in West Germany, and, the families allege, German intelligence sources had received at least three reports between August 21 and September 2 of Palestinian terrorists flowing into the region. Early in 2001 the Germans, who the families say had for years denied that a report on the disaster even existed, finally settled with the families, offering a pool of $3 million in compensation, to be paid out in equal thirds by the German, Bavarian, and Munich governments. (This was in addition to bereavement funds of $1 million doled out by the German Red Cross in the immediate aftermath of the attack.) But the families have yet to receive any money from this "humanitarian" fund, and they believe that the Germans haven't released all the evidence that exists. Moreover, they still wait for an expression of remorse or responsibility. "If they would only say to us, 'Look, we tried, we didn't know what we were doing, we didn't mean for what happened to happen, we're sorry' — that would be the end of it," says Ankie Spitzer. "But they've never even said that."

Sieber has never again worked with an organizing committee for a sporting event. "It's nothing but frustration," he says. "The officials aren't able to develop a tradition because everyone is a rookie. Nine out of ten aren't paid — they're volunteers — and the paid professional can't lead them. If you're not a professional, you incur no risk, take no responsibility. This disaster in Munich, it was a horror trip, the whole thing, a chain of catastrophes large and small. Who paid? Okay, the German government paid, but of those individuals who were responsible, no one paid. We can't change the past. But more important, we're not learning for the future, because nothing's really different."

In fact Munich changed forever how the Olympics are conducted. Athletes at the 1980 Winter Games in Lake Placid stayed in a Village built to be so secure that it was eventually converted into a prison. Later that year, in Moscow, the Soviets X-rayed every piece of incoming luggage at the airport and deployed 240,000 militiamen to show they meant business. Though the Soviet Union's boycott of the 1984 Olympics in Los Angeles was surely payback to the

United States for passing up those Moscow Games, the Soviets claimed they stayed home because of inadequate security, even as the L.A. Olympics introduced such gadgets as a remote-controlled robot that could examine suspicious objects. Sixteen years ago the IOC began to collect and share information related to security and in 1997 formally established a "transfer of knowledge" program so Olympic know-how — from the food tasters for athletes in Seoul to the palm-print recognition technology in Atlanta — could be passed from one organizing committee to the next. To help Athens prepare for 2004, security experts from Australia, Britain, France, Germany, Israel, Spain, and the United States are collaborating with Olympic organizers and the Greek authorities.

If you accept Santayana's maxim that those who fail to remember the past are condemned to repeat it, you could argue that Munich organizers recalled their past all too well, thereby inviting a horror of a different sort. But while the Greeks have their own historical baggage, they seem to be toting it more lightly. The military junta that ruthlessly ruled from 1967 to 1974 was detested by most Greeks, who pride themselves on living in the birthplace of democracy. A homegrown terrorist group, November 17, took its name from a bloody student uprising on that date in 1973, and over the past three decades its members have targeted various representatives of Western governments that supported that military rule, including the United States. November 17 has claimed responsibility for more than one hundred attacks that have killed twenty-two people and wounded scores of others, yet there hadn't been a single arrest in twenty-six years.

Then, in June, police caught a break. A bomb accidentally exploded in Piraeus, the port of Athens, gravely injuring the man carrying it. Tips poured in, and over the next several weeks police raided November 17 hideouts, seized weapons, and charged at least ten people with involvement in the group. A senior Western diplomatic official posted in Athens also points approvingly to the government's plan to deploy at least seven thousand armed troops in the streets during the Games. "The public reaction to that announcement was silence," he says. "Given the aversion of the average citizen here to anything that smacks of the junta, that was a big, big sign. But then this is a post–9/11 Olympics, and 9/11 changed the way all of us look at the world. Plus, people take a lot of pride in being Greek. They want to look good in the eyes of the world."

Those in the security field believe that no group poses a greater threat to the 2004 Olympics than al-Qaeda. Many experts suspect that "Afghan alumni" have joined up with al-Qaeda cells in Albania, the anarchic, predominantly Muslim nation that abuts Greece to the north. The challenge will be to secure a country that has long been a transfer point between Europe and the Middle East — to protect not only Greece's rugged mountain borders, but also thousands of miles of coastline and hundreds of ports. As one Israeli counterterrorism expert puts it, "It's so much easier to bounce from the Middle East to a barren island in Greece and then make your way to Athens than to travel halfway around the globe to prepare for an attack in Sydney."

The concrete structures of Athens' Olympic Village are sprouting at the base of Mount Parnis, on the northern edge of the city. Builders and suppliers desperately try to keep to a schedule, despite several work stoppages and four on-the-job deaths. Most of the 2,300 workers on the site are Greek, but scores of them aren't. "We don't screen everyone," says Katerina Barbosa, an official with the private company building the Village. "But at this point we have nothing to fear. By the end of the year this will be a very secure place."

Sieber is out of the business of tabletopping the Olympics and refuses to talk specifically about Athens. But he brings up one of his thirty-year-old scenarios, one that might give Greek organizers pause, especially in light of the dynamite and hand grenade discovered early this month buried next to the 1896 Olympic stadium, which is slated to be used as a venue in 2004. "[The Basque separatist group] ETA is very patient," Sieber says, his imagination vivid as ever. "They pick out a man they want to kill. They send one of their operatives, disguised as a worker, to the construction site for his new home and plant a bomb. For several years they do nothing. Then one morning, perhaps after he is married, with a family, they detonate it by radio. He finds himself up in the sky."

JULIET MACUR

Power Pact

FROM THE DALLAS MORNING NEWS

DAYTON, OHIO — The boy bounds into the gym looking like a regular kid, mounds of muscles under cover, hidden beneath a T-shirt and shorts that droop below his knees.

He is waving the Dayton phone book above his head, announcing that he's about to attempt a miraculous feat.

"Wait until you see this," he says, aglow with an eighth-grader's energy. "I'm going to rip the Dayton phone book in half, just like my dad does."

The gym, a small but specialized setup not far from the interstate, comes to a halt. High school girls in their tight T-shirts and short shorts stop jogging on the treadmills. Middle-aged men admiring themselves in the mirrors stop lifting barbells.

The kid's dad, once one of the world's strongest men, sidles up next to his son, one of the nation's strongest teenagers. He laughs, watching the kid wring the two-inch-thick phone book so hard that ink should drip from it.

"I'm gonna rip this thing," the boy says, straining. "I . . . am . . . gonna . . . do . . . this!"

He wrestles with the book, his body writhing as if he's trying to pry open the jaws of an alligator.

"Argh! Dad! How do you do this? You have to teach me!"

His father grabs the book, creases it, and tears it as if it were wafer-thin.

"It's easy," the dad says. "It just takes practice. I know you'll do it someday, Jimmie. I know you will."

*

In many ways, Jimmie Pacifico is your ordinary teenager.

He's a shy, handsome fourteen-year-old boy with dark, spiky hair, a baby face, and a shadow of a goatee. He walks his middle school girlfriend to classes, careful to keep Listerine breath strips in his pocket. He helps his mother take out the trash and cleans his room, for which he receives a $15 allowance every Friday.

He has two dreams. He wants to play football for Ohio State. And he wants to be just like his dad.

It's in chasing those dreams that Jimmie veers from the ordinary.

He may not be able to tear the phone book in half, but, at five-foot-eight, 187 pounds, Jimmie is a teenage bulldozer, stronger than most men at your neighborhood gym. His body is lean and ripped with layers of muscles. He can bench-press 305 pounds, the weight of a baby elephant. When he squats 500 pounds, so much weight that it threatens to crush him, he is Superboy defying gravity.

His father couldn't lift that much until he was twenty-one, which is significant. Larry Pacifico was perhaps the greatest powerlifter of all time.

In the 1970s, Pacifico was Hercules, a five-foot-six, 242-pound Michelin Man of muscles cut wide and rippled, his body a relief map of hard bumps and lumps. A nine-time powerlifting world champion, he went undefeated for ten years.

At the height of his success, he made weightlifting a career. He sold his own videos, apparel, and vitamins. He gave speeches and seminars. He worked as a network television commentator for weightlifting events.

From there, he moved into business in the Dayton area. Now fifty-six, he owns two gyms called Club Champions, and licenses three more.

All of that success came at a high cost. To keep up with his competitors, Pacifico says, he started using steroids, the muscle-building drugs that can be obtained legally only through a doctor's prescription. As a user of the drugs, he became part of their secret fraternity. He then became a dealer.

Soon enough, he paid the price.

He says that steroid use contributed to serious health problems. Three heart attacks. A seven-way coronary bypass. Fifteen orthopedic surgeries. Chronic pain in his joints. Advanced arthritis.

In 1986, two years before Jimmie's birth, Pacifico was charged with smuggling and selling steroids. Convicted of a felony a year later, he paid a $15,000 fine, served five years of probation, and did one thousand hours of community service, mostly speaking to kids about the perils of steroid use.

He acknowledges that his past has left him a broken man. Still, Larry Pacifico says he would live his life the same way, if given another chance.

"I would do it again because that's what I needed to win," he says. "Everybody was taking steroids. I know it sounds very nuts to you, but in those days that's what you had to do to keep up with the competition."

He lowers his clear, deep voice and whispers, "There's nothing like fame."

Pacifico is a likable character. He has a bald, shaved head and friendly eyes. He is brimming with energy. His personal training business is booming, and he has a loyal following. He wants his clients to lose weight, look good, and feel confident about their bodies.

Growing up in New York, he hardly ever felt confident about his body. He had rheumatic fever when he was nine and was scrawny and weak until he began working out in junior high school. He went from puny to powerful — just as his son has.

As soon as Jimmie started lifting, he grew fast. He remembers his own statistics: "In fifth grade, I was 105 pounds. In sixth, I was 146. In seventh, I was 170, and now I'm maybe 187."

His father interjects: "By his senior year of high school, he should be 230."

"But Dad! You said I'd be 250! I want to be 250!"

Pacifico shakes his head and says, "We'll see, Jimmie."

Jimmie's mother, Pam Masten, was Pacifico's fourth wife. After divorcing three years ago, they share custody of their son, and Masten worries about Jimmie's health. She questions how safe it is for Jimmie to bulk up and lift so much weight, but she can't argue with the results.

Despite being several inches shorter than his toughest competition, Jimmie is one of the nation's top shot putters and discus throwers for his age group. At this year's USA Track & Field Junior

Olympics, he won the shot put and finished second in the discus. His best throws in competition are 57 feet, 6½ inches in the shot put and 184 feet, 6¼ inches in the discus.

As a running back last year for the Morton-Smith Middle School football team in Butler Township, Ohio, he scored 23 of the team's 24 touchdowns. In the last game this year, he had 302 all-purpose yards and scored three touchdowns, including one on a 98-yard interception return.

When he was eleven, he was a world champion powerlifter for one of the many powerlifting associations.

None of it happened by accident.

Larry Pacifico has molded his son into an image of his former self. He is leading Jimmie down the same path he took, into a world of powerlifting and field events in track. Both sports are infamous for being riddled by steroid abuse.

"I know all about my dad and the steroids and the other problems," Jimmie says. "But that won't happen to me because my dad's training me the right way. He knows so much about the right and wrong things to do. I'm pretty lucky to have a dad like him."

Still, people are skeptical. If Pacifico said he would "do it all over again" and take steroids and sell steroids, they reason, why should anyone believe he wouldn't feed them to his son?

Jimmie hears it all the time. Kids tease him at school. Parents heckle him at football games and meets. They accuse him of being manufactured. They say he is a liar, a cheat, and a criminal.

"It used to bother me a lot, but not anymore," Jimmie says, staring at the floor. "Because I know I'm not taking them. I can get tested if I want to, but am I supposed to walk around with a piece of paper that says I'm not taking steroids? What do I do?"

When Jimmie won the shot put and discus at a local track meet last year, one of the parents demanded that Jimmie be tested for performance-enhancing drugs. Pacifico said all the kids should be tested if Jimmie is tested, so the parent dropped the subject.

Jimmie has never been tested, but his father is bracing for it.

"He'll be the most tested athlete in history because of my background," Pacifico says.

Even when Jimmie was in the womb, and Pacifico's federal case was concluding, Pacifico and Masten discussed how people would assume their son was "on the juice" because of Pacifico's history.

Pacifico bristles when he thinks about it. Can't people see the truth? He is not a monster. Simply, he is a man who knows the ins and outs of elite athletics and wants his son to benefit from it. But some people aren't buying it.

Jon Almquist, chairman of the Secondary School Committee of the National Athletic Trainers' Association, has never met the Pacificos, but he's concerned all the same.

"It's sad that this father is putting his kid in the same type of environment that he's lived through. In his [powerlifting] career, his choices weren't too good. Now is he making the same bad choices for his kid? Who knows? Is he throwing in a little andro [androstenedione, an over-the-counter steroid compound] into his protein shake? Who knows?

"With the horrible regime of maxing out with weight and taking creatine shakes, why can't someone just call child protective services and stop all of this?"

Pacifico is wearing a sleeveless T-shirt and his muscles are showing, veins nearly popping from his skin because his body fat is so low. He pushes back his shirt, exposing his shoulder and one of his many scars.

The marks from his wounds come in various sizes and shapes: a four-inch scar on his right shoulder from four operations, a seven-inch scar on his left knee from surgery after his quadriceps muscle snapped off, a nine inch scar down his chest from his seven-way coronary bypass, which happened when he was forty-five, a decade after his powerlifting career ended.

His first heart attack, at thirty-five, prompted his retirement. His second heart attack came four years later.

"Look what steroids have done to me," he says, pointing to his scars. "Listen to my horror stories.

"Everybody I've ever known [in powerlifting] has either died or had a heart attack from taking steroids, so why would I give them to my son?" he says. "We've started his training young enough and we're building a foundation. The people that need to catch up are the ones who look to do it the quick and easy way.

"I tell everyone: the sins of the father do not pass onto the son."

But the dreams of the father do.

The day Jimmie was born, he was seven pounds, fourteen

ounces, all wrinkly and soft like a worn pillow. Even then, Larry
Pacifico imagined the future: someday his little boy would be hard
and hulking.

"I always thought that Jimmie would be one of the strongest people in the world someday," he says.

Though Pacifico had two older children from a previous marriage, he saw something special in Jimmie. He saw opportunity. Divorce separated him from his other children before he could watch
them grow up or help them train for sports.

Jimmie was his last chance to share his joy of athletics with one of
his own children. And he planned to do it right.

Pacifico started Jimmie on a personal training program early,
carefully planning every step of his athletic career, from the first
time Jimmie picked up a one-pound dumbbell at age three to the
first time Jimmie drank a protein and creatine shake at thirteen to
the Junior Olympics gold medal Jimmie won in the shot put last
summer.

Soon after Jimmie's birth, Pacifico began to maneuver Jimmie's
chubby little arms and calves to increase the range of motion in his
son's joints. During playtime, Pacifico encouraged Jimmie to join
him for a set of sit-ups or invited Jimmie to jump on his knees, so he
could bench-press him — and teach his son the fundamentals of
weightlifting. By the time he was six, Pacifico says, Jimmie could do
fifteen pull-ups, while other kids could do only one, if that.

"Jimmie was learning what Larry's world was about," Masten says.
"To Larry, the physical has always been very important. Physique is
important. He has built his whole life around it."

To help him gain agility, flexibility, and strength, Jimmie took
gymnastics. Tae kwon do, for discipline, came later.

It wasn't until Jimmie was seven that Masten noticed the beginning of her husband's obsession with their son's athletic success.
During baseball games, the father stood behind the backstop bois-
terously cheering and encouraging Jimmie each time he was at bat.

"That's when I was like, 'Okay, this is a little too much,'" Masten
says. "I told him, 'Back off a little, ease up. This is not the most important thing in the world.'"

Soon, it became the most important thing. She couldn't stop it.

One afternoon when he and Jimmie were out by their pool,
Pacifico handed his nine-year-old son a shot and Jimmie threw it
about sixteen feet.

"From that moment I knew he was going to be a national champion," he says. "I knew he had a gift."

About a year later, Pacifico religiously began keeping tabs of Jimmie's workout sessions.

"I have every workout logged in a book since he was small," Pacifico says, opening one of Jimmie's eleven workout logs and grinning. "Ah, yes. Our first official workout was in November of 1998 when Jimmie was ten. He did legs and chest that day. Squatted ten reps with the thirty-five-pound bar. Bench-pressed thirty-five pounds . . ."

While Olympic weightlifting consists of two separate lifting events — the snatch and the clean and jerk — powerlifting is much different. It's a combination of a bench press, a squat, and a dead lift. Only the strongest overall lifters succeed.

To become the strongest powerlifter in the world, Pacifico decided to become the biggest. In the 1970s, he ate enough to feed a cavalry, horses included. His breakfast: fifteen eggs, half a loaf of bread, one pound of bacon, a half-gallon of whole milk. His lunch: three entire chickens. His dinner: two pounds of steak, plus potatoes.

He says that at one point, his cholesterol level, heightened by his steroid use and diet, was 601. A healthy level is under 200.

Still, on the back of one photo from the 1973 worlds, he wrote "at my happiest" and his measurements: 242, 21 neck, 51 chest, 38 waist, 21½ arm (pumped), 30 thigh. It was a photo from his scrapbook, which chronicled his athletic career, including his high school gymnastics and shot put and discus competitions.

He left out the stories about his steroid use.

After winning his fourth world championship, Pacifico says, he turned to steroids because he heard other people were using them and he feared those people would start beating him.

"I took five times the amount anyone else was taking," he says. "When I was going for my tenth title, I took 25 percent more than that. Too much. I was willing to do anything."

Soon, his body began to break down because his muscles were too strong for his bones and joints to handle. His left biceps popped off of his elbow. His right shoulder's rotator cuff was ground down to nothing.

Although Jimmie's mother insists that her son isn't on steroids, she is worried about the physical effects of his workouts just the same. So far, with his father teaching him the correct weightlifting techniques and monitoring his every move, Jimmie hasn't had a serious injury.

"How much can your knees take, how much can your elbows take, how much can your tendons take?" Masten says. "I worry about so much. I worry for his bones. I worry that he's not playing outside, not having a regular boyhood.

"I worry that if Jimmie is great now that he's not going to be great when he needs to be."

Though Pacifico says Jimmie sees an orthopedist several times a year to monitor his bones and joints, Masten still may have reason to worry. Some experts, such as pediatric orthopedist Dr. Eric Small, say that lifting so much weight is detrimental for kids Jimmie's age.

"We don't recommend maximum lifts for kids until full bone maturity," which varies from person to person, says Small, assistant clinical professor of pediatrics and orthopedics at New York City's Mount Sinai School of Medicine. "Excessive stress can cause stress fractures or tendinitis. It can cause overuse injuries or it can damage the muscles and soft tissue, the tendons and ligaments. It can cause early arthritis. He may have chronic pain for the rest of his life.

"But that may be just the tip of the iceberg," Dr. Small says. "This is scary stuff."

Just like many teenage boys, Jimmie dreams of becoming an NFL running back, or at least playing in college on a scholarship. His father, on the other hand, worries about injuries in football. Instead he wants Jimmie to make it to the Olympics in the shot put or discus — and he thinks Jimmie *can* make it, if he keeps training.

Training isn't always easy. Three years after his parents' divorce, Jimmie splits his time between their houses, which are about one mile apart. For Jimmie, life at each place is markedly different.

"His mother's first question to him is, 'Did you finish your homework today?" his father says. "My first question to him is, 'Did you finish your protein shake today?'"

"We have different ways of grooming Jimmie," Masten says. "I say his schoolwork comes first. Larry teaches him to be strong and work out. 'Let's be great. Let's be number 1.' It's important to him that Jimmie be good in everything he does."

Larry Pacifico moved into a new house three years ago. He wanted more land for shot put and discus circles, so Jimmie could practice in the back yard. He also wanted to bring in a pole vaulting pit, to make Jimmie a decathlete, but the equipment was stolen before he had a chance to pick it up from a local high school.

So Jimmie was left to throw the shot and discus instead, and his father wanted to give him the best training available. In 1999, he hired Randy Barnes, gold medal shot putter from the 1996 Atlanta Olympics, to give Jimmie pointers. The year before, Barnes, the world record holder, had been suspended for life from USA Track & Field after testing positive for androstenedione. In 1991, he served a two-year suspension for testing positive for the steroid methyltestosterone.

Above Jimmie's bed at his dad's house, there is an autographed poster of Barnes. It says, "Jimmie, you have the power to make your dreams a reality!"

Barnes was six-foot-four and about 300 pounds when he was competing. Jimmie, cursed with short parents, won't grow nearly that tall, which puts him at a disadvantage because tall throwers have more leverage than shorter ones. When Jimmie was tiny, his father was trying to combat that problem.

Pacifico says he stretched Jimmie and did yoga with Jimmie to elongate his son's spine. Periodically, he still sends Jimmie for X-rays to see how much room he has left in his growth plates and to see whether his self-proclaimed "growth methods" are working. Pacifico's plan is to let Jimmie continue throwing the shot and the discus after high school, but only if he gets to five-ten.

"I'm so nervous when I go in because once or twice before, the doctor said I won't grow that much more," Jimmie says. "It kind of makes me feel sick just thinking about it."

Jimmie tries to eat healthy but still gobbles up pizza with the works when given the chance. He goes out with his girlfriend, hangs out with friends, and heads to the movies on weekends, but never if it conflicts with his training.

He lifts weights with his father three times a week and throws the shot on Sundays. He also works with a trainer who helps him increase his speed, agility, and flexibility through various drills. Twice a week, he meets his uncle, Dick Pacifico, for tutoring sessions because he is struggling academically, and his father is worried his grades will be too low for him to play sports in high school.

Every night, Jimmie drinks a shake his father makes, containing PowerAde, whey protein, creatine, and an over-the-counter supplement called GHR-15, which claims to stimulate the pituitary gland so the body will release growth hormones. Pacifico says that Jimmie began drinking protein shakes at twelve and that they began adding creatine in March.

Pacifico is relentless at creating the cocktail of supplements, and he's determined that Jimmie drink it nightly. Even when Jimmie is at his mother's, Pacifico whips up the concoction, then drops it off. "Sometimes he comes knocking in the middle of dinner, and we're like, 'Can't he miss one night?'" says John Masten, Jimmie's stepfather.

"With me, he never finishes his drink," Pam Masten says.

The Federal Drug Administration doesn't regulate supplements such as creatine, and use of them is controversial because long-term effects are unknown. Creatine's short-term side effects are cramping and dehydration, if taken without enough water.

Pacifico recommends creatine to his clients fourteen and older to build muscle, increase speed, and recover from workouts quicker. He says it's okay because the International Olympic Committee doesn't ban it and the body produces it on its own.

"I have no fears. In moderation, it's fine," he says. "Anything taken in excess can hurt you. Drinking too much milk can hurt you."

Charles Yesalis, professor of heath and human development at Penn State University, is a nationally known expert on supplements and steroids. He doesn't recommend creatine for athletes of any age, especially children. One of his concerns is that many supplements aren't labeled correctly, that there may be things in the bottle (like testosterone or steroids) that people don't expect. That only makes the long-term effects of supplements even more uncertain.

"With creatine, we still don't know what will happen to you five, ten, or twenty years down the road," Yesalis says. "Will your kidneys be damaged? We don't know that. With any of these supplements, we're allowing our kids to play a game of chemical Russian roulette."

Larry Pacifico hurts.

In the mornings, he cringes when the pain surges through his creaky bones, yet he still rises quickly. Thinking about Jimmie is enough to catapult him from bed.

He says it's his job to keep his son on the right path, so he can live a good and happy life on top of the sports world, so he can feel proud of himself for training so hard and accomplishing so much.

As the days go on, he feels more urgency about making Jimmie into a successful young man. Memories of his own father's death of a heart attack at fifty-eight haunt him. Nobody knew his father had heart problems. After all Pacifico has subjected his body to, he wonders how long he will hang on.

The steroids. The heart attacks. Now the effects from pain medications are causing problems.

"I hope I'm there to the end to see Jimmie in the Olympics or in the NFL, but I worry about my longevity," Pacifico says, glancing at the rosary coiled inside the cup-holder in his truck. "I just pray I'll be around for him."

He keeps those worries from Jimmie because he doesn't want to upset him. Though he is Jimmie's coach and motivator, the guy who for so long has plucked him out of bed or dragged him away from friends or the TV to work out, the son still loves his father unconditionally.

"I want to be a champion like he was," Jimmie says. "Who wouldn't want to be like their dad?"

BILL DONAHUE

End of the Run

FROM OUTSIDE

THE HOUSE WAS EMPTY and it would soon be demolished —
wrecking balls and all that — so they decided to have one last party
there, the real estate agent and her friends. It would be a white-
trash theme party — the Corn Dog Hoedown. Guests showed up in
cutoffs and gingham halter tops. A tattoo artist named Bill Conner
laid out his needles on a table by the sliding-glass door overlooking
the pool and waited. Conner had traveled here to San Diego all the
way from Miami Beach, where he worked at Tattoo Circus, render-
ing Harley logos, pinup girls, whatever, for tourists. On this February night in 2000, he was doing tats for practically nothing.

Pretty soon along came this guy — muscular, intense, somewhat
inebriated. He would get in a fistfight later that evening, after trying to hit on some marine's girlfriend. Conner remembers seeing
him with a gash on the head, being escorted off the property. But
right now all he wanted was a tattoo, an over-the-top number he'd
thought of himself. "I drew up a little skull with flames coming out
of it and a banner underneath with the words 'Ski to Die,'" Conner
says. "He was stoked."

Drunk-guy tattoos are often a source of serious regret, but not
this time. The man who got it was an unrepentant speed demon, a
former world-class skier who'd attained a brief flash of stardom,
ages before.

On February 16, 1984, William Dean Johnson, then twenty-
three, won the men's downhill at the Winter Olympics in Sarajevo,
Yugoslavia. On that cold afternoon he became the first American
man in Olympic history to earn a gold medal in an alpine skiing

event. Perhaps you remember his run: the hissing violence of his skis as he knifed through the tight turns on the upper half of the course, the wild looseness of his body flowing over the jumps, that ultratight tuck, and the euphoria with which ABC announcer Bob Beattie shouted, "Yes, he's done it! He's done it!"

The spectacle was even more poignant because Bill Johnson was a working-class kid, a onetime juvenile delinquent snatching victory in a sport long ruled by the rich. Johnson had grown up near Portland, Oregon, in the logging town of Brightwood, and his family was so strapped for cash that at times they had to sleep in the car when they traveled to ski races. As a kid, Bill broke into houses for kicks. He once stole a Chevy; he spent three days in jail.

He was brash, abrasive, and wholly surprising. When he arrived in Sarajevo, he wasn't even among the world's top ten downhillers. Yet the course — relatively straight and flat — was tailor-made for fast gliders like Johnson, and he saw this, cockily predicting, "Everyone else is here to fight for second place." He backed it up, too, trouncing his closest competitor by 0.27 seconds. When one reporter asked about the value of his gold medal, he swaggered and said, "Millions. We're talking millions."

He was not a bad guy, actually. He responded to all of the fifty or so fan letters he got each week, and after winning the gold he remained the consummate buddy to a tight band of friends, most of them skiers. "He's loyal to the death," says retired U.S. Ski Team racer Mark Herhusky. "He's the kind of person you'd want on your side in a barroom scuffle."

But Johnson's crash-and-burn style was better suited to the slopes than to daily life. He drove fast, partied hard, shot guns, surfed at midnight, and in general carried on as if those clichéd extreme-sport adages — *Rip it! Tear shit up!* — were his holy credo. In the end, the fire that propelled him, that youthful fearlessness, would devolve into a sort of desperation — nihilism, even. He would become the stereotypical ex-jock who destroys himself trying to act young, and his life would serve as proof that you cannot burn on forever. There he was at the white-trash party — unemployed, of no fixed address, in the midst of a divorce, and pathetically intent on reconnecting to his glorious past.

Ski to Die. Right after the ink dried on his shoulder, Johnson — who was about to turn forty — launched a long-shot bid to make the 2002 Olympic Ski Team. Almost no one has stayed on the team past thirty. Johnson had retired from the World Cup circuit at twenty-nine and had spent much of the past decade off skis, working as a freelance carpenter. He had herniated five disks and his shoulder was held together with pins, thanks to old ski-racing injuries. Without any sponsorship of note, he had only one pair of new skis instead of the five or six that elite racers typically need.

Nonetheless, last winter he began tooling around the West in his '84 Ford pickup — going to races and slowly climbing out of the basement of the national rankings. By March 2001, when it came time for the U.S. Alpine Championships at Big Mountain in Montana, Johnson was starting thirty-third in a field of sixty-three racers. He hoped to triumph by skiing fast through an icy, rutted dogleg turn near the base. He hit the turn at fifty miles per hour. Then he caught an edge, his legs went spread-eagle, and his body flew sideways through the mesh fence marking the course. His helmeted head smacked the snow, hard; his brain rotated inside his skull, and tissue tore and bled. Within minutes he was in a coma.

It was early October, six months after the crash, and Johnson was sitting at the breakfast table inside his mother's home near Portland, puzzling over a legal form as the soft autumn light washed in through the window. He is five-foot-nine, with reddish blond hair, and he's still handsome in a ruddy, straightforward way. He'd gained twenty-five pounds and a slight paunch since his accident, though, and his movements were herky-jerky. He smiled, and it was a huge smile, simple and generous. I liked him.

"I have to fill this out," Johnson said, "for the state." I nodded, and then he said it again: "I have to fill this out for the state."

Johnson's fall made his brain swell, putting pressure on his upper brain stem and triggering the coma. By the time medics arrived, his pupils weren't reacting to light. A chunk of his tongue had torn free and blood was filling his lungs. On the Glasgow coma scale, which ranges from three (no brain activity) to fifteen (fully cognitive), Johnson was a five.

He was unconscious for more than three weeks, and when he came to it was like his brain, damaged by countless small tissue tears, was a computer whose wiring had frayed. He couldn't remember anything from the previous six years. He had to learn the

most basic human activities — walking, speaking, brushing his
teeth — all over again. After three months at the Centre for Neuro
Skills in Bakersfield, California, Johnson returned to Portland to
live with his mother, DB, and her second husband, Jimmy Cooper,
a machinist. Johnson continued to visit various therapists four or
five times a week, where he spent hours doing balance exercises
and memorizing words. He had the emotional outlook of a child,
and when he tried to talk, the phrases often floated loose in his
mind.

"I forget where I crashed," he said to me. "I think it was 1991, but
people tell me I was forty years old and that's amazing because I
didn't want to make a comeback when I was forty years old. It
doesn't make any sense to me. But I want to get prepared for next
year's racing. There's no way I can be on the U.S. Ski Team, the way
my body is now, but next year . . ."

Johnson's mother was in the garage, where she runs a small business selling flags and banners for sporting events, but eventually
she wandered into the room. DB Johnson is sixty-five, sturdily built,
with gray hair. She's brisk and upbeat in the manner of someone
used to making the best of tough situations.

"Bill," she said cheerfully, "tell him what you did yesterday."

"Caught a twenty-seven-inch steelhead. It was no big deal.
Normally I catch all the fish in the river."

"And what else?"

"Went mountain biking. I fell a lot. I fell four or five times and
my knees and elbows are scratched, but I made it six miles."

Johnson was also playing golf; recently he'd shot a 38 for nine
holes. His body, it seemed, remembered being an athlete. After
months of therapy, however, his brain was still faltering. "I'd place
his physical recovery in the upper third among brain-injury patients," says his doctor, Molly Hoeflich, a physiatrist at Portland's
Providence Medical Center, "but he will be left with permanent
cognitive deficits. It's impossible to say how much, but people with
brain injuries — they frequently have a hard time returning to
work. They need to live in a supervised setting."

Which means that, for the foreseeable future, Johnson will be
staying with his mother. His therapy could go on for years, and the
cost will be covered only partially by Johnson's insurance, so DB is
having him file for bankruptcy to protect himself from mounting

medical bills. Meanwhile, she will loyally shuttle him back and forth between therapists.

"We were prepared to walk him to the bathroom when he came home from Bakersfield," DB told me. "This isn't scary. We just hope he comes out of it. It's hard. It's very difficult." From the warmth of her words, it was clear that she loved the youngest of her four children and wanted to shield him from further hurt. *If you ask too much,* DB's crossed arms and hard glare seemed to tell me, *I'll cut you off.* She has always protected Bill — from the pain of her 1976 divorce from her first husband, Wally Johnson, and from the trouble that Bill never seemed able to escape both as a child and as a grown man. It was DB who lobbied principals to keep Bill in school despite his playground brawling. Later, in 1985, she quit her job so that she could travel the ski circuit and work as his agent, soliciting endorsements. Their relationship was at times contentious. In fact, they were enmeshed in a dispute over finances before Bill crashed. Even now he can get sour on her.

"I could live in this house forever," he told me as I was leaving one day, "but do I want to? It's not a question." He turned to his mother. "I don't want to live with you right now. It's just not part of my life."

"Well, where do you want to live?" DB said, unfazed.

"Alone," Bill said. He slumped in his chair and glowered.

Mark Herhusky flew to Montana immediately after the accident. He sat in Johnson's hospital room for five days, reading fan letters out loud. Other friends played Led Zeppelin and Stevie Ray Vaughn tapes, in hopes that the familiar tunes would jolt something deep in his memory. They stayed with him overnight, listening for a conscious moan, waiting for him to open his eyes. A guy who washed dishes with Johnson more than two decades ago recently launched the Bill Johnson Foundation, which has raised $6,000 toward Johnson's future living expenses.

Clearly, the best thing that has happened in the wake of Johnson's crash is the great outpouring of support he's gotten from friends, from what former pro downhiller John Creel calls "the ski-racing brotherhood." Creel, forty-five, is a firefighter who raced against Johnson in the seventies. Like Johnson, he is friendly and boisterous, with a testosterone-heavy résumé. He's a waterfall kayaker and was the first person to ski the crater of Mount St. Helens after it erupted in 1980. He entered Bill Johnson's story in the summer of 2000, when Johnson showed up at Creel's fire station, looking for someone to coach him through his comeback attempt.

"He walked in with an ice cream cone and ice cream dripping down his shirt, and he said he wanted my help," Creel remembers. "We weren't close friends. It wasn't like we'd chased chicks together, but he was part of the brotherhood. I told him, 'Follow me home. We start training tomorrow.'"

Creel still styles himself as Johnson's coach. Though he acknowledges Dr. Hoeflich's assessment — that it's extremely unlikely Johnson will ski at a top level again — he's reluctant to let go of the notion that he's orchestrating an Olympic comeback. All last fall, as Johnson struggled with ordinary tasks, Creel shepherded him through a training regimen he described as "riding the edge." It consisted largely of drinking beer, with a little golf and fishing thrown in. In late November, Johnson officially returned to the slopes with some mild runs at Mount Hood. The primary training camp was Creel's house in Maupin, Oregon, a tiny desert town on the Deschutes River, one hundred miles east of Portland. One morning Johnson and I decided to head out there with fishing poles. He wore a special T-shirt for the occasion. It read: "Goin' Richter."

We went with Petr Kakes, a Czech national who placed sixth in speed skiing (that is, shooting straight down a steep slope) at the 1992 Winter Olympics. Kakes drove at least seventy-five the whole way, and we pulled some serious g's on the winding turns of Route 26.

I asked Johnson if he liked driving fast. "It's more of a thrill to shoot a gun," he said. "I used to shoot birds that go in the ocean — any kind of birds that ate fish. I used to shoot them for themselves."

We arrived at Creel's around noon, and right away he forked Johnson a cold beer.

"His mom said only one an hour," Creel said, smirking.

"That's history now," Kakes said.

We walked over to the Rainbow Tavern to get some sandwiches and ran into Gary Odam, a retired sheet-metal worker who'd met Johnson a couple of times the summer before. Odam insisted on buying Johnson a beer. "What this guy's been through," he said, "I should buy him a jug of whiskey." He turned to Johnson. "You were fucked up, man. But you came through. You got a lot of guts, man."

"I do got a lot of guts, man," Johnson said. It was impossible to tell whether the comment was a wry quip or just vacant mimicry. But it carried a glint of the old cocky Johnson, and Odam loved it.

"Let me buy you another one," he said. "I can't think of anything that'd be more of an honor to me. What you did at the Olympics, it was phenomenal! Man, that was like those guys landing on the moon or something! All the bars and taverns in Portland were full, and everyone was ecstatic. I mean, people were going fucking crazy that night. Crazy!"

For a short while after he won the gold, Johnson was a national hero. He made the cover of *Sports Illustrated*. He got a Porsche 911 and an Audi Quattro, along with fat victory payouts from Atomic and his other gear sponsors. Corporations paid him to show up at their ski outings.

He did not, to put it mildly, husband his resources carefully. He bought a house overlooking California's Malibu Canyon; a pickup truck; a speedboat. He paid for most of it with cash. Herhusky remembers seeing him once with $40,000 worth of $100 bills in his pocket; the serial numbers on the bills were consecutive.

Johnson met and later married a waitress from Lake Tahoe named Gina Ricci, and the couple traveled in style. "I visited them once at a resort and they were in a high-rise suite, with flowers all over the room," says Herhusky. "We were eating chocolate-covered strawberries and drinking champagne."

Johnson lived like a rock star, and his skiing suffered for it. He showed up for the 1985–86 season out of shape and he crashed hellaciously in Italy, wrenching his knee and herniating disks in his back. "He came to Tahoe to visit me in a cast, bent and broken," recalls Herhusky, "and he just went crazy, gambling, partying. He went to the casino four days straight."

His fifteen minutes of fame were over. The endorsements stopped flowing, and in the late eighties he sold the Malibu house. He and Gina began wandering California and Oregon in an RV, with Johnson, a skilled carpenter, picking up money here and there doing renovation work. He eventually landed a job with Crested Butte Mountain Resort in 1990; as the mountain's "ski ambassador," he was paid to schuss with visiting journalists and corporate bigwigs. But Johnson had a bad habit of bombing the hill and leaving civilians in the dust. In 1995 Crested Butte canceled his five-season contract a year early.

As his old teammates built solid careers in the ski industry, the gold medalist found himself on the margins. "Americans want their Olympic athletes to be wholesome — to have integrity, pride, and sportsmanship," says Ryan Schinman, president of a New York marketing firm called Platinum Rye Entertainment, which has represented Picabo Street and other star performers. "Bill was outlandish, and he had his mother as his agent. What did she know about corporate America?"

For a few years after leaving Crested Butte, Johnson eked out a living on the appearance fees he made at King of the Mountain, a downhill series for retired greats. He never worked a steady job but spent his days scheming — trading stocks on the phone and laying plans to launch a senior ski-racing tour. After he and Gina moved to San Diego in 1996, he played tons of golf. "He fell in with a bunch of guys who had nothing to do but play golf with a bottle of Jack Daniel's," says Herhusky. "He'd stay out for days at a time."

There was tension in the Johnson household, and also bad luck. In 1991, while Bill was caring for his one-year-old son, Ryan, the boy quietly let himself outside and into the hot tub. He didn't drown, but he came so close that, after he spent three hopeless weeks on life support, the Johnsons made the agonizing decision to let him die. They had two more boys — Nicholas in 1992 and Tyler in 1994 — but the marriage ended for good in 2000.

Gina now lives with the kids in northern California, where she works as an orthodontist's assistant. She did not return my phone calls. Bill sees her and his sons rarely, and since his crash he has lost all comprehension of why she vanished from his life. "The real tough part is my wife, the thing with me and my wife," he says. "I don't understand why she doesn't want to be with me. I told her all I want is love. She doesn't understand I don't have a life. My whole life is lost."

The Deschutes River tumbles down from the high lava fields of central Oregon, through ranches and pine forests and over myriad whitewater rapids on its way to the city of Bend. It's a fisherman's paradise, and in October the returning steelhead are profuse if you know where to look. Creel took us a few miles outside Maupin to his favorite fishing hole, and we unloaded the rods and the beer. Gary Odam, the guy from the bar, arrived with a twelve-pack of Hamm's.

Johnson threw a hook into the water and Creel, who stands six-foot-two and weighs two hundred pounds, lingered on the bank, exuding the mangy power of an athlete just a few brewskis past his prime. He popped open a fresh beer, took a drag on his Marlboro, and began to describe his training plan for the upcoming winter.

"This year, we're just going to get our feet under us," he said. "It'll be about getting out there and skiing. We'll go poach a course now and then, and yeah, we're gonna play to win. It'll be extreme and it'll be flat-out because here's the deal: we can get back on the team. We just gotta pick the right courses. We don't want the turny ones. We want the ones where he can go seventy-five, eighty miles an hour."

I figured Creel was rhapsodizing like this for Johnson's benefit, but I looked around and saw that Bill was well out of earshot. I can only conclude that the beer was working its magic, because a few days later, in sober reflection, Creel would shun all talk of a Johnson comeback. "Trying to make the team was hard enough for Bill the first and second times," he would say. "What person in their right mind would want to be involved with that scenario a third time?"

On the river, though, Creel envisioned great things. "We're going to the Olympics," he said. "The drill is, we're trying to light the torch."

Creel meant the Olympic torch. He and other Johnson friends had been lobbying the U.S. Olympic Committee since last May. There was, of course, a chance that their man would be chosen, but it was very slim. By the time of his accident America had largely forgotten Bill Johnson, and that hasn't changed, despite the made-for-TV drama of his recovery from a coma. Even in the ski world he's inspired only qualified sympathy. The U.S. Ski Team posts Johnson updates on its website, but has yet to sponsor any fundraisers.

So Johnson was lucky to have someone like Creel. Here was a guy who truly believed in Johnson's greatness, even when doing so was absurd. Creel believed in the particulars — the torch, the fame that would have come after that dogleg turn at the nationals — and he did not regard this fishing trip as baby-sitting or an act of charity. He and Bill, he told me, were on a nonstop adventure.

We caught nothing all afternoon; we didn't even get a nibble. Everything was quiet and still until about four o'clock, when suddenly I heard something go splash. It was Johnson. He'd slipped and fallen into the river and now he was floating there, his head up and his eyes bulging.

Kakes got to him first. He anchored his powerful legs on the bank, pulled Johnson out of the water, and rushed him up to the picnic table.

"Take off your socks," advised Creel.

"Here, use this towel," said Kakes.

"Take off your shirt," said Creel.

"Aw, hell," said Odam, "why don't you just take it all off and give us a table dance?" Johnson threw his head back and laughed, and then we fished for a couple more hours.

DB picked us up near Kakes's house on Mount Hood that evening. She knew about Bill's fall in the river (he'd called her from Creel's), and she had the heat cranked up in the car for him.

"We forgot to pack you an extra set of clothes," said DB. "Next time we'll just send them along whether you like it or not. Are you warm enough?"

It was seventy-nine degrees in the car, according to the gauge on the dash, but he wanted it warmer. DB turned the heat up a touch and then smiled over at Bill. She was just recovering from abdominal surgery and yet here she was, driving an hour to get us.

DB told me she was prepared to care for Bill until infirmity stopped her, and I thought of what his doctor, Molly Hoeflich, had said about the importance of this kind of care and attention: "If you go into any city in the country, you see people with cognitive deficits who live on the streets because they can't function in the world; they have no one to take care of them. These people just spiral downward. They get in fights. Their brain damage gets worse. Bill is doing well largely because he's gotten tremendous love and support.

"But is this enough? I hear people say, 'I got better because I really wanted it, because my family really wanted it.' But there are people who really want it and don't get it. Bill's outcome," she concluded, "is becoming increasingly predictable. He will improve, but not drastically."

We drove on. Johnson told me he could hit a golf ball three hundred yards. He reminded me, again, that he'd won the gold medal. Eventually his mother mentioned that the next morning she'd be taking him to a health club for his first visit.

"You can lift weights, Bill," she said.

"That's good," he said, "because all I want to do now, all I want to do now —" We reached the Johnsons' driveway and DB turned in as Bill groped for the words. "All I want to do now is be a weight holder."

"Oh, Bill," said DB. She turned off the car and patted him on the back, gently.

Johnson smiled at the gesture. Then he followed his mother across the driveway and into the house.

Veteran Finds Greens Peace

FROM THE LOS ANGELES TIMES

First Hole

WALTER DONALDSON lowers himself on to a faded, dew-covered picnic table, the moisture seeping through the bottom of his jeans.

He slips on a tattered white golf glove until the tips of his fingers are visible through the cracks.

He slides into a pair of brown golf shoes with the initials VAGC written into the side, and the size 11½ written on the heels.

He picks up a soiled, sour green golf bag filled with mismatched ladies' clubs.

With the stare of Tiger Woods and the gait of a king, Donaldson then marches to the first tee.

It is 6:45 A.M. There is nobody else here.

For twenty-seven years, there has never been anybody else here.

In the early mornings on this tiny nine-hole golf course hidden in a corner of the sprawling Veterans Administration hospital grounds in West Los Angeles, the first twosome is usually Donaldson and his fears. A man using our gentlest game to battle the turmoil of schizophrenia and addiction.

"Fore!" he shouts into the empty mist.

Second Hole

Today we give thanks for things far more important than games. Yet there is a fifty-five-year-old Vietnam veteran who can remind us of their place.

Sitting in the dining room of his boarding house, Donaldson will give thanks for sports, because he believes a sport has kept him alive.

Donaldson is a golfer, only not like the ones you see on television or at the country club.

He uses clubs and a bag he found in a dumpster.

He plays with balls given to him by patrons at a Pico Boulevard diner.

His ball markers are bus tokens.

His shoes are rentals that the VA finally just donated to him.

And in his entire life, he has only played one course.

For nearly three decades, nearly every day, Donaldson has played the postage-stamp VA public course as consistently as he once heard voices and used drugs.

"With his medication, he behaves like any other person, you would never notice anything unusual," said Dr. Rochelle Reno, manager of the VA's Dual Diagnosis Treatment Program. "He just loves golf."

He plays it in the morning before his daily routine of workshops and therapy in the treatment program.

He might play in the afternoon during a break.

Sometimes he plays four rounds in a day.

In all, he has played more than six thousand rounds on the same nine holes.

Never once breaking par.

"But I'm getting better, getting closer," he says.

Donaldson has been around here so long that workers in the rusted Quonset hut that serves as a pro shop ask him to help newcomers and beginners navigate the sometimes confusing track.

One day this summer, he walked nine holes with a teenage boy who was so moved, he wrote me a letter about it.

I phoned the course and read parts of the letter to a man who laughed.

"So," said Dave Wall, "somebody finally found him."

The folks here refer to Donaldson as one of their treasures.

On the second hole this chilly fall morning, you can see why.

He hits his tee shot over a hill, into a seemingly impenetrable cluster of bushes.

All these years, and sometimes he still can't put it on a fairway.

Yet all these years he's never lost a ball.

"I'll find it," he says cheerfully, scurrying down a steep hill and off the course, a six-foot-five man hunched over a tiny bag like it was an oversized purse.

"I don't think so," I say, a lazy sportswriter standing next to his pull cart.

"I'll play it," he says.

"I don't see how," I say.

He finds it. He plays it. Knocks it out of the weeds and onto the green.

Because his larynx was partially paralyzed during lung surgery several years ago, his words run together like a stream over rocks. Initially, he is difficult to understand.

But listen long enough, and you figure it out. Listen long enough and you realize he is saying something worth hearing.

He taps his dirt-specked ball into the hole.

"A man can do a whole lot with faith," he says.

Third Hole

The voices began sometime after the end of the bombing and gunfire.

Donaldson grew up on Seventy-fourth and Avalon in south L.A., joining the Air Force shortly after graduating from Fremont High because he thought his parents could no longer afford to care for him.

"I thought it would be better if I wasn't around," he recalls.

Soon he found himself stationed outside Saigon, listening to battle rage nightly, one of thousands of kids forced to grow up too soon.

"I was just twenty," he remembers. "It was too much."

When he returned home in 1969 after a year in combat, everything changed. He heard things that weren't there. He saw things that didn't exist.

"He came back a totally different person," says his mother, Annie. "I believe it was Vietnam that messed him up."

Donaldson's marriage fell apart, his wife and child remained home in Canada while he returned to Los Angeles to live an itinerant life in shelters and labor camps.

"I don't know what I was like, but I know it wasn't right," he says.

One day in 1975, discovering him incoherent on the streets, his father finally took him to the VA hospital for help.

That day, during tests that would diagnose him as a person with schizophrenia, he wandered out of the large brown buildings to the golf course.

For the first time, his trembling hands picked up a club.

Nine holes and one hour later, he had calmed.

"I hit one ball, and I haven't stopped since," he says.

The emotion he felt that first day still erupts twenty-seven years later, on this third hole, when he sinks a thirty-foot putt for birdie.

"Ha-ha-ha-ha!" he bellows, his huge mouth opening wide around a thrusting tongue that has been compromised with medication.

He then sticks out his hand, not for a high-five or fist tap, but a gentlemanly handshake, because this is golf.

Fourth Hole

His day begins at 4:00 A.M., in a twin bed nudged into a matchbox room at a board-and-care facility on Pico.

He rises before his four housemates turn on the blaring television behind the paper-thin wall above his head.

He rises before the traffic outside his window fills his room with noise the decibel equivalent of a train station.

There is a stained coffee mug on his nightstand that reads, "I putt better than I drive." Next to it is a golf etiquette calendar. Today's topic: scuffs and spike marks.

He has no phone. He has no car, nor a driver's license. His disability and social security check, minus his room and board, equals about $126 a month in spending money.

He grabs his clubs out of the corner and boards a bus to a coffee shop named Rae's. "When the people on the bus see me with my clubs, they call me 'Tiger Woods,'" Donaldson says.

It is the only time that anyone would make that comparison.

At Rae's, he will drink four cups of coffee for $1.03 and load up on balls handed to him by golfers headed to a country club. After spending a half-hour on the same counter stool, he boards another bus for the VA facility, where he will be the first one to arrive at the course.

There, sometimes in the dark, he waits until somebody shows up so he can sign in. "I never play until I sign in," he says.

The patio outside the Quonset hut would never be mistaken for a clubhouse. There are a few weathered chairs and ashtrays, a tiny detached bathroom with a creaky door.

The entire 1,144-yard course, with its tiny green and small fairways, is invisible to most of the golf-mad city.

Just as Donaldson is invisible to them.

He knocks a tee shot alongside the fourth green, and shrugs. "Out here you're reminded, it's about just you and the ball."

Fifth Hole

Donaldson has only four golf shirts and two caps, but one of those caps says it all.

"Golf Is My Therapy" it reads.

"I know that golf has been his lifeline, and I am so grateful for that," says Dr. Reno. "Every patient needs a passion that lights up his life. Without golf, Walter's life would be much emptier and difficult."

Where did it come from?

Donaldson is asked that question as he tees up on a fifth hole that does not have a tee box or markers. After all these years, he knows exactly where to start.

"Golf is struggle, but if you work hard enough, you can achieve something in it," he says. "I need that. I need something I can work for. Something I can accomplish."

Golf is the quietest thing in his life. It is the most consistent event of his day. It does not criticize or judge. Golf is one of the few things that allows Donaldson to be happy with who he is.

Twenty-seven years, and only once has he even stepped on a different course. It was recently, when he accompanied a group of VA members to an eighteen-hole course in the Valley. Donaldson never left the driving range.

"I didn't feel right," he says. "It wasn't me."

Sixth Hole

Late last summer, a teenage boy and his mother stopped by the VA for the best deal in town, a quick round of golf for eight bucks a person.

As they were standing on the first tee, up walked a lanky, gray-haired man with a wandering tongue and mottled speech.

"He said, 'Mind if I join you?'" Margaret Foster Dubbins recalls. "It was a little scary," Andrew Dubbins, now fourteen, says.

Not knowing the course, and not being very good at the game, they agreed to let him join. An hour later, there were tears in the mother's eyes. Donaldson had worked his strange magic.

"It was an amazing experience," Margaret Foster Dubbins recalls.

Donaldson accompanied them around the course, telling them about his past, giving tips about the game, showing them every nook and cranny in the landscape and his life.

Recounting the round on the drive home, the boy became so moved that the mother encouraged him to write about it.

So Andrew Dubbins, now an eighth-grader at Corpus Christi school in Pacific Palisades, wrote me an essay about his experience.

On the sixth hole during our round, I ask Walter about Andrew. "What a nice boy," he says while sinking a par putt. "Young people today, they don't listen. That was a boy who listens."

Seventh Hole

With several groundskeepers watching on the seventh tee, Donaldson skulls his tee shot.

He smiles, waves to them, walks toward his ball. "Golf teaches you to handle anything," he says.

I walk ahead to my ball. A few minutes later, he joins me. After he sinks his putt, I pull out the scorecard.

"A four?" I say.

"A five," he says.

Eighth Hole

He has never shot better than a 29 on this par-27 course.

But as Donaldson deftly places his eighth tee shot close to the cup, he mentions that he has done something that few people have done in a lifetime.

And he has done it twice.

"Two holes in ones!" he exclaims.

Both were in 1987. One was in a club tournament, the other was during a daily round. In neither case did he save the ball.

"The club gave me the ball when I started the round," he says. "After I finished, I turned it back in. It was their ball."

Ninth Hole

At the edge of the ninth tee box is a club-handle monument to the course's former golf volunteer instructor, Anthony "Tony" Costello.

He first showed Donaldson the game. He has since died. Before Donaldson tees off here, he walks to the monument, puts his hands around the club handle, and bows his head.

"This game saved my life from destruction," he says. "I will never forget the man who taught me."

He finishes the round by sinking a forty-foot birdie putt, howling in glee, shaking the hand of his playing partner.

When the round started, I thought I could beat this crooked old man by a dozen strokes.

Turns out, he beat me by five.

I tell him this as he sits back on a picnic bench and carefully sticks his borrowed shoes into his dumpster golf bag.

"Oh yeah?" says Walter Donaldson, looking confused for the first time this morning. "I didn't know we were keeping score."

JOSH SENS

Good Karma, Bad Golf

FROM GOLF DIGEST

WHEN HE WAS SEVEN years old, living in a remote mountain village in Tibet, Losang Kunga Gyurme was identified by religious visionaries as the reincarnation of an eleventh-century lama. So he's got that going for him.

What he doesn't have going is his iron game. He's chewing up the fairway of a short par 4 at Stone Tree Golf Club in Novato, California — a wire-framed, wildly flailing figure in a saffron robe.

"That last shot had too much ego," he says. "This time, I need to clear my mind."

He clears his mind, but his 7-iron shot doesn't clear the water. Triple bogey for the man known today as Lama Kunga Rinpoche, esteemed Buddhist teacher and also a devoted student of the links.

In a game overrun with self-proclaimed gurus, Lama Kunga is the real McCoy, a spiritual guide dispatched to this country by the Dalai Lama to lead disciples toward enlightenment. That's one of his missions. His other: seeking out fairways and greens.

"Golf is a nice game, the best game," Lama Kunga says. "To play well, you need to let your expectations go."

The lama had agreed to an afternoon round at the swank course despite its strict dress code: no jeans, no tank tops. They don't have a policy on yellow robes.

I'd picked him up at his place, a large house that doubles as a meditation center, with views of the Golden Gate Bridge. He's a monkish sixty-five-year-old with buzzed gray hair and a Larry Mize build. There were piles of plush pillows, a colorful shrine, and an oversize snapshot of Lama Kunga's close friend, the Dalai Lama.

"No, the Dalai Lama does not play golf," says Lama Kunga. He looks disappointed. Last year, when the Dalai Lama was visiting the Bay Area, Lama Kunga considered dragging him to the driving range. Then he thought better of it. "One day I will say, 'Your Holiness, I would like to tell you about golf,'" Lama Kunga says. "He will be happy to know I play. He is very busy making the world a better place, but I think he could use the exercise."

On the way to the course, the lama expounds on the link between golf and Buddhism. In both religions, one comes face to face with the Four Noble Truths. The first truth holds that suffering is unavoidable.

"The second," the lama says, "is that the origins of suffering come from anger, frustrations, self-consciousness. If you play golf, you know what I mean." (The third and fourth truths may not fix your slice, but they do explain how to get rid of all this pesky suffering.)

Just then, the transmission in my Geo begins to suffer. We hit a congested merge, but the stick is stuck. A big rig roars behind us, blaring its horn. But the lama stays serene, gazing peacefully over the dashboard. "I'm sorry," I say. "I'd hate to be responsible for the death of a high lama."

"That would be bad karma," he replies. I can't tell if he's making a pun.

We sputter the rest of the way in the breakdown lane. Outside the course entrance, the car gasps and dies. I get out and push. The lama steers. When we park, I kick the tires and curse.

"If it can be fixed, it is not a problem," says the lama. "If it cannot be fixed, it is not a problem." He is sounding a lot like my mechanic. Still, he's right. The sun is shining. We're playing golf.

We're joined by Brian "Big Dog" Soczka, a local pro known for his prodigious length, who begins the proceedings with a Himalayan drive three hundred yards down the fairway. The lama pull-hooks his ball into the weeds — the golf equivalent of yin and yank.

What is the sound of one man hacking? You learn the answer quickly when you play with Lama Kunga. He first picked up a club at age fifty-seven while visiting Sweden on a spiritual mission. One pure show was enough to hook him. He took a lesson, learned a few fundamentals. Someone told him to visualize his shots, a simple hint that didn't help at all.

"To me, golf is 90 percent physical," says the lama. "Mentally I am very strong. How do you explain that my best score is 97?"

If only he had started younger. But there was no golf in tiny Black Horse village, where Lama Kunga was raised. When he was still knee-high to Willie Wood, members of a spiritual search-party showed up at his door. The child, they said, was the reincarnation of Sevanrepa, a disciple of Milarepa, the revered poet and lama who had lived nine hundred years before. He was whisked off to a monastery, ordained, and was serving as an abbot in 1959 when the Chinese invaded Tibet. Three years later, on orders from the Dalai Lama, he fled to the United States. He settled in New Jersey ("Very cold," he says), then moved to California, where he now tees it up several times a week. He never bets and rarely keeps score. Most days, he shows up as a single at a public track and introduces himself as George.

Although Buddha recommended the Middle Path, on the course Lama Kunga rarely takes it. Now and then, he admits, he feels the seeds of golf frustration growing inside him, but he chuckles at barbarians who fling their putters and snap their sand wedges. "They have not achieved consciousness yet," he says.

Soczka, meanwhile, is flat-out unconscious, blistering his drives and stiffing his irons. On the thirteenth green, he turns to the lama: "If you hit a good shot, does that mean you have good karma?"

Lama Kunga embarks on an elaborate description of the thirteen stages of enlightenment. A good shot, he says, doesn't necessarily imply good karma, but it can represent a small "rebirth."

On the fourteenth hole, the lama skids his drive into the trees, then drops another in the fairway without adding a stroke. His next shot plops in the bunker. A fried-egg lie. But the lama improves it.

"Would the Buddha say it's okay to move your ball?" I ask.

"Sure," the lama grins. "Why not?"

On the fifteenth tee, Soczka strolls over to the lama. "Try releasing your hands," he says. "Fire through at impact. Finish high."

The lama uncorks a beauty. He pumps his fist. There they stand, the golf pro and the guru, exchanging high-fives. It's a giddy moment, and Soczka can't resist the Caddyshack comment.

"Hey, lama," he says, in his best Bill Murray. "How about a little something, you know, for the effort?"

But the lama is unacquainted with the movie. So Soczka fills him in on the famous routine: how the Dalai Lama, instead of paying his caddie, promises him total consciousness.

"Yes, yes, very funny," says the lama. "I will have to rent that movie. And if you'd like total consciousness, you can have it. Why not?"

The round winds down. Soczka closes birdie-par-birdie. No one's keeping track of the lama's score, least of all the lama. If he makes bogey, it is not a problem. If he makes double bogey, it is not a problem.

I call for a tow truck. The lama lays a hand on my shoulder. "Don't worry about your car," he says. "Let go of your expectations. That is very important."

"Maybe one day my car will be reborn with a new transmission," I suggest.

The lama looks doubtful.

"I don't know about that," he says. "But I would like to be reincarnated as a better golfer some day."

ELIZABETH KAYE

Servant of the Cause

FROM LOS ANGELES

1. PJ at Fifty-six He speaks of matters he has lately experienced. "The luster of watching your hair recede." "Beginning to see the end of who you are." "This light my mother had about her just before she died." Each is or was, he says, "a very interesting process to watch."

Note the usage: *process,* with its suggestion of inevitability; the clinical ring of *interesting.* Do not expect him to linger on the tyranny of limits. What engages him is possibility. That's the way it's always been. At fifty-six, a man is who he is.

2. At the Bar in the Best Hotel in Portland PJ considers a double vodka straight up, orders vodka with cranberry juice. It's nearing midnight. He feels as worn as his sweater but doesn't dwell on this.

On the next bar stool, Steve Kerr nurses a club soda. Kerr played on PJ's Bulls during the championship runs of '96, '97, '98. He's the all-time three-point shooter, blond, blue-eyed, a white American in a sport where whites are generally coaches or Eastern Europeans. Like PJ, Kerr views the game with a certain impartiality despite his devotion to it or, perhaps, because of it. He now plays for the Portland Trail Blazers, the Lakers' nemesis and the team that will beat them tomorrow.

PJ asks about Kerr's children. He hasn't seen them in a while but remembers names, ages, hobbies. Kerr's oldest son plays basketball. PJ is delighted. How tall is he? he asks. Is he a shooter? It's a conversation between friends but not equals. Even in a hotel bar, PJ does not — possibly cannot — relinquish the standing of teacher.

Someone taps PJ's shoulder. It's Bill Walton, sports analyst, former thorn in the side of the Knicks teams PJ played on in the 1970s. Walton's presence stirs PJ's competitive juices. But then, they are easily stirred.

"What sign are you?" PJ asks.

"Virgo," says Walton. "What are you?"

"I don't have a sign," says PJ.

PJ recounts the night he scored twenty-four points for the Nets.

"I didn't remember you played for New Jersey," says Walton.

"Another night," says PJ, "I went for a steal and missed. They took the ball down fast and scored on the other end."

Yes, he still is chewing over a botched play from the 1970s. This amazes Kerr but doesn't surprise him. That's Phil, he thinks. Ten championship rings, and he's pissed off by a missed steal in an unimportant game, thirty years ago.

3. PJ's Fact Sheet PROFESSIONAL: Player, New York Knicks (1967–78). Player/Assistant Coach, New Jersey Nets (1978–80). Head Coach, CBA Albany Patroons (1982–87). Head Coach, Chicago Bulls (1989–98). Head Coach, Los Angeles Lakers (1999–present).

AS PLAYER: Two championships. AS COACH: Best record in regular season (Bulls, 1995–96). Best record in postseason (Lakers, 2000–2001). Highest career winning percentage. Only coach to win multiple championships with two different teams. Eight championships, second only to storied coach Red Auerbach of the Boston Celtics.

PERSONAL: Two marriages, five children, twice divorced.

4. PJ in Public He makes his way from the isolation of the coaches' room through the tunnel that leads to the Staples Center court. He looks neither left nor right. People strain across railings, reach out to slap hands, to touch him. He does not want to be touched. At this juncture, it can only deplete his energy.

If this gives offense, so be it. His fate is to be lionized by some, pilloried by others, granted no turf in the middle ground. They say: he is a genius, an inspirational leader. They say: he is the naked emperor leading the parade, purporting to be covered in finery.

5. Why They Dislike Him Reporters tend to dislike him because he tends to dislike them. It's not that he ignores them; he doesn't seem to see them. He addresses them when he must: before games and after, often with the resigned, dutiful air of a man seasoning a meal he has no interest in eating.

Still, the press can suit his purposes. Tell them Kobe is pushing too hard or that Shaq isn't pushing hard enough, and they will dispense the information, creating awareness of the problem among the public and the players. The press resents being used but cannot show their resentment, which they also resent.

His first season in Los Angeles, the Lakers play on Christmas Day. He meets with the press, does not wish them Merry Christmas. On Mother's Day he greets them by saying, "Happy Mother's Day to all you mothers."

6. *Why They Love Him*   The Laker players he most often seeks out are Brian Shaw and Rick Fox. Both are veterans known for being fair-minded, centered, perceptive.

Shaw: "He's not just giving us basketball knowledge. He opens up all kinds of areas. You come to practice thinking, 'What's he going to teach me, what's he going to show me?'"

Fox: "He shows men how to be men. What I picked up is that having control over myself, having a focus, a growth process, translates into being a better basketball player. No coach ever told me that. No coach ever took the time to know me. Look at all the guys who've played on his teams. They seem to be on a greater plane mentally. That's because he gives them a greater understanding of themselves."

Shaw: "When he was having us do yoga and Tai Chi, everybody kind of looked at each other at first and said, *He's crazy.* Then you see it's broadening your horizons. Then you get a sixteen-game winning streak, and everybody's saying, *Damn, he does know what he's talking about.*

7. *PJ in Private*   He eats Chinese food, listens to bluegrass, plays Scrabble on the beach. He cooks. He reads constantly, mostly contemporary fiction. He is not interested in parties, premieres, and other staples of the local scene. Can the term "homebody" apply to a man who spends weekends, holidays, and at least eighty-two nights a year in a packed arena? If so, PJ is a homebody.

Then there is Jeanie, whom he has in mind when saying, "It's nice to have someone to share life with." Jeanie Buss is the Lakers' executive vice president of business operations. Also the daughter of Dr. Jerry Buss, the team's owner.

When PJ joins the Lakers, the attraction is instant. She's charmed, but smart and experienced enough to be a bit wary of a man newly separated from his wife. "You know in that situation," she says, "that this person's heart is not fully there." The liaison, in conventional terms, is dicey. Before asking her out, PJ asks for Dr. Buss's blessing.

There is about Jeanie a sunniness, which he admires but does not possess. During games she sits across the court in his line of vision. He wants to be able to see her.

"What I bring to him," she says, "is that my feelings for him are unconditional. I understand the business he's in. I've seen couples get eaten up by this industry. The relationships are intense, then the other party leaves for a week. And then you've got to get back together and get back to where you were, but then they leave again. It causes a lot of turmoil. What makes us work is that I really just want to make his life as simple as possible. Things that *can* be made simple.

"I just like to hear him laugh. He's just so kissable and lovable. And I don't think anyone really ever told him that."

Minutes before a game they are observed kissing in the tunnel. At this juncture, it can only increase his energy.

8. How Jeanie Knows Something Is on His Mind   He bakes cookies. Kitchen drawers open; measuring spoons, cups, eggs, and sugar materialize on counters. Can it be that baking is an antidote to uncertainty in general and the uncertainty of coaching in particular? He prepares a batter, adds ingredients by half-cups and quarter-teaspoons. Coaching has no such formula. In many respects it is impervious to laws of cause and effect. Use the finest ingredients with the greatest care and still you cannot predict the outcome. He likes that, of course. Ultimately, the formulaic is tedious. Perhaps that is why he improvises with mixed batter, tossing into it, in unspecified quantities, nuts, raisins, oatmeal, chocolate chips.

9. PJ Defined by Steve Kerr   "He's a paradox."

As proof Kerr cites the Bulls' motto: never take less than success, yet don't let success go to your head.

He cites the saying PJ posted in the team room: treat your job and every day at work as if the fate of the world depended on it, but remember that nobody cares.

"He's obsessed with basketball," Kerr says, "yet doesn't let it consume him." But because PJ is a paradox, Kerr also recalls the satellite dish he installed outside his home in Chicago. "He'd come to practice and ask stuff like, 'Did any of you guys see that Clippers-Vancouver game last night?' We'd look at him like, *You gotta be kidding.*"

10. Baseboards   He believes that people operate from a basic premise. He calls these premises "baseboards."

PJ's baseboard: being raised in rural North Dakota by a mother and father who were ministers in the Pentecostal church. Pentecostals speak in tongues, believe this signifies possession by the Holy Spirit. They do not drink, smoke, dance, watch movies or television. They believe the day of judgment is imminent.

"My mother had this message," he says. "It was a Second Coming message. When I was just a wee little kid, Israel became a state. This meant the Rapture was close. We were warned to be watchful, ready."

He came home from school one afternoon and found no one there. He was sure the Rapture had taken place, that his parents and two brothers had ascended to heaven and left him alone on the imperfect earth.

11. PJ Enumerates Three Things That Shaped Him   "There's the religion. The severity of it.

"There's the austerity about life. The workmanlike approach that my parents had to it. You work real hard to do what you have to do.

"There's the fact that my parents gave their lives over to a cause. So your family's dedicated to it, you're dedicated to it. Your own needs don't matter. You're taught to be a servant of the cause.

"Those are the overwhelming things."

12. PJ in Wonder   He is an outsider, a preacher's kid. His activities are the few his church deems wholesome: school plays, orchestra, choir, also sports and reading. Basketball and baseball allow him to enter the bounds of normalcy. Reading allows him to exceed those bounds.

"By sixth grade I was taking books out of the library two or three times a week. Books became a reality to me.

"Books that mattered were Hemingway — *The Sun Also Rises, For Whom the Bell Tolls,* such a difficult book to read. *The Catcher in the Rye.* Those books opened up a sense of wonderment. Abortion. I had never thought of the concept of abortion."

13. Bones Anatomy is fate. In high school PJ grows to six-foot-six. Later he grows two more inches. He's so skinny his classmates call him "Bones." He is athletic. Agile. Has remarkably long arms. He wants to get out of Williston, North Dakota. "I was always looking off to other areas," he says. "New York City would be an experience I couldn't wait to have."

He wins a basketball scholarship to the University of North Dakota. In his junior year he averages 21.8 points a game. He's team captain, two-time All-American.

He reads two novels by the Greek writer Nikos Kazantzakis: "*Zorba the Greek* is about breaking free, about a guy who's controlled by his religious background. That this guy could live life so riotously was astounding. *The Last Temptation of Christ* opened up a door to understanding the human side of Christ, the man who lived expressively, instinctively."

What must Zorba's cry "To dance!" convey to a young man to whom dancing is forbidden? What hope does Christ's spontaneity represent to a young man who has had to suppress every impulse?

"By my religion, by my background, I had so many ideas ingrained in me. To break free, it took more than just living free like Zorba."

He graduates in 1967. He's drafted by the Knicks, the seventeenth pick overall. At last he's in New York City. Yet breaking free produces a certain ambivalence. When he stops playing basketball, he tells his coach, he's going to be a minister.

14. PJ As Number 18 He comes off the bench, plays an energetic game. He's not much of a scorer, but he's quick and tough enough to be nicknamed "Action Jackson." He likes rebounding and shot-blocking, things that help the team but get less attention than scoring.

PJ is quite a sight. He has bad teeth, a fuzzy beard. He yearns to be part of his generation, to do what he's never done: belong. He lives in a loft, has a Spiro Agnew dartboard. He opposes the war in Vietnam, practices yoga, describes his game as "rolling with the flow." Still. The counterculture's excesses make him uneasy. His shoulder-length hair makes his teammates uneasy. In the era's parlance, belonging is not his thing.

15. PJ Finds His Faith   "The fight I had as a Christian, when I stayed inside the Christian domain, is that it's so overwhelmed with guilt, your sins, and your crude sins. We missed out on the grace aspect, which is what the Christ brought. It's the same thing with Buddhism. It's not asceticism. Buddhism is compassion. Christ is grace and love. I thought, these are the illuminating lights of East/ West culture, the liberation from all these thousands of years of a belief structure that's about guilt and punishment. That really made sense to me. So that's how I came to the idea that I could be a Zen Christian."

16. Harbingers of His Future   The Knicks' coach, Red Holzman, is wise, fabled. PJ asks him, "How do you see the whole game?"

Holzman is not asked this question often. After games, he takes to asking PJ, "What did you see?"

PJ sees plenty. He sees that Holzman's player and ball movement and emphasis on defense propel the Knicks to two championships. He sees that Holzman's credo of team unity elevates basketball into something more than a game. When a back injury sidelines him for a season, he becomes Holzman's unofficial assistant. "You could coach this game," Holzman tells him.

Eleven years go by. It is time to let go of his life as a player. He grapples with the painful, predictable process he will call "the death of the professional athlete." He considers becoming a lawyer or a professor of philosophy or religion. A career guidance test affirms his aptitude in these areas; it also notes he'd do well as a trail guide or a homemaker.

In the end, it's all beside the point. "The game kept calling me back," he says.

17. PJ Doesn't Get the Job   PJ interviews to be an assistant to the Bulls' head coach, Stan Albeck. He shows up in a garish shirt, a Panama hat with a feather protruding from the brim. Albeck passes. The Nets' coach, Larry Brown, also passes.

It seems that PJ's bohemian bent is too, well, bohemian for the NBA. The Continental Basketball Association, the sport's minor league, is a different story. He signs on with the Albany Patroons, makes $26,000 a year, wins a championship. He waits for someone to recognize that what qualifies him to be a coach are the same idiosyncrasies that make people think he's not NBA material. He waits for five years. The person who recognizes this is Jerry Krause, general manager of the Chicago Bulls. PJ is hired as an assistant coach. It's 1987. The Bulls are recruiting gifted players to serve as planets revolving around the sun that is the twenty-four-year-old Michael Jordan.

Scottie Pippen is in his rookie year. He's worked hard, made his way out of the rural South. He's introverted, doesn't trust easily. Like his teammates, he's leery of the head coach, Doug Collins. "He would come in the locker room at halftime," says Pippen, "looking like he played the whole first half. Take his jacket off. Be soaking wet. Screamed at everybody on the court. Except for Michael."

PJ at forty-two is the Un-Collins, prematurely tranquil and wise. He's assigned to work with Pippen. "Soon as I laid eyes on him," says Pippen, "we had an automatic bond." PJ plays one-on-one with him to refine his shooting. He gives Pippen an understanding of the game: how to discern the moment of truth, how to get the whole picture right in front of you. PJ asks him, "What are you thinking? How can you help the team?" He asks the question Holzman asked him: "What do you see?" Like PJ before him, Pippen sees plenty.

Pippen will cherish this training. "It's one of those things," he says, "that you can't put a price on." He will go on to be one of the greatest players in the game.

18. PJ Takes Over   It's 1989. Collins has lost the ear of his players. PJ gets the job. He wonders if he's ready to coach an NBA team.

He instills toughness of mind, collective attitude; he teaches yoga, meditation, breathing together. His great strength is knowing his weaknesses. He's not an accomplished offensive coach. His assistant coach Tex Winter is. Winter developed a system known as the triangle offense. It calls for sharing the ball, passing to the open man. It's an egalitarian system that animates PJ's concept of a team as a community of players. He calls the triangle "five-man Tai Chi." For a coach who sees the game as an act of body, spirit, and mind, it's the ideal system.

19. Rick Fox Considers PJ and His Wiles   "I watch him during the regular season. He'll run the same play the whole quarter. I can tell that he's not going to show anything to the other team. He's just baiting those guys. He cares whether we win or lose. But he'll even tell you sometimes it's not best to win right now. When he's trying to win a game, he dictates the whole action.

"A lot of coaches have the focus: *I gotta make the playoffs or make the second round.* He coaches the regular season with the mentality of: *I gotta find out who responds well to what situations.*

"This game is about setting your opponent up to think they can stop you a certain way. So he'll call a solo to Shaq, which is just dump the ball in to Shaq. We'll run 20, 30 percent of the game solo. It's laughable. Because all he does in the locker room and at practice is scream about how we can't just dump the ball in to Shaq. Other teams get a false sense of security. They think, *Oh we got it figured out now.* Then you come out in the playoffs and just blitz them, and they're going, *What happened? We thought we had it figured out.*"

20. Defining Moment Number One   It's 1991. The Bulls make it to the finals. Their opponent is Magic Johnson's Lakers. The Lakers think they've got it figured out. "The pressure's on," says PJ. "You're not supposed to win. Don't play that way. Go out there and seize it."

It's a best-of-seven series. It's tied at 1–1 when the Bulls arrive in Los Angeles for three games.

At the start of the series PJ tells Jordan to look for John Paxson, a three-point shooter who's getting open when Jordan draws a double team. Instead, Jordan does it all himself, forgets his teammates. They win game 3, game 4. They're one win away from the title. In game 5, with six minutes left, they're down by one. PJ calls, "Who's open, Michael?"

Jordan ignores him.

"Who's open?" PJ calls. It's turning into a showdown, which PJ generally avoids. Especially with a brilliant, impetuous player known to retaliate when backed into a corner.

PJ calls again, "Michael, who's open?"

"Pax," says Jordan.

Then get him the fucking ball.

Jordan gets Pax the fucking ball. Paxson scores ten points in four minutes. In the final seconds, with the Bulls up by two, Jordan gets the ball. He doesn't head to the basket. He moves across the court. PJ wonders what he's doing. He realizes he's looking for Paxson. He finds him. Paxson hits a three. PJ becomes one of nine men in NBA history to win rings for coaching and for playing.

"That kid is a great coach," says Red Holzman.

21. *Defining Moment Number Two* It's 1994. Jordan is on his baseball sabbatical. Pippen and the Bulls' center, Bill Cartwright, carry the team through the regular season. Pippen helps and encourages other players. PJ's pride in him is, he says, "almost parental." Going into the playoffs, Pippen is a leading contender for league MVP.

The Bulls and the Knicks are tied 102–102 at the end of the third game of the Eastern Conference finals. With 26.6 seconds to play, PJ calls a play for Pippen.

"I said, 'Take the clock all the way down. Shoot the shot at the end of the buzzer. Whatever happens, the Knicks won't have recourse.' So Scottie was taking the ball down, and we cleared the side out. But Toni Kukoc ran back into the cleared side, which meant that Scottie had to back out and shoot a three that didn't hit the basket. So now the Knicks had two and a half seconds. They scored in two seconds. We had six-tenths of a second to play. Toni's screwup had cost us what Scottie thought was a win. I designed the last play for Toni, and that put Scottie over the edge."

The Bulls head onto the court. Pippen refuses to go back to the game. PJ is staggered. He can't believe it. He turns to his assistant coach Jim Cleamons. "What do I do?" he asks.

"Fuck him. We play without him," says Cleamons.

Kukoc makes the shot. The Bulls win. Pippen has relinquished his claim to be MVP.

PJ knows Pippen must be called to account. But who should confront him? "Players *expect* to be confronted by their coach. Their defenses are already walled in. They're ready to reject what you have to say."

In the locker room Bill Cartwright is sobbing. All season he's preached unity and teamwork, the principles that Pippen violated. "I can't believe he did that," Cartwright is saying.

PJ decides that the resolution of this situation must be left to Pippen's peers. He tells the team that Pippen must answer to them. Before he leaves the locker room, he gathers all the players together and leads them in the Lord's Prayer.

22. *The Price of the Game Number One*   PJ is of the players' world but not part of it. This is as it ought to be. They are all ballplayers, a natural bond, but he cannot allow this to interfere with his objectivity, his need to get the job done. "If you're in this basketball life, you can't just cry because somebody broke their leg or got left in battle. You've got to go on. That's just part of it."

Coaching is not without occupational hazards. "Through the pressures of the job," says Jeanie, "he really built a wall around himself."

He grows accustomed to the wall, feels — perhaps — safe behind it, takes it other places. Has PJ read Robert Frost on the subject of walls? "Before I built a wall I'd ask to know / What I was walling in or walling out."

Or are the dangers inherent in walls of interest only to poets?

One spring PJ's youngest daughter writes a poem about him. "I'm home and the playoffs were on, and her high school graduation was coming, and she makes a comment, and I say, 'Oh, that's nice, dear,' and walk out of the room. I was probably thinking about how I could play the screen-and-roll against the Knicks. I couldn't be there in the moment with her. That poem cut through everything. It was very painful."

23. *PJ Leaves the Bulls*   It's 1998. He knows a lot about winning. This is his time to learn about loss.

After twenty years, his second marriage is fragmenting. His eleven-year tenure with the Bulls has soured. Some of this is his fault; some comes with the territory. The NBA life is tough on wives. The Bulls' general manager, Jerry Krause, begrudges PJ his legend, bandies about the slogan "Management wins championships."

PJ calls his team together for a farewell ceremony. In seven years they have won six NBA titles. He asks them to write a few words about what being on the team has meant. One by one, they read them. They do what guys don't do: they say they love each other. When they finish their testimonials, they burn them in a coffee can.

24. The Price of the Game Number Two   For the first time in sixteen years PJ is not coaching. The servant has no cause. His players wonder what will happen to him. "He doesn't just love the game," says Steve Kerr, "he depends on it, really."

After years of cheering, PJ is left to silence. The silence prompts him to seek deeper silence. "I spent a month at a monastery," he says. "I didn't make it through. Actually, the relationship with my wife was in such a place that it was too difficult for me to settle in."

In the next months he considers feelers from several teams. His wife's reaction is unambiguous. "It let me know that if I went back to coaching, that would make it difficult for our relationship to continue."

For years PJ has had to have the answers for his players. He would speak of the value of recognizing feelings and sharing them. And yet: "When someone had a conflict with me," he says, "if they asked, 'What do you feel?' I would come up pretty empty."

Had you asked what he wanted, he would have said: "to emotionally connect, to listen, love, converse, care." Does he lack the vitality to bring these desires into being? "I guess," he says, "when you're in the heat of a breakup situation all those things are in doubt."

PJ has things to do but has no purpose. He does organizing for Bill Bradley's presidential campaign, gives motivational talks. "The inactivity was just so stifling," he says. "It was almost a matter of not paying allegiance to a way of life, to a gift I have that, if not used, would be atrophied."

Note the *almost,* a qualifier orphaned in a phrase that is otherwise unequivocal.

25. PJ Decides   PJ gets an offer from the Lakers. He knows what it will cost him. He also knows that he can't live without a goal, a passion. Before leaving for Los Angeles, he takes his twin sons fishing in Alaska; the trip gives him hope that his children will not be lost to him. His marriage is another story.

"I invited my wife to join me in Los Angeles if she wanted to." She doesn't want to.

His sorrow is pervasive. He will learn from it as he has learned, in the game, from loss of another sort. What is the precise cause of his sorrow? Does he grieve because of what he has lost or because, in the end, he was willing to lose it? He drives to Los Angeles from

Montana, listening to a tape his daughters made for him. It's filled with songs about loving again, starting over. Somewhere in the Sierra Nevada, he pulls off the road and cries.

In time he will say of his wife, "She was right about not joining me."

26. *PJ and the Lakers*   The Lakers he inherits are a morass of underachievement, of egos either too bruised or too assertive. He is the morass's designated savior, contracted for five years to perform miracles at the annual rate of $6 million.

He's come to the Lakers an NBA legend, has kids older than Kobe Bryant. With the Bulls it was different: he grew up with those guys. The first day of training camp he challenges each player. Shaq needs to work harder; Kobe needs to mature; Glen Rice needs to get in shape; Robert Horry needs to get back to the level he played on with the championship Houston Rockets.

There's just one problem: the players are gazing at the ceiling, at the floor, fiddling with their fingers. The most intellectual coach in the NBA has, it appears, unwittingly signed on to give remedial courses. "Stop what you're doing," he says. "Check your breath. Focus on what I'm saying."

27. *PJ and His Pupil*   The Lakers go 67–15 in the regular season. They make it to the 1999–2000 Western Conference finals. Their opponent is the Portland Trail Blazers.

The Blazers' new forward is Scottie Pippen. They're counting on Pippen to get them to the finals, though no player knows better that championships are not won by a single man. Even Jordan did not win with the Bulls, Pippen would say on occasion, until he and Phil got there. Now it has come full circle: the coach and his pupil are about to vie for their first ring without Jordan.

The series goes to game 7. In the fourth quarter the Blazers are up by fifteen. The prize is within Pippen's grasp. The Lakers surge. The Blazers are drained. Pippen fouls out. As the clock winds down he stands on the sidelines, rueful, suddenly defeated, as if making of himself a sacrificial offering. He is fierce, yes, not lacking in killer instinct. But there is in him a quality seen rarely in great athletes, something raw, even poetic, that has always intrigued PJ and moved him.

In sports each game ends in a small death and a small victory. On this night the father wins by killing the son. This is not the ending PJ would have chosen. He made no secret when he came to the Lakers that Pippen was the player he most wanted for the team.

"Yes," says Pippen, "we wanted each other."

28. Defining Moment Number Three The World Champion Los Angeles Lakers descend into operatics. Soon into the 2000–2001 season even the most casual sports fans know that the Lakers' much-lauded marquee players are not happy. Shaquille O'Neal and Kobe Bryant are the most gifted players of their generation, on the shortlist of the most gifted ever. That each is jockeying to be the team's dominant player is not altogether surprising.

To the degree that their rivalry is about what constitutes a leader, it is a battle over philosophy. Does leadership fall, by definition, to the player currently posting the biggest numbers? If so, Bryant is the leader. Does it belong to the player the coach designates as the offense's first option? If so, the leader is O'Neal. Or should it fall to the player absorbed not with his own accomplishment or privilege but with the welfare of the team? If so, the leader is Derek Fisher.

Weeks pass. O'Neal and Bryant become each other's leading opponent. The Lakers lose games, become the franchise in which the most riveting battle is the psychological mismatch between its leading players.

A reporter takes notes as Bryant speculates about playing elsewhere. Others position their recorders inches from O'Neal's mouth as he grumbles, "If the big dog ain't me, then the house don't get guarded. Period."

Their words turn up on newscasts and front pages. PJ is not pleased. Meeting with errant, meddling reporters, his eyes go narrow and cold behind the glasses. He is the coach as biblical prophet, daunting, imperious, towering, shoulders wide as an eagle's wings. "This isn't your business," he says. "It's our business."

His anger is proportionate to what is at stake: the vital quality of mind he calls team wellness, a curious term, but PJ is of the New Age. For wellness to exist, each man must be unselfish. How many teams lost their chance for a championship over petty carping forgotten long before the varnish darkened on the trophy of the winner?

He considers the options, sees two: Do something. Do nothing.

He would do something, provided that the something was effective. He can tell the players about the Native American custom of judging a person's wealth not by what they have but by what they give. He can tell them, "The more you give, the richer you are." But he cannot compel players into wellness.

He tells himself, "I have to give up my own desire to want to solve it."

He tells the team, "I have to step back and let you guys do this."

He does not expect anyone to apprehend that doing nothing is a decisive action.

29. A Death   "My mother became a minister at twenty-two. There was a fervor about her. She had great presence. She lived her life like a warrior ready to do battle with Satan.

"In the end my mother was almost eighty-five. She lived in a nursing home. She didn't know her sons when we walked in to see her. She didn't know about rapture. She didn't know about praying over the food before she ate. Yet there was still a brilliant presence to her. She comforted other ladies who were crying. There was this light about her. She said, 'I'm ready to go. I want to go home.'"

She dies in the summer of 2001 while he is at training camp. After the funeral he rejoins the team. "You could tell he wanted to see us," says Rick Fox. "I could see how drained he was, how emotional he was. He has such a persona. He's reached a level that so many other people haven't. It's almost as though he's figured everything out. So in that sense, to see him on a level that's human, to have that pain and have that sorrow . . ."

30. A Eulogy   "My mother had a style that was unique. Hats were in when I was a kid. She made her own hats out of a variety of things. One day we were out driving. My father hit a pheasant on the road. She made him go back and get the pheasant. It was a male bird. Its feathers were brilliant, beautiful. She made them into a hat, sort of a skullcap. She had that ability to turn something that we look at as a shame into something beautiful and meaningful."

The last year of his mother's life was also the year his leading players feuded, the year he witnessed the dispiriting sight of his team imploding. When they resurrected themselves, it was in large measure because of what he gave them: room to learn from error, the understanding that their chances for victory were equal to the vigor with which they fused themselves into a community. When they came together at the last breath of the season, their game was an exercise in flow and harmony. Their eventual victory was a triumph of spirit.

You see that he is his mother's son. He, too, has the ability to turn something that we look at as a shame into something of meaning and beauty.

31. New Season PJ maintains that players are coachable only when they have some success and some failure. The two-time World Champion Lakers begin the 2001–2002 season with seven straight wins.

"That was a great streak," says PJ's agent, Todd Musburger.

"Yes," says PJ, "and I'm damn happy it's over."

The season is oddly quiet. Events are difficult to interpret, elusive, as if played out underwater. There is, it seems, a hangover from the drama of last season's Bryant-O'Neal colloquy. This year's Lakers are subdued, chastened; they are in drama recovery. Early on, O'Neal flirts with old ways, hints of problems between PJ and himself, then abandons the topic. Perhaps he thinks better of it; perhaps he realizes that, weeks after September 11, nobody cares about the complaints of a man in reasonable health making more than $20 million a year.

The Lakers are a different team. Gone are Horace Grant and Ron Harper, grown men in a man's game, the last of PJ's Chicago Bulls to play for the Lakers. Without them, something is missing. The team is preoccupied with personal matters: O'Neal by an arthritic toe, Bryant by a new marriage, Horry by the limitations of a body that looks, PJ will say, "like it belongs to three different people." They beat good teams, lose to every bottom dweller in the league. Often they seem bored by the regular season.

Bryant and O'Neal lash out at demons, real and imagined. Fists fly; technical fouls are assessed, suspensions levied. They demonstrate solidarity, wearing, on jerseys and sneakers, their ousted comrade's number. This signals an obvious change. Other changes are less visible. Last season PJ gave Bryant a book, *Corelli's Mandolin*, the story of an Italian soldier who falls in love and ceases to be an outsider. PJ gives books to all of his players. They are his way of saying, I know who you are and what matters to you. Bryant's novel suited a young man raised in Italy, about to get married, and resistant to the community of the team. "You know I'm not going to read it, man," Bryant said at the time.

PJ got the message. "He doesn't want anyone else's ideas to penetrate his mind," he said.

O'Neal's book for last season, *Siddhartha*, is about the redemptive power of choosing love over hatred. O'Neal read it reluctantly. "Why does Phil keep giving me these Harvard books?" he asked. "He knows I don't have a big vocabulary."

That was then. Midway into the season O'Neal takes a swing at the Bulls' Brad Miller, gets ejected from the game. He waits for the team on the bus. While he waits, he reads this year's book from PJ, a classic work about man's spiritual liberation: *Steppenwolf.* Later he follows PJ's suggestion to write a book report. It is, says PJ, among the best book reports he's ever gotten.

This year he gave Bryant *Ishmael,* a novel that divides humankind into tribes called "Leavers" and "Takers." "He responded to it," says PJ.

"In the beginning," says Brian Shaw, "you saw Kobe fighting Phil all the time. Then he started to get it. Now he believes in it. It gives you a warm feeling when you see that change."

32. PJ Renewed   "Being a new person in a new place, being a single father of five kids, I had to reach out, connect, offer my place as a place to come visit. Now I've ended up with two kids living with me. It's really wild. My kids are always coming out to visit me. Maybe it's not me. L.A.'s a great place to visit. The reconnection gave me a lot of confidence . . . in my ability as a father, in my ability to do things I didn't think I could: emotionally connect, listen, love, converse, care, those type of things.

"I know how I feel now. I've been able to identify my feelings. And I know that being cool is a lot of times just to compensate for what we really don't have as a male, and that's the emotional equipment. My players are into being warriors on the court and mentally cool off it. I tell them, 'That's okay. As long as you know that you want to know more about how you feel. You'll find your emotional center later on in life.'"

33. PJ at Fifty-six   He never planned to coach past the age of sixty. Months into the 2001–2002 season he says he will retire in two years when his contract expires. Days later he says he would stay in certain circumstances. Either way, the end is in sight.

If he chooses to go, what can we say of him? We can say that his abiding victory is, finally, not the kind calculated in statistics. The victory is that his life has become what the game has been for him all along: "a liberating exercise," as he calls it, "a cathartic occupation." And should he choose to go, we can say of him what he now says of Michael Jordan.

"He proved himself. He doesn't have to come back if he doesn't want to."

REBECCA MEAD

A Man-Child in Lotusland

FROM THE NEW YORKER

SHAQUILLE O'NEAL, the Los Angeles Lakers center, lives, during the basketball season, in a large cream-colored mansion at the end of a leafy cul-de-sac in Beverly Hills. The exterior of O'Neal's house is discreetly opulent, and it is not until you approach the double front doors that you notice, etched in the glass, two large Superman symbols. The first superhero that O'Neal ever felt an affinity with was the Incredible Hulk, because, as he told me recently, "he was big and green." The young O'Neal knew what it was to be a physical oddity; when he was five years old, his mother was obliged to carry her son's birth certificate with her around their home town of Newark, New Jersey, to prove to bus drivers that he was not eight or nine. Somewhere around the age of seven, O'Neal switched over to Superman, and now, at the age of thirty, his allegiance is steady.

Today, O'Neal, who is seven feet one, has a Superman "S" tattooed on his left biceps, and when he slams the ball into the basket with a particularly incontrovertible defiance at the Staples Center, the Lakers' home court, the Superman theme is played over the loudspeakers. The Superman logo is engraved in the headlights of his silver Mercedes, one of about fifteen cars and trucks he owns. More than five hundred framed Superman comic-book covers hang on the wall of a corridor in his off-season house, in Orlando, where he also has a vintage Superman pinball machine. For a while, he had a Superman bedspread on his bed. O'Neal considers it lucky that he shares a first initial with Superman. "The only reason I call myself Superman is that it starts with 'S,'" he says. "If my name was Tim, I couldn't be Superman. It wouldn't look right."

One of O'Neal's grandmothers died recently, and at her funeral he contemplated the design of his own final resting place. "I started to think about what my mausoleum would look like, and I thought it should be all marble, with Superman logos everywhere," he told me. "There would be stadium seating, and only my family would have the key, and they would be able to go in there and sit down, like in a little apartment. My grave would be right there, and there would be a TV showing, like, an hour-long video of who I was."

O'Neal considers himself to have a dual nature. "Shaquille is corporate, nice-looking, soft-spoken, wears suits, and is very cordial to people, whereas Shaq is the dominant athlete who is the two-time champion," he told me. "They are the same person, but it's kind of like Clark Kent and Superman. During the day, I am Shaquille, and at night I am Shaq." O'Neal also has a nemesis, an evil twin, whom he calls Elliuqahs Laeno. "That's my name spelled backward," he said. "That's the person that I am not allowed to be because of my status. He does what a normal young rich guy would do — party, hang out, use bad language. He stays out all night, tries to practice the next day, isn't focused. That is him. He's dead, though. I killed him off."

We were talking in a back office at the Lakers' training facility, in El Segundo, a suburb of Los Angeles, after O'Neal had come off the court from an afternoon practice. His skin was tide-marked with drying sweat, and he sat with his legs spread wide, like those riders on the New York subway who laugh in the face of the one-man-one-seat convention. O'Neal, who weighs somewhere around 340 pounds, would need at least three seats, and perhaps four. His identification with Superman is based on his sense of himself as a crusading force for good — good being, for the moment, the continued success of the Los Angeles Lakers, who are currently in the NBA playoffs — but it is also grounded in a sense of physical supremacy.

O'Neal is one of the largest men alive. He wears size 22 basketball shoes, which are made for him by a company called Starter; they are all white and finished with a shiny gloss, reminiscent, in their sheen and size, of the hull of a luxury yacht. (When the Lakers' equipment manager, a rotund man in the mid-five-foot range named Rudy Garciduenas, carries the shoes into the locker room before a game, he cradles them in gentle arms, as if he were

the nursemaid of Otus and Ephialtes, the twin giant sons of Posei-
don.) O'Neal's cars must have their interiors ripped out and their
seats moved back ten inches before he is able to drive them. (His
most recent acquisition is a Ferrari Spider convertible, a birthday
gift from his father that was, as he pointed out to reporters in the
Lakers' locker room one night, bought with his own earnings.
O'Neal's Spider has its top down permanently, since he's too big
for the convertible to convert.) O'Neal's pants have an outside
seam of four feet six and a half inches. He has never encountered a
hotel-room showerhead that was high enough for him to stand under, an inconvenience for a man who spends months at a time on
the road. When he speaks on a cell phone, he holds it in front of
his mouth and talks into it as if it were a walkie-talkie, and then
swivels it up to his ear to listen, as if the phone were a tiny planet
making a quarter-orbit around the sun of his enormous head.

O'Neal isn't the tallest player in the NBA — that's Shawn
Bradley, of the Dallas Mavericks, who is seven feet six — and many
teams have at least one seven-footer. But Shawn Bradley is seventy-
odd pounds lighter than O'Neal, and when they are on the court
together it looks as if Bradley would be well advised to abandon
basketball and return to his former calling, as a Mormon mission-
ary. O'Neal is daunting even to the most accomplished of seven-
footers, like Dikembe Mutombo, of the Philadelphia 76ers, who is
an inch taller than O'Neal but, at 265 pounds, a bantamweight by
comparison. When the 76ers met the Lakers in last year's NBA
finals, Mutombo and O'Neal clashed repeatedly under the boards,
with Mutombo bouncing off O'Neal's body — the hulking, barg-
ing shoulder, the prodigious posterior backing into implacable
reverse.

Many centers move like articulated trucks on a highway filled
with Mercedes SLs — they can't weave from lane to lane or make
sharp turns or suddenly accelerate. But O'Neal's physical power is
augmented by an unlikely agility: he is able to jump and loft his
massive body above the rim, and his recovery when he hits the
ground is such that should he miss the basket on the first try he can
go up again, just as high and just as quickly, grab the ball, feint to
fool the three defenders leaping around him, and hit his mark. On
the official play-by-play reports that are given to reporters covering
the game, O'Neal's performance is condensed into a code: "MISS
O'Neal Lay-up/O'Neal REBOUND/MISS O'Neal Lay-up/O'Neal

REBOUND/O'Neal Slam Dunk" — all happening within the space of seven seconds. O'Neal was the second-best scorer in the league this season, with 27.2 points per game, after Philadelphia's Allen Iverson, who scored an average of 31.4. And he has been the NBA finals' most valuable player for the past two years.

O'Neal's body isn't as cut as he'd like it to be, and friends say that what he really wants is a six-pack stomach, but he takes pride in his solid muscularity. At one point while we were talking, he rose from his chair, hoisted up his yellow number 34 jersey, and invited me to pinch his fat. A brief investigation revealed that there wasn't any fat to pinch — though there was an acreage of belly, tattooed just above the navel with "LIL Warrior"; and, glinting on the higher reaches of his torso, a gold bar piercing a nipple. "Sixteen percent body fat, baby," O'Neal said.

It is perhaps inevitable that O'Neal is routinely described as having a huge personality, although his personality is probably the most ordinary-sized thing about him. Even when he is silent in the presence of reporters, which he often is, or when his public comments are restricted to mumbles, his importance on the court means that his pronouncements are invested with extra significance. When O'Neal does talk to reporters, after a game, they swarm around him, pointing miniature tape recorders up over their heads, toward his mouth. His voice can be so low that you don't know what he's said until you bring the tape recorder back down to earth and play the tape.

O'Neal's on-court persona is ferocious, and his comments about his opponents are usually of the standard aggressive-athlete variety. "They ought to make those lazy-ass millionaires play some defense," he told me one day. O'Neal aspires to a career in law enforcement after he retires from basketball, and his profile as a player is that of a crushing, point-scoring bad cop, with no good cops in sight. "He likes to enforce things," Herb More, one of O'Neal's high school coaches, says. But his disposition is fundamentally sunny, and if his sense of humor runs to the excruciatingly broad — he derives great pleasure from picking up a defenseless member of the Lakers' staff, or a reporter, and manhandling him like a burly father with a squealing three-year-old — it is deeply felt.

These characteristics, along with his enthusiastic if less than triumphant excursions into the territories of rap music and movie acting, have made him a central figure in the popular culture. His affability is currently being harnessed to promote Burger King, Nestlé Crunch, and Swatch; and his endorsements have been estimated to earn him between $8 million and $10 million a year. He offers a combination of cartoonish playfulness and wholesome values. He has never taken drugs, unless you count a brief dalliance with creatine and androstenedione, the legal bodybuilding supplements. He never drinks in public, unless it's a soda he's endorsing. He is well known for his rapport with children, and he does a lot of charity work with them. Every Christmas, he dresses up in a Santa suit and hands out gifts in an event known as Shaq-A-Claus, and he has granted twelve wishes through the Make-A-Wish Foundation over the past two years. He's not the kind of player you'd expect to see slapped with a paternity suit. (O'Neal has four children: two with his girlfriend of three years, Shaunie Nelson, one daughter from a previous relationship, and a son of Shaunie's whom O'Neal considers his own.) Nor is he likely to participate in any of those activities that advertisers most fear, and be charged with DUI, like Rod Strickland, who plays for the Miami Heat, or, like the former New Jersey Net Jayson Williams, have a chauffeur found shot to death in his bedroom.

O'Neal has had some misadventures in marketing, largely because he and his former agent Leonard Armato tried in the late nineties to sell Shaq as an independent brand, something that had never been done by a basketball player. They launched an online clothing-and-shoe company, Dunk.net, which never took off and went bust after the dot-com crash; another clothing line, called TWIsM. — "The world is mine," O'Neal's personal motto — was similarly unsuccessful. O'Neal and Armato parted ways last year, and O'Neal replaced him with Perry Rogers, a sports marketer who built his career on selling Andre Agassi; Mike Parris, O'Neal's uncle and a former cop, has become O'Neal's manager. "Shaq is a brand, and we are trying to match him up with companies that match his personality and caliber as an athlete," Parris explained to me. (This realignment has yet to be entirely accomplished — O'Neal has until recently been associated with a health-club company called ZNetix, whose founder was accused of bilking investors of millions of dollars.)

Apart from Michael Jordan, who has made more than $425 million from the likes of Nike and Gatorade during the course of his career, the only other player whose advertising deals rival O'Neal's is Kobe Bryant, his Lakers teammate. Unlike some Lakers before him, such as Kareem Abdul-Jabbar, O'Neal thoroughly enjoys being a celebrity. He considers it his duty to present a friendly face in public, even on occasions when he would prefer not to be badgered by autograph-hunters, and he accepts the inevitability of being recognized. O'Neal was startled to discover, after being stranded on September 11 in Baton Rouge for several days, that he was expected to show ID when boarding the charter plane he'd hired. "I'm not prejudiced, but those pilots had better have some ID," he told a friend.

O'Neal's public persona could not be more different from that of Jordan, who was the dominant force in basketball throughout most of the late eighties and the nineties, and is still the world's best-known athlete. Jordan, like the style of basketball he perfected, was transcendent. His athleticism resembled aeronautics, and he regularly evoked celestial comparisons: Larry Bird once described him as "God disguised as Michael Jordan." O'Neal, by contrast, is solidly earthbound. (On the court, Kobe Bryant is Ariel to O'Neal's Caliban.) Michael Jordan was a wise adult figure who invited aspiration: the elegant Nike commercials that urged fans to Be Like Mike encouraged an identification with his prowess, even as they celebrated his superlative capacities.

Being Like Shaq is demonstrably impossible, and more or less unimaginable. Instead, O'Neal, with his taste for souped-up cars, and his appetite for dumb jokes, and his tendency toward braggadocio, looks like a regular American guy, albeit a drastically oversized one. Shaq appears to want to Be Like Us.

The growth of professional basketball over the past twenty-odd years from a relatively minor spectator sport to a mass-cultural phenomenon is an example of the way in which all of American culture is increasingly geared to the tastes of teenage boys. Marketers hold that adolescent boys, with their swiftly changing appetites and their enormous buying power, are the most difficult and most critical consumers to reach. Basketball is a perfect game for teenagers: it's fast, it's energetic, it requires little equipment, and it can be practiced in driveways and on the playground without so much as an opponent; and it has been appropriated by products that have nothing to do with sports — Coke, milk — as an excellent way to reach that desired demographic. Teen boys function, in turn, as cultural emissaries to the global population: Nikes aren't cool all over the world because Vince Carter wears them but because cool American teenagers wear them.

Basketball itself is marketed with teen tastes in mind. The theater of a Lakers game has an adolescent-boy aesthetic: goofy and over-heated. There are the whirling spotlights when the players emerge from the locker room, high-fiving; the snippets of roaring rap music and of the teen-boy anthem "We Will Rock You," by Queen; the absurd contests held between quarters, in which competitors do things like play musical chairs on a set of huge inflatable seats. Should all this hilarity be inadequate to the task of holding a young man's interest, there is always the Laker Girls.

The prevalence of teen-boy tastes in American culture is something that suits Shaquille O'Neal, since those are also his tastes. There are, of course, certain adult dimensions to his life. He talks of marrying Shaunie — she wears a big diamond engagement ring — although he says he's not quite ready yet. And he speaks often of his responsibilities and the fact that he doesn't go clubbing the way he used to. "When I was by myself, the only people I had to take care of were my parents," he says. "But then I had my first child and I had to slow down; and now I've got four." But in many ways his lifestyle is a thirteen-year-old's fantasy existence. O'Neal has surrounded himself with cousins from Newark and old friends from high school, who share his interests in goofing off, breaking stuff, making noise, shooting guns, and driving a wide range of motorized vehicles, which include customized Harley-Davidsons and, on the lake at his house in Orlando, a fleet of Jet Skis.

O'Neal has installed one of his high school buddies, Joe Cavallero, to look after the Orlando house, which also appears to mean wreaking measured destruction. "We have food fights, where Thomas, the chef, will come in from the grocery store with all these things, and Shaquille will break a whole watermelon over my head, and I'll hit him with a pudding cake," Cavallero told me. "Shaquille doesn't really have many books, but he has got a big video collection: the whole Little Rascals series, and every kung-fu thing you can think of, and sometimes we play-fight like that, too. And every night he'll get on his DJ deck and play for a couple of hours, and he'll turn that thing up as loud as it will go, and everything in his house is marble, so it echoes through the whole house. And Shaquille likes to wake me up with a pillow smash to the face. You know how you get to being sound asleep, and someone smashes you in the face with a pillow? It is so funny."

The house in Los Angeles is home not only to Shaunie and the children but to Thomas Gosney, Shaq's chef, factotum, and close friend, whose loyalty is such that he responds to questions about O'Neal in the first-person plural: when I asked Gosney whether O'Neal was ever going to get around to marrying Shaunie, he said, "I think we will, but I think we need to get out of the NBA first." In addition to feeding O'Neal lots of fruit and vegetables and preventing him from indulging his particular culinary vice of eating sandwiches late at night, Gosney provides round-the-clock companionship if necessary. "The night before that first championship that we won, O'Neal was up all night," Gosney said. "He was stressing out, and I knew he needed a release. He came in and found me and said, 'Are you sleeping?' So we got up, and we rode go-carts, and then we rode motorcycles. He needed to get up and do these things in the middle of the night." O'Neal depends on his friends not just for entertainment but for home management, and Gosney told me, "Before Shaunie came and lived with us, I would say that I was his wife, except for the sex. Shaquille has said to me, 'If you were a girl, I don't know what I would do.'"

O'Neal's size gives him a storybook quality that also exaggerates the childish aspect of his nature. In myth, giants are primordial creatures, who are often beloved for their lumbering doltishness. O'Neal is much sharper than the typical fairy-tale giant, but the simplicity of his tastes and of his manner of expression has currency in a popular culture where childishness is valued above adult sophistication. "Kids like me because they see themselves in me," he said. "I don't speak with a Harvard-type vocabulary. I only wear suits when I need to. I don't talk about stuff I haven't gone through. I am just me. They like rims; I like rims. They like rap music; I like rap music. They like platinum; I like platinum."

A few years ago, O'Neal took up hunting, and one of his favorite activities is disappearing for the day into a game preserve in Florida with a few friends and a few guns. He is a bit defensive about this hobby. "It's not like I'm just sneaking around and killing animals. I am a law-abiding citizen," he told me. "What I like about it, first, is looking at the animals, and then I like getting the big ones. You can be out there all day, walking around, looking at leaves, looking at grass, looking at footprints." Off the marble entrance hall of O'Neal's house in Beverly Hills, there is a carpeted room, filled with his hunting trophies: mounted heads of antlered creatures cover the walls and, because the walls are filled, cover the floor, too, their noses pointing quirkily up at the high ceiling. There are a few animals that O'Neal bought already stuffed: a polar bear, and a taxidermic tableau of a lion attacking a zebra. The scent of the room is a pungent mixture of the chemical and the irredeemably organic, and the door is usually kept closed, like Bluebeard's bloody chamber.

A few days after O'Neal turned thirty, in March, he threw a party for himself at his house for a couple of hundred friends, family members, and business associates. An archway of red balloons had been set up at the foot of the driveway, which was covered with a red carpet upon which Superman logos were projected in spinning light. The red carpet led into a large tent behind the house, above the tennis court, which was decorated with long tubular balloons in red and yellow and blue, twisted together like something from a medical diagram of the lymphatic system.

Large Superman logos hung from the tent's ceiling, and on either side of a DJ deck were two telephone booths with Superman logos on them. There were buffet tables piled with food: steaming lobster tails and a pyramid of shrimp; a birthday cake featuring a cardboard image of O'Neal in full Superman attire, swooping up through a basketball hoop. Guests could help themselves to Häagen-Dazs from a refrigerated cart, and order drinks from bars sponsored by Red Bull and E&J cognac. A cigar company had set up a table arrayed with different kinds of cigars, each of them bearing a paper ring printed with the words "Happy 30th Shaq."

O'Neal, who had a cigar clamped in his mouth, wore a gray leather suit with a three-quarter-length jacket. (The suit required 150 square feet of leather, the skins of about 18 lambs.) He greeted his guests — his Lakers teammate Rick Fox and Fox's wife, the actress Vanessa Williams; Ray Lewis, the Baltimore Ravens line-backer; the actor Tom Arnold, who lives across the street; the rap musicians Lord Tariq and Peter Gunz; and any number of Shaq service-industry members, including his masseur and the guy who installed the audio and video equipment in his house — with un-flagging enthusiasm, hugging the men, bending down low to kiss the women's cheeks. Guests wandered in and out of the house, past the triangular swimming pool on the patio, in which a surf-board decorated with an image of O'Neal's Lakers jersey floated, and into the kitchen, which was filled with gifts that he'd received: sugar cookies, a big toy truck, a box from the Sharper Image. On the walls of the marble hallway leading out of the kitchen, there was bad basketball art — a painting of tall figures leaping around a basket, and another of an athlete's back as he holds a basketball on his shoulders, Atlas-like. There were photographs of O'Neal's children, and a framed clipping from the *Star* bearing the headline "Caught! Shaq Dating up a Storm with Halle Berry."

The living room, which has a view of the San Fernando Valley, is flanked by two fish tanks made from curving glass. The tanks are filled with brightly colored exotic fish, swimming flickeringly, and at one point in the evening O'Neal, coming into the house, found a few guests standing mesmerized in front of the tanks. He went behind a staircase that led off the hallway, where, hidden from view, was a smaller tank, filled with goldfish. He scooped into the goldfish tank with a net and filled a glass with slippery orange bodies. Then he climbed up a stepladder that was set alongside one of the big tanks, lifted its lid, and dumped in the goldfish. The angel fish and clown fish and puffer fish went wild, darting to swallow the flailing goldfish whole. A ruthless-looking barracuda snapped one up, and then went for the rebound and snared another. O'Neal looked extremely satisfied with the whole scene. "I love the sport of hunting," he said.

The host spent most of the night bopping among a crowd of his friends in the middle of the dance floor, head and shoulders and most of a torso above everyone around him. Halfway through the evening, the music was turned down, and O'Neal was summoned to the stage, where he sat in a chair and, along with everyone else, watched a video tribute devoted to the greatness of Shaq. There was O'Neal playing basketball at Louisiana State University, a spindly version of himself, breaking the hoop from the backboard. There was home-video footage of him on a beach, and playing with his kids, and dancing — to one Dr. Dre tune, he dropped to his knees, kicked his legs in the air behind him, and humped the carpet. There were also innumerable shots of him mooning the camera. The final image was of O'Neal, shirtless and sweaty, at the turntables; he unzipped his pants, shifted them gradually down his ample hips, hoisted his underwear up above his waist, and finally turned around and dropped his pants to show the camera his glistening rear. After the show was over, O'Neal stood up, unzipped his fly, zipped it up again, and said, "I never knew I had such a good ass until I saw that film. Damn, I'm sexy."

The reason O'Neal dedicated himself to the pursuit of excellence in basketball, he says, was to impress girls. "I was always the class clown, and always wanted everybody to like me," he told me recently. "Everyone else had a girlfriend, and how come I couldn't have a girlfriend?" We were at the Mondrian Hotel, in Los Angeles, where he was being photographed by ESPN while perched on top of a six-foot-tall flowerpot, a design feature of the hotel's pool area. When we sat down at a table to talk, O'Neal smashed his head against the light fixture hanging overhead. "I had to learn around age fifteen to accept my size," he said. "My father told me, 'You are going to be someone. Just keep playing and you are going to be a football player, a basketball player, or even a baseball player.' Around the age of thirteen, I got my name in the papers for basketball and the girls started liking me, and ever since then it's been nothing but up."

O'Neal gets his height from his mother's side of the family. Lucille O'Neal Harrison is six feet two inches tall, and her grandfather, who was a farmer in Georgia, was about six-ten. O'Neal met his great-grandfather once before he died, and says he is one of the people from history he'd most like to know. The others are Walter Matthau, because of the movie *The Bad News Bears* ("He was a drunk coach who got a bunch of misfit kids together — black kids, Chinese kids, girls — and they played baseball and won the championship"), and Redd Foxx, "because I used to watch *Sanford and Son* all the time, and laughter is the best stress reliever."

He credits Phil Harrison, his stepfather, actually, with having given him the emotional impetus to succeed in basketball. (Harrison married O'Neal's mother when Shaq was two. His biological father is Joe Toney, who, in 1994, appeared in the *National Inquirer* claiming paternity and thereafter did the talk-show rounds. O'Neal's response was to write a rap song called "Biological Didn't Bother.") Harrison, who was a sergeant in the Army, was a disciplinarian, the kind of father who wouldn't let O'Neal keep trophies in the house for fear that he would become conceited. O'Neal still gives all his trophies to Harrison, and he tends to treat older men with the utmost respect.

O'Neal's earliest years were spent in Newark, but when he was in the sixth grade the family was transferred to an Army base in Wildflecken, Germany. There O'Neal started to play basketball seriously, and though he was not a prodigious talent, he worked hard and was unfeasibly tall. As O'Neal recounts in his autobiography, *Shaq Talks Back,* he was scouted by Dale Brown, the coach of LSU, who had come to Germany to give a basketball clinic. Brown asked how long the six-foot-nine-inch O'Neal had been in the Army; O'Neal replied that he was just fourteen. By the middle of O'Neal's sophomore year in high school, when he was six-eleven, the family had moved back to the United States, to San Antonio, where he was on his school's basketball team. From San Antonio, O'Neal went to LSU, and after three years there he opted for the NBA draft and signed, in 1992, with the Orlando Magic for $40 million over seven years, which was then the most lucrative contract in NBA history. O'Neal spent four years in Orlando, long enough to earn a reputation as a weak playoff player and to endure an ugly falling-out with his teammate Penny Hardaway. And yet there was no doubt that he had the potential to be one of the most formidable centers to play the game since Abdul-Jabbar, and even Bill Russell and Wilt Chamberlain. In 1996, Jerry Buss, the owner of the Lakers, and his general manager, Jerry West, lured O'Neal to Los Angeles, at a salary of $120 million over seven years — the biggest contract in the game.

By that time, O'Neal had started to make rap records for Jive — for example, *Shaq Diesel,* which included songs with titles such as "Shoot Pass Slam" and "(I Know I Got) Skillz" — and had played a genie in the movie *Kazaam,* one of a handful of films in which he demonstrated the limitations of his acting ability. He had not, how-

ever, helped Orlando win an NBA championship, and critics suggested that his proximity to Hollywood would lead to similar results
for the Lakers. But O'Neal's performing career failed to take off;
and his game improved when, in 1999, Phil Jackson, the former
coach of the Chicago Bulls, took over the job of coaching the
Lakers. Under Jackson, O'Neal started to play more of a team
game, passing to other players rather than bullying his way to the
hoop. In 2000, the team won its first championship since 1988, the
era of Magic Johnson and Abdul-Jabbar.

Jackson is well known for applying the principles of Zen to the
game of basketball, and O'Neal says that Jackson's methods meshed
with his own strategies for victory. "I control my dreams," O'Neal
told me. "So-called educated people call it meditation, but I don't.
I call it 'dreamful attraction.' The mind controls everything, so you
just close your eyes and see yourself dribbling, see yourself shooting." Contrary to some reports, O'Neal says that Jackson has not in-
duced the team to practice yoga. "We tried Tai Chi one year, but
the guys didn't like it, because, even though it was stretching, it
would make us tight," he said. "Anyway, I don't stretch. I just play."

O'Neal is regularly described as the league's most dominant player:
there is no other single player who can match him physically, and
there is no defensive strategy that another team can devise which
will decisively shut him down. Jerry West told me, "If you could con-
struct a basketball player physically, Shaq would be the model.
He has this great size and incredible strength, but on top of that he
has unbelievable balance, incredible footwork, and a great sense
of where he is on the court." Most dominant isn't synonymous
with best, however; the players who usually win that accolade are
smaller, faster men like Kobe Bryant or Jason Kidd of the New Jersey Nets. And O'Neal's weaknesses, for all his power, are transpar-
ently evident. His free-throw average has been only around 50 percent for most of his career.

His detractors say that he is dominant only because of his size.
Whenever *Slam,* whose readers are the young fans upon whom the
game depends, puts O'Neal on the cover, the editors receive letters
complaining that Shaq is just big and fat and boring. O'Neal's
weight is given in the official statistics about the team as an implau-
sible 315 pounds. (People close to Shaq claim that he sometimes

hits 350.) When, in mid-March, I asked O'Neal what he weighed, he told me 338 pounds, though he said it in the slightly hesitant tone of a kid asserting that he has done his homework. "I'm just a big-boned guy," he said. "Muscle weighs more than fat, and a big guy has big muscles. People look at me and see this big guy and they think it's fat. How can I be fat and out of shape and do what I do? You could put me up against any athlete in the world, you could put them on a computerized diet, and on a treadmill and all that, and I will bust their ass."

Being called the most dominant rather than the best is fine with O'Neal. "They've changed the game because of me; other organizations whine and cry because of me," he said. "Being the best is too easy for me." His free-throw failings are spurs to his ambition, he says. "If I played the game I play and shot 88 percent from the line, it would take away from my mental focus, because I would know how good I was and I wouldn't work so hard." (In fact, O'Neal has been making about 65 percent of his free throws during the current playoffs.) "I'm not allowed to be as dominant as I want to be," he told me. "I would probably average fifty points a game, twenty rebounds, and the opponents would foul out in the first or second quarter." O'Neal suspects that his game is being reined in by the NBA referees. "I guess they have to keep it even so that the viewers won't get bored," he said. David Stern, the NBA commissioner, recently acknowledged to the *Los Angeles Daily News* that it is difficult to know when to call a foul on Shaq, and said, "We used to get the same calls on Kareem and every other big man that's been as great as Shaq is."

NBA viewing figures are well down since their peak of 6.6 million at the height of Jordan's career. Last year, an average of four million people watched the regular-season games on NBC. But a game in which O'Neal plays can sometimes make for dull viewing. His strengths aren't as thrilling to watch as those of a player who flies and leaps, and the defenses used against him slow everything down so much that a viewer's attention can dwindle. The most notorious of these is the Hack-a-Shaq, in which opposing players make repeated fouls on O'Neal by throwing their arms around his waist, hoping to regain possession of the ball at little cost by sending him to the free-throw line. Phil Jackson agrees that O'Neal is expected to play by different rules from everyone else. "It's totally unfair, but the referees have to be," Jackson told me. "Everybody fouls Shaq all the time, because they know the referees can't call every foul that is created against him. There isn't a shot in which he's not fouled except maybe twice a game. There are guys hitting him on the way up, hitting him at the top, knocking him around." O'Neal says, "The beating that I take is like wrestling. It ain't even basketball sometimes. I'm the NBA's best WWF wrestler, and I'm the WWF's best NBA player."

O'Neal has a tattoo on his right arm that says "Against the Law," and, since he's famously supportive of the uniformed services, I asked him what he meant by it. "It's against the law to be this talented, this beautiful, this smart, this sexy," he said. "I don't mean penal-code law. I mean laws of nature."

Like a Hollywood movie or a mass-market paperback, every sports season needs a narrative of conflict and resolution, and in the 2000–2001 season the story was the rivalry and animosity between O'Neal and Kobe Bryant. The narrative is crafted by the Lakers' beat reporters, who attend around a hundred games a season — hanging out in the locker rooms for their appointed forty-five minutes before the game — and show up at countless closed practice sessions. The structure of team coverage creates what a therapist would diagnose as a cycle of dependency and resentment on the part of the reporters, who are a group of mostly smallish men obliged to wait around grudgingly for a bunch of mostly huge men to stoop and speak to them. The reporters exercise their own power, of course, in making a drama out of the daily shifts in locker-room mood, which in turn earns them the occasional enmity of the players. O'Neal barely talks to the press for weeks at a time, or does what he calls "SHAM-ming them" — giving them the Short Answer Method. "They're yellow journalists," he said to me one day. "Don't focus on whether Shaq is having problems with Phil, or whether Shaq is liking Kobe or not, or what Rick and Vanessa are doing — if we're a great team, say we're a great team. I think they get so bored with us winning all the time, they focus on that other stuff."

But the Shaq-Kobe feud was genuine, and it provided excellent copy. O'Neal and Bryant had never got along. Bryant, who came to the league a polished eighteen-year-old from a wealthy family, seemed to find O'Neal's antic goofiness distasteful; O'Neal thought Bryant was a selfish player who was interested only in demonstrating his own virtuosity and was insufficiently deferential. O'Neal would say ominous things like "If the big dog don't get fed, the house won't get guarded," after nights of what he saw as Kobe hogging the ball, and Kobe would say to reporters, "Turn my game down? I need to turn it up." The whole affair culminated, happily enough for the team and its chroniclers, in a reconciliation senti-mental enough for the most golden-hued of Hollywood dramas, with Bryant shucking off his natural aloofness both on and off the court — he started to laugh at teammates' jokes on the bus instead of listening to his Walkman — and with O'Neal referring to the quicksilver Bryant as "my idol." (The saga forms the basis of a new book, *Ain't No Tomorrow: Kobe, Shaq and the Making of a Lakers Dynasty,* by Elizabeth Kaye.) This season, Bryant and O'Neal have been coexisting quite chummily. O'Neal took a few shots at Bryant while delivering an impromptu rap to the crowd at his birthday party, castigating him for not showing up ("Kobe, if you hear me, I'm talking about your ass," and so on), but the razzing seemed good-natured.

This season's master narrative has been Shaq vs. Shaq — O'Neal's battle with his own body and its ailments. Chronic pain in an ar-thritic toe and other injuries that have cropped up have been end-lessly inquired after by the beat reporters. "We started out with the small toe on his left foot — that was getting to him early — and at some point in the season we all made the transition to the right big toe," Tim Brown, who covers the team for the *Los Angeles Times,* ex-plained. The paper has been running headlines like "Lakers' Big Hopes Rest in Shaq's Big Toe," and reams of newsprint have been devoted to the orthotics that have been devised by O'Neal's podia-trist, Robert Mohr, to alleviate the strain on the big toe. Last week, the papers reported that not only had O'Neal cut his finger while playing against the San Antonio Spurs in the first game of the West-ern Conference semifinals but he had also required stitches to mend a cut sustained earlier that day at home while he was pre-tending to be Spider-Man.

This season, O'Neal has thought a lot about the toll the game is taking on his body. "I feel beat up," he told me a few days after his birthday. "I'm probably one of the only guys in history who has

taken a pounding night in and night out." He was sitting on a massage bench after a practice session, and he rubbed his arms and
slapped his biceps as if he were looking over a recalcitrant piece of
machinery. "With the last two championships, afterward I just had
to sit down for a week and do nothing, like this" — and he struck a
catatonic pose, stiff-limbed and staring into space — "and let all
the injuries go away. And then there's another week to do this" —
he stretched his thick, muscled arms above his head, exposing the
spacious geography of his armpits — "and then, by the time my
shit is all gone, we've only got another week until training camp."
He was worried, too, about the effects of the anti-inflammatory
drugs he was taking. "They are the same drugs they say might have
messed up Alonzo Mourning's kidneys," he said, referring to the
Miami center who missed most of last season as a result of kidney
disease.

Rick Fox, O'Neal's teammate, coming off the court after a practice in New Jersey a few weeks ago, said, "Shaq is dealing with injuries that he never thought he'd have to deal with. This is new to
him. Even Superman had his kryptonite, but after ten years there
are only so many hits of kryptonite you can take." One day, O'Neal
told me, mournfully, "When I was Kobe's age, I could play a mag-
nificent game and stay out all night, but now I am old, and my toe is
killing me." O'Neal, whose contract expires in 2006, has started to
say that he may have only two more years in the game, though in
1999 he told *Slam* that he thought he might be out by the time he
reached thirty.

O'Neal will be under pressure to keep playing. Jerry West told
me, "If I ever see him retire early, I'll kill him. You play until you
can't play. This is a tough guy, and he can play through things that
mortal people wouldn't want to." Sometimes O'Neal talks about
himself this way, too. Toward the end of this year's regular season,
he was out for two games, with a sprained wrist, causing the reporters to shift their focus from foot to arm. The Lakers lost both
games, and just before the next game, in which O'Neal was to return, against Miami, I asked him whether he felt responsible for being hurt or whether he felt as if his body were betraying him as well
as the team.

He rejected the premise of the question. "I don't get hurt — I
get taken out," he said. "My wrist is hurting for a reason — it's not

hurting because I fell on it. My stomach is hurting for a reason. My knee is hurting for a reason. I don't get hurt, baby, I get taken out. You can't hurt this" — and, with that, he flexed his left biceps, like a bodybuilder, and, with one huge fist, banged on his Superman tattoo. Then he went out and scored forty points against Miami, leading the Lakers to victory.

In other moods, though, O'Neal admits to his own mortality. "Everything hurts," he told me. "A pinch is a pinch. If you pinch an elephant, it will hurt him. Pain is pain, and pain doesn't care how big you are or how strong you are." One day, he said, "You know who my favorite basketball player is? People might be surprised when they hear this. It's Dave Bing." I said I didn't know who Dave Bing was. "I don't know who he is, either," said O'Neal. "Who did he play for? Detroit? He's retired now, and he owns a big steel factory in Detroit." Bing left the game in 1978, and subsequently became a Hall of Famer, and the winner, in 1984, of the National Minority Small Business Person of the Year and the National Minority Supplier of the Year awards.

O'Neal says he's starting to develop business interests that have nothing to do with basketball: he told me he'd bought a couple of car washes and strip malls, and had just signed a deal for some Burger King franchises. "Basketball is cool, but we can't do it forever. After basketball, Dave Bing is my guy," he said. "Those players who are smart enough save their money, so that after you stop playing you can keep it going — that is what I plan on doing, like the Kennedy money." I asked O'Neal whether he saw himself as Joe Kennedy, a patriarch establishing a dynasty. "No, I'm the one who passed away in a plane crash — what's his name?" he said. "The good-looking one. That's who I am: good-looking, educated."

On those few evenings and afternoons when O'Neal is not playing basketball or filming a commercial or visiting the children's ward of a hospital or otherwise engaging in the various duties of an NBA superstar, he is often in a classroom, studying penal-code law. O'Neal has always been fascinated by the police — both Mike Parris, his business manager, and Jerome Crawford, who serves as his bodyguard, are retired police officers — and some years ago O'Neal decided that he wanted to train as a cop himself, with the intention of pursuing a law-enforcement career after he leaves basketball, along with developing his business interests. He is already an honorary deputy for the Orange County sheriff's office in Orlando, where he once surprised an international group of SWAT-team officers who were performing a practice exercise of freeing a hostage from a bus by playing the hostage.

In Los Angeles, he is training to become an auxiliary member of the Port of Los Angeles Police, and he drives around with a senior officer, learning about how the law works. O'Neal frequently practices his law enforcement techniques on his teammates and the Lakers' staff: Mark Madsen, a six-foot-nine-inch, 236-pound twenty-six-year-old, who has become a close friend of O'Neal's since joining the Lakers, last season, told me, "He will come up to me and put me in all these police grips. He'll say, 'Which wrist did you have surgery on?' and then he'll do it on the other wrist. If I put up any sort of fight, I'm on the ground, quick."

O'Neal hasn't arrested anyone yet, but he does horse around by threatening to make citizen's arrests on Lakers employees, and regularly orders members of the team's support staff to stand against the wall with their legs spread. It's unlikely that he will ever be a beat cop, since what he really wants to do is be a chief of police or run for sheriff, either in Louisiana or in Orlando: "Sheriff is an elective position, and I don't just want to be a figurehead. And I don't want to win because I'm Shaq, but because I have the knowledge and understand what is going on." O'Neal generally avoids politics (though he recently went to a Nation of Islam meeting to hear Louis Farrakhan speak, and says that he is a friend of the Farrakhan family). He says that he wouldn't run for sheriff on either a Republican or a Democratic ticket, but as an Independent, "like Ross Perot." He told me, "Of course, I am not going to stop crime, make it zero percent, but I would try."

When O'Neal returns to Orlando this summer, with or without a third championship ring, there will be plenty to do. He may undergo surgery on his foot, which would put him out of action for six to eight weeks. "Without any surgery, nothing is going to change," Robert Mohr, the podiatrist, says. "For ordinary motion, you need about sixty degrees of pain-free movement in your toe. For jumping or running, you need close to ninety degrees. He has maybe twenty or thirty degrees. You imagine a 350-pound body coming down on that joint."

Fortunately, if O'Neal is recovering from surgery he will have the solace of various home improvements that are under way in Orlando, where his house measures 36,000 square feet, and faces 400 yards of waterfront. He has already added an 8,000-square-foot gym and a regulation-size basketball court, and contractors have started on the other side of the house, adding a new swimming pool and another 9,000 square feet of living space, including seven new bedrooms (O'Neal already has a master bedroom with a circular bed measuring 20 feet across), a recreation room, a cigar room, a movie theater, and a private dance club with a state-of-the-art DJ booth.

Injuries permitting, O'Neal will also be able to engage in one of his favorite activities — going on the Skycoaster, an amusement-park ride in Orlando, which combines the sensations of hang gliding, bungee jumping, and skydiving. Riders are strapped into harnesses and hoisted to the top of a hundred-foot tower, where they pull a release cord that puts them into a pendulum swing, above an expanse that is the size of a football field, at about sixty miles an hour. The sensation is as close to flying as anyone who is not Superman or Michael Jordan is likely to experience, and O'Neal is fanatical about it.

"It's like a roller coaster, and it is dangerous — if that cord breaks, you can die," O'Neal told me. "It's scary. It feels like you're actually flying. It's like you are falling from the top of a building, and someone grabs you and says, 'Okay, I ain't going to let you die.' And then they swing you — *whoosh*. I go on it all the time." One evening, he flew for two hours, in his own customized harness; and when other would-be Skycoasters asked for his autograph he offered instead to take them on a ride with him. So all evening astonished patrons stood in line to fly with Shaq, waiting for their chance to swoop through the air, the kind of thing that happens in dreams.

JAMES McKEAN

Playing for Jud

FROM WITNESS

FROM HIGH IN THE STANDS, Jud Heathcote looked tortured, a tragic figure in a grand opera, so consumed by sorrow or lamentation or anger that we feared what he might do to himself. His whining was a high tenor screech and his posture crushed. The stories about him were commonplace enough to approach the mythic — how he slammed a basketball to the floor in anger only to have it bounce straight up and strike him in the nose, hunched over as he was in his half-bear, half-wrestler crouch; how he struck his own head with the heel of his hand in frustration, a kind of audible self-mutilation; how he ripped the top of his socks off in anger or as some say, in the optical illusion of retelling, how he lifted himself off the bench by his socks until the argyle gave way and he fell back into his chair and over. Back and forth, pacing, hands out to plead with the officials, his own players, the very fates themselves. All punctuated by his out-of-tune aria of injustice and bafflement.

Twenty years after playing for Jud, I rediscovered close up his precarious balance of calm and catastrophe. At Iowa's Carver-Hawkeye arena, Jud's Michigan State Spartans, then in first place in the Big Ten, were being overrun by the fast-breaking, seemingly undisciplined hometown Hawkeyes. The noise was at ear-damage level. Managers quickly set out folding chairs for a time-out huddle. Sweating and exhausted, the starters watched Jud pound his fist into his hand, as if it were a gavel calling this game to order. But his voice was exact and even, laying out strategy and offering encouragement, and all those fine players at Michigan State — Steve Smith, Mike Peplowski, Kirk Manns, Eric Snow, Shawn Respert, some All-American, some All–Big Ten — all those players listened.

I listened, too. I remember how it felt. In the '60s I played for Jud and Marv Harshman at Washington State University. For more than twenty years, I've replayed those seasons over and over, the violence and pain and discipline and humor and anger, the wins and, of course, the losses. It was a classic education without books, corporal and exhausting. Sometimes I regret being so myopic during those turbulent years from 1964 to 1968. On campus, students protested, breaking from convention and authority and the war. I remember in 1968 feeling defensive about my letterman's jacket. "Establishment," someone sneered. "I'm cold" was my halfhearted response. The memories are complex and ambivalent and then as simple as the ball in hand, the echo of its bouncing in an empty gym. Years later, as I sat behind the Michigan State bench, the memories drew close. I was family again and from the first row could speak, with practice now, of family matters.

When I wrote Jud to tell him I was going to school in Iowa City and to ask if I could get tickets to the Michigan State game, he wrote back to say there would be tickets for me as long as I didn't root for those sons-a-bitches. When I picked the tickets up at Will Call, they read "row 2, court side." The usher pointed down the steps. The long descent felt nostalgic. Before sixteen thousand Iowa fans, our seats were directly behind Jud. Beneath the lights, the game was intimate again, the floor crowded and tense. I'd forgotten how much happens in so small a space, and how, Macbeth-like, the hand and mind act as one. I could hear the conversations again, between the players themselves, clipped, single-word information — left, right, switch, mine, my fault — all directed to honing the moment to a simple edge, your two points and their absolute denial. And audible through the roar, the one voice the players on the floor heard was Jud's song *verismo*, full of signals, melancholy, directions, spleen, admonishments, and finally, praise.

It's the praise I remember seeking. If I screwed up, I felt that I had let the coaches down, that this game meant everything to them. Returning to the bench, I knew I'd hear about my failure in a mix of analysis and despair. If I did well, the encouragement would be there. Once when our Washington State team played the University of Washington at Hec Edmunson Pavilion, I heard two words spoken clearly in a crowd of ten thousand and the noisy rush of the game. Guarded by Jay Bond, Washington's center, whose strategy was to front me at my low-post position, leaning with his right arm folded against me and his left in front waving in the passing lane, I kept trying to move farther out so that our guard Lenny Alien at the top of the key could pass me the ball. Jay Bond kept inching farther and more aggressively in front. I'd move out and so would he. Finally, I made a sudden move toward the ball, Lenny Allen pump faked, Jay Bond scrambled to front, and I changed direction with two quick steps toward the basket, leaving Jay Bond all by himself. It was a backdoor, a classic move, though a rare event in my repertoire; Lenny laid the pass in just so, and all I had to do was rise and drop the ball in. All timing and a wonderful pass. As I ran under the basket and back down court, I heard Jud say, "Nice move." Ten thousand voices and one clear in its weight and authority. The basket was worth two points and praise I've never forgotten.

It took a long time, however, to earn that praise. Gangly, awkward, and eager to play, I was recruited out of Wilson High School in Tacoma by Marv Harshman, the head basketball coach at Washington State, who explained in handwritten letters how badly the Cougars needed me. The center position would be mine when I was a sophomore. I could get a fifth-year stipend if needed. They'd throw in a pair of contact lenses. I remember Coach Harshman sitting in our living room and explaining to my parents and my grandmother the virtues of Washington State. They were building the basketball program and I could play a crucial role. Their main concern was my academics, of course. I would be a student first and an athlete second, a student-athlete, he called me. My parents were sold. I signed the letter of intent. I'd be a Cougar playing for Marv Harshman, a gentleman, an All-American hero at Pacific Lutheran University in Tacoma, and now the head coach at a Pac-8 division 1 school. I was ready for the big time.

The next fall I hadn't been on campus very long when Coach Harshman introduced me to a slightly balding man who looked like Don Rickles. This was the new freshman basketball coach. I don't remember Jud saying much. His tone seemed perfunctory, as if he was unsure about me. He asked something about my being in shape and getting ready for the season. What struck me immediately was that the basketball office in Bohler Gym looked no bigger than my room at home, with no window shades and only two desks, one for Harshman and one for Bobo Brayton, the head baseball coach, and substitute assistant basketball coach, whose favorite ex-

pression was "That's as obvious as a horse turd in a pan of milk."
They borrowed the secretary down the hall in the athletic director's office. Jud would be replacing Bobo. I wondered if they'd still
share a desk.

After the first week of practice, I had larger worries. So much for
recruitment promises and noblesse oblige. During the first team
meeting, the coaches explained that they had lied. We were not students first. We were basketball players first. They weren't going to
let us forget it. During the first week of practice, the tone was set
and the haranguing began. We were freshman, ex–high school
stars, and even Pete, the irascible equipment manager, ignored us.
Maybe I wasn't as ready for college ball as I thought I was. I'd never
been treated like a basic training recruit.

"What the hell is that! Take that damn Wilson High School turn-
around stick shot and leave it in your high school drawer," Jud
barked. "There's no way you can play at Washington State if . . ."
and then followed an infinite number of transgressions to complete the sentence. Technical problems rated eyebrow-raising im-
patience and a short demonstration. More egregious errors, such
as lack of hustle and stupid choices, earned serious upbraiding and
questions that have no good answer: "When are you going to learn,
son? What does it take? What do I have to do?"

As the year progressed, we learned to take cover. When the whistle shrieked in the middle of a drill, and you heard "No, no, no" or
"Please, how many times . . . ," your first wish was that the tolling
wasn't for you. In the Midwest, tornado sirens get the same effect.
Everyone seems torn, looking up to see what's coming while heading down to the cellar to hide. We would wander to the edge of
the court, shuffle, look at our feet, catch our breath while the chosen one suffered. After a while we played with a kind of running-
scared and oh-no demeanor, which I've seen even on Jud's Michigan State teams. It's a your-father-knows-you-broke-the-neighbor's-
window look; all that's left is the sentence, the long walk back to the
bench or Jud's bearlike shuffle walk toward you for an explanation.
In a *Sports Illustrated* article that celebrates his career, Jud admits
that "like Bobby [Knight] I'm a negative coach. I'm always harping
on what's bad rather than praising what's good. Yes, I've hurt some
kids, and I've been bad for some kids. But one thing I'm always
proud of is that our players get *coached*. And I think most of them
get better every year."

For the 1964–65 season, the Jud-coached freshman basketball team at Washington State had twenty-two wins and no losses. We were balanced and deep. The highest individual scoring average on the team was twelve points per game, and the entire team average was eighty-two. Freshman games at Bohler Gym in Pullman had always been the opening act for the varsity, the rookies with their hand-me-down uniforms and bad passes playing to empty stands. As the season progressed, however, interest in our team began to grow, and at the halfway point, we were even getting statewide news coverage. The *Tacoma News Tribune* noted that "Washington State's freshmen own the state's longest collegiate basketball winning streak — eleven straight. The Coubabes beat North Idaho JC 102–61 on Friday night, then came back Saturday to upend Columbia Basin 63–59 to snip the Hawks' victory string at thirty-seven in a row. Marv Harshman lauded the Coubabe-CBC game as the finest freshman game he's ever seen. 'It wasn't run and shoot. It was just a real basketball game,' he said." I would add that it was a real game because of Jud's coaching. We played with a mix of desperation and pride. We wanted that clean record and we wanted to stay in Jud's good graces. By the end of the season, our record and the rumor of the red-faced, hair-tearing, combustible freshman coach named Jud had filled the stands.

Those players who made the transition to the varsity team, indeed, got better the next year. Out of sixteen freshman players, six made the varsity team, but several of the best players on the freshman team decided not to play at all. Some dropped out of school for academic reasons. Others decided they couldn't survive another year of Jud. "How do you put up with all that yelling at you," someone asked. I remember saying that I tried to listen to what he had to say but not necessarily how he said it, that he had good things to teach. I was young and deferential. It was 1965, and on campus, ROTC was still a major. Cadets wore their uniforms to class and in the evenings saluted officer upperclassmen at a soda joint called the "Coug," where the Stones and Buffalo Springfield played on the jukebox and fifty years' worth of names were carved into the wooden booths.

Shawn Respert has said that Jud is a great shooting coach. Yes, I agree. I remember many times Jud walking over to me as I was warming up before practice and saying, "Go ahead, shoot a couple." I would turn and shoot a jump shot from fifteen feet and then another and another until he said, "Okay, I see." Then he would explain what I was doing and where I might change the shot, an adjustment here or there, hand on top of the ball he would say or elbow in and stop the ball. "This is a shot, not a throw," he'd say. Or turn and square up. Use your legs. Follow through. What I remember is how easily he seemed to analyze what I was doing, spot my problems in rhythm and form, and offer up a solution. A prosodist of the jump shot, he'd explain what I might look for — how the ball should spin slowly backward, how it should die on the rim when it hits, how a good shot hesitates in the net, falls through, hits the floor, and bounces back to you. "Ready, shoot," is the drill we would run and run. He'd pass the ball and I'd catch it and set in a shooting position, right hand behind and up on the ball, left hand supporting, elbow in, eyes on the basket, wait, wait, wait . . . "shoot," he called, never quite when I expected it, shot opportunities and choices never the same twice, the theory goes, but the setup, the shot, the rhythm, the follow-through — these stay the same, practiced over and over until shooting is second nature.

Although his patience was suspect, Jud's motives never seemed in doubt. He wanted to win and he wanted us to be better basketball players. The outcome of the game mattered to him, but the more I played for Jud, the more I realized that how we reached that outcome mattered just as much. "Do what you can do. Leave the freelancing at home! Where in hell did that come from? That's not your shot! Play the game we practiced." Each season I understood more how playing well meant balancing control and enthusiasm, how the discipline in practice showed in the games, and how focus during the game was a learned skill. If we were asleep on the floor, Jud provided a wake-up. Ironically, it's as if his strategy was to drive his players away from him and completely into the moment. The choice was either total concentration on the game or a bench-side critique with Jud.

Many factors provide tension in a game — the crowd, the opposing team, the fear of losing — but Jud provided the means, the reason, and the urgency. He was conductor, expert guide, ally, and scold. An event both of character and outcome, each game meant more to him than we could imagine. A national champion handball player who coached high school basketball as vigorously as college, who arranged his marriage and married life around a basketball schedule, who never in my recollection missed a practice or a game, this was a man whose life was competition. "Why don't you hang around the gym more?" he asked me one day. I didn't understand then what he was asking. The gym was where he lived. And it wasn't until in the locker room after one home game against California, when he called me a "hot dog" and an "embarrassment" for my mouthing off to the officials, for kicking the ball away and for my self-righteous, prima donna antics, that I realized what Jud meant by playing well. It didn't seem to matter that their center, Bob Presley, kept barking in my ear that he was going to kick my honky motherfuckin' ass, or that I scored over thirty points. We won the game, but I had lost something in Jud's eyes. When I was back in my own room with the door locked, alone and fighting back tears, I realized how painful it was not to be in Jud's good graces. He was my father, I think now, or perhaps my very own Orwellian headmaster, "goading, threatening, exhorting, sometimes joking, very occasionally praising, but always prodding away at one's mind to keep it up to the right pitch of concentration, as one might keep a sleepy person awake by sticking pins into him."

My antics that evening had earned Jud's worst criticism: "You're not *thinking*."

There has always seemed to be a constructive tension between us. Even now. In one letter written a week or so before a 1992 Michigan State–Iowa game, he said, "Again we need all the help we can get in Iowa City; you have four tickets. We'll be staying at the Holiday Inn. Give me a call or drop by practice as we will be practicing 11:00–12:00 on February 6. I look forward to seeing you. Maybe you can work on Pep's stick shot and the roll hook, or has memory and age dimmed your talents with both?" Sitting behind the Michigan State bench during warm-ups for that game, I tried to field a ball that had bounced off the floor, hobbled it slightly, and threw it back out to the players just as Jud walked up. "You could shoot but still can't catch," he said, shaking his head. I thought, how typical.

Ambiguity honed to an art form, his give-and-take language maintained a kind of suspension between reinforcement and criticism, between satisfaction and wanting more. He was pleased yet hard to please. "So far so good . . ." he seemed to be saying, "all right as far as it goes." I remember an awful shot I took once, too far out, a turnout, the stick shot that Jud despised but begrudged

by the time I was a junior for want of something better, a shot I had
no business taking, having decided ahead of time I was due. I sailed
back in my fadeaway, twenty feet out, and hoisted the ball toward
the basket, the arc high as I heard from the bench, "No, no, what
the hell . . . no business . . ." and "nice shot" as the ball fell through.
No one was immune. "You know better. You're the best jumper
(shooter, defender, ball handler, etc.) on our team, so when are
you going to play like it." Such undercurrents. Such riptides. There
were no opportunities to float on what he said. I remember his
saying before a practice one day, "I want you to be a great basketball player, not just a good one." Was it praise or criticism, I
still wonder. When I heard Stanley Kunitz say once that he didn't
worry about all the bad poems being written, only about the ones
just good enough, I thought of Jud's high standards and pressure
to meet them, his urgent and focused poetic of concentration,
thought, rhythm, and movement.

It was inevitable, I guess, that such a dynamic tension might find
its limits. Coaches and players define each other's roles — a player
learns from the coach and plays for him, and the coach sees the results of his work through the performance of his player. Given the
pressure and the application of power in such a relationship, the
tolerances need to be clearly defined. Some players early at Washington State had no tolerance whatsoever for Jud. Others never
seemed bothered. When I was a freshman, for example, the seniors
of the varsity — Dale Ford, Ted Werner, and a few other players
who seemed far older, rougher, and wiser than I — listened more
to Harshman and less to Jud, unfazed, it seemed, by his tirades.
Green and heedless, I tried to stay out of each coach's line of fire. It
was a strategy that worked until my junior year when the falling-out
came.

On the court, the first string was assigned to defend the "gray"
squad in a half-court defense drill. The gray squad had been taught
the opponent's offense, and we were supposed to stop them with
our man-to-man defense. I was guarding Dave Kessler, an All-American high hurdler, who was six-foot-six and constructed entirely of
elbows, knees, and angles. Obedient and enthusiastic, Kessler, who
played the game at two speeds — fidget in place or full ahead —
had the dubious distinction on our team of having shot, during
games, air balls on three successive lay-ups, the most infamous of

which hit the backboard and bounced twenty feet back onto the court. Though he lacked a delicate touch, he was extremely fast and eager to please, sporting, despite the '60s, a flat-top which stood up on its own.

It was late in the practice. I was tired and needed to sit down. My job was to prevent Kessler, the mock center for the opposing team, from breaking from his low post position across the key and establishing position on the other side. His movement was predicated on following the ball around the perimeter, forward to point guard to opposite forward. When the ball left the point guard's hand, Kessler was supposed to break. I was supposed to block him high or low, forcing him high toward the free-throw line or low toward the out-of-bounds line under the basket. Then I had to front him to spoil the pass in from the forward. All this meant I had to have an idea where he was going and move quickly enough to get in his way.

Jud set the play up. Kessler bounced on his toes as if he were ready for the starting gun. I got into position, anticipating the break. Standing beneath the basket, Jud blew the whistle. The ball went from one forward to the point guard who caught it and Kessler was simply gone. I don't remember if he went right or left, but I spun around just in time to hear Jud's whistle, strident and prolonged. "There's no way, son, you're going to stop anybody, standing around flatfooted. Jesus, move your feet." He had taken two steps toward me and then turned back. "Again, please." Most of the team had wandered some, hands on their hips, looking at the floor or the empty stands, trying to stay out of the mix, but Kessler had stayed in position, ready to go. I was the first-string center, the big shot. I was supposed to make this play.

Back now. With the whistle, the ball went from forward to point guard who passed; Kessler jack-stepped me left — I fell for it — and then bounced right, buzz cut, elbows and knees zipping by in a blur. I didn't even have time to grab his jersey. Jud's whistle reached a new octave. Here he was, red-faced in front of me. I backed up. He followed, hands out demanding. "What the hell are you doing? Are you going to get this right, today?" Out of the side of my eye, I could see Kessler grinning. Everyone else found something else to look at. This was the dreaded inquisition, Jud's auto-da-fé, and I was the heretic, singled out and guilty of slow feet and fatigue and a timid heart.

My final mistake, a response to embarrassment and a bruised ego, was to cheat, Kessler having won the moment and being anxious, I could see, to win the next. "Let's get it right this time," Jud said and blew the whistle. Forward to point guard who passed just as Kessler tried to jack-step again; I met him with a forearm shiver just beneath his armpit and punched, driving up and out so his upper body stayed put while his feet kept going up. Horizontal before he landed with a "whump" on his back on the floor, Kessler never got to the other side of the key. Vindicated and stupid, I didn't help him up.

Jud erupted, his whistle boiling over in the middle of a face as red as I'd ever seen. He shuffle-trotted out toward me, fists clenched and head down, bull-like. Embarrassed and frustrated before, now I was scared, backing up as he got to me. I don't remember what he said for the ringing in my ears. I do remember my peripheral vision closing down as if his anger had grabbed at my shirt. My mouth was open, though I couldn't breath. And then, bang, bang, he started with his index finger pounding on my chest, once, twice . . . "Don't you ever . . ."

At the third bang, I broke ranks.

The telling takes far longer than my blocking his right arm away with my left hand and stepping with my left foot toward him, cocking my right fist so I could deliver the punch with authority. "Keep your fucking hands off me," I said quicker than the instant, a slur muddled by fear and anger. I was pushed into a corner and snapping. He took two quick steps back and dropped his whistle, and in that moment we both stood on intolerant ground, far beyond any diagram, watching each other.

Until Coach Harshman stepped in.

"Now, now," he said as if we were boys in a school yard. "We have a game to get ready for." The pontiff had spoken. Harshman, the final authority, refocused our energies on the abstract and holy. Jud was pit boss and teacher, but it was Harshman's team.

Jud and I didn't talk for the rest of the practice. That evening and all the next day, I agonized over what had happened. Fairy tales have this as the defining moment. The final breaking away. Conflict leads to self-sufficiency and independence. Jack cuts the beanstalk down. A mythological son strikes down his father when they meet anonymously, face to face on the road. I had never been so defiant of nor as violent with an authority figure. I was immediately lonely. Should I quit the team or was I already off? Independent for a day, I wanted back in the fold. But that seemed impossible.

The next day, in language as sweet as a good play, Jud fixed it. I heard him behind me as I warmed up early before practice, by myself, at a far corner basket in Bohler Gym. After the boundaries had been overstepped and the tolerances squeezed down to zero, the first thing he said to me was, "Mind if I throw you a few passes?"

"Sure," I said, turning and bouncing the ball to him to get ready for the "ready, shoot," drill.

"That is," he said, "if you don't hit me in the mouth."

"No," I said, "as long as you don't pound me in the chest if I make a mistake."

"Sounds fair to me" was all he said.

I have learned over the years that I am not the only player to have taken a swing at Jud. Rumor has it that one of Jud's West Valley High players connected with a right cross, and Jud's response after he got up from the floor was, "That's the most heart you've shown all day." It seems in character. That a player-coach relationship would break down and even turn violent is no surprise. Coaches, from high school to professional, pressure their players, set goals, and make demands. Players need a coach to convince them the pain they're going through is worthwhile. There's a fine line here between push and shove. When that line is obliterated, it's the coach's job to redraw it. That's what Jud did. He took charge and we all moved on.

When I was a senior, Pete the equipment manager finally talked to me. After three years of machinations and trials and seventy-four games, I felt as if I had earned respect from the coaches and my teammates and could watch at the far end of the court the new freshmen squirm and grimace under their first year with Jud. Despite such seniority, however, the pressure was always on, though the tolerances had been discovered and respected both ways, coach and player.

Perhaps what tempered Jud's maniacal intensity for the game was that he seemed capable of perspective, whether through humor, self-parody, or simply looking the other way. *Sports Illustrated* explains that "Heathcote . . . has a warmth about him, an awkward, gruff-uncle charm. He is most comfortable when turning the needle inward, and unlike Knight, he is incapable of taking himself seriously." True, there are many examples of Jud's self-deprecating humor. "Sooner or later, the game makes fools of us all," he has been quoted saying. "And I guess I'm living proof." And I remember his being able to poke fun at himself — the time on a road trip, for example, he backed the car over his own suitcases. For thirty miles no one dared speak until someone said from the back seat, "They were easier to get in the trunk." Even Jud had to laugh. Or the time we finally beat Oregon State at Corvallis in the season's next to last game and spent the night in downtown Portland at the Benson Hotel. Dick Vandervort, the trainer, gave us each five dollars to get something to eat. Then we were on our own in downtown Portland late on a Saturday night. I don't know whose idea it was to spend our five bucks at the topless nightclub three blocks north of the Benson, but six of us, four of whom were starters, headed for the nightlife, dressed in our crimson blazers with the Cougar insignias. We might as well have been wearing overalls and straw hats, as obvious as we were spread out in the front row, our five dollars spent on the two-drink minimum, the glasses weeping on the miniature tables. In blue light and fine timing before us onstage Fatima of the Nile rotated her tassels in opposite directions. We were near deep hypnosis when the door opened and in walked Dick Vandervort, Coach Harshman, and Jud. They took pains not to trip over us as they walked back behind us into the dark. No one turned to look. As the tassels slowed and we froze, out the door filed Dick Vandervort, Coach Harshman, and then Jud who turned to us, one hand on the door, and said, "This isn't the place we thought it was." The next day was a 250-mile trip from Portland to Pullman — a long, silent car ride home.

On the other hand, it's simply not true that Jud is "incapable of taking himself seriously." None of his players worked for Jud's sense of humor. To see the look on his face when the Spartans won the national championship in 1979 or his despair in 1990 when Georgia Tech's Kenny Anderson tied the game on an unwhistled, after-the-buzzer shot, a game Georgia Tech then won in overtime, is to see a coach for whom the game means everything. Lear couldn't have looked more tragic. Basketball was always first. Opinions, one-liners, wit, green blazers, and a bad hairstyle notwithstanding, the forty minutes on the court is serious business indeed.

Watching Michigan State practice on one of their visits to Iowa City, I realized that Jud's teams have always been a reflection of his character — serious, playful, and urgent. There was Jud on the floor at the end of practice trying to face-guard Shawn Respert, who moved left and right and called for the ball. "Mismatch, mismatch," Respert yelled, laughing. How true, both ways. Jud was sixty-four with a bad knee, but Respert played Jud's game.

So did we all. I'd like to think I took from my four years a sense of form and rhythm, of creative tension, the ability to concentrate, the need to get things right, and a friendship that has lasted years beyond my eligibility. In 1986, when *Headlong,* my first book of poems was published, I sent a copy to Jud. He wrote back, "Thanks so much for your book of poems. This is the first of many you will be famous for some day and I will be able to say, 'I knew him when.' I do hope sooner or later you will be able to figure out one that rhymes. Remember, you can always start, Roses are red, Violets are blue and go from there. I do plan to study them all and maybe sooner or later it will make me a smarter basketball coach." He ended his letter by saying, "I am looking forward to seeing you February 6. Count on four tickets as usual as we need all the support we can get."

I wrote back to thank him for the tickets and to say I wasn't sure if my poems would make him a smarter basketball coach but I knew playing basketball for him certainly made me a better poet. My legs are gone but my memory hasn't dimmed. Michigan State won by a point that evening on a three-point shot at the buzzer, picked up their water bottles and towels, and escaped to East Lansing before the Iowa crowd had a chance to sit back down. As the gym emptied out, I sat and waited, thinking of my divided loyalties. An Iowa alum now, I live in Iowa City and follow the Hawkeye basketball team, but here I was sitting all evening in a row of green sweaters, rooting for Michigan State. No, I was rooting for Jud. Ever since I left Washington State University, left home in effect, I've been loyal to Marv Harshman and Jud. They helped me grow up. And even though I don't play basketball much anymore, preferring the humility of tennis after a day of words, I still hear their voices. They have left me something parental, a kind of conscience that speaks from court side, saying in reference to whatever I do or make, "Too much here or not enough there," or "effort, please, effort," or "terrific," followed always by "try again."

RON C. JUDD

Race a Memorable First
for Seventeenth Man

FROM THE SEATTLE TIMES

ON BOARD *USA-67* — They told me where not to put my hands. If I could only figure out where not to put the rest of me.

Out here on the angry waters where the America's Cup will be won, a strong nor'westerly has kicked up, bringing with it swells of six to ten feet. We are powering upwind through a seventeen-knot breeze in *USA-67*, the sleek blue-and-black boat representing Seattle's hopes for sailing's greatest prize.

An Aussie is at the wheel. Kiwis are at the grinders. About $100,000 worth of sails are snapping and popping overhead. I'm sprawled spread-eagle astern, flat on my back, arms clutching a rail overhead, feet against the other side. Hanging on for dear life. Wishing, like a freshly gaffed ling cod, for that sweet, final bonk on the head.

On upwind legs in heavy seas, riding as the "seventeenth man" observer in the back of the OneWorld boat is a little like trying to stay seated in the middle of the bed of a pickup truck careening down a mountain pass. Each time the boat tacks, I spin around on my weather-suited body's stern end and point my bow the other way, struggling to stay on the uphill side of a deck slanting what for all the world seems like forty-five degrees.

"Bad wave coming!" yells a gray-jumpsuited crewman.

They don't kid about these things.

Ka-whump! The big, blue boat slams into it, blasting spray and sending a tsunami into the back of the boat, my little nesting place for the most fantastic two-hour ride of my life.

Here's the thing: no matter how wet, windy, turbulent, or tumultuous it would get this day, I kept catching glimpses of myself in crewmen's sunglasses to realize something I couldn't have dreamed: I never stopped grinning.

Which is saying something, considering how this thrill ride came to be, when the phone rang at 8:30 this morning.

"Ron," declared the voice of Bob Ratliffe, OneWorld's executive director. "Your country needs you."

My mind spun.

"The crew has specifically requested you," Ratliffe continued.

They probably wanted some quick-witted repartee to entertain the troops. Or an opportunity to absorb some of my, ahem, extensive sailing knowledge. Or . . .

"It's blowing big today. They need you as ballast."

He was serious.

I hesitated. See, I can get seasick staring into a chai tea latte whipped up by a light westerly breeze off the coast of Lake Sammamish. And given this day's blustery forecast, lunch could be lost.

But Ratliffe was persistent: OneWorld was up against Prada of Italy, the defending Louis Vuitton Cup champion. And the forecast called for breezes of twenty-five to thirty knots.

In sailboat racing, extra weight on the deck is actually a good thing in heavy winds. And it just so happened that I had trained extra hard all week for this gig, with a rigorous ballast-boosting training regimen that included ordering extra hollandaise sauce on my daily eggs Benedict.

I felt rested. Ready. Bulky. Needed. I swallowed hard. "I'll be there," I blurted.

Two hours later, after signing release forms I am fairly certain included the words "last rites" and "not our bloody fault," we were racing toward New Zealand's Hauraki Gulf in an inflatable chase boat, careening off green, wind-whipped waves bigger than Range Rovers.

Before I had a chance to rethink things, I was being transferred, along with other cargo, onto another inflatable, which caught up with OneWorld just outside the race course. In rolling seas, connecting with the big sailboat is not unlike an aerial refueling operation: a delicate dance in which the heaving chase boat makes contact with a heaving race yacht, then presses hard at midship while the transfer is made.

Skipper Peter Gilmour greeted me with a firm handshake, and quickly showed me the ropes. Namely, the halyards and lines to avoid.

"We've already lost one finger on this boat," he pointed out, matter-of-factly, tapping on a block. Say no more, captain.

With the start rapidly approaching, crewman Brian Ledbetter of Seattle popped back to offer some valuable advice. He outlined a three-by-four-foot area where, essentially, nothing can kill you, and you can't screw anything up. At the start, he said, get in it, crouch on all fours like an animal, and hang on.

Ninety seconds later, I saw what he meant. Prada's *Luna Rossa* and our boat circled each other like twenty-five-ton house cats in a shoebox, their crewmen shouting in Italian, our crewmen shouting in Aussie, Kiwi, Japanese, and Ballard American English.

The start is the one part of the race when the other boat is in close quarters, its reactions completely unpredictable. It is a total, undeniable rush.

At one point, our boat was bearing away from the start area and I completely lost track of the *Luna Rossa* — only to turn and see the gray bow headed dead for my head, less than a dozen yards away. "Stern! Watch the stern!" someone shouted. They veered off, barely, and our young Aussie helmsman, James Spithill, made a smart tack and beelined for the start, with another crewman counting down the seconds to another trademark OneWorld clean start.

Life gets a little more normal when the race is on. I scrunched up into position against the uphill side of the boat, watching the crew work its magic as we tacked upwind on a hard sideways slant.

It's clear that too much credit is given to the boat design; too little to the crew. Their clean, athletic movements in this precarious, upwind dance/slugfest — throughout which the boat's carbon-fiber hull and titanium rigging moan and screech in protest over high tensions and heavy loads — is a sight to behold.

Everyone is doing at least two things at once, monitoring their own equipment — and every single perceived movement of the opposing boat. After each tack is called and flawlessly performed, crewmen shuffle silently back to their posts — heads and bodies low to the deck, anything to reduce drag.

Before you know it, crewman Tatsuya Wakinaga is calling off boat lengths to the first upwind mark: "Four . . . three . . . two . . . one!" Synchronized chaos ensues as the boat tacks gracefully around the mark. Every man aboard, it seems, grabs on to a grinder and cranks furiously, at the same time keeping a careful eye on *Luna Rossa,* at this point still clinging within shouting distance to our port side.

At times like these, communication is constant. Some crewmen wear wireless headsets to receive commands from the helm. But most striking is the way they seem to read each other's minds, communicating through smooth movements honed by months of practice. When a small mistake is made on this boat, nobody yells to point it out. Everybody feels it, files it away — and goes on. It's the stuff for dissection later, on the tow in, not blame games in the middle of a race.

Magically and instantly, the spinnaker billows and we're running with the wind. Downwind runs, by comparison, are pure serenity — a chance to catch your breath. Seated cross-legged, facing astern on the deck, I watch in wonder as the big boat, under full sail, surfs down those big, whitecapped Hauraki Gulf waves with graceful, almost silent, ease.

On these runs, Aussies Gilmour, facing astern, and Spithill, steering forward, seem to have a unique language of navigation and wind.

Gilmour, the coach/general manager of this team, constantly scans the horizon to the rear, watching for puffs of wind, or, on this day, particularly strong swells to steer into and ride like a body surfer.

"Big puff coming in five, Jimmy," he says calmly to Spithill. The grinders roll, the sail is trimmed — and, like magic, you feel the boat surge with that puff, pushing forward like a revved-up car with the parking brake removed.

"Nice gain on that one," Gilmour says calmly, then adds, "Big wave on the side, Jimmy." Spithill turns slightly into it, and again, you feel the boat rise almost imperceptibly, riding the crest downwind with a perceptible forward surge.

It's pure magic.

It was so transfixing downwind and so tumultuous upwind that, ninety minutes into the race, it occurred to me I'd been riding on such sensory overload, I'd never even had time to think about getting seasick. I felt good — and lucky.

At the finish line, the crew is subdued. A handshake here, a "nice race" there. If you weren't listening closely, you'd never know we'd crossed the line.

By the time *Luna Rossa* gets there, OneWorld's chase boat is pulling alongside with lunch and fresh water. Everyone dresses down and relaxes. On the hourlong tow into port, Gilmour and the crew casually discuss what went well, and what needs work. They swap tales about life in Auckland, life in Seattle, and the next opponent.

It's just another day at the office for Seattle's America's Cup syndicate. And a lifetime memory for me. At the dock, I thank Gilmour and crew for the ride, telling the skipper if he needs the big ballast, he knows where to call.

As I climb off the boat, I tell one crewman a part of *USA-67* will always stay with me — and a part of me will always stay with it.

He thought I was waxing philosophic. But I really meant it. Years from now, when *USA-67* is decommissioned, having fought and won many a battle at sea, I'm fairly certain of one thing: they'll still find traces of my fingernails on that black nonslip deck.

SUSY BUCHANAN

Appetite for Destruction

FROM PHOENIX NEW TIMES

IT'S SATURDAY NIGHT. The air reeks of transmission fluid, scorched steel, and horse manure. A man jumps up and down on the roof of his car like a chimpanzee on a Samsonite. John Denver warbles "Sunshine on my shoulders . . . makes me hap-py" from tinny loudspeakers. Another man sheds his shirt and lays into his car with a sledgehammer. The thuds overpower the music, echoing into the night like a .357 in an elevator shaft. This is what makes these men happy. Fuck sunshine.

"I'm going to destroy my car tonight," vows Ryan Horn, a blond, blue-eyed twenty-six-year-old with a face better suited to a boy band than demolition derby.

"I'm going to kill it!" he sputters. "I've had enough! I want there to be nothing left when I go home tonight!"

Despite his apparent desperation, Horn knows just how he wants the car he's spent months working on to die. Although there will be forty other cars in the arena tonight, he'll plow through them all to reach just one, his target, Eric DePoy.

"I hate Eric, I hate him!" Horn says, looking over to where DePoy stands next to his black hearse-like station wagon, the same car that won him first place at the State Fair two weeks earlier.

"I'm sick and tired of hearing him whine about how we tag-teamed him at the fair," Horn continues. "I don't ever want to hear him whine again after tonight, except maybe about how he lost."

If Horn seems intense, he is only reflecting the intensity of the sport he loves. With its unholy industrial-strength carnage, only America could have birthed a spectacle like demolition derby. It is poetry and violence, a ritual Tristan Tzara would have loved.

"We are a furious Wind, tearing the dirty linen of clouds and prayers, preparing the great spectacle of disaster, fire, decomposition," Tzara wrote in his Dada Manifesto of 1918, but he might as well have been talking about demolition derby.

Drivers strip the biggest, baddest, and boldest carcasses of Detroit steel of the comfortable interiors and safety features that defined them in their genesis, and return these machines to a stark fury truer to their steely essence. They give the cars their souls back for one shining moment, and the results are intentionally disastrous.

As the creations of man lash out in the arena, these wagons and sedans that suffered through thirty years of slowing for speed bumps and carting around grocery bags are no longer safe and comfortable transportation. They are as much gladiators as the men who drive them, man and machine simultaneously, and seemingly, demonically possessed.

The rulers of the Arizona demolition derby scene are an elite, wizened coven of drivers who have run together for decades. Horn's nemesis, Eric DePoy, is their reigning champion.

The crew of middle-aged men who accompany him to battle are a select few who have through the years proven their worth in the arena. They know the deep, dark secrets that will keep a car running through fire and ruthless destruction. Most of them are balding.

The clan gathers before a derby to build cars together and trade wisdom. They consistently place in the top five and work hard to keep it that way. Their camaraderie extends to inside the arena as well. DePoy and friends band together to take out newer drivers they view as threats. Drivers like Horn, and his friends Justin Suhr and Jolee Murdell.

But tonight, in Buckeye, vengeance is burning in the young challengers' veins. DePoy was on Suhr two weeks ago at the State Fair, tag-teaming and pounding him as best he could through the thick mud.

Not this time.

"This is a small, fast track," Horn tells the small huddle of younger drivers, friends all. "There's no mud to protect [DePoy] tonight."

Tonight it is kill or be killed, and probably both.

*

Kevin Temple is one of DePoy's minions. A laid-back general contractor with thinning red hair, Temple is a derby junkie. Lured in after helping a friend build a car, Temple drove his first derby in 1986 and has been addicted ever since.

"It only takes one time to get the bug. Everybody loves derbies. Kids really love derbies," he says. "Most people enjoy seeing things destroyed."

But there is more to driving derbies than most casual fans recognize. It can take years for a novice driver to learn the secrets necessary to be competitive, Temple says, and these secrets are not something veteran drivers are willing to share.

"You have newer people who come up to you and want to be your friend and want you to tell them all your tricks," he says, shaking his head slowly. "That's not the way this works. You have to go through a lot of years of losing. You have to pay your dues and figure things out on your own."

A month before the fair, Temple surveys his '76 Impala and points out some of the modifications he has made.

The gas tank has been removed and replaced with a smaller, military gas tank that has been chained to the floor behind the front passenger's seat. The exhaust has been rerouted to sprout through holes cut into the hood with a blowtorch, resembling a half-dozen skeletal ribs. The motor has been chained and welded to the frame to prevent it from ending up in his lap. A crude roll cage has been added. The dashboard has been removed completely. Strategic cuts have been made to sections of the sides and trunk, which upon impact will cause the back end to crumple into a more effective weapon.

"It's funny to think that once this was somebody's pride and joy, sitting in their driveway as they showed it off to their friends," he says, pausing as he surveys his handiwork.

And then there are the tires, a demolition driver's Achilles' heel. Drivers have been known to fill them with cement to keep them from puncturing.

"Cement is illegal, of course," Temple says quickly. "I like to put a tire inside a tire, double tires, we call 'em." Double tires are also illegal, but not *as* illegal, Temple reasons. "It's not cheating, really. Just because I have an edge doesn't make me a cheater." Temple refuses to comment on other edge-garnering techniques. "I can't go there. Let's just say I don't do anything no one else can do."

Temple classifies himself as a semiprofessional. He attends twelve derbies a year around the state, and usually wins money. Although his winnings have bought him a new video camera in the past (to film derbies with) and a color TV (to watch derbies on), most of the dough goes to support his habit. "Say I win four derbies a year; that's four thousand dollars. I can buy a lot of cars with that money."

And if Temple is not in the money, he knows one of his friends will be. "There's a small group of guys who really know how to build cars. We work together. We race together. We help each other take out the other cars, then at the end we battle each other."

To hear him talk, there's not much competition. He searches his mind for names. "I think there's one younger driver named Justin who's pretty aggressive," Temple adds, "but I guarantee you it'll be one of us who wins it."

Justin Suhr has a baby swing in his living room and shells of dead cars in his back yard. He's twenty-six, a married father of two who works for a pool company. His wife doesn't care much for his hobby. "It's not the derbies she minds, but the time I spend on them," he says.

Suhr looks like a jock: tall, broad shoulders, slate blue eyes, earring, baseball cap, lip full of dip.

Five years ago his life changed. "I don't do anything else anymore for fun. I used to play basketball and stuff, then I got into this and it takes up all of my time. Besides work, it's just derby."

Suhr flips through a thick album of derby photos, depicting startling before and after shots, and a trophy here and there. "My dad [Jim "Slick" Suhr, who pits and builds cars with his son] drove for a few years in South Dakota. I remember when I was six or seven years old watching him work on cars, smashing in windshields," he reminisces. "It looked awfully fun to me. One day I came across a cheap car, entered a derby, and got hooked." The first car he ever owned ended up in a derby, he says. Wrecking it, he adds, was richly satisfying.

Suhr likens demolition derby to bumper cars for big boys. It's a chance, he says, to break all the rules of the road. "It's a weird, wonderful feeling when you run into people. The expression on their faces is great. You really find out what one car can do to another." He smiles shyly and nudges the carpet with his toe. "You can take your aggression out . . . and I have a lot of aggression."

In Suhr's back yard, Ryan Horn applies house paint to the '76 Impala. The color? "Recycling-can blue," Suhr says. Horn and Suhr met at a derby four years ago, discovered they lived near one another, and became close friends and teammates. Horn, too, was just starting out in derbies. "I can't really explain the feeling except to say it's a forty-five-minute adrenaline rush. The first time I went out, I was like, 'What have I gotten myself into?' Now I can't wait to get out there." Horn placed fourth in his first derby. "[Suhr] has more trophies than I do," he says, "but I'm more consistent."

Both are meticulous mechanics, and maniacs behind the wheel. "I think we've gotten a lot of respect out there," Horn says. "People watch out for us now. They don't want to make us mad or we'll destroy them."

Horn looks at Suhr. "Shall we start her up?" he says as he climbs up on the hood and lowers his wiry frame in through the windshield, snaking into the driver's seat. Horn and Suhr glance around the quiet street for a split-second, then Suhr removes a series of soda cans sitting on the exhaust pipes to keep rain and dust out. He takes a step back, Horn flips a switch, and the old Impala wails like a wounded animal, shattering any semblance of peace in the north Phoenix neighborhood. Exhaust screams out of the hood through the pipes that sputter and wheeze for a moment, then rumble violently enough to rattle the windows.

Horn and Suhr are momentarily mesmerized, as if the revving engine were an aria instead of a potential noise pollution citation. Horn guns it a few times, then switches it off.

A subdivision has moved in across the street in the last few months. The first families have taken up residence. It means the boys must be a little more restrained than they once were. Before construction began, the land the homes now sit on was a big dirt field, and Justin and Ryan could not resist taking a couple of cars out there for some one-on-one.

The following Friday night at the State Fair, both camps are assembled for what should be the greatest derby of the season. The evening is dark, pungent, and velvety smooth. The air shudders with drumbeats and piercing screams. Sparks shower and steel burns white-hot. The atmosphere is decidedly tribal as the rival teams and rogue individual challengers ready themselves for a fight to the death.

The cotton-candy crowd pays little attention to the brewing drama deep in the pits, where, oblivious to the midway's Ferris wheels and fried Twinkies, drivers put the finishing touches on their cars. It's not a delicate business. Engines rev, and blowtorches bore into bumpers as inspectors check for violations and safety features, ordering duct tape here, chains there.

In one corner: a fleet of shiny, sleek station wagons belonging to DePoy and his crew. On the opposite side of the pits: Horn, Suhr, and their friends prep their fleet of banged-up Impalas.

This is the first of three scheduled nights of racing at the Arizona State Fair, a tradition for thirty years. The grandstands hold seven thousand people, and before the event can begin they are completely full. Jon Sellers, the derby's promoter, is the Don King of motorized events in Arizona. He's hard to miss in his ever-present black Stetson, bulging belt buckle, and cowboy boots, but in case you did, somehow, miss him, his announcers remind the crowd over and over to "look for the Jon Sellers name" at every motorized event they attend.

Sellers took over promotion of the derby shortly before retiring from the Phoenix Police Department, where he worked as a detective. (Sellers was the chief investigator on the Don Bolles case.) Besides promoting the derby each year, Sellers sings country-western music and calls women pretty little fillies, oozing honky-tonk charm.

Sellers is as organized as he is personable. During his tenure at the fair he has transformed what could be a chaotic, rule-bending free-for-all into a smooth, crowd-pleasing spectacle of family entertainment. His events start and end on a schedule as precise as Stalin's trains.

But try as he might, Sellers can't control every variable. The derby arena has just come off four nights of monster trucks and remains muddy and sticky like chocolate cake batter.

The traction his drivers need to obtain to make walloping hits isn't there, and the drivers are complaining. Suhr, Horn, and their

teammate Jolee Murdell mostly spend their time in the arena trying to get unstuck instead of attacking. Sellers promises the arena
just needs another day to dry out, and that the action will be much
faster Saturday night. Nature has other plans.

Saturday a hard rain saturates Phoenix, turning the arena into a
swamp. Sellers cancels his "rain or shine" derby for the second
time in thirty years. Sunday, as clouds circle, Sellers rounds up a
fleet of derby crews with four-wheel-drive trucks and has them drive
around and around the arena for hours trying to pack down the
mud. They drive until they run out of gas, but the ruts are still deep
enough to lose a sheep in.

Despite their efforts, the main event that night is a big disappointment. The crowd thins midway through the show, tired of
watching a parking lot of stuck cars spin their wheels. The drivers
are frustrated, too. All except Eric DePoy, who manages to win
without receiving or inflicting any real damage. This means his
wagon will be at the Buckeye derby, the last of the season, in two
weeks.

So, the young challengers vow, will they.

Two weeks later, as the sun sets in Buckeye, Horn and Murdell
head to the concession stand to grab a hot dog. Suhr's father, Slick,
looks around the crowded field for his son. "Aw, he's off talking to
somebody," Slick says, lighting a cigarette. "He's kind of the social
butterfly. Maybe he's talking to the Shoeless boys."

The Shoeless boys are exactly the type of demolition derby drivers Suhr says fans expect to see. It makes him cringe. "You know,
the media always picks some scraggly haired redneck with a cigar
butt hanging out of his mouth in a '6os helmet driving some heap
into the arena." There is that element, Suhr says as he walks over to
talk to a prime specimen, "but most of us are real respectable."
He's proud of his sport, and he and Horn both shower and put on
clean clothes before a derby.

By all appearances, Shoeless Jim does not know a shower nearly
as well. He still draws a crowd; a Springer-esque celebrity even
in Buckeye. Tonight, Shoeless Jim talks with Suhr in front of an
unrecognizable heap that looks more fragile than a wadded-up
Kleenex.

Shoeless Jim Wagner and his brothers are full-time demolition derby drivers from Missouri, where they drive forty to sixty derbies from May to October every year. They spend the offseason working as ranch hands in Arizona, and racing in derbies they aren't banned from.

Shoeless Jim is twenty-six years old with thick glasses and a permanently dazed look on his face. He's been racing since he was thirteen. The shoeless nickname stems from the fact that he and his kin don't wear shoes — ever — because "that's the way our daddy raised us. That's how everyone is back home."

Going barefoot can be a hazard as a ranch hand, and can be downright dangerous in the arena, especially since Shoeless Jim prefers to drive a manual transmission. "Remember that time you duct-taped a boot to the clutch so your foot wouldn't slip?" asks Suhr with a smile. "Uh, yup," says Shoeless Jim.

The Shoeless boys are no longer welcome at the State Fair. Sellers, and other drivers, cite sandbagging (hiding from the action), but Shoeless Jim says he's been banned for "political differences. My daddy was the only man in history to win all three nights at the State Fair with the same car. We don't fit in with the promoter's idea of who should win, so he don't want us there." Buckeye isn't so picky.

A few yards from the Shoeless boys stands Eric DePoy, holding court. Suhr may enjoy making the rounds and trading small talk with other drivers, but DePoy stays put. People come to him. DePoy is tall and clean-cut, with rust-colored hair, an orange APS shirt, and snug black jeans that he likes to adjust when he talks with Justin. Eric adjusts, Justin spits, almost as if trading dance moves while DePoy's prize-winning wagon lurks behind him.

He's still strong competition, and no car should look so good after doing in forty-two others.

DePoy's prepared the wagon with the utmost care. His precision is diabolical. "Look at that," says Horn, peering inside the stark interior of the long, ebony body with wide eyes. "You see all those seams where he's welded? I did that once. Once," he gulps. "You have to go through after you strip it and scrape off this shiny glue they put on the seams, then weld to reinforce them. It takes, like, months!"

The drivers' meeting is called next. The typical warnings include no sandbagging, no hits to the driver's-side door, as well as cautions against arena hits (speeding from one end of the arena to another to nail someone) and T-boning.

Because of the number of cars, organizers decide to run three heats and take the top eight cars from each for the main event. As they call out the names for each heat, Suhr, Horn, Murdell, and three other sympathetic young racers find themselves together in the first heat. DePoy is in the third heat.

The challengers converge in front of Suhr's car and assess the competition. With six out of the top eight in their heat being friendly, they must move aggressively on the other cars, and keep their objectives straight. "There's a mean-looking '50s Mercury wagon and an old Buckeye cop car that need to go away," Horn says. "The cop car and the Mercury are the ones we need to pound," Suhr agrees. "You got that, [Murdell]?" jokes Slick. "Do you want me to write their numbers on your visor?"

The announcer begins calling drivers into the arena. Suhr dons his helmet, spits, then slips gracefully into his car. "I don't care what they said at the drivers' meeting about arena shots," he says. "I'm gonna come out there and make some really hard hits. We need to get the crowd behind us."

The boys back out of their slots and rumble toward the arena gate. Slick talks about his son's first derby in Buckeye as he clambers up the grandstand, a video camera in hand.

"He was smoking so bad you could barely see him, there was this white cloud all around him." Suhr won that year, and his dad says proudly, "It was a heck of a finish. As soon as he shut off his engine, the car burst into flames. The crowd loved it."

Two factors make his son competitive. "Mainly it's the driving," he says. "He knows how to watch for cars in the right place and where and when to hit. Also, he's kind of meticulous about the way he builds things."

Then Slick smiles without turning his head. "Here comes Jolee [Murdell], here comes my car," he says. "I can tell by the sound of the motor." Murdell dates Slick's daughter, Suhr's sister, and is the least experienced, and most nervous, of the three.

As the rest of the cars line up backward on either side of the arena, a firefighter stationed along the edge motions to Murdell to leave the arena. There is a confusion over car numbers. With the cacophony of revving engines, this is no place for a discussion, so

Murdell pulls out of the arena, back into the pit. Slick is puzzled, but mostly worried. "I don't know what happened; they'll probably put him in another heat, but that's not good. I hate to see Jolee out there alone."

10, 9, 8 . . .

Slick focuses his video camera . . . 4, 3, 2, 1! The crowd shouts, and suddenly it sounds like a swarm of bees as cars shimmy across the arena to make contact.

After a few soft hits and maneuvers, Suhr breaks away from the pack and skates quickly around the dusty arena looking for his targets. But before he can do much damage, the action is stopped.

A devastating hit has knocked the hood of a black sedan straight through to the passenger's compartment. The driver is pinned underneath and safety personnel can't tell if he's conscious or decapitated.

The firefighters slide the hood back to where it belongs, the driver climbs gingerly out of the window, apparently unharmed, and jogs out of the arena. The crowd applauds and begs for more. The green flag waves again and Suhr and Horn work both ends of the Mercury for a while before Horn gets spun around and moves toward the cop car.

Suhr is enraged, though, and begins a series of devastating hits on the Mercury that push it closer and closer to the concrete barriers at one corner of the arena. The crowd cheers, dogs bark. "Boom! Boom!" yells a toddler, laughing. Slick, one eye glued to the camcorder, says softly, "Right on target."

The Mercury is pinned in the corner and can neither avoid Suhr's pummeling nor inflict any real damage of its own. Suhr backs up and flies forward at him one last time, shoving the Mercury up and over the concrete barrier where he high-centers.

Although the Mercury flounders, paralyzed, Suhr backs up and pounds him again. The Mercury driver reaches out angrily and rips the flag from his window, disqualifying himself.

Suhr wheels around quickly and looks for Horn. Horn, however, is dead in the water. Red flags wave again and the heat is over. Suhr drives out of the arena, but not Horn. His steering column is useless, and as a tractor drags him to the pits, he shrugs and spins the steering wheel like a top.

"I gotta do something fancy here," says Horn after reviewing the problem. He jacks the car up, changes a shredded tire in seconds, and goes to work on the steering with friends gathering around to offer advice.

Meanwhile, Murdell is sent out alone in the second heat. Although he is known as an easy target, most of the older drivers have chosen a different sacrificial lamb, Shoeless Jim.

They move in on him like orcas on a seal, tossing him to and fro hard enough that he bounces off every surface of what's left of his car. He's obviously out of commission, but the feeding frenzy continues until Shoeless manages to stick one arm out through his windshield and raise a middle finger. He breaks off his flag with the other. His face is dripping with blood.

In the third heat, DePoy is virtually untouched, protected by his horde.

Murdell, Horn, and Suhr prepare for the main event, eyeing DePoy every now and again. Horn has pounded, twisted, and finally blowtorched his way around the steering problem. He fires up his twisted ride with a relieved smile. "God, I love that sound right there, it makes me feel all tingly!"

DePoy stands tall in his pit, unflinching, pokerfaced. "I can only worry about myself," he says. "I can't control the other cars. There are teams, you know. Justin and them . . . and us. I'm only saying I'm going to try not to hit my friends."

DePoy glances over at what is left of Suhr's and Horn's cars. "They're very competitive when they have fresh cars, but they're kind of beat up tonight," he says dismissively.

The organizers draw out the suspense between the third heat and the finale, running lawn mower races for an hour as drivers prepare, and wait. Finally they are summoned back to the arena.

Murdell straps on his helmet and waves good-bye to his nine-year-old brother Jordan. "Jolee, watch out," the boy says, gripping his mother's hand. "I will, Jordan, I will," Murdell vows.

When the melee begins, Suhr homes in on DePoy and slaps him with a hit on the rear driver's-side door. DePoy's buddies move in to block Suhr, but he spins around and nails him in the back end hard enough to make the crowd gasp.

Horn moves in to protect Suhr, blocking a potentially devastating hit from DePoy's friend Glenn Grim. DePoy's out of reach now, so Suhr moves to the Mercury he picked on in the first heat, slamming it once, then backing into it again, ripping into its side with his rear end that has been bent and twisted into a battering ram.

Horn chases down DePoy and aims for a radiator shot that just misses. DePoy's friends come to his rescue, and now there are four of them on Suhr at once, delivering blows from all four sides, crunching him for a good three minutes until he manages to break free.

Horn and Suhr resume their abuse of DePoy, making him the meat in their sandwich as they slam him from both sides.

DePoy is hobbling now, but so is Suhr. He's giving as good as he's getting, but a rear end to the grille sends a geyser of steam shooting into the air. "That's Justin losing his water," Slick narrates for the camcorder. There are just over a dozen cars left when Horn also runs into trouble. He's trying to extricate himself from a pile-up when the competitor lying on his hood is black-flagged. Horn can't move. Murdell is in a similar heap at the far end of the arena with a busted transmission.

Suhr circles around the dead cars, trying to find DePoy, but without a radiator he hasn't got much time. Suddenly he's T-boned hard, knocking his car a good ten feet sideways. The radiator quits, and he's disqualified. DePoy soon follows. David Schueller, a DePoy teammate, wins the derby a few minutes later.

Horn and Suhr regroup in the pit area. "Oh well," Suhr says. "At least we took out Eric."

Tractors pull off body after body, but not Horn. His mortally wounded Impala is still running, much to his dismay.

This was meant to be a suicide mission. Horn looks at the mutilated heap in disgust. It's either finish it off tonight, or live with it until the next derby, in April. "No way am I taking this thing home," he vows.

Although the main derby is over, the women's powder-puff remains. It's Horn's last chance. With his radiator gone, he knows his car has just a few minutes of life left. All he needs is a woman. "Maybe we should put a wig on Jolee and let him race," Slick suggests.

Horn kicks a tire, then turns to survey the pit area where a few wide-eyed fans wander between wrecked cars.

The furrows in his brow disappear as he spots a woman standing nearby. He's on her in an instant. "I'm begging you to kill my car.

There's still just enough life left in it that I can't stand it, please, please."

The woman does not say no immediately, and that's all Horn needs. "Listen, after your first hit you're going to love it. Forget your instinct about not hurting other people, forget everything but reverse and forward. And no brakes, there's no need for brakes here." The woman remains unconvinced. "How hard are the hits?" she asks.

Horn is honest. "The last powder-puff here was brutal, worse than the men. It's like women don't care about the rules." She takes a step back but he continues. "Look, you're not going to go much faster than twenty miles an hour, maybe thirty. Of course, a head-on when you're both going thirty is like hitting a brick wall at sixty . . . but you'll be okay." She looks terrified. He realizes he's losing her, and pulls out his trump card. "Here, get in. Just sit behind the wheel and see how you feel."

She lets loose of her daughter's hand, steps up on the hood, and eases into the seat. Grabbing hold of the steering wheel, a wide grin blooms across her face. "Um, can I start it?" she says. "Sure," Horn says, smiling widely. He shows her the switch, she flicks it, and the roaring engine makes her shriek in delight. "All right!" she shouts over the engine, "this is great! Now what do I have to do, just go hit people?"

STEPHEN J. DUBNER

Life Is a Contact Sport

FROM THE NEW YORK TIMES MAGAZINE

THE BANANAS are distributed first. Young women from the league office tote them on their hips in big wicker baskets. Then come the condoms, in smaller baskets. Given the sheer plenitude and the wicker, the enterprise almost has the feel of a summer-camp picnic. One banana and one condom for every young man in the hotel ballroom, 262 of them, the entire rookie draft class of the National Football League. Then the woman onstage, a grandmotherly dynamo named Sandra McDonald, commands the rookies to practice technique. The condom is a condom, and the banana is. . . .

There is a fair amount of snickering. In her sweetly hectoring southern accent, McDonald, an AIDS counselor, tries to shush the rookies. "Someone in this room," she says, "is gonna go get AIDS because y'all are not listening."

If the bananas don't get their attention, the photographs do: extreme close-ups of gonorrhea and syphilis and herpes infections. The room quakes with groans and wails.

Now they are listening. Now they are grabbing for the microphone. How did Magic Johnson really get HIV, they want to know. ("I don't know," says McDonald, "I'm not Magic Johnson. But we need to respect what he said — that he had a lot of sex with a lot of different women.") Is it true, they want to know, that AIDS was invented in a laboratory to kill off young black men? ("Baby, we're in the fire now; we don't have time to find out who struck the match.") One rookie asks about oral sex — can you get AIDS that way?

"I know that one's close to y'all's hearts," McDonald says. "And I wish I could give you a blanket permission, but I can't. I would not want you to be the first person in the world to get AIDS that way."

Another rookie waves his hand. "I've heard a lot of horror stories about women setting up guys," he says. "So, is it true that if a woman puts K-Y Jelly in her vagina, it'll, like, burn up a condom?"

Such woman-as-predator tales are common among professional athletes, and McDonald has come to expect them. "No, baby, that's not true," she says, "but that's a real good question."

And so it goes for the rest of her hour onstage. She knows how to talk to the rookies. She knows that, physically, they are grown men (and then some), but in other significant ways they are not. The average rookie is a man-child in the promised land. He has some growing up to do — and the promised land, Sandra McDonald and others are here to tell him, is not quite as he imagined it. Some of the rookies will make a great deal of money, but many will not. Some of them will bring home trophies, but most will not. And a few of them will get in big trouble.

The sports pages this summer have been full of mayhem and stupidity. Baseball suffered the triple threat of steroids, strike, and Seligry. Vacationing basketball writers were kept busy covering the former all-star Jayson Williams (who is charged with aggravated manslaughter in the shooting of a limousine driver) and Allen Iverson (who supposedly threw his naked wife out of their house in the middle of the night — "in the manner of an aggrieved Fred Flintstone putting out the cat," as *Sports Illustrated* blithely put it — and then went looking for her). Al Unser Jr., who has twice won the Indianapolis 500, was arrested on charges that, while drunk, he hit his girlfriend in the face and abandoned her beside an interstate, also in the middle of the night. As Unser admitted after the charges were dropped, "I made some very poor choices."

In late June, the NFL convened its rookies in the hope of teaching them to make choices that aren't so poor. For the better part of four days, the league commandeered La Costa Resort and Spa, north of San Diego, for a "rookie symposium." Every drafted rookie was required to attend (or pay a $10,000 fine), from the number-one pick, David Carr, to the lowly seventh-rounders. They were not allowed to leave the premises without permission, or have guests, or drink alcohol. Cell phones and pagers were banned from the proceedings, as were do-rags, bandannas, and sunglasses. The

NFL is working hard to breed the thug life out of any rookie so in-
clined. From 8:00 A.M. until 10:00 P.M., the players would sit
through lectures about the pitfalls that await the unwary: paternity suits and domestic abuse charges, bar fights and drug stings,
crooked financial advisers and greedy hangers-on. The symposium
would play like a blend of motivational seminar, boot camp, and
Scared Straight, full of cautionary tales.

The greatest cautionary tale, however, was an unspoken one.
The NFL has been holding this symposium for six years. Major
League Baseball and the National Basketball Association began
similar versions even earlier. Which means that, of the relatively few
professional athletes who do hit the crime blotter, the vast majority
have already heard and not listened.

In the ballroom, Harold Henderson, the executive vice president of labor relations for the league, welcomes the rookies with
congratulatory vigor: "You're in the NFL and your life will never be
the same again!" They respond with a round of prideful tittering.
"The average rookie makes $460,308," says Henderson. "We might
have our first $100 million career player here in the room!" They
sit back in wide-body leather chairs, a sea of Fubu and Sean John,
of cornrows and farm-boy buzz cuts. And yes, they are huge. Huge
in a different way than in seasons past — since the NFL outlawed
steroids more than ten years ago, football bodies are more KFC
than AAS — but still huge. At the sign-in desk, I came upon Bryant
McKinnie, a six-foot-eight, 343 pound lineman from the University
of Miami; it was like coming upon an upended SUV. He smiled,
gently, from high above.

Having pumped the rookies up, Henderson now deflates them.
"Seventy percent of you in this room will make the opening-day ros-
ter — and 30 percent of you won't," he says. "Almost 50 percent of
you will not be in the league after four years."

Mike Haynes, a Hall of Fame defensive back who is now vice president for player and employee development for the NFL, joins
Henderson onstage. "How many of you guys know what you want to
do when your NFL career is over?" he asks. Only a few dozen rookies raise their hands. Haynes gives a chiding smile. This is a paradox the rookies would confront throughout the symposium. As
athletes, they must have blinding confidence in their abilities; now
they are being asked to envision their careers flaming out at any

moment. "The NFL," as Sandra McDonald would say later, "stands for Not For Long."

The opening-night panel discussion, "Life as a Rookie," features four budding NFL stars who were rookies last year. Kendrell Bell, a Pittsburgh Steelers linebacker, tells of his great awakening to the verities of income tax: "I got a million-dollar signing bonus. But then I got the check, and it was only $624,000. I thought, 'Oh, well, I'll get the other half later.' Then I found out that's all there was. I thought, 'They can't do this to me.' Then I got on the Internet and I found out they can."

Richard Seymour, a defensive tackle for the New England Patriots, describes the hazing a rookie should expect: at the very least, running errands for the veterans and carrying their sweaty pads. (At the worst, a veteran may try to break a rookie's skull — for it is the veteran's job, after all, that the rookie is trying to win.) One night, Seymour recalls, the Patriots rookies had to take the Patriots veterans out to dinner. The veterans ate aggressively and drank Cristal. Seymour's share of the tab: $15,000. That, he says, was when he decided to put himself on a budget. And he decided that, when old friends came looking for handouts, he had to say no.

One rookie in the crowd stands up. "People have been investing in me all my life," he says. "I can't just shut them all off."

Seymour shoots him a look. "Now that you're in the NFL, everybody's going to say they be for you," he says. "But all they're going to be for me is leeches."

The next day, over lunch with the Oakland Raiders rookies, I learned that the leeching had already begun. The phone calls started back in April, when the rookies were drafted. "Some of my homeboys were wanting to put together a rap group, and they needed $8,000 to shoot a video," says Keyon Nash, a defensive back who grew up in Colquitt, Georgia. "I said, 'Man, I never even heard you rap.'"

The other Raiders laugh knowingly. Most of them have taken to carrying two cell phones: one for family and "real" friends, the second sometimes called a "girlfriend phone."

According to a loose survey I conducted during the symposium — of players, counselors, and league and union officials — roughly 50 percent of the rookies have fathered children. (About 10 percent, meanwhile, are married.) The mothers of those children are often shunted to that girlfriend line.

"I heard from an uncle I hadn't seen in six years," says Napoleon Harris, a linebacker whom the Raiders drafted in the first round. "He wanted two things. He wanted free tickets, and he wanted me to set him up with girls. And I started hearing from a cousin I hadn't seen since I was ten. He's been in jail and everything. He was calling me every day, sometimes twice in twenty minutes. A couple weeks ago, I had to snap. He says, 'I'm just calling to tell you how happy I am for you.' I had to say: 'Look, dog, I know you're happy for me. I'm happy for me, too, and I'll get a lot happier when you stop calling my [expletive] phone.'"

Harris grew up in suburban Chicago (he made the National Honor Society in high school) and graduated from Northwestern. He is sharp, funny, confident. Some rookies at the symposium seem cowed by the step up to the NFL; not so Harris. "This is what guys like myself dream about all your life, to be a superstar," he says. "When I'm done, twelve or fourteen years from now, I want these guys sitting here saying to you, 'Hey man, I want to be like Napoleon Harris; he changed the game.'"

Harris was considered the best linebacker in this year's draft. (One scouting report called him a "big hitter with a touch of nasty.") Like many of the rookies, he hasn't yet signed a contract, which means he hasn't yet been paid. Contracts would be signed in the coming weeks, toward the start of training camp in late July. But Harris knew what to expect. As the number 23 pick overall, he would be paid about $3 million as a signing bonus, plus a salary of at least $225,000, the rookie minimum. (A sixth-round pick like Keyon Nash, meanwhile, would get a signing bonus of just $45,000 and, if he makes the team, his salary.)

Although they would hear a great deal during the symposium about not spending money that wasn't yet theirs, about the wisdom of buying mutual funds versus $60,000 SUVs, a lot of players are already driving SUVs. Their agents or bankers have been only too happy to extend them credit. Some of them buy cars for all their old friends. Andrew Park, a social worker who led sessions during the symposium, told me why: "They lack refusal skills because they've never had anything to refuse before."

I ask Napoleon Harris what he has spent so far. "All I spent was $8,000 last Christmas," he says. "But $6,000 of that was for a mink coat for my mom. My father, he passed away when I was sixteen. I'm the oldest in the family." Harris is wearing a pair of small hoop earrings with tiny diamond chips. I ask how much they cost. "No, I got these for free from a jewelry store back home. I gave them some autographs, sent some friends there." What, I ask, will he do with his signing bonus? "I think I'll just put it up. They told us about the NFL having a 401(k) with a two-for-one match, so that's a win-win situation. There's only one thing I want to do now, which is get my mom a house. That's a must." Harris fingers one of his earrings. "I'm a mama's boy," he adds, matter-of-factly.

The rest of the Raiders, half-listening to Harris over their plates of roast beef and fried chicken and macaroni and cheese, start nodding in agreement. "Gotta get Mama that house!" one of them says. And they all burst out with a laughter beyond happy.

Most of the rookies admit they would rather be elsewhere. The symposium cuts into the last vacation they'll have until midwinter. Where, I ask Joaquin Gonzalez, a seventh-round pick of the Cleveland Browns, would he be if not here? "To be totally honest?" he says. "I'd be home, sleeping off a hangover." Between lectures, and sometimes during them, rookies bolt themselves into bathroom stalls for half-hour phone calls to their agents.

Back in the ballroom, Zachary Minor has taken the stage. "Character," he tells the rookies, "is what you do when you're angry, afraid, or bored, and no one is watching." Minor is an educator and actor from New York who, with his troupe of seven other actors, stages bad-news scenarios for the rookies in all four major sports leagues.

Minor writes the NFL scenarios in consultation with the league. They are meant to be ultra-realistic, and they are. In one scene, two actors play a pair of rookies who discover that the woman they shared in a hotel room eight months earlier — consensually, they thought — is charging them with sexual assault. As the real-life rookies watch, they probably know that Darrell Russell, a Pro Bowl defensive tackle for the Oakland Raiders, is currently awaiting trial on similar charges.

Between scenes, Minor adopts the mien of a prison counselor or storefront preacher. His mantra: "Choices. Decisions. Consequences." He'll say it a thousand times by symposium's end, and although the rookies start to mock it, they can't seem to forget it, either.

In another scenario, a ballplayer decides to kick his live-in girlfriend out of the house. "You better think long and hard about telling me to walk," she tells him, "because I'm going to walk with half." It turns out that his girlfriend has already seen a lawyer. She and the ballplayer have been cohabiting long enough, she explains, to be considered legally married.

En masse, the rookies boo. "That's not fair!" they shout, and more unprintable terms. Minor calms them down. "Every state has its own common-law marriage statute," he says. "When you get to your states where you're playing, please make yourself aware of what that statute is."

The scene continues. The ballplayer badly desires to smack his girlfriend in the head. That desire, encouragingly, also brings boos.

"Good!" Minor says. "Remember: Choices. Decisions. Consequences. We all get angry. But you've got to deal with it appropriately. Each of you has a player-development representative on your team — use them. Go to them for help. You're not a bad person for going to counseling."

Domestic and sexual assaults are hardly new problems. In early 1996, shortly after O. J. Simpson was acquitted of murder, two members of Congress wrote to NFL Commissioner Paul Tagliabue, urging him to address "repeated tragic examples" of football players' violence against women. The league held its first rookie symposium the following summer. A year later, in *Pros and Cons: The Criminals Who Play in the NFL,* the authors Jeff Benedict and Don Yaeger argued that violence against women was only part of the problem. "Our research," they wrote, "shows that 21 percent — one of every five — of the players in the NFL have been charged with a serious crime."

The league is still steaming about that claim. At the symposium, I spoke with Milt Ahlerich, a former FBI assistant director who is now the NFL's security chief. "The guys who wrote this book *Pros and Cons* took players from something like the time they were fifteen years old until they were forty-five, and showed that they had criminal records over that time," he said. "Give me a break!"

Before each year's draft, Ahlerich's office compiles a criminal background report on all likely draftees. Those reports are hardly exhaustive, Ahlerich said. "We're not going out and knocking on doors and saying: 'What kind of kid was Johnny Johnson when he was around here? Did he smoke dope in the back yard?'"

But, increasingly, individual teams do go knocking on old doors.

They track down high school girlfriends and guidance counselors. They also put the players through strenuous predraft interviews and psychological testing. One night during the symposium, between the end of lectures and the 12:30 A.M. bed check, I sat up talking with Jeff Hatch, the New York Giants' third-round pick. (He was bleary-eyed. La Costa Resort is overrun with rabbits, and one of them got in Hatch's room two nights earlier; its rustling kept him awake.) Hatch is a six-foot-seven, 310-pound offensive lineman, a Penn graduate and this year's only Ivy draftee. "It was unbelievable," he said of the predraft testing. "You're just being grilled by these people. I must have talked to fifteen or sixteen teams. The Giants, you may or may not know, are notorious; they give you this 438-question test. It takes an hour and a half if you're moving decently. Questions like, 'Did you ever put a dog in the microwave?' Or like, 'If there's no cops around, do you speed?'"

Milt Ahlerich contended that the NFL, its teams, and the players' union are conspiring to minimize the crimes committed by players. "This symposium is very successful," he said. "It's a tone-setting device; it raises the expectations with the players. But we will not save all souls here, and it's hard to measure the souls that were saved."

Ahlerich further contended that, despite the claims of *Pros and Cons,* NFL players are in fact arrested at a lower rate than young men in the general population. And a variety of independent studies back him up. But the perception of NFL gangsterism was fixed, perhaps indelibly, three summers ago, when two players stood charged with murder in separate incidents. Ray Lewis, a Baltimore Ravens linebacker, ultimately pleaded guilty to obstructing justice and returned to lead the Ravens to a Super Bowl victory. Rae Carruth, a wide receiver for the Carolina Panthers, went to prison for helping gun down his pregnant girlfriend.

Since then, the NFL has freighted the symposium with speakers who try to scare the rookies into lawfulness. Irving Fryar, a recently retired wide receiver, is such a speaker. "We're going to have some idiots come out of this room," he begins. "Those of you feeling good about yourselves, stop it. You ain't did nothing yet." Fryar recites his career stats: seventeen NFL seasons, a drug habit since he was thirteen, and four trips to jail. "The first time, I was stopped in New Jersey," he says. "I was on my way to shoot somebody. Driving my BMW. I had guns in the trunk, and I got taken to jail. The second time, also guns. Third time was domestic abuse. Fourth time, it was guns again. No. Yeah, yeah, it was guns again. Things got so bad for me, I put a .44 magnum up to my head and pulled the trigger." Now Fryar is a minister. "When I was a rookie," he says, "we didn't have anything like this. I had to learn it the hard way. Don't use me as an example of what you can get away with, brothers. Use me as an example of what you shouldn't do."

Fryar exhorts the rookies to, among other things, dress with class. "Why," he asks, "do you guys wear your pants down below your butt?"

It's plainly meant as a rhetorical question, but one rookie stands up to answer. "Najeh Davenport, Green Bay Packers," he identifies himself. "It's comfortable. That's what this generation is about. Kris Kross did it, and we do it."

The other rookies laugh, and Fryar pounces: "You're going to tell me you follow some little boy?"

Davenport keeps talking, digging a deeper hole. His tone, though, is less defiant than vacant. He used to cinch up his pants with his shoestrings, he says, but now he uses his shoestrings in his shoes. The other rookies start to jeer him; Fryar stops just short of cursing Davenport. Finally he sits down.

There are more scary stories. Marcus Spears, a veteran offensive lineman with the Kansas City Chiefs, tells the rookies about sitting out his first season with an injury. "I turned to drinking a lot," he says. "And on occasion, I'd smoke some sticky. We'd go to these strip clubs, and I would get so drunk, I'd drive home and not even know I drove home. Four, five, six times a week. And in the offseason, I really thought about trying to kill myself."

Alongside Spears onstage is Luis Sharpe. The rookies are informed that Sharpe is attending the symposium "through a special arrangement with his parole officer." With his short-sleeve shirt, plain tie, and high-water pants, Sharpe has the determined look of a repentant. A onetime first-round draft pick and All Pro, Sharpe now lives and works at a drug-rehab center in Phoenix. In a grave voice, he recalls how he was making $2 million a year when he was shot twice and then — though Sharpe doesn't detail his own crimes — landed in prison. "One day, a guard was killed," he says, "and everybody was locked down. They took us outside, in the Arizona heat, laid us down with our hands behind our backs, on concrete for four or five hours. One guard came up to me and said, 'Yeah, Sharpe, you're not a Pro Bowl player now, are you?'"

The rookies are edging forward in their seats. A couple of them dab at tears. Sharpe's voice is so brittle with longing and regret that you cannot help feeling for him — and hope that your own life unspools in exactly the opposite direction.

Then, as if pained over the gloom he has cast, Sharpe offers a bouquet: "I know that Christ is alive today, and that he wants to touch each and every one of your lives. So listen to the guys on this stage. And go to your Bible studies."

The rookies applaud robustly. Marcus Spears and Irving Fryar, too, will tell the rookies that things got better only when they turned their lives over to Jesus. Again, heartfelt applause. At such moments, all the raunch and bravado washes away; the symposium feels like a church sleepaway camp.

If it is generally agreed that Jesus is the force that will lift up a football player, it is also agreed that two other forces exist only to bring him down. The first is the media. "When you mess up, they'll be all over you like bees on honey," Greg Aiello, the NFL's chief media spokesman, warns the rookies. But without the media, Aiello reminds them, there wouldn't be fans, and without fans, there wouldn't be million-dollar paychecks. The All Pro receiver Keyshawn Johnson advises the rookies to play the media game before it plays them. When he was drafted six years ago by the New York Jets, he says, the first thing he did was investigate all the New York beat writers to learn their tendencies.

The other great destructive force? Women. "The CIA has nothing on a woman with a plan," Irving Fryar tells the rookies. "There are women who have a plan to trap you. It's going to happen to somebody in this room." Marcellus Wiley, a San Diego Chargers veteran, advocates "keeping a stable" of women to avoid undue complications. "You ugly?" Wiley says to the rookies. "Don't matter no more. Green, dog, it's all about the green, and you got green. The root of 'dating' is 'data,' and that means you gotta find out some information on her." In one of Zachary Minor's staged scenes, a ballplayer recounts to a teammate the fight he just had with his girlfriend. "She wanted me to hit her!" he screams. "She wanted me to hit her!"

Later, through his rabbit-induced weariness, the Giants' lineman Jeff Hatch reflected on the symposium's teaching about women. "If you came down from Mars and saw all this," he said, "you'd think that women were an evil, evil species."

Despite spending $750,000 on the symposium, the NFL would not, as Ahlerich predicted, save all souls. On July 2, Rodney Wright, a Buffalo Bills rookie, would be arrested on felony hit-and-run charges. A week later, Najeh Davenport, the baggy-pants defender, was also arrested, on charges dating back to April. In the wee hours, Davenport supposedly entered a women's dormitory at a Catholic university in Florida, found his way into a sleeping student's room, and, for reasons that remain unclear, defecated in her laundry basket.

But the vast majority of rookies I spoke with as the symposium wound down seemed grateful for the experience. A cynic might view the symposium as nothing more than the NFL's effort to protect its costliest investments. Any rookie who was willing, however, could learn a great deal — about medical benefits and identity theft and investment strategy — that could only better his chances for a sane life off the football field.

Now the symposium is over. Outside La Costa's main building, the rookies stand in the sun, waiting for the airport buses. I fall to talking with Larry Ned, a running back drafted by the Raiders. A sixth-round pick, Ned isn't banking on a marquee career. "It didn't scare me," he says of the symposium, "but it did put everything in perspective. I'll be all right, though. I'm a businessman. I have a formula I'm going to stick with, which is investing in things where there's high demand and low maintenance. Like storage bins in university towns. Laundromats in lower-income areas. Things like that."

Alan Harper, a New York Jets fourth-round pick, also found the symposium helpful. As for dating, however, he already has a system in place. "When you go to a club and you meet a lady, if you tell them you're from the Jets, they're going to think one thing: money," he explains. "And we don't want them to think that. We want them to look at you for what you are."

Harper glances over my shoulder, distracted. A dozen rookies have clustered in a tight, noisy swarm — is it a fight? — and are quickly joined by another dozen. After a moment, the object of their attention is revealed: a shiny black Cadillac Escalade. Its doors are open, its music pumping, its rims gleaming. Word spreads quickly that Keyshawn Johnson drove it down from Los Angeles. It has been fully customized, at a total cost of $105,000. And Johnson, at the center of the rookie swarm, is handing out business cards — for the car-customizing shop he owns in Los Angeles.

Alan Harper returns to his nightclub story. "So when me and Bryan go out" — Bryan Thomas, the Jets' first-round pick — "and we're talking to some ladies, when they ask, 'What do you do,' we say, 'We pick up garbage.' And if they're willing to talk to you if you pick up garbage, and take you for what you are, you might have something."

How long, I ask, does he keep up the act?

"Once you talk to the girl, you get to know her a little bit," he says. "You let her know, 'I play for the Jets.' Or, usually, when they see your car."

What kind of car, I ask Harper, does he drive?

"An Escalade." He nods toward Keyshawn Johnson's. "But mine's maroon."

PETER RICHMOND

Rulon Gardner Wants
a Third Helping

FROM GQ

Go WEST, then go even more west, until you've just about run out of Wyoming, until you've passed through Frontier and Cokeville and Smoot, until you've arrived in Afton, population 1,818, nestled between Idaho and the Salt River Range. Drive up Main Street, beneath the arch fashioned entirely of elk horns, beyond the Red Baron Drive-In, where blond, milk-fed high school girls offer curbside service, French fries with pink sauce, cheeseburgers with pastrami, and wholesomely homegrown smiles lit by the brilliance of a sky wider than anything you could possibly imagine.

Rulon Gardner Avenue is on your left, an arrow-straight quarter-mile of pavement that dead-ends at the new high school, but don't go there: Rulon and school were never the best of friends. Take a right instead, into the parking lot of the supermarket. Walk through the automatic doors, hang a left toward the pastry case, and there he is: a guy with the body of the Michelin Man and the face of a Teletubby. He displaces a lot of space, but there's a buoyancy to all that weight. He'll probably be laughing.

On this morning, he's piling a cardboard tray with doughy concoctions, studying the selections the way a rare-book expert might peruse a shelf of Prousts. It's a good two hours to lunch, and in Rulon-stomach years, two hours is an eternity. Between 1:00 and 8:00 P.M. one day, I watched him eat a chicken hoagie, fries with pink sauce, an order of Tater Tots, an order of onion rings, a Butterfinger milk shake, a large cup of Mountain Dew, a square strawberry ice cream cone, an order of chicken fajitas, three more glasses of Mountain Dew, a large bag of Swedish Fish candy, a beef-jerky stick the size of a Little League bat, a liter bottle of Mountain Dew, an apple Flavor Burst soft vanilla ice cream cone, and a dozen of Mrs. Powell's Cinnamon Rolls. (Note: He chose the chicken hoagie because it's healthier than a cheeseburger; also, he didn't actually eat the cinnamon rolls. He had ordered them, but because he'd detoured to the pet store to buy some hamburger treats for his dog, we arrived at Mrs. Powell's store after it had closed.)

Most of the people in Afton, a deeply religious town in a deeply religious valley settled by Rulon's deeply religious ancestors, ascribe Rulon's miraculous escape last February from a snowy ravine in the Salt River Range to a Higher Power, who had an as yet unrevealed purpose for keeping him alive. A few opine that Rulon's size made it harder to freeze him, even at twenty-five below zero over the course of seventeen hours. But what really kept Rulon alive that night was his gulping, carnivorous appetite: the pioneering high-risk hunger of the American settler. The kind that ate up the frontier until there was no frontier left to claim. Befitting those who came to Star Valley before him, Rulon Gardner must devour everything in his way, literally and figuratively, with pink sauce or without.

It was Rulon's appetite that beat Alexander Karelin, the shaven-headed Goliath, to secure America's greatest Olympic upset in twenty years. It was Rulon's appetite that propelled him ten thousand feet into the mountains in a snowmobile in February. And when it became clear he wasn't going to beat the mountain — when, in fact, the mountain was poised to beat him — it was Rulon's appetite that kept him alive, even though technically he was not qualified to stay alive, given that his body temperature when they rescued him was eighty degrees and life generally doesn't like to linger in a human body that's lost nearly one-fifth of its heat.

It was certainly Rulon's appetite that made it difficult for the helicopter to lift off once they'd hefted his body on board, the way you'd shove a half-frozen walrus onto a beach. And that's the appetite that has driven him, famished, this midmorning to the pastry counter, where he runs into a friend, a local citizen, who congenially asks, as everyone in Afton is wont to ask, how Rulon's feet are healing up.

And so, as he is wont to do, Rulon peels off his sock to let the foot speak for itself. The foot speaks loudly. It is large and swollen, and where the middle toe should be, a little flipper of pink flesh winks out, all that's left of the digit that failed to survive on the evening his dad likes to call the Longest Night. The other toes are also pinker than you'd expect, not just because they're being displayed beneath the fluorescent lights of a supermarket, held aloft by a 286-pound man doing a pirouette dainty enough for a *Fantasia* elephant, but also because the skin is out of place. When the original skin froze off of seven of his toes and the pigskin transplants had done their job, surgeons replaced them with skin from the ample supply on Rulon's thigh.

The shopper's expression is hard to read. He hadn't expected to meet Rulon's foot this early in the morning. He allows as to how it looks like it's coming along real well. Then he disappears down an aisle. Rulon puts his foot back in his sandal and turns to make a final assault on the pastry case. He pulls out a couple of rectangular things slathered in a frosting the color of swamp mud. "Maple flavored," Rulon explains. They are the kind of mutant pastry no one ever eats. Rulon will eat them. And come back for more.

The idea was to see God's country the way it's meant to be seen: from the top. The idea was to ride into the Salt River Range on snowmobiles with Danny and Trent at about one in the afternoon, tear up the chute to the peak of Wagner Mountain, and ride the high ridges down, be out by dinnertime. In hindsight this was a tad unrealistic, but you have to understand how absolutely dumbstruck in *love* Rulon is with Star Valley, every peak, every bluff, every sunglinting river ripple. He's as astute as an Arapaho guide when he's reading its topographic clues. I have seen him stop his Jeep to admire a mountain hare and say — and here I quote — "Aw, little bunny foo foo." I have heard him propose to sell the acreage in Yellowstone for condos, so as to keep the goddamn Feds from putting a velvet rope around it.

As befitting any anti-big-government man (and who wouldn't be, if he spent each day of his life in the company of these peaks next to whom all mortals shrink to insignificance?), Rulon has distinct theories about many things, from gun control (he owns a .45) to selective breeding (he's all for it, although he suspects he'd lose out in the deal), but the land-management issues are closest to his heart. And Rulon loves the land most when it's frostinged in deep midwinter snow.

And so Rulon, Danny, and Trent set off for a quick glimpse of God's white acres from the vantage point of the Cosmic Architect. But when they hit the slopes, the snow was blowing hard in their faces, the going was slower than they had anticipated. By midafternoon they had decided to settle for some joyriding on the lower ridges, then weave their way back, letting the channels cut by the narrow Snake River guide them home.

Danny was the first to descend; he had to attend a daughter's basketball game. Rulon was to meet Danny and his family for dinner at six, back on planet Earth.

"Call me at 4:20 so I know you're all right," Danny told him, and Rulon called at the appointed time.

"Where's Trent?" Danny asked.

"I don't know for sure," Rulon said. "I'm going to drop down and look for him. Then we're coming out."

"Where are you?"

"On this four-hundred-foot cliff. I'm on top of the world!" Rulon shouted into his cell phone. "It's so great up here! It's awesome!"

Six o'clock came and went. Rulon didn't show. Danny knew something was wrong: Rulon is routinely late for almost everything, but he's never late for dinner.

Rulon's first mistake, of course, was wearing only a few layers of clothes: T-shirts, a snowmobiling bib, a fleece jacket. The second was dropping down into a ravine to look for Trent; the slope was much too steep to reascend. Over the next few hours, he tried to find another ridge to climb, but eventually it became clear that the only way out was to follow the river. His third mistake was failing to do what the most amateur outdoorsman would do once the sun started to set: build a snow hut, climb inside, and wait for rescue. But waiting has never been part of the Rulon creed, and waiting for rescue was unthinkable.

The terrain was now winning, every step of the way. At one point, Rulon plunged blindly over a small ridge only to find a near vertical slope; he barely kept from flipping over. He tried to Evel Knievel his way across the river twice. The first time, he soaked himself to the thighs while lifting the sled out. The second time, he slipped and fell backward into the water. In the end, his snowmobile wedged between some rocks. Fine, he told himself, I'll walk out. But the snow was so deep he had to struggle to raise his legs.

Finally, the dim voice of judgment made itself heard: Stop. Wait. Danny and Trent will find you in the morning.

As darkness fell, he discovered a grove of pines and sat down. By now it was twenty-five below zero. His feet were wet; his hands were wet; his legs were wet; his back was wet. His cell phone could get no signal. It could only tell him the time. He vowed not to open it, not until it was near daylight, to make the night go faster. He stood up, so as to stay awake, propped his head on a branch. Nodded off. Nodded on. Sat down. Stood up. He could feel the ice between his toes.

When he could wait no longer, he extracted the cell phone from under his frozen fleece using two fingers peaking out from his sleeve. The time flashed: 12:30 A.M.

This was as low as Rulon would get, the single moment when he didn't know what resources he could summon to weather the night, the moment when he allowed himself to look for hope and found very little. But the moment was brief. For he had a strategy, one he'd used to motivate himself many times before. On the mat, when he wasn't reaching inside, he'd degrade himself. Insult himself. You're a piece of crap, he'd say, and notch it up a level. A year ago at the Worlds, when he was losing to Karelin's successor, 3–0, with less than a minute to go, Rulon ramped it up so ferociously he flipped his opponent onto his head, then pinned the guy as he lay there flopping weakly.

Now, on this night whose silence was broken only by the faint ripple of ice-cold water, Rulon put the cell phone away.

"You'd better notch the stinkin' intensity up," he said to himself, more than once, as the moonless dark stretched on.

Alexander Karelin didn't underestimate Rulon's strength. He simply underestimated how much Rulon wanted to win. Without a doubt, the Ph.D. who holds a seat in Russia's Duma had perused his opponent's dossier. He knew the farm kid had never finished higher than fifth in international competition. Knew he'd been DQ'd during the last Summer Games for missing the weigh-in. Observed, during the nationalistic introductions for their match, how Rulon was fighting back tears, having to take deep breaths just to keep from bawling at the sheer emotion of it all. He looked weak, undisciplined, like his homeland.

What Karelin could not see was the heart. He couldn't possibly know how hardy Gardner blood could be. How Rulon's great-great-grandmother had been the eleventh wife of Archibald Gardner, the sawmill builder who had settled Star Valley. How one winter day late in the nineteenth century, Mary Larson had sheared 128 sheep. How Mary's great-grandson Reed had spent his childhood felling trees and lugging them to the sawmill before siring nine children of his own, five sons and four daughters. The last child would be named Rulon.

"The wayward son" is what Reed Gardner, a hoary old guy with a rasp of a voice, calls his boy. Reed and his wife, Virginia, shake their heads in mock dismay at Rulon's headstrong manner, but make no mistake about the degree of pride in their split-level ranch house. Reed wants to nail a wooden sign with the legend THE LONGEST NIGHT to the pine tree that sheltered his son on February 14. He lugged Rulon's world-championship belt to a sports conference in Pocatello, Idaho.

Unfortunately, Reed lost the belt. This is troublesome for two reasons. One: the world title means as much to Rulon as the gold medal, because some say the wrestling he did in that tournament was the best wrestling that's ever been done. Two: in Rulon's mind, Reed's careless treatment of the belt is an insult, yet another snub in a lifetime of disrespect.

You see, Rulon wasn't even the best wrestler in his family. That title belonged to Reynold, the fourth son, until Rulon beat him in an exhibition. The house shook for the next three days. Reynold wrestled for Oregon State; Rulon settled for a community college in Idaho. It took two full years for Nebraska to recognize his prowess and admit him to the big time.

"I was always too fat, too lazy, too stupid," Rulon says. The words slice through the buffeting winds and the Foo Fighters slamming from his Jeep's speakers on a ninety-mile cruise to the hospital in Idaho Falls. "Having your high school counselors say you're never going to go to college? Going to Nebraska and having your adviser say, 'You're not smart enough to be here'?"

The Miracle of the Mat was every bit as astounding as the Miracle on Ice. But because Greco-Roman wrestling is unintelligible to most fans, because Rulon beat an opponent who hailed not from the Evil Empire but from the global equivalent of a postbankruptcy

Kmart franchise, the scale of his achievement was easy to overlook. Television-wise, the highlights were far too subtle: Rulon sliding an inch or two on his belly to keep Karelin from flipping him, Rulon flexing his back muscles to break Karelin's grip and score the only point of the match.

But the discerning viewer would have sensed the depths of his determination, picked up Rulon's signal at the match's end: the curious hand gesture, motioning as if to deflect something sinister into the crowd.

"That was me throwing the negativity at all the people who cheered against me and told me I couldn't be successful," Rulon says. "I grabbed that and threw it right back."

The more worked up he gets, the more he tries to outrun the blacktop. Soon the wayward son is steering the Jeep with his knees, and then he turns around to fumble behind his seat for a liter of Mountain Dew, just as the road, a two-lane highway high above the Salmon River, curves to the left. The Jeep continues straight ahead. We are a half-second from a gory, flaming death.

"LUGGGOUTTTT!!!!!" is what I hear myself screaming.

Rulon pops his head above the dash, grabs the wheel, and wrestles us back onto the road.

"Hyuh! Hyuh! Hyuh!" he says.

This is the first occasion on which he nearly kills us both. It will not be the last. "I'm not absolutely nuts," Rulon explains. "I just live life and enjoy it. I mean, if you're going to live your life, why not live your life?" And like so much of Rulon's wilderness logic, it is inarguable, unless you think it through, follow it to its logical conclusion, which in this case would likely have been fatal. But once I learned to keep an eye on the road and a hand on the roll bar, it became increasingly apparent that Rulon's madness had a method. When I asked him if his over-the-top behavior had something to do with his instincts as an athlete, he thought for a moment. "People say athletes don't know when to turn their engine off," he said. "But you know what? You're a product of your environment. If people treat you a certain way, you'll act that way. My family has always treated me like a knucklehead, so I'm a knucklehead."

I turned to look at him, saw the Wyoming landscape streaking past. "Nobody listened to me my whole life," he continued. "It's interesting that people listen to me now." He paused, then added: "You didn't care before."

He was talking to the wind.

Let's be perfectly clear about one thing: in the darkest hours of the Longest Night, Rulon was not caught in some ethereal limbo, suspended in a white glowy tunnel, enwebbed in the pull between the quick and the afterlife. He was simply having a dream. In the dream, his brother Roland looked like a grown man instead of the fourteen-year-old boy who had died of aplastic anemia when Rulon was eight. Jesus had soft skin, and his hair was pulled back over his ears. God's appearance remains vague to this day, because Rulon didn't look at God. Even in a fitful sleep, even with his body temperature inching toward your basic Slurpee, Rulon's unconscious was alert enough to understand that looking the Big Man square in the eye might be tantamount to surrendering to the Big Sleep.

He had two visitors during the night. The first was a lost head of cattle that froze to death before dawn. The next was a rescue party, led by Danny, which came within a few hundred yards of Rulon around 2:00 A.M. Danny's snowmobile stalled upriver. Rulon heard it die. He whistled. No response. The party pulled out and decided to start from the bottom of the mountain on snowshoes in the morning.

They left at dawn. They never would have made it in time. But Mark Heiner did. Heiner is a test pilot for Aviat Aircraft, a small company that hand-manufactures single-engine stunt planes down in the valley. When he got the call from search and rescue, Heiner wasn't surprised. Over the years, he had pulled six men from the Salt River Range. He himself had walked out of the mountains after ditching a plane into some pines.

On this night, his favorite aircraft wouldn't start; it was too cold. He took off in another at first light, ignoring the coordinates he'd been given. No way Rulon would have made as much progress as search and rescue had figured.

So Mark Heiner flew to a spot eight miles lower and bingo: there was Rulon, sitting on a rock in the stream. With his feet in the water. At subzero temperatures, flowing water, even if it's literally ice-cold, is warmer than the air. Rulon had waded into the current just before dawn for a drink of water. He didn't have the strength to get back out. So he cleared the snow off a rock and sat down. With his feet in a stream of liquid far more fluid than the synapses of his brain, he watched, marveling, as the stars winked out one by one. Then he heard the plane. Saw it. Waved in slow motion. Heiner dropped to forty feet and threw his coat out the window. Rulon watched it fall. Slowly moved out of the stream. Tried slip-slopping through the thigh-high snow. Gave up, sat on the snow, his head slumped, his body slumped, the slump of a dead man frozen. Heiner radioed for a rescue helicopter and started to circle. The next two hours were the toughest of his life.

When the copter arrived, Rulon's heart did not soar. It sank. Because now there'd be headlines; all the triumphs would be wasted, dwarfed by the night the fat kid fucked up on the mountain.

They airlifted him to the hospital in Afton, cut off his boots, saw the color of his feet, and flew him to Idaho Falls, where Timothy Thurman, a hand surgeon and plastic surgeon, blanched at the sight.

"I was literally sick to see what his feet looked like," he says. "To see this guy who has accomplished so much, and by the looks of things, he's going to have to do without a lot of toes. And portions of his feet." When I ask him if Rulon will wrestle again, Thurman says, "I believe his toes will work. They won't work as well as they did. They'll probably be stiffer. I think . . . I really think he'll be able to go back and wrestle, if that's his goal."

Has the recovery been a success?

"So far . . . if I can keep him chained down," he says with half a laugh, because Rulon was riding his four-wheeler two weeks earlier when he struck a piece of metal behind his parents' farm and nearly lost control. He managed to run over his left foot. The good one. The wounds are healing nicely.

"I'm going to go back in," Rulon says over an iron skillet of sizzling fajitas. "The challenge has been laid."

"Mother Nature doesn't issue challenges," I reply.

"Doesn't she? Why do people climb Mount Everest?"

"Well, she's not saying 'Come on, you knucklehead; I dare you to try again.'"

"Yes, she is. Yes, she is."

"So you're going to go in, strand yourself at the same spot, and walk out?"

"No, I want to go up, say, at 7:00 A.M. Drop down in the same path. With seven more hours of sunlight, I could work the sled, side-hill it, and work my way out."

"And your friends? Your family? They'll let you do this?"

"I'm going to say, 'I'm going up Wagner. You're coming.' And they'll say, 'You're crazy. Yeah. Let's go.'"

"Why?"

"Personal destiny." [*Chewing.*] "Stupidity." [*More chewing.*]

"You're not stupid."

"If you're crazy, you're stupid," he says.

"You're not crazy, and you know it."

"By my actions, I am. I do things I shouldn't be doing. But give me an opportunity to seize and I'll enjoy life."

"Well, at the very least," I say, "make some money off it this time. Sell the rights to Fox. Don King. Showtime. A helicopter with a camera. *Rulon Versus Mother Nature: A Wyoming Death Match.*"

"Bring them on," he says, reaching for a slug of Mountain Dew.

Rulon wants to take me into the mountains — not the Mountain, but a mountain with a good view of the Mountain — and I go, because in Star Valley bypassing the mountains is not an option. Their pull is like gravity.

We are climbing in Rulon's Jeep. It has an altimeter mounted on the dash. We are climbing next to Danny, who drives his own Jeep. We will make a great deal of noise as we cleave the wilderness, but this does not worry Rulon. Did you know studies show that snow-mobiles do not startle wildlife as much as cross-country skiers do? That's what Rulon says. Stinkin' cross-country skiers give the elk heart attacks.

Whatever's out there today is sure to hear us coming, because we don't so much climb the mountain as *take* the mountain. First by dirt road, then by rutted trail, then by anything in our path. Rulon hurtles past the U.S. Forest Service sign that says NO VEHICLES BE-YOND THIS POINT. He vaults the three-foot earthen humps laid by the service to stop any and all vehicles. All but Rulon's Jeep. And Danny's. Danny is a lot like Rulon, except he seems to know what he's doing. Danny's Jeep has a top on it, Rulon's does not. For half the climb, defying the laws of physics as I understand them, great clods of mud kicked up by our tires rain down on the cab and somehow find their way into my face and, on occasion, into my slack-jawed mouth. Weeks later I will find dried clods of dirt in the pockets of my jacket.

Eventually, all that stands between our Jeep and the summit is a stream bed, but we don't have to cross it. We have to climb it. Danny gives it a few tries. He backs out. Rulon and I move into the lead. Five or six times, we charge up the sharp, slippery boulders, and five or six times we fail. Rulon calmly rocks us out to plan a new strategy. I suggest we hike to the ridge on foot. But this, of course, would be surrender. We return to the river bed instead, the Jeep rocking and vibrating so violently that it's not the tires I'm worried about now but the very frame. And then, suddenly, like a bone caught in Mother Nature's throat, we dislodge, upstream, into the meadow. Danny soon follows.

Only a soft blanket of wildflowers stands between us and the wide-open sky. But rather than basking in his triumph, Rulon, being Rulon, challenges Danny to a duel. I am the passenger in a drag race on a sloping plane ten thousand feet above sea level.

We near the ridge and the Great Beyond: air and space and distant mountain peaks. Danny slows and stops. Rulon does not.

"RULLLONNNNN!!!!!" is what I hear myself scream, for I am terrified. This is sheer madness.

We are no more than ten yards from the top when he hits the brakes. We skid. Over grass. Through a patch of snow. To within two, maybe three yards of the ledge. I jump out as quickly as my fingers can fumble with the seat belt and look over the precipice. I see not a sheer drop but a steeply sloping field and a line of trees about two hundred yards down. If the brakes had failed, if we'd kept skidding, if Rulon's wounded, half-functional foot had slipped off the pedal, we'd have gone airborne, then rolled and rolled, perhaps all the way to the trees.

Rulon is laughing. Danny would like to but cannot. The three of us assemble at the ridge for a full view: Wagner Mountain off in the distance, snow-capped, imperious, waiting. And for the first time, I see something you couldn't possibly notice from down below, in the real world: it's not the height of these mountains that inspires the awe; it's their incredible breadth.

And that, of course, is what makes them killers. The space between the peaks. An area so wide and woolly it could swallow a man whole. Even a big man. One looking to be even bigger or — in the spirit of all who came before him — die trying.

MICHAEL LEAHY

Gambling Man

FROM THE WASHINGTON POST

CARDS. Cards sliding his way. Aces, kings, diamonds, spades — losers, all losers. The man in Pit 21 had been losing for a good hour by then. Losing what for most people would have been their life's savings. "Yeah, give 'em to me, give 'em to me," Michael Jordan commanded, pushing another $5,000 chip forward. He loved games but craved risky games more. He feasted on adrenaline, the big jolts that mortals don't know.

Besides accounting for a basketball comeback, it had propelled him to this high-stakes blackjack game late on an October evening in Uncasville, Connecticut, just hours after having played a preseason contest there against the Boston Celtics.

"Give 'em to me," he said to the dealer.

More than mildly addictive, his many games over eighteen years necessarily had meant that real life, so devoid of spectacular risk, so steeped in tedium and low on euphoria, had been hard on him during the past three years. Sometimes in his old office at MCI Center his body language had said it for him, when he slid down in his desk chair while talking about his routines as a Washington Wizards executive.

He relished uncertainty, a mindset that had led him back to basketball and, a little after 11:00 P.M., past a cacophony of clanging slots and to this table in Pit 21 of the Mohegan Sun Casino, behind a red rope designed to keep $100-a-hand plebes at a distance. He sat alongside young Boston Celtics star Antoine Walker, whom he'd known since Walker was a promising junior high player in Chicago, and across the table from his Wizards teammate Richard Hamilton, with whom his relationship had yet to define itself. Jordan played blackjack into the early morning hours, down half a million dollars at one point, refusing to quit, sinking deeper into the red, trying to recover his losses by succumbing to the sucker's gambit — raising his bets and playing multiple hands simultaneously.

Around 3:00 A.M., about the time his prospects looked the dreariest, he called for coffee to replace his drink and lit another cigar. The Jordan party — bodyguards, teammates, his personal trainer, a few friends — settled in for what appeared to be an all-nighter. Someone in the party whispered to Jordan that perhaps he ought to get some sleep, particularly as, in only three days, he would be in Madison Square Garden for opening night against the New York Knicks.

Jordan ignored the questions, the veiled admonishments that it was getting late. When he would miss critical shots down the stretch and seem to have nothing in his tank late in the fourth quarter during a narrow loss to the Knicks, it would leave at least one Wizards official wondering what price, if any, he had paid for Casino Night. But no one ever pressed him about such things.

It spoke of the bargain that basketball had made with him long before: coaches and executives agreed implicitly to take on the burdens of his appetites. They lived with his vicissitudes, realizing that the very restlessness in him that sometimes triggered whispers was the flip side of a bottomless will without rival. He regularly subjected himself to grueling private workouts while his teammates slept. He arrived at regular practice before anyone else, did more stretching, came alone into the Wizards' MCI practice gym after a red-eye flight to shoot for an hour, and then another hour, a solitary figure attempting to regain the old touch of his three-point jump shot and turn back a clock. He was, in most things, a portrait of excess.

And any loss was a shaming for him. "Cards," he called, and a dealer in Pit 21 flicked out three more hands to him — three more busts, as it turned out, at about ten grand a hand. He was hemorrhaging cash and chips now. He raised the stakes, playing $15,000 hands, drinking more coffee, finally turning around the game near 4:00 A.M., drawing about even.

By breakfast he was moving ahead, winning three hands at a time over and over, going up about $600,000, exultant, manic now.

Wanting his victory proclaimed, he began happily trash-talking, "Give me those cards, *give me those damn cards* . . . You're gonna have to rob a register to pay me" — not quitting until about 8:00 A.M., when he walked toward an exit of the Mohegan Sun with arms raised, as if he'd won game 7 of a playoff series. Chattering. Woofing. Sleepless in Uncasville.

"I returned . . . for the love of the game . . . and to teach," he liked to say, but Jordan's comeback was always more complicated than that. He didn't love the game so much, after all, that he hadn't left it twice already — the last time in early 1999, when he cited mental exhaustion on his way out the door.

The years that followed were never so much a tale of longing as they were a tale of loss — the difference between wanting something badly and going back to it because nothing else in his new life was half as thrilling. It was the contrast between exhilaration and emptiness, between having a compass and feeling adrift.

"It's hard for anything to be as good as playing for him," his personal trainer, Tim Grover, had said casually the previous winter, when Grover was still permitted by Jordan to talk. But "loss" was a dirty word in the Jordan camp; "loss" carried with it the image of a void, of something desperate. Jordan and his publicity personnel instead talked about love, which sounded cheerier, as if he were answering a calling instead of fleeing a void. "I have an itch that needs to be scratched," he said winningly.

The basic truth, as former Chicago Bulls and current Los Angeles Lakers coach Phil Jackson privately observed to a friend about the player whom he most treasured, was that Michael liked to dominate.

From its first days to the last, his comeback season was like stepping outside at night and running in pitch blackness, risky to the body, riskier still to the ego, but absolutely thrilling, in the not-knowing, in the equal potential for magic and catastrophe.

The turning point arrived early, if unseen. During a summer scrimmage at Grover's gymnasium with a corps of NBA players, Jordan was hurt: two broken ribs, suffered in a collision with an intense, powerful young Chicago Bull named Ron Artest.

He needed four weeks to mend, four weeks during which he sat idle, four weeks in which all the training he had done to that point went for naught — and after which he maniacally rushed back into his workouts and scrimmages, trying to make up for time lost. Driving at such a furious pace presented its own dangers, thought Grover, who warned Jordan that to play so hard after weeks of inactivity — and three years of indulgence before that — would leave him susceptible to tendinitis and worse.

Jordan ignored him.

Now Grover tried to paint a picture of possible calamity looming, putting himself in the unusual position of trying to cajole Jordan into doing what in the old days constituted a training sin: think of going easier, or not at all — at least for a few days.

Jordan, more firmly than ever, answered that he understood his body's limits in a way no one else did. *Just get me ready,* the boss ordered.

The story of Jordan's troubles began in that moment, not with the right knee that would become so famous but the little-scrutinized left one. The tendinitis there troubled him from the first practices in the Wizards training camp in Wilmington, North Carolina, where Jordan denied the problem even as he ended every practice with a grapefruit-size ice pack fashioned around it. Privately, Grover believed that Jordan was favoring the sore knee, which, if true, meant his right knee already had begun absorbing more stress, leaving it vulnerable to tendinitis, too — physiology's equivalent of the Domino Effect.

It was the comeback's real crossroads — Jordan's last chance to attend to his knees' problems before they escalated into something chronic and season-threatening. Grover persisted. Jordan nonchalantly resisted. The unspoken question hung there between them: Do you ease off the pedal or possibly risk the unraveling of a season?

Jordan later found the media and made a vow: "I'll be ready for the opening of the season."

And the unraveling began.

"Whatever happens, happens," Jordan liked to say at different points in the season. At thirty-eight years and eight months when the season began, he tried playing the part of the stoic about nearly everything, from his knees to his erratic young team. But, privately, he fumed.

What's going on? he privately asked coaches and others in the organization early, when the team was losing eight straight. *What the [expletive] is going on? You're watchin' us, what the [expletive] do you see wrong?*

Nearly everyone with whom Jordan spoke counseled calm and patience. Most of his young teammates, already accustomed to losing as Wizards after gilded college careers, were sad but philosophical, having perfected that impassive and amiable mien of trampled athletes everywhere, a glazed look that said, *I work hard but this is my fate.*

At week's end, an outraged Jordan told them that their play was *unacceptable, losing like this is [expletive] unacceptable.* Only it wasn't, not really; very few things were immediately unacceptable in the NBA so long as big money rolled in. In Washington, more money poured into the Wizards' coffers than ever in the team's history — despite a team on its way to losing eight games in a row, for nearly three winless weeks.

All the normal gauges of sports — team standings, wins and losses, playoff possibilities — had a curious irrelevance by then. A Jordan game throughout most of the year was not basketball so much as a transcendental event, and the Wizards less a losing NBA team than a novelty act, a touring troupe led by a charismatic figure aiming for nothing less than his professional resurrection. It was basketball's equivalent of a fantasy Beatles reunion at Wembley Stadium.

The Wizards were on the way to leading the NBA in total home and road attendance for the first time in franchise history, selling out each of the team's forty-one games at MCI, increasing its home attendance by a league-high 32 percent, and banking what some industry experts estimated to be an extra $450,000 per home game in ticket revenue — which translated to a gaudy boost of more than $18 million by season's end. "Michael's impact already has been dramatic," Wizards principal owner Abe Pollin happily said early, already aware that the years of his team's financial malaise were ending.

But even the team's new profits in the 2001–2002 season paled against what Jordan the gold mine meant to the NBA as a whole. In the last year of the league's existing television contract, ratings climbed for NBC and Turner, including among eighteen- to thirty-four-year-olds. Thirty-eight of the Wizards' forty-one road games were sellouts. Coupled with a coming-out of new stars and a surge in NBA merchandising, Jordan triggered a tsunami of new gate and ancillary income for the league.

Best of all, for several owners, the new money sparked a casualty. The NBA's so-called luxury tax — a levy imposed on high-spending teams whose player salaries exceed a ceiling reflective of a defined ratio of league revenue — has likely disappeared for the season, in large part because the jump in revenue from Jordan's presence pushed the year's salary cap beyond even the most profligate teams' expenditures. Three NBA big spenders originally projected to be hit by the tax — Dallas, New York, and Portland — consequently will pay nothing, saving their owners an estimated $60 million among them.

Add in the higher gate revenue from Jordan's road appearances and his impact on television ratings, and Jordan's financial boost to the NBA was ineffably high. "If the league wrote Jordan a check for $100 million, the league would still be getting the better end of the bargain," said Alvin Gentry, the Los Angeles Clippers' head coach. "We wouldn't be able to give him enough."

Such gratitude toward the Jordan comeback sparked a powerful deference throughout the NBA, a reluctance to press Midas to do anything he didn't wish, even when his disenchantments prompted the Wizards to break league rules.

Wanting to minimize scrutiny of his practice habits, particularly after his right knee began troubling him, Jordan and the Wizards casually flouted league rules governing the relationship between the media and the players, including those guaranteeing reporters the opportunity to observe the last half-hour of team practices. The vast majority of practices were closed altogether, a decision made mutually by Wizards Coach Doug Collins and Jordan, the coach typically exchanging a glance with his star when a Wizards public relations official asked whether the media could be admitted that day.

"No," Collins said, dispatching the PR man to tell the media to stay put.

Usually, Jordan would be riding a stationary bike by then. From the start of the season, as his tendinitis worsened, he seldom played any basketball outside of games, participating in about one-quarter of the Wizards' practices, according to team observers. He would do a few drills — a series of sprints, some shooting on undefensed fast breaks, a brief run-through of plays — before muttering to Collins, "I'll go to the bike." Or Collins, wanting to save the troubled knee for a grueling game coming, would sometimes call to him, "I think you've done enough. Go to the bike."

Consequently, the Wizards seldom scrimmaged full-court, with one team observer saying he had never been part of an NBA organization that practiced so little under game-like conditions.

Once a fierce practice player who had taken pride in driving and schooling those around him, Jordan had been responsible in Chicago for dramatically improving the play of several Bulls teammates, most notably Scottie Pippen. Pippen had arrived in the NBA with a reputation as a sieve on defense but who, relentlessly abused in scrimmages by a merciless Jordan, lifted his game to become a premier defender. "You either sink or swim with Michael in practice, and Scottie made it," said Tex Winter, a Bulls assistant who had moved on with Coach Phil Jackson to the Los Angeles Lakers. "You either work hard or Michael has no use for you."

The Wizards had hoped that Jordan's ruthless practice style, particularly his zest for preying on even the weakest in drills, might transform Richard Hamilton and Courtney Alexander, two offensive talents tagged by coaches and foes as serious defensive liabilities. But Jordan's knee made any tough tutelage impossible.

So instead he aimed to play the role of mentor. It was not something that came to him naturally. When injured, he wasn't around much, and when around, his advice had limits. He counseled Hamilton on pump-faking before his jump shot, and Tyronn Lue on making wiser decisions from the point guard position — but he was not given to lengthy, soul-searching discussions. He'd give Alexander a pair of shoes and snicker that maybe they would lead him to pull down a rebound. End of discussion.

He needed avid listeners but not more friends; friendships invited risk, and he preferred to confine his risks to games. In time his new teammates understood this, but even as familiarity diminished their awe for the icon, their curiosity about Michael Jordan remained. Young men, some of whom had grown up looking at his poster above their beds, sometimes wondered what it might be like to hang with him, if only for a single night on the town. It wasn't going to happen. "Nobody *meets* Michael," said Jordan's handpicked first-round draft pick, the highly touted nineteen-year-old Kwame

Brown. "You gotta know somebody who knows somebody before you meet Michael."

It was, as Jordan emphasized once to an aide, nothing personal, just habit, the tic of a man who derived comfort from routine and secrecy, dating to his Chicago days, when he would hang out with veteran Bulls teammates like Charles Oakley and Pippen but not younger players. "One of the Jordan rules when he went places with friends was that they respect confidentiality, that what they did together was not to be regurgitated," said an agent representing a Bulls friend of Jordan's. "Younger players were seen as too risky. They might get excited and brag."

As a consequence of needing games, however, Jordan required foils. On many days during the season, it meant finding a young teammate whose money he might be able to take in a post-practice shooting contest.

In Chicago, the day after a January game there against the Bulls, the Wizards had just finished a practice at Grover's gym when Hamilton accepted Jordan's challenge to a shooting competition while the team bus waited for them. The competition dragged on. Ten, fifteen, twenty minutes. No player but Jordan would have dared to keep a team bus waiting. On this day, the contest involved shooting from midcourt. Hamilton went up several hundred dollars early, happily yelling, while the attendants, fetching balls, kept glancing at watches. Someone finally said: "Probably time to get going, Michael."

No, he said coolly.

Finally, Jordan started finding his range and hit eight of his last thirteen shots to win more than $1,000 off the day's prey, now at last wrapping up. He grinned and whooped — "coo, coo, coo" — a signal that he had fleeced another pigeon, then pointed in a gesture of amused supremacy at the defeated Hamilton, who, turning his back, quietly walked to the back of the gym to retrieve his sweats, while a delighted Jordan fitted an earring into his left lobe and kept teasing. Hamilton never stopped walking. Jordan stared at Hamilton's back, calling out, "Rip, we'll do it again."

The moment revealed all his sides — a need for dominance, the compulsion to find another rush, his avuncular instinct to soothe the bruised foe.

He was an alpha personality in a profession teeming with alphas,

which necessarily meant there were ebbs and flows to his relationships with ambitious young teammates like Hamilton. From about
the midpoint of the season, as Jordan's tendinitis took an irrevers-
ible hold, the team's number-two star made a frequent point of em-
phasizing, casually and without edge, that Jordan would not be
around in another few years, that the team's future hinged on
younger players — the New Jacks, as Hamilton had referred to
them. "I just wish people would see we're more than a team with
Michael Jordan; we got the pride to win without Michael, and we're
stepping up because we know we got a lot of talent here, and we're
going to be the leaders somebody soon," he said.

Never had anyone stated the obvious so directly. It reflected a
steadily ebbing veneration of the idol as the season wore on, a new
daring among a few players making clear where the future rested.

But even so, most were cautious. Kwame Brown became a case
study in the risks of angering Jordan, a man famously intolerant of
slackers and mediocrities.

When Brown arrived at training camp in October woefully out
of shape after a summer illness, Jordan had been patient for a
week, draping his arm around Brown and praising his ability to
Wizards officials. But Jordan's fascination for his protégé swiftly
waned. Brown didn't work hard enough sometimes for Jordan's
tastes, and it did not help that many in the organization, from officials to teammates, thought that Brown showed no willingness for
either accepting criticism or honoring an old basketball tenet that
said rookies should play hard, accept bruises, and complain about
nothing.

For his part, Brown had become maddeningly frustrated, a kid
who thought that he was being repeatedly fouled in intrasquad
games. He would drive toward the basket and feel himself being
bumped by a hard hip off the ball, infuriated that the referees
wouldn't blow a whistle. "That was a foul," he finally groaned.

There was an electric silence then. Play had stopped. A wide-
eyed Jordan walked toward Brown. "You [expletive] flaming fag-
got," he exploded. "You don't get a foul call on a [expletive] little
touch foul, you [expletive]. Get your [expletive] back on the floor
and play. I don't want to hear that out of you again. Get your ass
back and play, you [expletive]."

Brown would only say later, "It was pretty rough, but that's Mi-

chael Jordan; you deal with it. You learn you're a rookie and you're
not going to get calls."

Jordan continued to express hope that, while "lost out there"
and not likely to be an immediate star, Brown would be able to con-
tribute in game situations. When Brown didn't, when he couldn't,
the question arose whether Jordan had been overly optimistic; that
he and Collins had unrealistically tried to rush Brown, even messed
with his psyche in publicly skewering his play. When Brown broke
down one day in Houston and sobbed, Jordan comforted him, but
by then Brown's season was in tatters, and Jordan's relationship
with most of his teammates defined.

Jordan had stopped talking about the brilliant future ahead for
Brown. "[Before then] Michael [had] shunned him for a while,"
the Wizards official said. "Kwame went from having the biggest guy
on his side to having nobody. It was a long freeze. Michael helped
him later when Kwame broke down and cried at practice. But
things were done by then."

Ironically, by late in the season, some players expressed relief to
friends that Jordan had never sought to hang out with *them*, wondering whether he would have scrutinized their after-hours life
for signs of misbehavior. One player's agent said, "[The player] always asked, 'Am I playing alongside a teammate or my general
manager?'"

There were generational and class differences, as well. "They
didn't have much in common," the agent observed. "[The player]
said it was like playing with an older uncle at a barbecue." Jordan
sounded as mystified as a forty-something when sniping about hip-
hop — "the kids' noise" — blaring through speakers in the locker
room. "I'd get amped up and be throwin' balls away and [exple-
tive] if I had to listen to that [expletive] all the time," he said, re-
treating to his headphones.

But on the court he played uncle and leader, and they looked to
him to save them more often than not, particularly in a game's
final minutes, which generally reflected the Wizards' utter reliance
on Jordan. In the 2001–2002 season, he hit no fewer than three
game-winning shots in the last seconds. And, at any point in a game
when players looked lost, the ball went to Jordan, underscoring his
position as a crutch for everyone else.

"I looked at tapes and saw that we basically only scored when

Mike is hot and Mike's got it going," said forward Tyrone Nesby. "Mike was doing it all. When he wasn't on the court, everybody looked at each other, like: *What are we gonna do?*" Nesby didn't learn that Jordan's season had ended until, walking through a Milwaukee hotel lobby, he heard the news from teammates. Jordan was already headed to an airport by then, having broken the news to Collins and packed some bags.

Few things spoke more simply about the remove the idol had perfected. He appreciated teammates for how well they could play games, the bond between them in their shared risk, which is where it ended. One winter day, a group of people that included Wizards guard Chris Whitney walked through the players' underground parking lot at MCI Center, when suddenly they heard a car screeching. Swiveling their heads, they saw an Aston Martin whipping around the tight little turns of the lot at seemingly upward of fifty miles per hour.

Alone, Jordan hit the brakes and squealed to a stop in front of Whitney. "See you at the airport," he said. There was no conversation, no need for one. He had a crowd marveling. He laughed. It was enough.

But he wanted order in a locker room. He told aides he wanted *everybody* focused on preparation. He wanted no autograph signings, no posing for photos, no distractions. Later, when skeptics began raising questions about his right knee and endurance, he used the pregame to work himself into a simmering furor, doing what Michael Jordan did better than anyone else in sports — convince himself that he was being dismissed and disrespected.

"Scoring six points, my career low, I'm pretty sure you guys were saying how old I was," he said, forty-eight hours after a poor December performance in Indiana, looking for payback. He shot a look at his inquisitors, searching for confirmation of his suspicions — a nodding head here, a telling chuckle there. Nobody around him so much as flinched, nobody said a thing. He wasn't through. "I knew with that game, you guys would say I'd lost whatever I'd gained; that maybe the [comeback] wasn't a great idea."

Playing in a frenzy at home against Charlotte, he scored twenty-four points by the end of the first quarter. He berated veteran referee Derrick Stafford after having one of his jumpers partially blocked by Hornet P. J. Brown and receiving no foul call: "Derrick, what game are you [expletive] watchin' out there?"

Stafford wheeled. Other players gaped.

Jordan kept letting Stafford have it. "How's that not a foul on him? What game are you [expletive] watchin'?"

Stafford looked at him but did nothing, just one more ref being reminded of the uses of Jordan's power. Late in the fourth quarter, with a last binge and a short fadeaway jumper, he scored his fifty-first point, the oldest player in league history to total as many as fifty. MCI Center became a din — *Jorrrr-dan, Jorrrr-dan*. On his off nights, he had been a sad reminder of mortality. But on this evening, he was the flickering ember who would not go out — and so, transfixed, they screamed.

Slightly raising his hand, he finally called it a night. He exited as he had entered — as a flesh-and-blood Rorschach test: people saw in him what they wished. He was, depending upon the set of eyes observing him, the ultimate representation of male physicality and beauty; he was the post-9/11 symbol of indomitability; he was an earnest superstar trying only to reclaim what he loved; he was a guy who craved the spotlight too much; he was an older dude who did not have the same ups, as kids say of the aging, low-altitude leaper.

Of all these things, only the last judgment visibly nettled him. "I am not the *same* player," he said, "but when I get going, I believe I can still hold my own . . . Even in the past, I wasn't dunking *that* much . . . I do other things now."

When on a roll, he lost himself in basketball, and on New Year's Eve, as if to prove his masterpiece against Charlotte two nights earlier was no aberration, he scored forty-five in a blowout victory over Eastern Division powerhouse New Jersey.

He looked beatific afterward, in a way he never would again that season. Other players rushed out to New Year's parties. Facing the media about 11:30 P.M., his silver earring glistening, Jordan talked longer than usual and, even after saying good night, he lingered, basking in the good feeling, wanting to talk a little more. Somebody in his retinue said, "Gettin' late. We better be goin', M.J."

Jordan raised an index finger like a sword: *wait.*

He turned and told a couple of reporters that another fifty-point game had been within his reach that night.

There had been only five back-to-back fifties in NBA history, and, though his name was already on that list, oh, man, he muttered exuberantly, how he would have loved to do it again, especially at age thirty-eight. "And I *would've* had it," he insisted, "if I didn't miss that last one" — an allusion to an errant three-point attempt, after which he'd allowed Collins to take him out for good. "If that one goes," he said, "I'm there [at forty-eight points] and then . . ." — he grinned, and flipped his wrist, in a gesture that meant fifty would have been only a hoop away, a done deal.

He insisted he felt great, answering a question no one had posed, talking about his bad knee although he'd spoken about it to the media horde two minutes earlier, preoccupied by the subject. "I'm getting treatment [for it]," he said. "If I can keep this tendinitis away — knock on wood" (he audibly conked his shaven head with a half-formed fist again, in what was becoming a favorite Jordan gesture) — "then obviously, you'll see how I can move."

It was 11:40 P.M. now. Another voice began pleading: *Let's go, Mike.* He happily relented, starting off on his night, yelling at something in the air, something only he could feel. "Yeah, yeah."

The euphoria would last for all of one more week.

The new year brought two slices of hell — one he saw coming only too late, and one he saw coming not at all. His right knee apparently sent no signals he could recognize. But a divorce petition seldom sneaks up on a man; a spouse's estrangement is a palpable thing. Twenty-four hours after his wife, Juanita, had filed her petition, Jordan candidly, if curtly, acknowledged his marriage's strains and alluded to his concern for his children — the first small tentative steps toward trying to effect a reconciliation with her.

Sealed off, Jordan could see little or nothing coming at him. In Cleveland, Robert Mercer — who made his living as "The Rumpshaker," an exotic dancer who could boast of a brief appearance on HBO's lurid little slice of Americana, the series *Real Sex* — had mailed a registered letter to Wizards executive and close Jordan friend Rod Higgins, alleging Jordan's involvement in an extramarital affair. Jordan's Chicago attorney, Frederick Sperling, dashed off a response to the dancer, threatening legal action if he made his claims public.

Years earlier, Jordan had empowered Sperling to deal with Bobby Mercer. He wanted to be left alone to concentrate on basketball, and this had happened.

Such a splendid isolation required the vigilance of the Wizards coaches and the club's PR staff, which came to serve as his official gatekeepers. Even with the tight controls, however, people talked, information seeped out: Jordan's knee had grown worse, according to insiders watching him walk more gingerly than ever at closed-door practices that he increasingly sat out. Jordan's personal publicist, Estee Portnoy, made a phone call in an effort to learn the identities of those in the Wizards' circle who had privately — and without Jordan's authorization — spoken about the boss. "Michael doesn't like it when people try to make money off him," she told a reporter.

She recited a favorite Jordan aphorism: *Those who know don't speak, and those who speak don't know.*

It was, among other things, a cryptic order to those in his circle: *Don't talk.*

If October, November, and December had been physically demanding, January was the death march for Jordan's knees. He played forty-one minutes a game during one especially brutal road stretch. Phil Jackson privately told people that Jordan was playing too many minutes. Tex Winter, Jackson's highly regarded assistant, said it publicly: "I think he's running a real possibility of injury in the second half of the season if he keeps playing these kind of hard minutes."

His right knee gave out on a balmy February Sunday in Miami, and surgery for torn cartilage swiftly followed. After only a three-week rehab, Jordan, the shadow boss, returned to tell Collins when he would play and, generally, for how long. Collins had earlier expressed disbelief that Jordan could possibly return from surgery without practicing several times, only to see Jordan show up in Denver, wanting to play.

As the most famous knee on the planet came back from arthroscopic surgery and swelled yet again, Collins increasingly found himself the subject of questions about the reasons for allowing Jordan to play at long stretches, or play at all.

By then, the coach's self-interest merged with Jordan's desires. In need of inspiring a banged-up squad that had difficulty scoring points, Collins began citing Jordan as the model of the hurting warrior who pushed on. But when Jordan's season ended with a ballooning right knee in a Milwaukee hotel room, the Wizards' playoff hopes succumbed with it, and something changed in Collins. His hazel eyes stopped flashing irritably at questions about Jordan's health. He began searching to explain why the comeback had imploded.

By the regular season's final day, he confessed that his younger

players' struggles early in the year "probably seduced me" into playing Jordan too many minutes, noting with regret that Jordan had
controlled their relationship.

"Michael has such a dominant personality," he said softly, "that
he tells you he's feeling good and you want to believe it even when
he's not. There are games when I played him forty-one minutes
when I probably should have played him thirty-five. But I kept saying to myself, 'There's no back-to-back. He doesn't have to practice
much tomorrow.' That [approach] took its toll, no question."

And then came the most surprising disclosure, one that seemingly nullified everything Collins had said for six months. "That
knee wasn't right all season long," he said. "He probably hurt it in
the summer."

He wondered what Jordan's attitude about such things as playing
time might be if he came back for another season. His minutes
would have to be cut, Collins said. "And the thing about it is, if it
means he gets mad at me, then I'm gonna have to do it, anyway, because" — Collins paused for a split second, looked up in the air,
said it — "he won't do it on his own."

He never had, he never could. His appetites prevented that. Collins knew it now, too.

During the last days before his season's end, if only for a moment, the idol pulled up the shade on a mystery. He talked candidly about his tendinitis for the first time all year, grimly offering a
theory about the origin of his troubles. His explanation eerily echoed the words and warnings of Tim Grover, six months earlier. The
problem began, he said now, with his broken ribs, and the favoring
of his hurting left knee. "I came back without that period of building myself up and from there it started: the flaring of the knee, the
tendinitis. And parts of the body start to break down. *And you start
compensating and other things happen.*"

The next day, April 3, he was gone. He has not spoken publicly
since his knee gave out in Milwaukee, leaving unanswered what the
season meant to him and to the Washington Wizards.

For their part, Collins and other coaches have told the Wizards
brass that the team cannot improve as it stands, triggering uncomfortable questions: How does one rebuild a team around a man
just three months shy of forty at the beginning of the next NBA season? What happens when his departure necessarily means the team

must retool? How long are the New Jacks willing to be the chorus for the Michael Show?

Not all his friends are anxious to see him return. In public, they usually praise his comeback, their reservations expressed only in private or in rare slips of public candor. Jordan was "a shadow of himself," Jackson said after the legend's final game against the Lakers, and few assessments could have cut deeper.

Jordan has spent parts of the last few weeks, friends say, in Monaco and Las Vegas, doing the predictable. There is always a Pit 21 somewhere out there, always a pile of blue chips waiting. Twenty years of breathless gambles played out in the din of arenas have left him with fewer interests than raging appetites, in love with adrenaline rushes that necessarily put a strain on real life to measure up. It hasn't, it can't. Where does he go to find what he wants?

About a week ago he resumed light workouts. No one knows, least of all Michael Jordan at midlife, where all this is going, or for how much longer. He always has given the impression he craves even this. The uncertainty. Some exquisite doubt. He is in love with risk.

MARK KRAM JR.

"I Want to Kill Him"

FROM THE PHILADELPHIA DAILY NEWS

HACKENSACK, N.J. — Cold fear gripped George Khalid Jones as he boarded the Acela Express in Newark that summer day last July. Over and over he pondered: What would people say when he showed up in Washington at the funeral? Would they spot him in the crowded church and whisper among themselves, *"There he is. The guy who did it!"* He could feel their eyes upon him, the anger, the accusation, welling up from behind shiny pools of tears. And what would the widow say when she saw him? Would she become hysterical and scream, *"You killed my husband! You killed my husband!"* She would be there with her three children, suddenly fatherless because of him. How could he ever face them? How could he ever face any of them?

"George, come along with me to the funeral," Lou Duva, his promoter, had told him. "View the body, see the family, and go to the reception. Go down there and let people see you."

Two weeks had passed since Jones had stopped Beethavean "Honey Bee" Scotland in the tenth and final round of their light-heavyweight bout aboard the retired aircraft carrier USS *Intrepid* on the Hudson River in New York. Carried unconscious from the ring on a stretcher, Scotland underwent two surgeries at Bellevue Hospital Center: the first to gauge the pressure building up in his brain, the second to drain blood in an effort to relieve that pressure. He lingered in a coma for six days, during which Jones found himself overwhelmed with an ever-deepening anxiety. Nightmares filled what few hours of sleep he could get, spooky harbingers of the phone call that would finally come on July 2: Scotland was dead at age twenty-six of a subdural hematoma, a rupture of the veins between the brain and the skull. Uncertain if he could bring himself to attend the funeral seven days later, if only because of the profound shame that had enveloped him, he agreed when Duva told him simply, "George, this is the right thing do."

So they settled into their seats for their three-hour journey, during which Jones somberly peered out his window at the passing factories and rivers. The then seventy-nine-year-old Duva looked over at Jones and said of Scottland, "It was his time, you know? Whether it happened in a boat or car or in the ring, God has a set time for everyone." He told Jones there had been an insurance policy on Scottland, that his widow and children would get "a nice piece of money." The *New York Daily News* reported after the death that the promoter took out two insurance policies — a $20,000 medical policy and a $50,000 life policy. And Duva added this, "Remember: it could have happened to you." He told him boxing was a rough game, that he should get what he could out of it in the way of financial security and get out while he still had his faculties. Buy a house, get a college fund started. As they drew into Union Station, Duva said, "You have to leave this behind you today. You have to get closure."

A car picked them up at the curb and drove them to Metropolitan Baptist Church in Northwest Washington. Jones cautiously blended into the big crowd that had formed there, which included some boxers with whom he was friendly. They told him, "It happens. Keep your head up." Some relatives of Scottland were surprised to see him, but an uncle came up to Jones, held out a hand, and said, "We're so happy to see you." The uncle told him that he should go on with his boxing career because "Bee would have wanted you to do that." The widow was equally gracious, her face sad yet forgiving. As he filed by the open coffin, which was surrounded by stands of flowers, he wondered how she and her children would be able to cope in the years to come. And suddenly it occurred to him: How could there ever be closure? *A piece of me is going along with him to the grave.*

Whenever a fighter kills another in the ring, he is always the forgotten victim, walled in by heavy shadows of guilt, fear, and remorse. You cannot know how it feels until it has happened to you, which is why George Khalid Jones found himself so distressed when he picked up the sports section a few weeks ago and saw a quote from Mike Tyson. Outrageously, Tyson had said of Lennox Lewis, his opponent Saturday in Memphis, Tennessee: "My main objective is . . . to kill him. He should want to kill me, too, because I want to kill him." It sent a wave of terror through Jones, who said that while Tyson was probably only trying to psyche himself up, he wondered if he truly knew what he was saying. Jones remembered what he had said a few days before the Scottland bout: that he had worked so hard in the gym that "I pray I don't kill anybody." They were only words then — typical prefight hype — but they have since come back to him as an unintended prophecy.

"Be careful what you say: it could come true," said Jones, seated at a corner table at an empty North Jersey diner. "And when it does come true, then you suddenly find yourself caught in a horrible nightmare. Sometimes you just say things, but you never think it'll happen."

The year that has passed since Beethavean Scottland expired has been a search for life after death for Jones, thirty-four. When he came back from the funeral in Washington, he became overwhelmed by the tragedy that had befallen his opponent, who everyone said was "a good guy who loved his wife and children." Thoughts of his own mate and five children, of how precious they were to him, would leave him in a state of anguish, his tears streaming down the side of his handsome face. A voice inside his head told him: quit boxing. Yet even as he packed up his gear and stowed it away in the attic, a part of him knew that the sport had provided him with the only piece of thread he ever had to weave a worthwhile existence. No one is exactly sure if he will ever again be the same fighter — and that includes himself. But he is certain that "some good has come out of the death of Beethavean Scottland," if only that he now understands something that had eluded him for years: the value of life.

That has been a revelation to Jones, who grew up in circumstances where life had no value. With soulful eyes that exude a mannered gentility, Jones said his late father had twenty-six children with a variety of women and abandoned him while his mother was six months pregnant with him. He fell into drugs at an early age. Jailed at age seventeen for shooting "a guy who tried to rob me and a friend on a corner" in 1985, Jones spent four years behind bars. Said his mother, Ruth Ann Jones-Mass, who remembered how a drug-crazed Jones once had to be led away in a straitjacket to the hospital to keep him from jumping off the roof: "Sometimes our children just go astray."

He sold drugs to support a gambling addiction and was arrested again in 1997. He came before a judge who told him, "Mr. Jones, you are a menace to society." So he went to prison again for a four-year term, only this time he was leaving behind a woman, Naomi Del Valle, and their small children. Jones and Del Valle had been together since December 1991 and not a week passed that she did not go to the prison with her children. "Seeing him there was the hardest thing I ever had to do," said Del Valle, employed in customer services by The Bank of New York. "I cried every visit, but I did every second of his time with him. I just knew there was a better person somewhere deep inside of him."

Some boxing talent was in there, too, if only he could clean himself up. He had begun boxing in jail in 1985 because he discovered that boxers received certain privileges, such as Sunday ice cream and unlimited cheeseburgers. He began to spar in some local gyms in 1994, then turned pro that September against Marty Lindquist in Minnesota. He was supposed to go there as an "opponent" — which is to say he was supposed to lose — but he won a four-round decision. He then strung together ten straight victories — including eight by knockout — when his career was interrupted by that four-year jail stint, of which he served thirty-four months. When he came out again in May 2000, he clicked off four straight victories, three by knockout. His opponent for that ESPN2 *Tuesday Night Fights* date, June 26 on the USS *Intrepid*, was supposed to be David Telesco, but Telesco begged off with a broken nose sustained in training, and Scottland stepped in as his replacement.

"What would have happened if I had fought Telesco instead of Bee?" said Jones. "I ask myself 'What if . . .' every day."

The bell tolled: ten strikes in honor of a popular boxing figure who had recently died. In the ring before his comeback fight against highly rated Eric Harding at the Mohegan Sun Casino in Connecticut, Jones suddenly found himself overwhelmed by the tragedy he had just endured. Walking into the ring that evening he had been fine — or thought he had been fine — but he had not expected there to be a call by the ring announcer for a moment of silence. As he stood there listening in his corner, he wondered to himself, "Man, is somebody playing a trick on me or what?" His eyes began to well up with tears.

"Every time I heard that bell 'ding,' the only thing I could think of was what had happened," Jones said. "And I began reliving the whole thing again."

Until he stepped into the ring on the USS *Intrepid,* Jones had been unacquainted with Scottland, a southpaw who fought out of a gym in suburban Washington called Round One Boxing. Scottland (20–6–2) worked as an exterminator to supplement his earnings from boxing, which were minimal in light of his inability to connect with a big promoter. He had married his childhood friend, Denise Lewis, and they had an eight-year-old daughter and two sons, ages two and six. Ironically, the opponent he had been lined up to face for the Maryland State 168-pound belt last June 20, Dana Rucker, withdrew because of a hamstring injury, so Scottland was available when Duva began looking for a replacement for Telesco. Scottland had to jump up a weight class; he weighed in at 170, four pounds lighter than Jones. But Scottland jumped at the opportunity because it would pay him more than he had ever earned for a bout: $7,000 plus $1,000 in expenses. Said Jones, also a southpaw, "We both wanted the same thing: a shot at something better."

But it soon became clear that Scottland was in well over his head. By the end of the fourth round, CompuBox statistics showed Jones had landed sixty-four more punches than Scottland. During a forty-two-second span in the fifth round, Jones pummeled Scottland with forty-three shots; Scottland landed only three. Cries of "Stop it! Stop it!" rang out from the crowd, and even ESPN2 commentator Max Kellerman observed, "This is how guys get seriously hurt." Ring physician Dr. Barry Jordan told referee Arthur Mercante Jr. before the eighth round not to allow Scottland to "take many more blows," but Scottland, who Mercante later said still was defending himself, rallied to narrowly win the eighth and ninth rounds. When the fighters came out at the beginning of the final round, Jones said Mercante told them as they touched gloves: "Show me who wants it more."

"And the only thing I could think was: 'I gotta get this guy out of here,'" Jones said. Scottland was felled by a combination with forty-five seconds remaining and was immediately attended to by Jordan and two other doctors. Jones climbed up on the ring ropes to salute the crowd in victory.

But that joy turned to horror as it became obvious Scottland was seriously injured. While the doctors found him initially to be conscious, they said his condition quickly deteriorated. Concerned, Jones looked on as paramedics strapped Scottland to a stretcher, which they would have trouble squeezing into the elevator of the World War II–era *Intrepid*. As Jones walked back to his dressing room, he reminded himself, "This is just part of the game." Johnny Bos, his booking agent, assured him Scottland would be fine, but when Bos telephoned him later at home, the report he had was not an encouraging one. Nor were any of the subsequent reports from Bos, who called Jones six to eight times a day with updates. Said Jones, "All I could do was pray: *please let him live.* It was the longest six days you could possibly imagine, then Johnny called to say, 'He died.'"

A depression fell over Jones that summer. He attended the funeral in Washington, but only when a close friend who had helped him conquer his gambling addiction told him, "What are you going to do? Are you going to punk out again, the way you always used to do? Or are you going to stand up and be a man?"

Going there had a soothing effect on him, yet if he discovered that others had forgiven him, he still was not at a point where he could forgive himself. When he attempted to go back to the gym a few weeks later, he broke down in tears and told Del Valle he was through. He began getting up late every day, at which point he would brush his teeth, then go back to sleep again. Del Valle told him, "This is not who you are. You have to get over this." And yet whenever Jones looked at her and his children, it reminded him of how Denise would never again be able to hold her husband, and how the children would never be able to say, "Daddy, we love you." Said Jones, "You know, it takes two parents to raise a child. No one knows that better than me." Weeks of inactivity had passed when Bos spoke up.

"George, you drive a cab for a living, and you hit someone, and they die, you have to get back in that cab and drive it again," Bos said. "This is the same thing. You have to get back in that cab."

You can never predict how certain fighters will come back after they have killed an opponent; fine talents such as Ray "Boom Boom" Mancini and Gabriel Ruelas were never the same again. In the case of Jones — who began training again in the fall — Bos said he never would have booked him against Harding last December if he had been aware of just how emotionally fragile he was. But Bos said he figured it could set him up for a big-money title shot against light-heavyweight champion Roy Jones Jr. A victory would give George an undefeated record with "the rep of killing an opponent," which Bos said could only enhance his desirability. But in the week before the Harding bout — for which George wore trunks emblazoned with the words "Bee" and "R.I.P." — he did a television interview in which he began crying. Asked in the interview how he has fared since the tragedy, he said: "This is the first time I have ever felt compassion." Bos was aghast.

Compassion is not an attractive feature in a fighter.

"Naaahhh," said Bos. "You do not want a compassionate fighter."

The Harding bout did not go well in any way. Duva, who ordinarily works the corner, was rushed to a hospital when his heart defibrillator malfunctioned. And then Jones fell to pieces during that unexpected moment of silence. While Jones would say later, "The better man won that night," Bos said Jones was holding back with his punches, that he had Harding in early trouble but would not step in aggressively enough. Harding wobbled Jones toward the end of the sixth round, then finished the job in the seventh with a seven-punch combination. As Jones slid helplessly to the canvas, Del Valle looked on from her ringside seat and saw his eyes roll back into his head. "Oh God!" she yelled in terror. "Now this is happening to me!" Eleven-year-old daughter Aisha began crying hysterically. When Jones recovered back in his dressing room, Bos approached him and said, "This cannot be. Either you fight the way you're capable of or you're packing it in. I'm not letting you go out there and get hurt."

Bos said, "He called me and begged me for another chance."

He got it against Karl Willis in April. Jones (17–1, 13 KOs) fought well enough to win by a third-round technical knockout, but as Bos said, "Willis is no Eric Harding." Bos just said he told Jones to get some work in and that was what he did. Jones had command of the bout from the opening bell, got his punches off cleanly, and said that he only once drifted back in time to the

Scottland fight. It was when a fan stood up at his seat and shouted at him for everyone to hear: "Come on, George. Kill the guy."

Change has come over George Khalid Jones. Small things he does every day convince him of that. Once, he would have become enraged if another driver had cut him off. Today, he said he just shakes his head and sighs. In fact, he said you can slap him in the face and "the only thing I will do now is smile." It was not long ago, on a Saturday night, he happened to be watching the fights on television when it appeared to him that the referee should stop it. Suddenly, he began shouting frantically at the television screen: "Stop it! Stop it!" Only later did it occur to him he never would have done something like that before Scottland.

Preparing for a bout that could come as early as next month, he goes to the Police Athletic League gym in Hackensack every weekday at 4:30 P.M. He goes there after he gets off work at a printing plant, where he is the inventory manager. There, he works out until 6:30 or so and is surrounded by friends, every one of whom says what a fine fellow he is. "I told him to get rid of those damn trunks he wore during the Harding fight," said an elderly trainer at the PAL. "All that does is bring up bad memories." Whenever Jones hears someone say that, he smiles politely and explains that Scottland is a part of him now, that he has dedicated his career to him. He hopes to help his widow in whatever way he can in the years ahead and even hopes to begin a college fund to help the children. Said Jones, "What I realized is that life is short, and you have to ask yourself: How do you want to be remembered?"

What Bos and others say is that Scottland died needlessly, that the bout should have been stopped in the early rounds. They say Scottland was a victim. His widow sued New York City, which owns the *Intrepid,* in March, for allowing her husband to be "unreasonably and violently pummeled." What has gone unsaid is that the burden of grief is a shared one, and that it extends far beyond the gravesite, where Jones stood that July day a year ago and peered into eternity. He did not "punk out," the way he once would have done, but faced up to a difficult thing and has become stronger — if not as a fighter then as a man. Somehow he knows that Scottland has forgiven him. A certain inner peace has come with that realization. He can finally forgive himself.

BRUCE FELDMAN

Out of Control

FROM ESPN: THE MAGAZINE

BIRMINGHAM clings to its nickname with white-knuckled fists: "The Football Capital of the South." (At least that's better than "Bomb-ingham," the moniker it earned in the 1960s as America's most ra-cially charged city.) And while the place no longer hosts the annual Alabama-Auburn slugfest, it does have a new team to cheer: the University of Alabama at Birmingham.

UAB may be just a commuter school lost in the shadow of two in-state behemoths, but it is a commuter school hell-bent on raising its profile. And in Alabama, the land of Bo and The Bear, the quick-est path to getting on the map cuts across the gridiron.

In fact, UAB took a no-huddle approach to building its pro-gram. Just five seasons after its launch as a D3 doormat in 1991, Blazer football hit the big time. The school had plucked Watson Brown — folksy and funny and carrying deep-fried cred on the re-cruiting trail — from Oklahoma's staff. Ol' Watson assembled a crew of gridiron grunts, fielding twenty-two transfers when UAB made its 1A debut on August 31, 1996. The Blazers got whupped 29–0 at Auburn that day, but Brown flashed that televangelist smile and doll-eyed his way through the postgame. "Soon," he promised in a kudzu-thick Tennessee drawl, "evah-one'll know 'bout UAB football."

The most important recruit in UAB history was a freckle-faced, carrot-topped fourteen-year-old named Brittany, who finished high school in under a year. UAB pursued the five-foot-one, 120-pound bookworm like it would a quarterback who could rope the deep out.

Brittany, who looks like a cross between Little Orphan Annie and Molly Ringwald, grew up an hour down Route 280 in tiny Childersburg (pop. 4,900). Frank and Jackie Benefield, as country as cornbread, had been trying for a child for twenty years before Brittany was born. They called her the miracle baby. When other children were stuck on c-a-t, Brittany could rattle off b-l-u-e-b-e-r-r-y. Her second-grade teacher suggested Brittany jump through to third grade. Jackie Benefield wasn't sure, but figured the teacher knew best.

The Benefields were protective of their only child, who had her dad's wide smile and her mom's soft eyes. Brittany's social life revolved around a church youth group, its skate parties and Bible classes. Her folks were strict about what she could do. While other sixth-graders rehashed *Home Improvement,* Brittany kept quiet about her favorites — Bugs, Daffy, and *Mister Ed.* When Brittany was in seventh grade, Jackie bought her a new dress for the spring dance. But when a student threatened to bring a gun, the school canceled the event. That's when the Benefields decided to home-school Brittany.

The child prodigy earned her degree at thirteen. Still, Frank, now sixty, and Jackie, fifty-four, worried about Brittany's future. "I always thought, if we just lived to see her educated and able to take care of herself, she'd be okay," says Jackie.

In March 1999, fourteen-year-old Brittany was accepted at Auburn, making headlines in the *Birmingham News.* When her scholarship money got lost in a bureaucratic maze, Auburn told the family not to worry, they'd hold her place for the next class. A few weeks later, though, Jackie got a call from UAB. They wanted Brittany, too, and they were offering full tuition. Jackie was thrilled — and nervous; Birmingham, after all, was the big city. Brittany, having spent day after monotonous day at home, couldn't stop smiling.

Her plan was to finish law school before she turned twenty-one. As it turns out, Brittany Benefield's day in court arrived three years ahead of schedule — not as a lawyer, but as a plaintiff accusing twenty-six UAB athletes of sexual abuse and a university for its culpability in the matter. Acting through her mother, Brittany Benefield has filed lawsuits under Title IX in state and federal courts. The Benefields are suing UAB trustees, administrators, coaches, athletes, resident assistants, police, and others. At the time of publication, the Benefields were seeking $80 million in compensatory and punitive damages.

This is the story of what happens when a naive fifteen-year-old prodigy collides with an upward-reaching football program, some of whose players feel like they own the campus.

When the Benefields first met then-UAB president Ann Reynolds and VP of student affairs Virginia Gauld, they made their reservations known, according to statements contained in their complaints. The Benefields say they told the UAB brass that Brittany had never been away from them for more than a day. "I was worried about her crossing the street or someone snatching her," says Jackie. A meeting was set up with Warren Hale, director of student housing, and Susan McKinnon, assistant VP of enrollment management. The Benefields claim they were assured by talk of security escorts. According to their complaints, they were told the dorm to which Brittany would be assigned, Rast Hall, housed only freshmen and had security every night, and that residents needed a key to enter the building. The Benefields allege Hale and McKinnon also promised that one of the girl's suitemates would be a resident adviser, a student who would monitor Brittany's activities and mentor her. The UAB officials wanted Brittany to enroll immediately for the winter quarter in December 1999. Her folks wanted to wait until she was fifteen. They agreed that Brittany would begin in the spring, a month after her fifteenth birthday.

From the start, Brittany was a minor celebrity at UAB, although she says the other students saw her as more circus freak than star. "I felt very out of place," she says. "When people found out my age, they were like, 'What are you doing here?' I mean, it was okay to hear that now and then, but ten times a day? I was pretty lonely."

Her suitemates, who'd been on campus for six months, had their own friends. With no one to talk to — or watch TV or grab a burger with — her days dragged by in solitary routine: wake up, go to class, head back to the dorm, study. Her parents brought her home almost every weekend, with Jackie working longer shifts just so she could pick up Brittany on Thursdays.

Brittany carried a 3.5 GPA in basic freshman courses in her first quarter. The Benefields say they wanted her to take the summer off, but she was adamant about continuing classes so she could graduate in three years. "I figured if I made her come home, she'd just be staring at the four walls," says Jackie. "I guess that was my mistake." To Brittany, the only bummer was that she'd have to change dorms, because hers would be used to house summer-camp students.

Drenched in sweat on a steamy Louisiana night, helmets in hands, the UAB squad stomped and hollered and let the football world know they could no longer be ignored. As eighty-six thousand dazed LSU fans watched, the visitors jumped on the Tiger's face at midfield. On September 23, 2000, the Blazers — upstarts with a cartoon dragon on their helmets — took home a 13–10 upset victory and a $410,000 paycheck. Who-AB? Not anymore.

Man, you should've heard Ol' Watson before the game that night, down in the bowels of Tiger Stadium just before his Blazers took the field. The air was heavy with sweat and menthol; Brown was all fire and brimstone: "Fellas, lemme tell ya 'bout the irony we have here tonight," he told them. "Those guys in the other dressing room are no better than you. Every day you go up against guys who are as good as they are. I know that. You know that. They just don't know it yet. But tonight — tonight! — they're gonna *fiiind* out."

Brown took a long slow breath, and the team recited the Lord's Prayer. Brown glanced around the room like a proud father. His baby had sure grown up fast. The 2000 UAB Blazers looked nothing like the ragtag squad that got blistered by Auburn in '96. Out were the D1 castoffs. In were speedy cover-corners and run-stuffing linemen from Atlanta, the Florida Panhandle, and every holler in Alabama. Brown turned sleeper recruits into nasty playmakers. He took Prop 48 kids, gave 'em some love, and sharpened the chips on their shoulders. It worked in the weight room, on the field, and in the classroom. (More than 60 percent of the team members were honor students.) Sure, they had a few renegades. Heck, everybody's got a few, right?

Everyone inside that cramped room knew they were building something here. Most teams have more cliques than a sorority house, but the Blazers were different. They were tight. Maybe it was Coach Brown's pep talks. Maybe it was month after month of gut-busting practice. Or maybe it was the players' visibility. Of the roughly seven hundred men who lived on campus, nearly one in nine played for Brown. They literally had the run of the place.

*

Just a post pattern from the UAB practice field is Blazer Hall, a twelve-sided, eight-story, antiseptic building that resembles a hospital ward more than a dorm. In the summer of 2000, Blazer housed mostly football players, a few basketball players, a handful of women — and one fifteen-year-old girl.

The family's complaints allege that when all of Blazer's residents assembled for an informal introduction on a June evening, an RA scanned the crowd and paused on Brittany, uttering an introduction that still rings in Brittany's ears: "Okay, this is the fifteen-year-old y'all been hearing about." Brittany remembers a split-second of silence giving way to the sound of forty heads turning at once.

If Brittany had been lonely from day one on campus, she felt absolutely isolated during those first days in Blazer Hall. The Benefields say in their complaints that, because the school didn't offer her another RA for a roommate, they chose a single room for Brittany. They say they preferred Brittany living alone to her sharing space with female students who might have beer in the fridge and boyfriends staying over. On her third day in Blazer, Brittany says, she entered the elevator and encountered a mountain of a man, a Blazer football player with a bushy afro and hands as thick as cinder blocks. Brittany tried to avoid making eye contact, but the man faced her as the doors shut. "Whussup, shorty?" he huffed, according to Brittany. She remembers feeling the blood drain from her face. He said he knew her; she was that child genius. He asked if she'd help him with a paper. Brittany panicked and stammered: "I'm fifteen."

"Well, you don't look it," she says he told her.

Brittany's emotions swirled as she stepped off the elevator. The comment about her appearance transformed her initial fear into a feeling that surprised her: acceptance. Maybe she belonged in this strange place after all. "That made me feel a lot better," Brittany says. That night, she says, the player brought his paper — and a six-pack of beer — to her room. Brittany says she had never had a beer — or any kind of alcohol — but felt compelled to accept when she was offered one. According to Brittany, one led to another. And another. Brittany got wasted. She'd never even kissed a boy, and now she was making out with the player. Then they had sex.

The next morning, the burly football players seemed a lot less menacing to her. In fact, Brittany says, they began to treat her as if she belonged. That night, another player asked for homework help, and brought over more beer. Brittany says she got drunk again and the player persuaded her to perform oral sex. The next day, she says she got drunk and had sex with a third player, who introduced her to pot. "I felt accepted," Brittany says. "I felt like they were my friends."

The players joked with her that she was becoming their "plaything." She began hanging with them all the time. They'd sit outside Blazer downing beer, bumming cigarettes, watching cars go by.

On August 7, the school got the exposure from its star recruit that it had hoped for. The *Birmingham News* ran a front-page story about Brittany and a sixteen-year-old male student, headlined "Whiz Kids." On campus, though, Brittany was no longer known as a fifteen-year-old prodigy, but as that fifteen-year-old rumored to be doing half the football team.

According to an e-mail from Hale attached to the complaints, he states, having heard the rumors, that he called Brittany in for a meeting with a UAB police officer. They asked if she was having sex with football players. She said no. The complaints allege the school didn't investigate any further, nor did it notify the Benefields or Alabama's Department of Human Resources of their concerns of drugs and sexual activities, despite a state law requiring they do so in the case of a minor. However, the e-mail reflects that Hale did talk to the Benefields regarding Brittany "hosting guests." The Benefields acknowledge Brittany stopped coming home as much, and that she slept all weekend when she did return. But they say they figured she was just overworked.

An e-mail from Hale, included in the complaints, indicates that he did meet with Blazers special-teams coach Larry Crowe, letting the coach know that school administrators had heard rumors about his players and Brittany. According to the e-mail, Hale told Crowe that a girl Brittany's age could not consent to sex. No matter the situation, it was statutory rape. Later that week, the complaints allege, Brown told his team to stay away from Brittany. "If this gets outside of me," he said, "I can no longer help you." He allegedly added that it could mean "jail time."

Apparently the Blazers didn't heed the warnings. Some team members interviewed by *The Magazine* echo comments in the complaints that a few days later Coach Crowe pointed to Blazer Hall and told his players to stay out of Brittany's room. The next week, according to the complaints, the players got a warning from "Officer Andy" — a.k.a. Anderson Williams Jr. — a UAB cop who was moonlighting as the team's unofficial speed coach. Before lecturing the Blazers about lengthening their running strides, he allegedly reminded the players to "be careful" with the underage girl.

The Blazers opened the 2000 season on September 7 with a 20–15 home victory over Chattanooga. Brittany recalls feeling like she was part of the program, cheering like they'd just beaten Alabama. She'd grown even more alienated from other students, but now she didn't give a damn what those losers thought. Though she had moved back into her old dorm, Brittany's partying escalated from beer to whiskey to vodka. Other students say her room reeked of weed, but that was just the beginning. She told *The Magazine* that the players turned her on to coke, ecstasy, and LSD, and she says one player even tried to turn her out. She declined to let him pimp her, but she kept sleeping with football players and began hooking up with some members of the basketball team. She was being passed around like a mix tape. In all, she alleges, more than two dozen Blazer athletes took their turn. The complaints even allege that an employee of the UABPD and the student who plays Blaze, the school's mascot, came knocking on Brittany's door.

Experts say her attitude was not unusual for a female who has been sexually abused. "It's not uncommon for a woman who has been raped to engage in promiscuous behavior," says New York–based sports psychologist Mitch Abrams, who specializes in trauma-abuse counseling. "People say, 'See, she's a slut,' or 'See, she loved it.' But rape is about power, not sex. Someone took her power and now she was trying anything to get it back."

Brittany tells of one especially harrowing night, when she was invited to the room of two football players. When she walked in, she says, two other men were there as well and each of the four took his turn with her. She recalls leaving the dorm in tears, telling no one.

Later that September, a UAB police officer and other administrators called in Brittany to discuss a curfew, according to the complaints, and Brittany was again asked about her sexual involvement with athletes and drug use. She denied it all. The complaints allege they didn't push the matter further, nor did they alert the

Benefields, who weren't even notified when her GPA plummeted to 1.9.

That Saturday, the Blazers — following their huge win at LSU — crushed Louisiana-Lafayette, 47–2.

Meanwhile, Brittany's downward spiral continued. She stopped going to class and got high day and night. When some of the players stopped coming around, Brittany began using meal and rent money to buy drugs, and, according to the complaints, on November 7, the school sent an eviction notice to Brittany rather than her parents, even though the Benefields were financially responsible for her room and board. The Benefields allege UAB didn't contact them until five weeks later, when Jackie received a shocking call telling her that her daughter was getting kicked out of her dorm for not paying rent.

The Benefields raced to UAB, but Brittany was nowhere to be found. Frank Benefield says he could barely speak when he filed a runaway report with the UABPD. The next morning, the Benefields' phone rang. It was Brittany, asking to be picked up at the local airport. Her parents made the twelve-mile drive, but Brittany wasn't there. Instead, she and a friend, a reputed Birmingham drug dealer, were breaking into the Benefield home, swiping a handgun and blank checks.

The next day, Sunday, December 17, the Birmingham police nabbed Brittany and her friend at a pizza parlor for trying to pass a bad check. When they arrived on the scene, says Jackie, Brittany broke down. Their miracle baby, tears streaming and body trembling, admitted she'd spent all her rent money on drugs and that she'd passed a couple of dozen bad checks. The Benefields took their daughter back to Childersburg, but Brittany disappeared again after one night. Four days passed before she called her father from a gas station near campus. She told him she'd been staying in a boarded-up apartment. She wanted to kill herself. "I was a zombie," Brittany says. "I was a broken person. The things I'd been through were unreal."

Two hours later, Jackie opened her front door, laid eyes on her baby, and winced. "I didn't know her," she says. "I saw her face. I saw her hair, but when I looked into her eyes, they were hollow. I didn't see who was behind them." The Benefields put their daughter in rehab. It was Christmas Eve.

Four days earlier, according to the complaints, UAB president Ann Reynolds had received an e-mail from VP Virginia Gauld, telling her that the prize recruit had tragically spiraled into drugs, alcohol, and degradation. The e-mail's last line was chilling: "Sometimes we win and sometimes we lose!" Reynolds's reply was just as cold. The Benefields' suits allege that Reynolds quipped the Whiz Kid's story had the makings of a "B movie," and that "she was clearly overprotected and doted on by elderly parents. Warren Hale and others are to be praised for trying."

So if everyone was "trying," is anyone to blame? None of the defendants will comment on the case, but all have either denied the Benefields' allegations or moved to dismiss the complaints in court. "We're not called on to defend factual statements," says Doug Jones, who represents six UAB administrators. "We're called on to defend legal allegations." Ken Lay, a public defender for seventeen Blazer athletes, released this statement: "Most of the athletes we represent know little or nothing about Ms. Benefield or her allegations."

Brittany's story may prove to be the most extreme recent case of sexual abuse in college sports, but it is not unique. Since August, athletes have been accused of sexual assault and rape at Colorado, Georgia, LSU, Notre Dame, and Oklahoma State. And those are just the public accusations. In many college football towns, police forces have long had officers designated to deal with athlete-related investigations. They're often the first dispatched to the scene and have a prior working relationship with coaches. The Oklahoma State victim, for instance, has alleged that a police officer tried to coerce her into signing a prosecution waiver while she was in the ICU.

"There is such an incestuous relationship [between police and athletic departments]," says Kathy Redmond, founder of the National Coalition Against Violent Athletes. "It's very frightening." Seven years ago, Redmond accused Huskers DT Christian Peter, who'd already been accused twice of assaulting women, of raping her four years earlier. No criminal charges were filed against Peter, but Redmond's lawyers brought a civil suit against him and the university. Soon, she was taking on an entire football-mad state.

Redmond's lawyer filed a Title IX lawsuit contending the school was liable under the federal law because the university failed to provide a safe environment from sexual harassment — and that inhibited Redmond's right to an education. NU and Peter settled out of court without admitting liability. Says Redmond, "I don't think anybody understands the power that law has over college sports."

Here's where that power lies. Rape and sexual assault are harder to prove in criminal court than in civil court, so many victims find their only recourse in a civil case. Title IX suits offer an opportunity for the victim to be heard away from potentially biased local jurisdictions, plus access to the deeper pockets of universities rather than just to individual defendants.

Dr. Abrams, the sports psychologist, agrees that victims and lawyers don't know the ramifications of Title IX — yet. "You could see hundreds, if not thousands, of silent victims come forward," he says.

On August 30, 2001, the same day the Blazers opened a new football season by beating Montana State, 41–13, John Whitaker and Terry Dytrych, lawyers for the Benefields, filed a civil suit in state court against forty-four people, including members of UAB's administration and police, two coaches, twenty-six athletes — and the mascot.

Turnovers! Watson Brown sweeps sweat from his shaggy mop of hair, crinkles his nose, and shakes his head. Just forty-five minutes into UAB's 2002 spring game, and Ol' Watson is a plastered hair from his boiling point. It's bad enough that his QB has tossed four picks in the first half. Did he have to throw one in the doggoned red zone? At least the QB levels the dude who picked him off. That almost makes Brown crack a smile. Over the past month and a half, Brown's boys have surprised him with the best hitting since he came to Birmingham.

UAB is on a roll, on the field and off. Brown has inked the school's strongest recruiting class and the Blazers beat mighty Tennessee for a prized QB recruit. Two of his kids (not named in the lawsuit) went high in the NFL draft: DE Bryan Thomas (first round, Jets) and DT Eddie Freeman (second round, Chiefs). Mirroring the rise of its football program, out-of-state enrollment at UAB has nearly doubled, and total enrollment is up 20 percent since 1998. Still, Brown figures if the Blazers pull a 3–8 this fall after last year's 6–5, they'll be just another flash-in-the-pan. Brown refuses to blame the lawsuit for his team dropping four of their first six in 2001.

The Benefields say they couldn't care less if their daughter's lawsuits are a distraction for the Blazers. They want justice. They want someone to pay. In April they filed a Title IX suit, this one in federal court, against the university trustees. No criminal charges have been filed against the defendants in either of the Benefield lawsuits.

Six projected UAB starters are defendants. But there's little locker room talk about Brittany or her lawsuit. Some players don't deny bad things happened with the fifteen-year-old prodigy, they just downplay how bad things really were. "We think they're just trying to get money out of the school," says one player not named in the suit. "There's not much we can do about it. I just hope it doesn't make the team look too bad."

The miracle baby is seventeen now, but despite a heavy dusting of midnight-blue eye shadow, she still looks like an apple-cheeked fourteen-year-old. She does clerical work in her mom's office; she can't afford to go back to college. Instead, she attends weekly substance abuse sessions. Her meetings with a rape counselor are down from four a week to just one. Three years ago, she chased life at warp speed. Now she barely makes it from day to day. There are moments when she'll sit on her bed and just zone out.

At a crowded Birmingham barbecue joint on a sunny April day, Brittany sits beside her mom and talks about her nightmare. Conversations at nearby booths clatter to a halt, but Brittany refuses to speak in hushed tones. This is her life. She has learned not to be ashamed, only reflective. She admits she was naïve and maybe not as smart as she thought. The big lesson she has learned? Brittany pauses briefly before the words spill out.

"Never trust anyone."

UAB football opens at Florida on August 31.

MICHAEL AGOVINO

My Dad, the Bookie

FROM GQ

IT WAS SUPER BOWL SUNDAY, the only day of the year my mother
served dinner in front of the television set. She knew that my father
had a vested financial interest in the game and that I was a boy who
cared deeply about sports. So she conceded: dinner in the living
room, in front of the Trinitron. I suspect she enjoyed it.

The menu was a concession, too, solely for me this time. Gone
was our usual midwinter southern Italian Sunday feast: a home-
made *ragù* over rigatoni, with braciola, sausage, broccoli rabe on
the side, and a carafe of Valpolicella. No, on this day, my mother,
ever so desperate to put meat on my little bones, served up my favorite: roast beef, potatoes, Boston lettuce, and mountains of green
beans sautéed with garlic and olive oil.

My older sister refused to take part. She always hated two things
— red meat and sports. Above all, she hated my father's gambling,
the ebb and flow of anxiety that came with it, the screaming matches
it provoked between my parents, the dark silences after a bad day at
"the office," the absurdity of risking our future on Tampa Bay or
TCU or some horse, maybe Foolish Pleasure.

For my father, gambling and bookmaking was a second job, his
clandestine second life. He had been gambling in some form or another since FDR's second term. By the 1980s, it had become his
main source of income.

On that Super Bowl Sunday in 1984, in our Bronx apartment
twenty-two stories above the rickety treetops, the three of us — my
parents and I — watched the Washington Redskins play the Los
Angeles Raiders. The Redskins were the defending title-holders

and a three-point favorite. My father had wagered heavily on the Raiders. How heavily, I don't know; I knew not to ask.

He never had favorite teams — gamblers and bookmakers can't get attached, can't afford to — but he had a thing for the Raiders. Kenny Stabler might have started it; my father had a predilection for lefties. And the Raiders were always the bad guys. That helped.

Washington had the self-aggrandizing quarterback Joe Theismann and the impudent receiving corps known as the Smurfs. The Raiders had the stoic Tom Flores and the unfashionable Jim Plunkett — two scions of industrious Chicano laborers who came up the hard way.

In the third quarter, when the game was still a game, there was a play — a very famous play. Perhaps you remember it. Marcus Allen, bright, young, stealthy, took a handoff from Plunkett. He ran left to the line of scrimmage, saw it was clogged, "stopped on a dime," spun 180 degrees to the right, got a feeble but well-intentioned block from the creaky-limbed Plunkett, and turned upfield. For a few interminable seconds, we didn't talk, we didn't chew, we didn't breathe. Our eyes widened, and we watched Marcus Allen run. He kept on running, a silver streak, away from the pack for some seventy yards and a touchdown. Roasted potatoes flew into the air, and green beans, and shouts of joy. My sister, eavesdropping, came out of her room, relieved. For now it was apparent the Raiders would win. Her perpetually overdue tuition at Clark University would be paid. Outside, the Bronx resonated with horns and howls, at least our multiracial, multi-ethnic, occasionally tensioned corner of the Bronx, an eyesore of gray schematic towers called Co-Op City. Marcus Allen saved the world that night.

This is what it was like to live with a bookmaker. When my father won, we saw things. Doors opened, views expanded. He liked to think of himself as a capitalist hero. He would tell us over dinner that he "made the wheels turn." For him, money was something you enjoyed. It went to things like books, food, wine, delicacies, opera tickets, music lessons, and trips to museums — in Delft.

How much did my father win? There was never a final tally, not that Sunday nor any other. As in any business, he had a gross and a net, the difference being how much he owed. When he didn't win, when things hit rock-bottom, bills would not be paid. The fee for his gallbladder surgery at New York Hospital in 1977 wasn't settled until the early '90s. He'd go six months without paying the phone bill and the telephone company would shut off our service or at least prevent us from making outgoing calls. "God forbid of an emergency," my mother would say.

To buy time, my father raised the already fine art of check bouncing to something metaphysical. Eventually, people wouldn't accept anything but cash from him. He probably averted trouble, narrowly, a dozen times, maybe more. What kind of trouble, I'm not sure. I know he borrowed from people, maybe bad people, borrowed from one to pay another.

When I worked up the gumption, and as a child I wasn't blessed with gumption, I'd ask how much he'd won or lost and he'd simply say, "Don't worry," or, "Worry about your schoolwork." By the time I was in college, I was more aggressive in my questioning, especially when I'd meet him on a corner near the NYU campus in the final hour of late registration, two weeks into the semester, and he'd be in a cold, panicked sweat, bank check in hand, with me thinking he'd have a stroke between Greene and Mercer. He was fifty-eight then, no longer permitted to have a credit card. I was eighteen, a freshman in college, making four-something an hour at the NYU bookstore, and I had my choice of Visa, Mastercard, or Discover. He wouldn't answer. He would just turn reticent.

My mother tried to save. She would stash what she could in her James Beard cookbook so he couldn't get to it, squander it on the early daily double. She made my sister and me swear not to tell him where the money was. Not that there was much: a few fives, tens, and twenties. Just enough to pay the pharmacist and maybe a taxi driver if sickly me needed to see Dr. Printz on Burke Avenue. When my mother knew my father was short on cash — that is, when he came to me or my sister for change to buy subway tokens — she began to worry. As far as I know, he never did try to uncover her cache, not unless he searched the house at night, when we were all asleep. He never could sleep very well.

Other people, most others we knew, had assets — houses, cars, savings or retirement accounts: "security," as my mother would say. Even my father's "customers" — that's what he called them — had plenty put away. Mostly Wall Street types, Jews, Italians, Irish, the odd Wasp, they gambled simply for sport. One of them, my mother reminded us, had a Swiss bank account. "A Swiss bank account!" My father borrowed from his pension and his IRA.

"It's not normal," she'd say loudly, decrying our lifestyle.

"I know it's not normal," he'd say.

Sure it was odd, but it was all we knew. My sister and I couldn't have friends over between six and eight at night, between noon and two on weekends. Our phones — we had two extensions, one private, one for the customers — would ring off the hook. It would look suspicious to visitors.

Not that our neighbors could afford to pass judgment. Co-Op City had a cast of fifty-five thousand oddball characters. Who drank, who smacked around his wife, who was a degenerate horseplayer, who was a petty gossip, who never should have been a parent, who scrawled graffiti in the stairwells, who pissed in the elevators, who was a corrupt cop or a junkie-to-be — this was common knowledge in Co-Op City. We had no Main Street or Pine Street or Fourth of July parade. Just cherry bombs in garbage cans. But my family seemed odd to the oddballs. We were the freaks. Jetting off one day, finding eviction notices on the door the next. Steven Shligger, half-Italian, half-Jewish, would ask me in third grade, "Is your father in the Mafia?" The kids, even teachers, would look at me and wait for a response. They didn't know what to think when we went round the room, reporting on summer vacations. Everyone else said Lake George or Shorehaven. I said Lisbon or Rabat or Amsterdam. My teachers thought what Shligger thought. They had the same mentality as a third-grader.

But Shligger was wrong. We weren't connected. And we certainly didn't look like we were. My mother was taken for an elementary-school teacher. Old Jewish women would say to her on Friday afternoon, "Shabbat shalom." People mistook my father for my grandfather. He looked as conformist as they come, bifocaled, in conservative matte blazers, no jewelry, a balding head, hair mostly gray. And he was terribly hard of hearing — except when the phone rang. Sometimes he'd run to the receiver, pick it up, and discover nothing but a dial tone. Often the phone hadn't even been ringing.

My father had a full-time job — quotidian bureaucratic work for the city's Department of Welfare. He hated it, for thirty-five years. It was there, at his day job, that he struck up a friendship with the playwright Loften Mitchell and with the artist Romare Bearden, who was a caseworker. Getting to know these men was a bright spot, one of the few, in my father's workday.

That was in the late '50s, early '60s, when our country was less educated but smarter somehow, more engaged. My father and Bearden would talk about Coleman Hawkins and Johnny Hodges, Vermeer and Giotto, the Rock and Clay. One day the humble Bearden said, "Hey, come to my studio; I make these collages." He offered to make one for my father. Not wanting to seem presumptuous (*scustumad*, in the Neapolitan dialect of my father's birthplace, East Harlem), my father said, "No, no, really, I couldn't."

"What that would be worth today," my mother would say for years afterward. Then my father would say it again: "What that would be worth today." When I was much older, I went to the Harlem home of author Albert Murray. There, in the bathroom, was a very small work of Bearden's. It was exquisite, teeming with humanity and language, so much happening in so small a space. It was the kind of collage I now imagine Bearden would have given my father. As I stood in Murray's bathroom, I thought, Why couldn't we have one of those, something of rare beauty and value?

Of course, my father might have sold our Bearden in a fit of financial desperation. Then again, I have to remind myself that art was sacred to him, that Bearden was much closer to Albert Murray than he was to my father. Murray had fourteen original Beardens, large and small, around his apartment. Still, there is a photograph that exists somewhere of my father and Bearden taken after my father was one of a handful of people who spoke at a farewell party for Bearden when Bearden left the department to devote himself to his art, and I can't help but think that one day, a special day or a sad day, that photograph and a transcendent little Bearden collage will be brought to me. I know in reality this will never happen. My father's story is true: he didn't want to be presumptuous. His collage exists only in Albert Murray's bathroom or in a gallery on Fifty-seventh Street between Madison and Park.

Unlike Bearden, my father stuck it out at the Department of Welfare. He had no viable alternative — it was the best he could do with a high school education. Stuyvesant High School, but still high school. After the service, after the war, Colgate University was an option, but he didn't go that way. Joining the Genovese crime family was another option. Frank Costello was the man in charge in East Harlem, and he was looking to recruit bright kids from the neighborhood. My father had a willing and able sponsor, but he didn't go that way either.

My father had a talent for something; for what, I've never been sure. It was something intangible, something suited to his strengths: the inherent disposition of a gambler, mettle, nerve, out-and-out gall. I wish I had some of these things, more guts, more guile, a romantic sense of risk, equanimity, smarts. Instead I have the college degree he never got.

When the two of us ended up alone, at a ball game or walking around the city (never camping, never golfing), he would talk to me — his nine-year-old — man to man. He didn't want to put me on the spot, but he couldn't help himself. By rationalizing to his son, he rationalized to himself: "Your mother doesn't understand" . . . "My job can barely put food on the table" . . . "It's a business; please understand." I would nod plaintively; by now the ball game or whatever outing we had planned was ruined.

He had to do whatever he did. For whatever reasons, however opaque, he didn't go to college. Instead, he split his time between the Garden and the Met, read books, gambled, did some bookmaking. He also did tax returns, first for a professional outfit, then mainly for friends and their friends. He worked cheap; word got around. He just hinted at a figure — something below reasonable — and often got in return only a bottle of hard liquor, which he never drank.

He wasn't alone in his odd, elliptical sort of defiance, his hostility. A lot of the East Harlem recalcitrants he grew up with tried to tweak the system and give scapegoat society a collective fuck you, from Pleasant Avenue to the world. Some played it safe, bought two-family houses in the Bronx or Queens, but others grew bitter, self-destructed, or vanished off the face of the earth. We heard stories, the same ones again and again, from my father, of Bense. I don't even know his real name. He was an East Harlem boy, my father's best friend, and all I remember from those stories is how he choked a dog to death because it barked at him the wrong way. Bense was one of those who fell off the earth, but I can't recall how. My father said he was a great friend: fiercely loyal, free with a buck, would challenge guys twice his size to protect his friends. My mother just talked about his disconcerting gaze. She did everything she could to keep us away from the Benses of the world.

My father couldn't work for anyone; that was another of his defining traits. He was a Manhattanite, but he was never invited to its upper precincts. He'd see art (Mantegna, Velázquez, and Rubens were his Ruth, Gehrig, and DiMaggio), see the latest Kurosawa or Fellini, read the Greek tragedies or Seneca the Stoic, or venture up to the decaying Polo Grounds to "lay a few dollars" on Warren Spahn when the Milwaukee Braves played the Giants. Spahn was his boy. Later Ron Guidry, good Cajun, was his talisman. Nolan Ryan, as my mother never let us forget, brought nothing but dread.

Most Sunday afternoons in autumn and winter, some of the biggest gambling days of the year, my sister would lock herself in her room, listen to Blondie records, and immerse herself in homework, obsessed with good grades. I didn't study as much, just enough to get by, and for the most part I didn't mind my father's second job. Only when we went to a game and he needed the other team to win would it dampen my mood. Imagine rooting for the Kansas City Kings against the Knicks, the San Diego Padres against the Mets, because you fear your father might get hurt if the visiting team doesn't cover. When you're a boy, your father is still more important to you than Louis Orr or Dave Kingman.

In later years, I resented him and admired him. I learned to see things. He taught me how to improvise. And we had Tommy Hearns. Sugar Ray Leonard versus Tommy Hearns, September 1981. We went to Madison Square Garden for the closed-circuit telecast. My father met me at Twenty-third and Broadway; there was a bus from the Bronx that let out there. We took a short walk to Paul & Jimmy's on Irving Place for dinner. Then he took this little seventh-grader, the envy of I.S. 181 that day, to the fight with a New York crowd, twenty thousand, no kids, all grown-ups, all men, some scary. In the thirteenth round, when a desperate, puffy-eyed Leonard, behind on points, threw a last-ditch roundhouse right and Hearns's spindly legs buckled, we yelled together, "Stay up, Tommy." Tommy went down — three times — and one round later the ref stopped the fight. We rushed out onto Seventh Avenue, rancid and teeming.

My mother worried. She thought I would grow up to be a gambler. I would casually ask at the dinner table, "Daddy, what's a parlay? What's a two-team teaser? How much is a nickel? How much is a dime? What's a wheel bet? What's the line on the Vikings game this week? . . . *Three and a half,* that's it?"

"See what you're teaching him?" she'd say.

He would send me to the candy store to get the *New York Times,* the *Post,* and a touting sheet called *The Sports Eye* before I could even reach the countertop. Some of the old men — two-dollar bettors whom my father looked down on — thought it was cute. Who knows what else they thought?

We never owned a house, had virtually no savings, and barely owned a car — you couldn't really count the used-up gray-and-black 1960-something Buick LeSabre that was stolen twice, both times when we were in New Orleans. But we saw places: Italy in '73; Spain, Portugal, and Morocco in '76; England and Holland in '79; Martinique in '80; St. Martin in '81; the Dominican Republic in '82; Mexico, Canada, and Charleston, South Carolina, in '83; Switzerland in '85. Six times we went to Puerto Rico, where my father had two gambling friends, a Romanian and a half–Pole, half–Puerto Rican, who would pare down their debt by letting us stay in their Santurce apartments.

One night in the early spring of 1984, with those Super Bowl winnings still trickling in, my parents talked about the summer. The Bronx would be unforgiving in July, they reasoned; France would be nice. (At last they agreed on something.) Two months later, we were bound for Orly Airport. Off to Paris, Chartres, the Loire Valley, then Versailles for an afternoon, across to Strasbourg, down to Lyon, then to Nice, where the people looked like us, tiptoeing around dog shit in Aix-en-Provence, west into Languedoc, to Carcassonne in the foothills of the Pyrenees. "On a clear day," a man said to a child, "you can see Spain if you squint." We went way up north, fourteen hours by overnight train, to Rouen, the bane of Joan of Arc, before returning to a Paris, bright and perfect.

It was a special trip. My sister and I were getting older; more and more of those tuition bills dotted the horizon. My father's losses were mounting. Already, U.S. marshals had rung the bell to remind us we owed four months' rent, handing my mother the eviction notice.

We managed Geneva the following year, unexpectedly, thanks maybe to Villanova. But in 1984, we figured France to be our last trip together, though none of us said so. We talked about staying in Paris, for a week, a month, forever. It was comforting. Eight francs to the dollar. We met only one haughty Frenchman the entire month. But we had to get back, back to reality, back to our waiting, anomalous Bronx. A new football season was about to start. Doors would open or close with each Monday-morning line. On Sunday nights, I would peek into my father's bedroom, sometimes pitch-black, after his screeching big-band tapes were through, Benny Goodman and Basie and Jimmy Lunceford, and see him staring straight ahead, sometimes muttering softly the line: Cincy minus seven, Denver plus two and a half, Texas Tech pick 'em. Now, when the sun is just right, at such an angle where you have to use your hand as a visor, and the air has the warmth of July in it, numbers like that can carry me back to southwestern France, standing on a dusty bluff in Carcassonne. If you squint hard enough, on the clearest of days, you can see Spain.

TED LEVIN

The Birds at Oriole Park

FROM WASHINGTONIAN

ORIOLE PARK AT CAMDEN YARDS is the quintessential ballpark. It sits close to Baltimore Harbor, which empties into Chesapeake Bay. On a Friday evening last summer, the sky is the color of bruised fruit and the air hot and humid. Rain is imminent. A breeze pushes westward at three or four knots, not enough to alter the path of a fly ball but enough to lift a wayfaring butterfly up and over the right-field grandstands.

The patrons in the box seats along the first-base line ready their umbrellas as the visiting Red Sox suspend batting practice and head for their dugout. When the rains come, the ground crew rolls the tarpaulin over the infield, while the sky above Camden Yards fills with herring gulls, ring-billed gulls, starlings, pigeons, and chimney swifts that dart back and forth above the field like a flock of frenetic shortstops.

As the rain falls harder, my five-year-old son Jordan squeezes my hand and asks if Cal Ripken is dry.

Jordan, his fourteen-year-old brother, Casey, and I retreat to the shelter of the press box and wait for an announcement that the game will be canceled. In the meantime, out of the rain and enjoying free hot dogs, we comb the sky for more birds.

At 6:34 P.M., Casey spots ten great egrets flying in loose formation above left field, white birds against a dark sky, like a bevy of outfielders dressed in immaculate home jerseys. A ring-billed gull lands in shallow center field, walks around in tight circles, wet to the bone. Mercifully, the game is canceled.

*

Birds are so much a part of the scene at Camden Yards that Al Capitos, the head groundskeeper, told me that last spring, while the Orioles were on the road, a pair of Canada geese tried to nest in the outfield until they were chased away.

This past summer, Capitos had his hands full with a pair of amorous mallards. During a game, the ducks flew in from the harbor and landed in short center field, the male bowing and strutting. Not ready to consummate their nuptials in front of the home crowd, the female played hard to get and led her suitor on a jaunt around the outfield. The ducks could not be persuaded to leave, so the Orioles played around them, Mr. Mallard showing off, a swagger more emblematic of after-touchdown football than the genteel game of baseball.

The one bird Capitos has never seen in Camden Yards is a Baltimore oriole. "Come to think of it," he adds, "I've never seen a raven in Baltimore either."

For two decades, ballparks have fueled my twin passions: baseball and bird watching. Many major league stadiums hug migration routes, and Camden Yards is no exception. Located on the Atlantic flyway, Camden Yards offers the bird enthusiast a glimpse of both spring and fall migrants.

When visiting ballparks, I consistently record more species per game in late summer and early autumn, when bird numbers include migrating juveniles. But ballpark birding is not limited to the migratory seasons, particularly at a waterfront stadium like Camden Yards. During summer night games, insects assemble around the stadium lights, which causes an avian feeding frenzy.

Several years ago, an archaeologist estimated that seven to eight million spiders hung their webs in the lights above Cincinnati's Riverfront Stadium. He figured the spiders were attracted by the uncountable numbers of insects that had left the Ohio River for the lure of the lights.

The insects draw birds as well as spiders; when the Reds hosted the Dodgers in the summer of 1978, I paid more attention to the pirouetting purple martins, the spiders' chief competitors for insects, than I did to the ball game.

The next afternoon, a Saturday, we are at game two in the series between the Red Sox and the Orioles. The sky is again overcast and still threatening rain. I tally birds and watch the Sox take batting practice. Manny Ramirez launches a ball that hits far back in the center-field bleachers as a pair of mourning doves flies across the field and lands on the roof between home and third.

While I record the doves, our first species of the day, Jordan is enchanted by the oriole weathervanes above the bleachers, and Casey is equally taken by the historic Bromo Seltzer clock tower beyond left field.

"What's Bromo Seltzer — pop?" he asks. I explain that it's a remedy for an upset stomach, a malady both Orioles and Red Sox fans often endure in late summer.

In more than twenty years of watching birds and baseball, I've never seen a real oriole or blue jay or cardinal at a major league ballpark. (I've never seen a diamondback rattlesnake either.) But I have seen birds associated with the wilds of North America winging past a baseball game — a barn owl and a kestrel at Yankee Stadium; a merlin, an osprey, and a great blue heron at Fenway. At old Candlestick Park in San Francisco, two red-tailed hawks fastened their nest in the stanchions of the lights above left field.

Now, as the boys and I wait for the Orioles to take the field, a barn swallow — small, swift, and colorful — enters the airspace above left field, cuts sharply to its right, pivots like Roberto Alomar turning a double play, catches an insect or two, then passes over us, heading southward toward Brazil. Species number two.

Casey and Jordan are talking to Alan Mills, a right-handed relief pitcher for the Orioles, who happens to be relaxing by the seats next to us. He offers the boys gum, and during the exchange a pair of crows passes in front of the Bromo Seltzer tower, angles over left field, then lands on the roof of the third deck. One crow squawks at the other, leaning into each vocalization, like Earl Weaver barking at an umpire. Species number three.

I spot a dozen pigeons (species four) flying in and out of the grid work of the overhanging roof. These feathered miscreants, reared in the framework of the stadium, lullabied by the roar of the crowd, feast during Orioles home stands. For them, Camden Yards is one of Baltimore's premier feeding grounds.

An usher leads me beneath a horizontal support beam, a notorious pigeon roost. "This row below the beam can be messy," he says, wiping a line of guano off the seat next to him. A starling arrows past, stiff-winged and short-tailed, a little, dark crescent. Species number five, another miscreant.

A grackle, glossy purple, long-tailed, and bold, lands on the back of seat six, row FFF, the lower boxes, scanning for food. Number six.

Josh Towers takes the mound for the Orioles. Three up, three down, a perfect first. David Cone pitches for the Sox. The game moves quickly despite being interrupted by a forty-nine-minute rain delay. By the bottom of the fourth inning, the Orioles are up 4 to 0, Towers is totally in control, and I'm stalled at six.

Jerry Hairston's on second, Melvin Mora's up. A yellow-shafted flicker flicks in and out of the firmament above center field as Cone gloves Mora's sacrifice bunt. A woodpecker out of its element and soon to be out of the ballpark, the heavy-chested flicker passes over the pitcher's mound, above home plate, a slow, steady roller-coaster flight like Boog Powell tottering to third. Number seven for the day and a baseball first for me. "Hey, guys, a woodpecker. Look, it's heading for the bat rack in the Orioles dugout." Jordan believes me. "No, no, just kidding, it's just passing through."

In the top of the sixth, Trot Nixon homers on an 0-and-2 count. The score is 4 to 2. In the bottom of the sixth, Cone is gone. Big Rich Garces is pitching; one out, the bases are empty. Garces is called El Guapo, the handsome one, by Sox fans. Casey decides to call him El Guano, the bird dropping. "What's guano?" Jordan asks. Mora strikes out as a purple martin, the largest swallow in North America, pirouettes above the field, mouth wide, snagging moths the way Brooks Robinson snagged line drives. Number eight.

Top of the eighth, Buddy Groom is pitching for the Orioles, who still lead by two. As Scott Hatteberg flies to left, Casey spots a peregrine falcon, the grand slam of ballpark birding, high above the warehouse behind right field, floating on the breeze like a lazy fly ball. A peregrine is a franchise bird; it stoops on ducks and pigeons and, yes, even on Baltimore orioles at speeds in excess of 180 miles per hour. A pair nests on the Bank of America building on Light Street, near the Inner Harbor, a good glide away from Camden Yards, and appears over the ballpark from time to time, perhaps searching for pigeons or starlings. The bird hangs for a moment, then tucks in its wings, pinches its tail feathers together, and streaks lights-out, like a Randy Johnson fastball. Number nine and another baseball first.

During a game, species, like runs, come in flurries or trickles or not at all. I once had thirteen species in Fenway Park in less than an hour but none after the first inning. If the quality of baseball is good, I'm caught up in the action and my bird counts tend to be low.

The opposite can be true. I once missed a ninth-inning, two-out Don Baylor home run that turned a Boston lead into a Yankee victory because migrating nighthawks had ridden into view.

Casey, Jordan, and I return to Camden Yards the next afternoon for the final game of the three-game series. Twenty starlings perch on the left-field lights, and a mixed flock of hundreds of tree swallows, barn swallows, and chimney swifts swirls over the playing field. Again, the game is delayed by rain.

In the top of the first, as the swallows and swifts troll for insects, the Sox score six unearned runs, aided by three Oriole errors. By the bottom of the third Boston is ahead 6 to 3. Ripken doubles to left, base hit number 3,153. Two runs score.

On the mound John Bale replaces Jason Johnson, and in the air starlings replace swallows and swifts. A monarch butterfly flutters over the infield, bullied by the wind. For the Sox, Tim Wakefield replaces Rolando Arrojo, and his pitches — most knucklers that are slow, slower, slowest — float toward the home plate like a butterfly.

Top of the eighth, Alan Mills pitches for the Orioles. Runners on first and second. Carl Everett, something of a bird-brain himself, launches the first pitch 430 feet into the right-center-field bleachers. Three mourning doves glide in off the warehouse roof and circle the field, unsure of their next move, like Mike Hargrove, who paces in the dugout. The next batter, Manny Ramirez, homers on a 3–2 pitch. Hargrove leaves the dugout and Mills is gone. So are the doves and the Orioles.

After a wet weekend, we leave Camden Yards with two new ballpark birds — yellow-shafted flicker and peregrine falcon — and a combined total of thirteen species of birds, which equals my single-game American League record.

I also tally four species of insects, including a praying mantis that got squished when the tarp was rolled out and a morning-clock butterfly.

Casey leaves having coined a new nickname for Rich Garces and having spotted the peregrine, the coup of the weekend.

Jordan leaves with an official Major League baseball given to him by coach Sam Perlozzo and a fondness for the third baseman of the Orioles.

"Papa," he tells me later in the week as I tuck him in bed, "whenever bad dreams get into my head, I just think of Cal Ripken, and that makes me feel better."

His Role on Team Is Beyond Words

FROM THE AKRON BEACON JOURNAL

You HOLD the water bottles.

You are six feet tall and 275 pounds. Some people see you and wonder why you are not wearing shoulder pads and a helmet like the other players.

You'd love to tell them. You want them to know what it means to be you. You want to explain, to answer, to just say SOMETHING!

You hear the words in your head. You know what you want to say. But the best you can do is make sounds: moans, screeches, laughs, grunts.

And no one understands.

They say you are autistic, something like Dustin Hoffman in the movie *Rain Man*. Only you can't talk at all, while Hoffman spoke in a distracted monotone. They say there are a lot of people like you, about fifteen of every ten thousand births, and it's four times more likely to happen to males.

They can say all they want, but they just don't know.

They don't know how your brain works.

They don't know that when Hudson High football coach Tom Narducci said you could come to practice, you thought it was to play, that you crashed into the tackling dummy like a charging bull.

But they led you to the water and the bottles, saying you're a team manager. You're one of several "special needs" students who help the team, but none of the others is battling the obstacles you face.

Your name is Mark Mesko.

Your father and mother are John and Phyllis Mesko. They love Narducci for doing what no coach was willing to try before — letting you be a part of the team.

You're eighteen years old. Your favorite color is red. You love football teams that wear red, especially Ohio State and Nebraska. You like fire trucks. You sometimes carry a red book bag with your pictures of fire trucks. You have a fire truck as a screen saver on your computer. You have a framed picture of you in a fire truck. Your older sister, Heather, drives around with a camera, and when she sees a neat fire truck, she takes a picture for you.

You'd like to be a firefighter, or a football player.

But it probably won't happen.

If only you could talk. If only you could be like the other kids. As your oldest sister, Jennifer, said, "If only I could know if he's happy."

You are happy. And you're frustrated. And you're lonely. And you feel loved. And sometimes you don't know how you feel.

That's how it is for many teenagers.

You get mad at your parents, you glare at them, you stalk off, you slam the door and hide in your room. You're likely to put on a videotape of Scooby Doo or the Care Bears. But Heather has seen you with a Victoria's Secret catalog. You seem to have one foot in a child's world, another leg in the life of any teenage boy.

Heather understands this. She bought you a poster of Pamela Sue Anderson. She says, "I wish Mark could go on a date, just do the things everyone does in high school."

Sometimes, Heather takes you to the Stow Cafe, where you get hamburgers together. You love hamburgers. You love your twenty-three-year-old sister. Sometimes, she holds your hand. Sometimes, people think you're her boyfriend. She doesn't care. She loves you.

You're her brother, you're special, and you know that.

One day, your mom found her eyes tearing up, her throat going dry as she sat next to you by the computer. She told you how much she loved you. She so wanted to hear that voice from your soul, to know what thoughts are in your heart.

Phyllis Mesko whispered, "Mark Mesko, why can't you talk?"

You typed: TOO HARD.

*

They say that for the first two years of your life, you were like most
infants. Your mother insists that you said "Mama . . . daddy . . .
cookie" and about thirty other words.

Then something happened. Those words are gone. Except you
do hear them in your head. Sometimes, you can even type them on
the computer. Sometimes, you can't.

You don't know why that happens; it just does.

Just like you don't know why the words fail to come out. They
just don't.

They say it's a neurological problem; the brain didn't develop in
the usual way. They took you to doctors in Cleveland, Baltimore,
and North Carolina. By the time you were seven, they finally put a
label on you.

Autistic.

How much of this you comprehend, it's hard to know. You're just
aware that you're different, that you really don't have friends like
most of the kids at Hudson High. Sometimes, you feel walled in.
The walls are glass. You see them. They see you. But communication is lost.

You give water to football players such as Toney Morton and
Tyson Meikle. They say thank you. Once in a while, they pat you on
the back. You whack their shoulder pads, as you've seen the other
coaches and players do.

Meikle says the team respects you, that you're at practice every
day, and at every game. Morton wishes he could talk to you, that
you could "play football like the other guys."

They don't know that one day you brought your mother into
your room, pointed at a football player on TV who looked like you,
and then pointed at yourself. Yes, you wanted to play, and you knew
you had the right size.

Your coach, Tom Narducci, says, "Mark is so big, sometimes I
think I should put him in pads and a helmet and let him stand on
the sidelines just to scare the other team."

But he can't do that. Just like you want to play, but you can't.

Your mom recalls meeting Narducci at Holy Family Church in
Stow, how Coach Narducci shook your hand, stared you in the eye,
and introduced himself. Talked to you like you were a regular person, which is how he sees you. A regular person with unique circumstances, but a person who needs football.

At Hudson, football is about kids being involved. It's about seventy-eight players on the varsity and junior varsity. It's about another thirty-five on the freshman team. And about three hundred marching band members.

And some special needs kids on the sidelines.

Narducci says you're "the most severe" of the challenged managers he has had in his twenty years of coaching. But he believes in giving people chances.

It goes back to 1972, when he was a young coach at Padua Franciscan High School in Parma. He was asked to teach a Wednesday night religion class for special needs kids at St. Anthony of Padua Catholic Church. It hurt to see them dealing with their disabilities, yet it raised his spirits to watch them battle, to feel their love.

He never forgot that.

Narducci is impressed by your progress. He says he barely notices you, which is a compliment, because it means you're doing your job well.

"The other day, Mark really became a member of the team," says your coach. "He was a little late getting into the dressing room at halftime, and I screamed at whoever was at the door. It was Mark and his dad."

Narducci laughs.

"I tell everyone that they really know they're with us when I yell at them," he says. "That goes for Mark, too."

At games and practices, you need help.

Often, it comes from Charly Murphy, a health aide who has his own photography business and is studying to be a minister. He was hired last fall to be with you at practice.

He wasn't sure it would work. You seemed to take an eternity, just finding a way to turn the knob on those huge orange igloos that hold the water, and then correctly lining up the plastic bottles so the water flowed inside.

"At first, Mark couldn't even fill a single bottle by himself," says Murphy in front of you. "Now, look at him. He does about all the work; I just make sure he's concentrating."

You had to learn every step. It wasn't easy to unscrew the plastic caps, then screw them back on. It took practice to get all the bottles in the carry-case, so you could then take them to the players.

Then there's walking.

You move slowly, sort of dragging your feet. At least most of the time. Once in a while, you sprint for fifteen to twenty yards. Then stop. No one is sure why.

Mostly, you seem to plod, plod, plod. One foot in front of another.

In the past, people with your disabilities were dismissed. Locked away and forgotten. Some people still think like that.

They don't know that when you want pizza, you cut a coupon out of the newspaper and give it to your parents. Or that you load the dishwasher. You make your bed. You've done some woodworking. You've had part-time jobs stocking shelves at a grocery store.

You need supervision, but you can do it.

You just have to practice, over and over. People don't know what you can do.

There's something else they don't know.

The noise. The lights. The crowds.

It's called "overstimulation."

When all that hits you, it scares you. It pushes your nerves to the limit. You take six pills a day for problems such as anxiety and attention deficit disorder. When you were small, you'd get upset and bite your sister's shoulder as she held you, trying to calm you.

You're much better now.

But the games are hard because there is just so much — of everything.

You began by barely tolerating it for one quarter, and finished last year being able to stay until the fourth period. The goal for this season is to make it through an entire game.

Your coach says, "I just want Mark to show up and do his best for as long as he can. It's not like he has to punch in and punch out."

Sometimes, you don't feel like going to practice. You hide your Hudson cap in the cupboard right before Charly arrives to pick you up. Other times, you are dressed and ready, waiting outside for him, rushing to his truck when he pulls into the driveway.

At the end of last season, you were awarded a varsity letter.

How could they know what it means to you? You used to wear your oldest sister Jennifer's cheerleading jacket. A few years later, it was Heather's softball letter jacket from Hudson. Your mother said,

"Mark Mesko, one day you will get your own letter jacket," but she had no idea how that would ever happen.

Only, it did.

You're like many teenagers. Right before dinner, you wander into the kitchen and sneak doughnut holes for snacks. You get on the computer and order things, surprising your parents.

Once, there was gutbuster-type exercise equipment that arrived at the door. You pointed to the TV and then your abdomen, telling your mother you wanted to lose weight and saw something on the screen that would help.

Another time, you locked your father out of the house because you wanted some ice cream, and he had a different plan. He was furious. You thought it was hilarious.

One of your favorite places is the beach, where you ride the waves, build sandcastles, chase the sea gulls. You also like the beach because you don't have to wear shoes, and you sometimes get tired of shoes.

But other times, you don't make eye contact. You seem somewhere else, distracted, depressed. You have routines, always wearing a golf shirt and khaki pants to school.

Your family worries that someone will hurt you, but you won't be able to tell them. When you were five, you asked for a Popsicle. You put it on your arm. Turns out, the arm had been fractured at least three days earlier.

No one knew.

You couldn't say.

Heather is still embarrassed about the time many years ago when she threw a ball through a window, but blamed you. It took three months for her to finally confess.

One day, a stranger sits next to you by your computer.

He has given you an Ohio State football guide. You type: THANKS.

A while later, the two of you are the only ones in the kitchen.

The stranger asks, "Mark, how does it feel not to be able to talk?"

In your left hand, your roll a rubber band, over and over.

With your right hand, you type: PIG, BLUE, GREEN, NEWSPAPER.

You know the stranger is from a newspaper. You don't know what he really wants. He tells you about his father, who couldn't talk either.

You roll that rubber band some more.

You type: PIG, BLUE, GREEN, NEWSPAPER.

Over and over: PIG, BLUE, GREEN, NEWSPAPER.

And roll the rubber band, over and over.

That's how you feel when you're anxious. You fall into a routine. You try to get some control of your life. You long for a comfort zone, where you could be like everyone else, and everyone could understand you.

You're Mark Mesko.

Your sister, Jennifer, was just married to Chris Kimmick. He had to first pass "The Mark Test." He didn't know it, but he had to show he liked you.

"When Chris spent thirty minutes on the floor watching a football game with Mark, just the two of them in Mark's room, I knew our relationship had a chance," says Jennifer. "I'm a package deal."

Your family is like that. They don't know what the future is for you. Maybe a group home setting. Maybe something else. But they vow to be there for you, just as they have been for eighteen years.

Your dad is a postal worker, your mom a nurse. They combine with your two older sisters to form a special family, one they say God set aside for you.

Down deep, you know that.

You hug them. You hug them a lot.

And there's no need for anyone to say a word about love.

BETH KEPHART

Of Sound and Ice

FROM THE WASHINGTON POST BOOK WORLD

ALL SUMMER LONG I waited for the weather to change. For the breeze to chill and kick the color off the trees. For fall, which would herald winter, which would finally bring me calm. I am a cold-weather woman, graceless and insufferable during months of summer heat. I am a sweater writer who finds her words in frozen ponds and rinks, in the hold-fast sound of a blade against the ice. I was eight going on nine when my parents first took me to a hardened pond and helped me strap on a pair of skates. It was the hour before dusk, still sun enough to see not just the surface of the routed ice but all the rot trapped deep beneath — tubercles of trees, broken twigs, last summer's dragonflies. I tossed off my hat and flew. Caught the wind in my ears, felt the frost on my face, and imagined all those stiffened wings unfurling.

Life would never be the same for me after that. I'd go on to coaches and sequins, to mohawks and spirals, to footwork, to training before dawn. I'd do all I was taught to do: delay my Axel, tuck a flip inside my splits, toe in for the double Lutz and spin — once, twice. The music would fall, and I with it. It banged and chattered, pulsed and sighed, and so, of course, did I.

Most writers grow up with books, but I grew up with all the things a sheet of ice can teach you. I grew up knowing that you quick-step your way through a pizzicato, that you deepen your edge to the soar of the violins, that when the bass laments you lament with the bass, that you open your arms wide to a plainchant. A held note is a spread eagle. A sudden polyphony is a combination jump. And when they play "Somewhere" from *West Side Story*, you are Maria —

yearning, weightless, prayerful — and when they play a little *Bolero*, you do as Torvill and Dean did: knee low, rise high, reach far. Music was my first language — ice my first page.

The past is never really past; it carries forward. I carried ice and sound into the books I began — later than I should have — to read. Melody, rhythm, tone color, harmony, form: such is music, and such is what I looked for when I turned to books. I found those elements of music first at the age of sixteen, in F. Scott Fitzgerald's *The Great Gatsby*, a symphonic composition, an urgent book — so many instruments and interludes, so much raucous, furious speed on its closing pages. I found it next in James Agee's *A Death in the Family*, which plays like a bow against a string and left me physically quavering. William Faulkner was choral, as was the early Louise Erdrich, and when I discovered Michael Ondaatje's books, I knew I'd finally found another skater. Ondaatje writes the way champion skater Kurt Browning moves on ice: hypnotically, with a technical sophistication that yields up his soul. The truth is, I cannot fall into the thrall of a book unless it resonates with song.

From skating into reading, and from reading into writing: it was a precipitous slide. I went from oboes, violins, and bass to grammar, phrases, metaphors; and then from there to chapters, to books, and finally to my own life, exposed. Who knows what one is doing when one begins to write? I didn't. I knew only that I'd turned to words as a cure. I'd begun to feel hollow, vaguely dissatisfied, and words seemed like weights in my hands, real, purposeful. But I wanted to do with them what I'd learned to do with movement. I wanted to do more than tell a story: I wanted to choreograph it — throw my body against the words.

The more I wrote, the more it felt like skating. The blank page is like the lull before the needle drops on the phonograph record. The flow of chapters is like the linking of flips, toe loops, footwork, lunges, and supining layback spins. The final edit is like my final competition dress — beaded, delicate, trimmed to the essentials, a banishment of excess.

I chose memoir or perhaps memoir chose me, the prose growing out of so many swanning questions. I wrote a book about a son who taught me patience. A book about the friends who shaped my heart. A book about the man I married and the country that he came from. For fifteen years I skated toward words, and, at the end,

I had three slender volumes to show for it. All three are haunted by the riffle of the wind, by ice.

I am old enough to know that it's too late to change my ways. Old enough to recognize that I'll always be a skater among books. Now, in my writing life, I wake in the hours before dawn. After all these years, I still love — I still require — the essential qualities of darkness, the chill upon my face. Downstairs, I stand before the large old windows and peer out across the yard. When I convince myself I'm ready, I slip into my office, sling myself across the couch, and read what I've written the day before, scratching most of it into oblivion. I'll add a line or two, snap the piece apart, circle back, connect two fragments, hunt down the minor chords and melodies. By 7:00 A.M., I'm out of words, and so I turn on the music — Schubert, Loreena McKennitt, fandangos, Nelly Furtado, Bach — it doesn't matter. What matters is that it is loud, that I can dance to it, that it rattles my bones and loosens my thoughts. What matters is how far the music takes me, and who I am when I return. After I have stood inside that crush of music, remembered my necessary patch of ice, I start stringing together the words, choreographing the memories. It seems, at first, as if nothing much is happening, but almost everything is: I am skating, I am writing, I am moving with the story. And so it goes, and so I go, and so books are made and finished, and new books are dreamt about.

I will fall, I know I'll fall, but I will get back on my feet — toe pick to blade to stroke to speed to a suspended, soaring Axel. It is dangerous here, out on this pond with nothing but my words, but the ice, I trust, will hold me. The ice and all the frozen debris beneath it.

Biographical Notes
Notable Sports Writing of 2002

Biographical Notes

MICHAEL AGOVINO is an editor at *Newsweek*. Previously he was an editor at *Esquire*. His writing has appeared in those publications as well as in the *New York Times, New York*, the *New York Observer, Spin, Mirabella, Vanity Fair, Outside, Book Forum*, Salon.com, the *Independent, ESPN: The Magazine, Time Out, Vibe*, and *People*. His profile of Albert Murray was featured in the anthology *Conversations with Albert Murray*. He is a native of New York City.

SUSY BUCHANAN, originally from Anchorage, Alaska, is a staff writer at *New Times* in Phoenix, Arizona. In her four years as a journalist she has covered midget wrestling, skijoring, quadriplegic rugby, ice fishing, extreme fighting, and paragliding, yet has found nothing comparable to the rock-'em-sock-'em action of demolition derby.

RENE CHUN lives in New York and is a frequent contributor to numerous publications, including *Esquire, Playboy*, and *New York*.

BILL DONAHUE is an *Outside* magazine correspondent whose writing has appeared in *The New Yorker*, the *New York Times Magazine*, and *DoubleTake*. He lives in Portland, Oregon.

STEPHEN J. DUBNER is the author of *Confessions of a Hero-Worshiper* and *Turbulent Souls: A Catholic Son's Return to His Jewish Family*. A former writer and editor at the *New York Times Magazine*, he has also written for *The New Yorker, Time*, and *New York* magazine. He holds degrees from Appalachian State University and Columbia University; in between, he started a rock band that was signed to Arista Records. He lives with his family in New York City and is now writing a book about the psychology of money.

BRUCE FELDMAN is a senior writer for *ESPN: The Magazine* and ESPN.com. His first book, *Death to Dynasty*, is scheduled to come out in 2004. Before working for ESPN, he played semiprofessional football in the Empire Football League as a wide receiver for the Hudson Valley Vikings. He lives in New York City.

ELIZABETH GILBERT is the author of two books of fiction, *Pilgrims* and *Stern Men*, and one book of nonfiction, *The Last American Man*. She has been a finalist for the PEN/Hemingway Award, the National Book Critics Circle Award, and the National Book Award, and she was also the recipient of the *Paris Review*'s New Discovery Award. For the past four years she has worked as a writer-at-large for *GQ*, where she has three times been a finalist for the National Magazine Award. Her article on bullfighting, "Near Death in the Afternoon," appeared in *The Best American Sports Writing 2002*. Her work has appeared in such publications as *Esquire, Spin*, and the *New York Times Magazine*. She lives in New York City and participates in no sports whatsoever, although she was once a halfway decent field hockey player.

DAVID GRANN is a frequent contributor to the *New York Times Magazine*. His stories have also appeared in *The New Yorker*, the *Atlantic Monthly*, and *The New Republic*, as well as in several collections of nonfiction, including, most recently, *What We Saw: The Events of September 11 in Words, Pictures, and Video*.

RON C. JUDD has written on a wide variety of subjects at the *Seattle Times* since 1988. For the past six years he's been a columnist covering the great outdoors, general sports, the Olympic Games, and, most recently, the thirty-first America's Cup in Auckland, New Zealand. A 1985 graduate of Western Washington University, he is the author of four outdoor guides to the Pacific Northwest and lives in Bellingham, Washington.

ELIZABETH KAYE is a contributing editor of *Los Angeles* magazine. She formerly held similar positions with *Rolling Stone, Esquire*, and *George*. She is the author of *American Ballet Theater* and *Mid-Life: Notes from the Halfway Mark*.

BETH KEPHART is the award-winning author of three memoirs, *A Slant of Sun, Into the Tangle of Friendship*, and *Still Love in Strange Places*. Frequently anthologized, her essays, profiles, and reviews have appeared in the *New York Times, Washington Post, Chicago Tribune, Real Simple, Parenting*, Salon.com, and elsewhere. Her new book of nonfiction will be published in the spring of 2004, and she is at work on a novel. Her piece "Playing for Keeps" appeared in *The Best American Sports Writing 2001*.

MARK KRAM JR. is a sportswriter for the *Philadelphia Daily News* and contributing writer to *Philadelphia* magazine. This is his third appearance in *The Best American Sports Writing*.

MICHAEL LEAHY has been a staff writer for the *Washington Post* since 1999. Raised in Los Angeles, and a graduate of Yale, he was formerly a magazine writer in California and a feature writer and columnist for the *Arkansas Democrat-Gazette*. In 2001 his story on the life of a paroled murderer won the Washington, D.C., Society of Professional Journalists' best feature story award, and "Best of Show" honors from the Maryland-D.C.-Delaware Press Association. His feature stories on Cal Ripken Jr. and Michael Jordan have been honored by the SPJ and the Associated Press. He lives with his wife Jane and son Cameron in Virginia. This is his third appearance in *The Best American Sports Writing*.

When TED LEVIN isn't at the ballpark watching birds, he's busy at his desk. He's written four books for adults and five for children. *Liquid Land: A Journey Through the Florida Everglades* will be published by the University of Georgia Press in the fall of 2003. His photographs have been published worldwide, and his essays have appeared in *Audubon, National Wildlife, Yankee,* and *Sports Illustrated,* among many other publications. When he was a teenager, he saw a barn owl at Yankee Stadium, which he claims is still his best ballpark bird.

JULIET MACUR is a features writer in the sports department of the *Dallas Morning News*. She grew up in New Jersey and has undergraduate and graduate degrees from Columbia University. Her narrative of a long-distance runner struggling with eating disorders appeared in *The Best American Sports Writing 2002*.

Poet and essayist JAMES MCKEAN is a graduate of the University of Iowa Writers' Workshop and received his Ph.D. from the University of Iowa. He has taught writing at Columbia Basin College and the University of Iowa. In 1987 the University of Utah Press published his first book of poems, *Headlong*, which won the Great Lakes Colleges New Writers Award. He is the recipient of an Iowa Poetry Prize for his book *Tree of Heaven*, published by the University of Iowa Press. His poems have appeared in *Poetry, Prairie Schooner,* and the *Atlantic Monthly*. He is now associate professor of English at Mount Mercy College in Cedar Rapids.

REBECCA MEAD has been a staff writer at *The New Yorker* since 1997. Before that, she was a contributing editor at *New York* magazine and a writer for the *Sunday Times* of London. She received her B.A. from Oxford University and her M.A. from New York University.

BILL PLASCHKE'S "Her Blue Heaven" appeared in *The Best American Sports Writing 2002*. An award-winning sports columnist for the *Los Angeles Times* since 1996, Plaschke has also worked for the *Fort Lauderdale News* and the *Seattle Post-Intelligencer*. He is the author of three books, most recently, *Plaschke: Good Sports, Spoilsports, Foul Balls, and Oddballs*. He loves L.A. and lives there with wife Lisa and children Tessa, Willie, and Mary Clare.

Columnist TERRY PLUTO of the *Akron Beacon Journal* is the author of several books, including *The View from Pluto* and *Loose Balls: The Short Wild Life of the American Basketball Association*.

Senior writer S. L. PRICE of *Sports Illustrated* is the author of *Pitching Around Fidel*. A graduate of the University of North Carolina, he lives in Washington, D.C.

PETER RICHMOND is a senior writer for *GQ* and author of *My Father's War*.

JOSH SENS is a former columnist for the *San Francisco Chronicle* and the current restaurant critic for *San Francisco* magazine. It shows in his golf game. He has written for *Golf Digest* and *Golf for Women*. He lives in Oakland, California.

GARY SMITH is a senior writer for *Sports Illustrated* and author of *Beyond the Game: The Collected Sportswriting of Gary Smith*. This is his eighth appearance in *The Best American Sports Writing*, more than any other writer.

ALEXANDER WOLFF has been a member of the *Sports Illustrated* staff since 1980. Wolff has written or cowritten six books, most recently *Big Game, Small World: A Basketball Odyssey*, an account of a year spent chasing basketball around the world. A native of Rochester, he lives in Vermont.

Notable Sports Writing of 2002

COMPILED BY GLENN STOUT

SCOTT REID
Missed Opportunities. *Orange County
Register,* June 2, 2002
RICK REILLY
The Gold Standard. *Sports Illustrated,*
March 4, 2002
CARLO ROTELLA
Champion at Twilight. *Washington
Post Magazine,* November 17, 2002
LORNE RUBENSTEIN
A Must-Wind Situation. *Golf Journal,*
September 2002

TOM SCOCCA
Blackballed. *Transition,* no. 90
LORI SHONTZ
Fast Forward. *Pittsburgh Post-Gazette,*
May 5–9, 2002
BRYAN SMITH
To Hell and Back. *Chicago Sun Times,*
February 3, 2002
STEVE SPRINGER
Buss — The Next Generation. *Los
Angeles Times,* November 24, 2002
GEORGE SULLIVAN
The Kid and I. *Bostonia,* Fall 2002
JOHN JEREMIAH SULLIVAN
Horseman, Pass By. *Harper's
Magazine,* October 2002

WRIGHT THOMPSON
Finding Elvis Grbac. *Kansas City Star,*
October 27, 2002

DENNIS TUTTLE
"All I Can Do Is Be Excited About
Today." *The Sporting News,* April 17,
2002

KYLE VELTROP
Remembered in His Will. *The
Sporting News,* August 5, 2002
TOM VERDUCCI
Totally Juiced. *Sports Illustrated,* June
3, 2002

JAMES WALKER
Act of Kindness Speaks Volumes
about Football's Spirit. *Huntington
Herald Dispatch,* November 7, 2002
JOAN WALSH
Trouble at Pac Bell Park.
SanFrancisco, September 2002
CRAIG WELCH
A Question of Balance. *Seattle Times,*
June 23, 2002
L. JON WERTHEIM
When Fans Cross the Line. *Sports
Illustrated Women,* May–June 2002
JACK E. WHITE
Spare the Tiger. *Time,* December 16,
2002
WOODY WOODBURN
Mills Went Distance for Unity. *The
Daily Breeze,* July 14, 2002

THE BEST AMERICAN SHORT STORIES® 2003
Walter Mosley, guest editor • Katrina Kenison, series editor

"Story for story, readers can't beat the *Best American Short Stories* series" (*Chicago Tribune*). This year's most beloved short fiction anthology is edited by the award-winning author Walter Mosley and includes stories by Dorothy Allison, Mona Simpson, Anthony Doerr, Dan Chaon, and Louise Erdrich, among others.

0-618-19733-8 PA $13.00 / 0-618-19732-X CL $27.50
0-618-19748-6 CASS $26.00 / 0-618-19752-4 CD $35.00

THE BEST AMERICAN ESSAYS® 2003
Anne Fadiman, guest editor • Robert Atwan, series editor

Since 1986, the *Best American Essays* series has gathered the best non-fiction writing of the year and established itself as the best anthology of its kind. Edited by Anne Fadiman, author of *Ex Libris* and editor of the *American Scholar*, this year's volume features writing by Edward Hoagland, Adam Gopnik, Michael Pollan, Susan Sontag, John Edgar Wideman, and others.

0-618-34161-7 PA $13.00 / 0-618-34160-9 CL $27.50

THE BEST AMERICAN MYSTERY STORIES™ 2003
Michael Connelly, guest editor • Otto Penzler, series editor

Our perennially popular anthology is a favorite of mystery buffs and general readers alike. This year's volume is edited by the best-selling author Michael Connelly and offers pieces by Elmore Leonard, Joyce Carol Oates, Brendan DuBois, Walter Mosley, and others.

0-618-32965-X PA $13.00 / 0-618-32966-8 CL $27.50
0-618-39072-3 CD $35.00

THE BEST AMERICAN SPORTS WRITING™ 2003
Buzz Bissinger, guest editor • Glenn Stout, series editor

This series has garnered wide acclaim for its stellar sports writing and top-notch editors. Now Buzz Bissinger, the Pulitzer Prize–winning journalist and author of the classic *Friday Night Lights,* continues that tradition with pieces by Mark Kram Jr., Elizabeth Gilbert, Bill Plaschke, S. L. Price, and others.

0-618-25132-4 PA $13.00 / 0-618-25130-8 CL $27.50

THE B·E·S·T AMERICAN SERIES ™

THE BEST AMERICAN TRAVEL WRITING 2003
Ian Frazier, guest editor • Jason Wilson, series editor

The Best American Travel Writing 2003 is edited by Ian Frazier, the author of *Great Plains* and *On the Rez*. Giving new life to armchair travel this year are William T. Vollmann, Geoff Dyer, Christopher Hitchens, and many others.

0-618-11881-0 PA $13.00 / 0-618-11881-0 CL $27.50
0-618-39074-X CD $35.00

THE BEST AMERICAN SCIENCE AND NATURE WRITING 2003
Richard Dawkins, guest editor • Tim Folger, series editor

This year's edition promises to be another "eclectic, provocative collection" (*Entertainment Weekly*). Edited by Richard Dawkins, the eminent scientist and distinguished author, it features work by Bill McKibben, Steve Olson, Natalie Angier, Steven Pinker, Oliver Sacks, and others.

0-618-17892-9 PA $13.00 / 0-618-17891-0 CL $27.50

THE BEST AMERICAN RECIPES 2003-2004
Edited by Fran McCullough and Molly Stevens

"The cream of the crop . . . McCullough's selections form an eclectic, unfussy mix" (*People*). Offering the very best of what America is cooking, as well as the latest trends, time-saving tips, and techniques, this year's edition includes a foreword by Alan Richman, award-winning columnist for *GQ*.

0-618-27384-0 CL $26.00

THE BEST AMERICAN NONREQUIRED READING 2003
Edited by Dave Eggers • Introduction by Zadie Smith

Edited by Dave Eggers, the author of *A Heartbreaking Work of Staggering Genius* and *You Shall Know Our Velocity*, this genre-busting volume draws the finest, most interesting, and least expected fiction, nonfiction, humor, alternative comics, and more from publications large, small, and on-line. *The Best American Nonrequired Reading 2003* features writing by David Sedaris, ZZ Packer, Jonathan Safran Foer, Andrea Lee, and others.

0-618-24696-7 $13.00 PA / 0-618-24696-7 $27.50 CL
0-618-39073-1 $35.00 CD

HOUGHTON MIFFLIN COMPANY www.houghtonmifflinbooks.com